EDITION

Web Performance Tuning

Patrick Killelea

O'REILLY®

Beijing · Cambridge · Farnham · Köln · Paris · Sebastopol · Taipei · Tokyo

MAY   '02

Web Performance Tuning, Second Edition
by Patrick Killelea

Published by O'Reilly & Associates, Inc., 1005 Gravenstein Highway North, Sebastopol, CA 95472.

O'Reilly & Associates books may be purchased for educational, business, or sales promotional use. Online editions are also available for most titles (*safari.oreilly.com*). For more information contact our corporate/institutional sales department: (800) 998-9938 or *corporate@oreilly.com*.

Editor:	Linda Mui
Production Editor:	Mary Brady
Cover Designer:	Edie Freedman
Interior Designer:	Melanie Wang

Printing History:

October 1998:	First Edition.
March 2002:	Second Edition.

ISBN: 0-596-00172-x

[M]

Table of Contents

Preface

In the four years since the first edition of this book, enormous fortunes were made and lost in a speculative bubble based on the potential of the Web. Thousands of web companies were founded with very thin business plans, and most are now floundering. Older companies, such as Cisco, Sun, and Oracle, rose to dizzying heights as the primary suppliers of equipment and software that was to revolutionize our lives, but they too have fallen greatly from their peaks. Microsoft continues its near-monopoly of the desktop, and yet it finds that monopoly increasingly irrelevant in a networked world. Meanwhile, mainstream media has had success in bringing much of television's low quality and intrusive advertising to the Web.

Now that the revolution is over, what has really changed? The change is that the Web has moved from novelty to an essential utility for the distribution of information. URLs are everywhere, as well as understood everywhere. Phone lines now carry more data than voice traffic. Almost every company and government agency has a web presence, along with millions of individuals. The Web is now taken for granted, though it has huge beneficial effects on our lives. Thanks to the Web, it is cheaper, faster, and easier to communicate than ever before.

Yet web performance is a bigger problem than it was four years ago, because of the ever larger volume of information and the critical nature of modern transactions. Fortunately, we know much more about web performance, what works and what does not, how to watch for problems, and how to fix them. That is what this book is about.

This edition contains far more software that you can use to monitor, load test, and analyze web site performance than did the first edition. All of the software is available at *http://patrick.net/software/*. I've also included many more graphs and analyses of real performance problems that I have come across in the last few years.

What Is This Book Good For?

This book is good for improving web site performance, estimating web site hardware and software requirements, and clarifying scaling issues. It covers client and network issues as well as server-side issues, because many web sites are on intranets, where a system administrator has control over the client and network, as well as the server. While most web performance discussion centers on the HTTP server, the server itself is not usually the performance bottleneck; rather, client connection speed, dynamic content generation, and database performance are. To improve performance, we must also look at these and other issues.

The performance I care about is from the end user's point of view: how quickly the Web satisfies the user's request. There are other kinds of performance, such as throughput, but this book focuses mainly on the user's perception of speed. I have also included a chapter on reliability, which is yet another kind of performance.

Although this book presents some general principles of performance tuning, it concentrates on practical advice much more than on theory. I hope to make performance tuning simple by providing the algorithms to follow and tools to use that have helped me in real-life situations. Another goal is to present a clear picture of the chain of events involved in viewing a web page. Having a clear mental model of exactly what happens is critical to reasoning through new performance problems and finding solutions.

The best tool for improving the performance of your web site is a good understanding of your own application and your architecture. Software tools can help, but their value is proportional to your understanding of what they do. In the end, performance tuning is about spending money and time wisely to get the most out of your resources. Much of life is like that.

Audience for This Book

Web Performance Tuning will be of interest to anyone working on a web site, from a personal site running off a Linux PC at home to a large corporate site with multiple enterprise-class servers and redundant Internet connections. The book assumes you are familiar with the fundamentals of setting up a web site and getting connected to the Internet. If you need advice on setting up a web server, see *Apache: The Definitive Guide* by Ben Laurie and Peter Laurie (O'Reilly & Associates). If you need advice on how to get connected to the Internet, see *Getting Connected* by Kevin Dowd (O'Reilly & Associates).

This is a book of practical advice about the configuration and application-level programming of commodity components. In other words, the book covers what you can change right now, including design content, system administration, and application programming.

To some degree, you are at the mercy of the market to supply good building blocks. Since the performance of a web site is a function not only of tuning parameters and options, but also of the raw hardware and software products involved, this book includes information on how to select the appropriate products. I also cover the issues of scalability and conformance with open standards.

Here are some representative titles of people who might have an interest in this book:

- System administrator
- System architect
- System integrator
- Web applications programmer
- Web content developer
- Webmaster

Assumptions of This Book

This book assumes a basic familiarity with the technical components of the Web. Throughout the book I've included descriptions of the events that occur in a typical HTTP operation. There are also references in the text and the appendixes to other books and web sites for those who need more background or want to explore a subject in more depth.

The server examples are drawn from the Unix world because about 75 percent of all web servers use a Unix operating system or clone, and an even higher percentage of commercial web sites use Unix. Most of the other 25 percent are Windows-based web servers, so I tried to include more information about Windows in this edition. I've assumed that the reader has some programming experience with either C, Java, or Perl, but this is not a requirement for using this book.

How This Book Is Organized

The first part of this book covers topics of general interest to anyone running a web site, including quick and simple performance boosts, estimating what hardware and software you need for a given load and level of performance, common measures of web site performance, real case studies of some web sites, and principles of performance tuning.

The structure of the second part of this book is modeled on what actually happens when the user of a web browser requests an HTML page from a web server (see Figure P-1). We'll follow an HTML request from client to network to server to middleware to database. From the browser's point of view, after the request is sent, the answer magically appears on the network. From the network's point of view, the answer magically appears at the connection to the server, and so on. We'll trace the

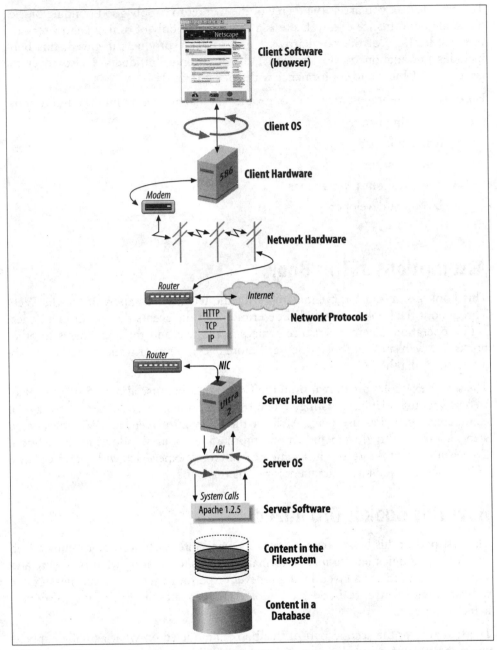

Figure P-1. The chain of events

process back one stage at a time to point out performance issues along the way and to eliminate the unknown. I'll also give tips for finding out which side of each interface is slower so that you can figure out where the bottleneck is and how to bring the performance of that section into line with the rest of your web site. Here is a break-down by chapter.

Part I: Preliminary Considerations

Chapter 1, *The Quick and the Dead*
> Describes a set of questions useful to find common performance problems and quick tips to increase your site's performance.

Chapter 2, *Web Site Architecture*
> Helps you make decisions about what kind of hardware and software you'll need to allow your site to perform well and scale for the future and describes major commercial web sites, including what hardware and software they use.

Chapter 3, *Capacity Planning*
> Describes how to estimate how much hardware you'll need.

Chapter 4, *Performance Monitoring*
> Gives software and examples for how to watch your site's performance.

Chapter 5, *Load Testing*
> Helps you design and run relevant load tests of your web site.

Chapter 6, *Performance Analysis*
> Discusses how to figure out where the bottleneck is.

Chapter 7, *Reliability*
> Provides many examples of problems than can crash your site.

Chapter 8, *Security*
> Explains the performance you give up in exchange for security.

Chapter 9, *Case Studies*
> Gives some real examples of performance problems and solutions.

Chapter 10, *Principles and Patterns*
> Describes some general principles to keep in mind when thinking about the performance of your web site.

Part II: Tuning in Depth

Chapter 11, *Browsers*
> Tells you what's going on in your browser and how to help it along, especially when it seems to be hanging.

Chapter 12, *Client Operating System*
> Gives tips on the differences between the various operating systems and how these affect browser performance.

Chapter 13, *Client Hardware*
> Describes what the bottlenecks are on the client hardware and what you can do about them.

Chapter 14, *Lines and Terminators*

Describes the hardware of the Internet. There's not a lot you can do about hardware that belongs to someone else, but you can at least choose the parts of the Internet you use. If you're running your own intranet, you can modify many parameters to tune performance.

Chapter 15, *Network Protocols*

Describes the protocols at the core of the Web and gives you tips on how the protocols interact and how to get them to play nicely together.

Chapter 16, *Server Hardware*

Describes issues constraining the server, such as disk bottlenecks.

Chapter 17, *Server Operating System*

Gives tuning hints for the typical Unix web server.

Chapter 18, *Server Software*

Discusses the free and commercial HTTP server software available.

Chapter 19, *Content*

Goes over the various kinds of data you return to the user and the performance implications of each.

Chapter 20, *Custom Applications*

Gives you tips and tricks for reducing the amount of time spent generating dynamic content.

Chapter 21, *Java*

Goes over some issues in optimizing your Java applications.

Chapter 22, *Databases*

Describes the performance and cost of some database systems.

Appendix, *Web Performance Product Lists and Reviews*

Offers my opinion on many performance products.

Font Conventions

Italic

Is used for URLs, filenames, program names, commands, hostnames, and for emphasizing words.

`Constant width`

Is used for HTTP headers, text to be typed literally, and function and system call names.

`Constant width bold`

Is used for user input.

How to Contact Us

We have tested and verified all the information in this book to the best of our ability, but you may find that features have changed (or even that we have made mistakes!). Please let us know about any errors you find, as well as your suggestions for future editions, by writing to:

O'Reilly & Associates
1005 Gravenstein Highway North
Sebastopol, CA 95472
(800) 998-9938 (in the United States or Canada)
(707) 829-0515 (international/local)
(707) 829-0104 (fax)

There is a web page for this book, which lists errata and any additional information. You can access this page at:

http://www.oreilly.com/catalog/webpt2/

To comment or ask technical questions about this book, send email to:

bookquestions@oreilly.com

For more information about books, conferences, Resource Centers, and the O'Reilly Network, see the O'Reilly web site at:

http://www.oreilly.com

Please write the author with comments, criticism, and suggestions at:

p@patrick.net

Web Site Updates and Code Examples

Be warned that web pages frequently change without regard to references to them. For the latest corrections and collection of my links, and also for the book's code examples, see *http://patrick.net/*. You can also find the code examples at *http://www. oreilly.com/catalog/webpt2/*.

Other Books and Resources

While this book is an excellent place to start learning how to improve your web performance, by no means is it the last word. So here I've listed some books, URLs, and newsgroups that you should examine if this book doesn't answer all your questions, or if you simply want to know more.

Books

In reading this book, you'll find that I frequently refer to other books that explain concepts more completely than I can (at least, not without making this book twice its size). Here are books with good explanations of the details.

Albitz, Paul and Cricket Liu, *DNS and Bind* (O'Reilly & Associates, 1997).

Back, Maurice, *Design of the Unix Operating System* (Prentice Hall, 1986).

Ballew, Scott, *Managing IP Networks with Cisco Routers* (O'Reilly & Associates, 1997).

Blake, Russ, *Optimizing Windows NT* (Microsoft Press, out of print).

Brooks, Fredrick P., Jr., *The Mythical Man-Month* (Addison Wesley, 1995).

Chapman, Brent and Elizabeth Zwicky, *Building Internet Firewalls, Second Edition* (O'Reilly & Associates, 2001).

Cockcroft, Adrian and Richard Pettit, *Sun Performance and Tuning, Second Edition* (Prentice Hall, 1998). Everything about tuning Solaris and Sun hardware.

Cockcroft, Adrian and Will Walker, *Capacity Planning for Internet Services* (Prentice Hall, 2001).

Dowd, Kevin, *Getting Connected* (O'Reilly & Associates, 1996).

Frisch, Æleen, *Essential System Administration* (O'Reilly & Associates, 1995).

Gancarz, Mike, *The Unix Philosophy* (Digital Press, 1996). Wonderful explanation of what makes Unix Unix.

Garfinkel, Simon, *PGP: Pretty Good Privacy* (O'Reilly & Associates, 1995).

Gray, Jim, *The Benchmark Handbook for Database and Transaction Processing Systems* (Morgan Kauffman Publishers, 1993).

Guelich Scott, Shishir Gundavaram, and Gunther Birznieks, *CGI Programming with Perl* (O'Reilly & Associates, 2000).

Gurry, Mark and Peter Corrigan, *Oracle Performance Tuning, Second Edition* (O'Reilly & Associates, 1996).

Harold, Elliotte Rusty, *Java Network Programming, Second Edition* (O'Reilly & Associates, 2000).

Laurie, Ben and Peter Laurie, *Apache: The Definitive Guide, Second Edition* (O'Reilly & Associates, 1999).

Musumeci, Gian-Paolo D. and Mike Loukides, *System Performance Tuning, Second Edition* (O'Reilly & Associates, 2002). The standard text on Unix system performance.

Nassar, Daniel J., *Ethernet and Token Ring Optimization* (M&T Books, out of print). The accumulated experience of a network tuner. Includes TCP/IP tips.

Orfali, Robert and Dan Harkey, *Client Server Programming with Java and CORBA* (John Wiley & Sons, 1998).

Partridge, Craig, *Gigabit Networking* (Addison Wesley, 1994).

Stern, Hal, Mike Eisler, and Ricardo Labiaga, *Managing NFS and NIS, Second Edition* (O'Reilly & Associates, 2001).

Stern, Hal, and Evan Markus, *Blueprints for High Availability* (John Wiley & Sons, 2000).

Stevens, Richard, *Advanced Programming in the Unix Environment* (Addison Wesley, 1993)

Stevens, Richard, *TCP/IP Illustrated, Volumes 1, 2, and 3* (Addison Wesley, 1994).

Stevens, Richard, *Unix Network Programming* (Prentice Hall, 1998).

Tannenbaum, Andrew S., *Computer Networks* (Prentice Hall, 1996). The canonical networking book.

Tannenbaum, Andrew S., *Modern Operating Systems* (Prentice Hall, 1992).

Ware, Scott, Michael Tracy, Louis Slothouber, and Robert Barker, *Professional Web Site Optimization* (Wrox Press, Inc., 1997).

Wall, Larry, Tom Christiansen, and John Orwant, *Programming Perl, Third Edition* (O'Reilly & Associates, 2000).

Wong, Brian L., *Configuration and Capacity Planning for Solaris Servers* (Prentice Hall, 1997). See especially Chapter 4, which is about configuring web services.

Wong, Clinton, *Web Client Programming with Perl* (O'Reilly & Associates, 1997).

Web Sites with Performance Information

The following URLs also include indispensable performance information:

http://help.netscape.com/kb/server/971211-7.html
   A Netscape-tuning page.

http://www.apache.org/
   The Apache home page. See especially *http://www.apache.org/docs/misc/perf.html*.

http://www.apacheweek.com/tips/
   Tips for running Apache.

http://www.cmg.org/
   The Computer Measurement Group's home page.

http://www.cs.cmu.edu/~jch/java/optimization.html
   Jonathan Hardwick's Java optimization page.

http://www.sysopt.com/
   Very popular page packed with information on optimizing PCs.

http://www.1computers.com/f/ftomhardware.html
Tom's Hardware Guide. Rightly famous for PC hardware information.

http://www.nlanr.net/Papers/data-inet97.html
Excellent review of performance measurement of the Internet.

http://www.rational.com/
Includes some papers on application performance tuning.

http://www.cerberus-sys.com/~belleisl/mtu_mss_rwin.html
The definitive site for Winsock tuning.

http://www.w3.org/
Has the RFCs on which the web is based.

http://www.usenix.org/events/usenix99/full_papers/maltzahn/maltzahn_html
Reducing the Disk IO of Web Proxy Server Caches.

http://www.opensta.org/
Open System Testing Architecture "The completely open way to test your systems."

See also:

- *http://dir.yahoo.com/Computers_and_Internet/Internet/World_Wide_Web/HTTP/Performance/*
- *http://www.yahoo.com/Computers_and_Internet/Hardware/Benchmarking/*
- *http://linuxperf.nl.linux.org/*
- *http://www.w3.org/Protocols/HTTP/Performance/Pipeline.html*
- *http://www.w3.org/Protocols/HTTP-NG/*
- *http://ircache.nlanr.net/Cache/reading.html*
- *http://www.sun.com/sun-on-net/performance*

Newsgroups with Web Performance Content

Also, check out these newsgroups:

- *comp.benchmarks*
- *comp.infosystems.www.authoring.html*
- *comp.infosystems.www.misc*
- *comp.unix.solaris*

Disclaimer

I hate to yell in all caps, but here it is:

THE INFORMATION IS PROVIDED "AS-IS" AND WITHOUT WARRANTY OF ANY KIND, EXPRESS, IMPLIED OR OTHERWISE, INCLUDING WITHOUT

Not a single suggestion in this book is guaranteed to help any particular situation. In fact, if you simply change configurations and parameters without analyzing the situation and understanding what you are changing and why, you may experience hardware damage, data loss, hair loss, dizziness, and nausea. Back up everything, don't work directly on production servers, and be careful.

Also note that the opinions expressed in this book are those of the author and have nothing to do with the author's employer or with the book's publisher, O'Reilly & Associates, Inc.

Acknowledgments for the Second Edition

Thank you again to Linda Mui, my editor at O'Reilly, for her patience. Thanks to my father, Thomas, for instilling ambition, and to my mother, Diane, for saying I ought to write a book. My wife Leah and son Jacob and daughter Genevieve deserve enormous credit for giving me enough time to finish. I told Robert Hellwig I'd mention him here. And thanks to everyone on the Internet who is willing to share what they know just because it's a nice thing to do. Thanks to Dean Gaudet and Jens-S. Voeckler for letting me include their material as appendices in the first edition. Much of the information from those appendices has been integrated into this second edition.

Second edition thanks to Sam Brodkin for a Java script tip and Daniel Lewart for suggestions and errata. Tony Pugliese provided many interesting leads and papers. I learned as much about performance working with John Nevins and Tori Walsh as I did before ever meeting them. Brian Robinson of Harvard University provided an excellent case study. Thanks to Adrian Cockcroft, Dave Loughlin, John Mani, and Joey Trevino for their useful comments. Thanks to Ron Walters for showing me the Perl Telnet module and to Naf Furman for introducing me to the Perl DBI. Pavel Semfield also provided many links to the new information.

Preliminary Considerations

The Quick and the Dead

While this book contains a lot of detailed information about monitoring, load testing, problem analysis, and background about how things work, I often find myself referring to this small set of questions and answers I wrote up to quickly diagnose and treat the most common problems. Since a majority of problems can be solved by simply reading through this list and checking things off, I provide it here right up front. There are many references to concepts that have not been discussed yet, but they are explained later in the book.

Questions for the Browser Side

First, here are the things you might try if your browser seems slow or unresponsive:

Is Your Modem On?

If you have an external modem, the power light should be lit to indicate that the modem is on.

Is Your Modem Connected to Your Computer?

If you have an external modem, make sure the modem cable is connected to your computer. Then try manually sending something to the modem. From a Linux shell you can do this:

```
% echo AT > /dev/modem
```

From a DOS prompt on a Windows machine you can do this:

```
% echo AT > COM1
```

If your modem is connected, you will see the send and read lights flash as the modem responds OK to the AT command. If the lights do not flash, either the modem is not connected, or you have configured it for the wrong COM port, PCMCIA slot, or other attachment point.

Did the Other End Hang Up on You?

External modems should have a light labeled CD (Carrier Detect) to indicate whether there is a carrier signal; that is, whether you are online. If it is not lit, it may be that the remote end hung up on you, or you lost your connection through too much noise on the line or an inactivity timeout.

Are You Sending Data over the Modem?

Look at external modem lights when you request a web page. The read and send lights should be flashing. This is also true for DSL modems, cable modems, hubs, and other network equipment. The send light will tell you that your modem is trying to send data out to the Internet. The read light will tell you if your modem is getting anything back from the network. If you cannot see these lights flashing, there is no data flowing through the modem.

Do You Have a Valid IP Address and Gateway Router?

On Windows, check that you actually have an assigned IP address by using the *ipconfig* command from a DOS prompt. On Linux, use the command *ifconfig -a* to check that you have an IP address. An IP address consists of four numbers between 0 and 255, separated by periods.

If you do have an IP address, you still may have forgotten to set a gateway router entry in the operating system. Use the graphical configuration tools under Windows or the Mac to enter a valid gateway router for your IP address. Under Linux, you can use the *route* command, like this:

```
% route add default gw <router IP address>
```

If you can use *telnet* or *ftp*, then you are definitely connected with a valid IP address. If you can hit *http://www.yahoo.com/* or other well-known sites from your web browser, you know you have a valid address and gateway. Try to hit a site with constantly changing content to be sure you're not just seeing a previously cached page. Stock quote pages are good for checking whether you're getting cached or viewing current data.

Is the Browser Hanging?

Browsers have been known to hang. On the other hand, your browser may just be thinking some deep thoughts at the moment. Give it a minute, especially if you just requested a page. The system call to resolve DNS names may hang the browser for a moment if the DNS server is slow. If you give it a minute and it's still stuck, kill the browser and try again.

Is Your Browser in "Offline" Mode?

Many browsers have an offline mode where they disconnect themselves from the Internet even if the PC is still connected. Make sure your browser is not offline. If it is offline, you may see a little "disconnected wire" icon in the lower left corner of the browser.

Can You Still Resolve Names?

Maybe your DNS server is down or not configured. Try a known IP address in the browser. In case you don't keep the IP addresses of web servers around, try hitting *http://204.71.200.66* (which is *http://www.yahoo.com/*). If this URL works, but *http://www.yahoo.com/* does not, your problem is DNS resolution and you need to set a DNS server using one of the graphical tools on Windows or the Mac, or by entering the IP address of your DNS server in *etc/resolv.conf* on Linux. Case does not matter for DNS names, but it does matter for the part of the URL after the machine name, which is confusing.

Is an Intermediate Router Down or Very Slow?

If you can, try opening a Telnet session directly to the web server. For example:

```
% telnet www.yahoo.com 80
```

Note how long it takes before Telnet returns a "connected" response. If it is consistently a second or more, try a *traceroute* to the server to see how far you can get. The *traceroute* program comes packaged with most versions of Unix, but there is also an imitation called *tracert* on NT and a commercial version called Net.Medic from Vital Signs Software. If *traceroute* stops within your ISP, it could be that your Internet provider is down, i.e., not connected to the rest of the Internet. Sometimes your whole region may be down because of a regional NAP (Network Access Point) or Internet backbone issue. There's not much you can do about that.

If any of the routers along the way show times of more than a few tenths of a second, consider which router it is. If it belongs to your ISP, you may benefit from changing your ISP. If it belongs to a large network provider such as MCI or Sprint, you may still benefit from changing your ISP because a different ISP may use a different route. But if the slow router belongs to the target site's ISP, all you can do is complain to the webmaster of the target site. Quite often their email address is given on the site. Other times they fit a pattern like *webmaster@targetsite.com*. If you don't have *traceroute* or *tracert*, you can simply try to Telnet to some other web servers. If the connect time is long for each of them, the problem is probably with a router in your own organization or your client machine itself.

Is the Remote Site Overloaded?

If you are on a Unix system, you can try pointing *rstat* at any remote server to see if you can find out something about how loaded it is. Running *rstat* won't hurt anything; if that server does not run the *rstatd* daemon, or if *rstat*'s request is blocked by a firewall, you won't see any response. See Chapter 4 for more about *rstat*.

Is the Remote Site Down?

An immediate "connection refused" message means that the remote web server software is down, yet the remote web server machine is still up and working well enough to send a TCP reset packet, telling you that nothing is listening on the web server's port. If the attempted connection hangs, it probably means you cannot get a connection to the remote web server machine at all, perhaps because it has crashed or is turned off or disconnected. You can check whether you're getting any packets at all from the remote side by using the *tcpdump* tool on Linux or the *snoop* tool on Solaris.

Is There a Mirror Site?

If you're trying to read a popular site, consider that there may be mirror sites that are less heavily loaded. Mirror sites are usually mentioned on the home page of a site. The Apache Web Server site (*http://www.apache.org/*), for example, has mirror sites around the world.

Did You Already Get Most of the Page?

Maybe everything is working fine, but you are stuck waiting for that last few bytes of data. Hit the Stop button and see if the page renders.

Is Your MTU too Big, or too Small?

The Maximum Transmission Unit (MTU) is the largest packet your network interface will send. If you set it too big, packets will be rejected by the interface and returned to be split up. This will slow down your browsing. If you set it too small, you will send many small packets when you could have been more efficient and sent a few large ones. This will also slow down your browsing. See Chapter 12 for information about how to adjust your MTU.

Do You Need to Use a Proxy Server?

Most large companies do not allow internal users to connect directly to the Internet, but instead require that they go through proxy serves, both for security and performance reasons. All browsers allow you to set a proxy through a preferences dialog box. Your organization can tell you the proxy settings to use. If you can telnet to port 80 of well-known web sites, then you are directly on the Internet and do not need to use a proxy server.

Does Your Proxy Handle https URLs?

Note that some proxy servers cannot handle the Secure Socket Layer (SSL). If your proxy cannot handle SSL, and you have to use that proxy, then you just can't see any SSL-protected pages. SSL-protected pages are the ones that start with "https" rather than "http". Most commercial web sites use SSL for transaction security.

Is There a Faster Proxy Server?

Most large organizations have several proxy servers, some more loaded than others. You can often see a dramatic increase in performance just by picking the right proxy. If you are within an organization with multiple proxy servers, try to find the most lightly loaded proxy. If your proxies run on Solaris or some other OS that supports the *rstatd* remote statistics daemon, you can use *rstat* or *perfmeter* to get an indication of which one is least loaded. See Chapter 4 for more information about *rstat*.

One problem is simply figuring out the names of your proxies. You can ask around in your company, or if your browser is automatically configured via a *proxy.pac* file, you can manually get the *proxy.pac* file through Telnet and look through it for the names of the proxies. It would be nice if browsers had the ability to automatically switch to a faster proxy based on *rstat* statistics or response times, but as far as I know, they do not. On the bright side, most proxies do not require any authentication, so you can switch to a faster one at will.

You can also see how fast the target site is by putting the URL into the web site analysis tool at *http://patrick.net/*. If the analysis tool reports that the site is fast, but you are getting it slowly, that also indicates that your proxy or some other network component may be to blame.

Are You Being Blocked Deliberately?

Some "network nanny" software may be installed on your PC to prevent you from viewing certain sites, or a proxy may refuse to access certain sites.

Are You Running too Many Programs?

Check whether your client is overloaded from running other tasks in addition to the browser. On Linux, *top* will show you the top processes by CPU usage or memory usage and let you kill them. On Windows NT, Ctrl-Alt-Delete will bring up the task manager, which is an imitation of *top*.

Fewer processes are always better, but be sure you know what you're killing, or you might crash your machine. If you aren't completely sure that you know what you are doing, consider rebooting to get rid of processes that are leaking memory or otherwise abusing the system. Your initialization files may start them up again, but at least they will be starting small.

Do You Have Enough Memory?

The classic sign of a memory shortage is very poor performance and a constantly working hard disk. This is because your operating system will try to use hard disk as "virtual" memory when there isn't enough RAM. Unfortunately, disk is extremely slow compared to RAM. The solutions are to run fewer or smaller applications and turn off Java in the browser, or buy more RAM.

Is Your CPU Fast Enough?

Yes, your CPU is fast enough. By comparison with network and memory, CPU is almost never a problem for web browsing.

Do You Have Enough Bandwidth?

On the client side, the most common performance bottleneck is lack of bandwidth between ISP and PC. If you have to use a modem, it is well worth the money to buy the fastest modem available, but make sure your ISP supports that speed. ISDN is better than a modem, but difficult to configure. ADSL and cable modem are the best options for home users. If you are on a LAN, 100mbps "fast" Ethernet is noticeably better than standard 10mbps Ethernet. Fast Ethernet can be configured to run full-duplex, increasing its advantage even more.

Are Excessive Images Dragging Down Your Performance?

Turning off autoloading of images will help performance dramatically if the problem is simply that your bandwidth is limited to that of a modem on a regular dial-up telephone line (also known as a POTS line, for Plain Old Telephone Service). Of course, without graphics you won't enjoy a lot of what the Web is about, which is, well, graphics. On the other hand, you'll escape most advertising. In Netscape, turn off automatic loading by choosing Edit → Preferences → Advanced and then unchecking the Automatically Load Images box.

Even if you turn off automatic loading of images, you can load and view an interesting image by clicking on the associated image icon. Your next question should be how to tell whether an image looks interesting before you've seen it. This is exactly what the HTML <ALT> tag is for: the HTML author is supposed to add a text description of the associated image, which the browser will display if image loading is off. ALT stands for "alternate text." Here is an example:

```
<img src="images/foo.gif" alt="Picture of a Foo" width=190 height=24>
```

Most browsers also have a button that forces all unloaded images to load. Many sites offer a light-graphics or text-only link for the bandwidth-impaired user. Another option is to use a text-only browser such as *lynx*, which also has the advantage that it can be run remotely over a VT100 or other terminal-mode connection rather than requiring a TCP/IP connection all the way to the client. That is, your ISP may let you dial up and run *lynx* on the ISP's computer rather than on your computer at home.

Internet Explorer is faster than Netscape in displaying images that do not have associated size parameters in the HTML.

Is Browser Startup Time Getting You Down?

It is frequently helpful to set the browser to start on a blank page, so that you do not have to wait for a default page to load when starting up. The Netscape home page can be particularly heavy with graphics and features, so it's a poor choice to leave as the default. To change the startup page to blank in Netscape, choose Edit → Preferences → Navigator and then click the radio button for "Navigator starts with blank page."

If you don't care about graphics, you could use the *lynx* browser, which starts instantly.

Are You Using a Slow Browser?

Newer browsers take advantage of the newest performance improvements in the HTTP protocol, but they also tend to get slower and fatter with each generation. On the other hand, Netscape 6 is a complete rewrite and much faster than Netscape 4. (Apparently Netscape has simply skipped the number 5.) IE 5 is also an improvement over its predecessors.

Very old browsers are usually very simple, and so they may not have support for SSL, JavaScript, Java, and many other features you may need, but in their favor, they are generally very small and quick on current hardware. The Opera browser, from *http://www.opera.com/*, is very small and very fast, but is not free unless you are willing to put up with advertising.

Is Your Cache Big Enough?

Set your browser's memory and disk caches to 25 percent of your memory and 10 percent of your disk. That's aggressive, but should still leave enough room for other applications to run.

Are You Wasting Time Verifying Cached Pages?

Browsers cache the documents you view and then retrieve an item from the browser's cache if you request it again. Because the document may have changed in the meantime, the browser will by default contact the original server to validate the freshness of every cached page. If the document has changed on the server, the new version will be downloaded. If the locally cached copy is up to date, then it is displayed.

The validation request may require only a little network traffic if the document has not been modified, but you'll still get better performance from using what's in the cache without verification, and you won't have to download any pages with trivial changes. You may get stale pages, but at least you'll get them quickly.

To get the performance gain from not verifying cached documents in Netscape, set Options → Network Preferences → Verify Document: to Never. If you suspect you've got a stale page, it's an easy matter to force Netscape to get the current version. Simply hold down the Shift key and hit Reload. Setting Verify Document: to "Once per Session" is second-best; this will verify the timeliness of the document just once for that Netscape session. Setting Verify Document: to "Every Time" is worse from a performance point of view. This instructs Netscape to check with the original server for a fresher version every time you view that page.

Is Java Startup Time Annoying You?

It can take 15 or 20 seconds to start up the Java virtual machine the first time you hit a page with Java in it. This Java initialization freezes the browser and cannot be interrupted, which can be very annoying. One solution is to turn off Java in the browser unless you know you want a specific applet. Another solution is to try the latest Java "Plugin" from Sun, which is capable of caching applets indefinitely, so you won't need to download a particular applet more than once. However, the Plugin itself is very large and takes a long time to download when you first install it.

Could You Benefit from Using a Specific ISP?

If you are spending most of your time getting data from one server, it may be worthwhile to get an account with the ISP that connects that server to the Internet. You'll probably see better throughput and latency working from an account on the same ISP than from somewhere else. Telecommuters probably want an account with their company's ISP.

Are You Surfing at Slow Times?

If you are on the West Coast of the U.S., be aware that there is a lot of network traffic in the morning because the East Coast has been up and surfing for three hours already. So the East Coast gets better speed early in the morning because the Californians are asleep, and the West Coast is faster late at night because the East Coasters are asleep.

Could Your Organization Benefit by Installing a Proxy Server?

A proxy server between your organization and the Internet will cache frequently requested pages, reducing the load on your connection to the Internet while providing faster response time to the users for cached pages. The benefit you see depends on the number of times the requested page is in the cache. If all web requests were for unique URLs, then a proxy would actually reduce performance, but in practice, a few web pages are very popular and the cache is well used.

The proxy server has a particular need for speed, since it must act as both client and server. Proxies are write-intensive, so they can benefit significantly from a caching disk controller.

Keep in mind that proxies may make some Java applets unusable, since applets can currently connect only back to the server they came from. The server they came from will be the proxy, which is not where the applet probably thinks it came from.

Questions for the Server Side

Now let's look at things from the server side. Here's what you should look at if your web server seems sluggish.

Is Your Server Sleeping?

If you are running a web site from a PC, be sure to disable the power conservation features that spin down the disk and go into sleep mode after a period of inactivity. Sleep mode will slow down the first user who hits your site while it is sleeping, because it takes a few moments for the disk to spin up again. Some operating systems—for example, Mac OS X—are capable of quickly serving pages in their sleep; but even they will eventually have to wake up to log to disk, so it is best to turn off sleep mode.

Is Your DNS Server Overloaded?

DNS servers can become overloaded like anything else on the Internet. Since DNS lookups block the calling process, a slow DNS server can have a big impact on perceived performance. Check whether your DNS server's CPU or network load is nearing its capacity by monitoring that machine's hardware statistics. See Chapter 4 for more information on monitoring.

If you determine that your DNS server is a problem, consider setting up additional servers or simply pointing your DNS resolver to another DNS server. Using a different DNS server is done by modifying */etc/resolv.conf* under Linux or using the Network Control Panel on Windows.

Do Your Images All Have Sizes and ALT Tags?

Netscape browsers do not display a page at all until all images sizes are known. If you do not include the images sizes in your HTML, this means that the browser must actually download all the images before it knows the sizes, resulting in a long delay before the user sees anything at all. Many users also do not download images for one reason or another, but would like to know what kind of image it is they are missing, especially if you use images for navigation tools. So for best performance and usability, make sure all your images have size parameters in the HTML like this:

```
<img src="images/foo.gif" alt="Picture of a Foo" width=190 height=24>
```

Do All Your Applets Have ALT Tags?

Similarly, many users turn off Java because VM startup time and applet download time are very annoying. Like the ALT text for images, any text within the <APPLET> </APPLET> tags will be displayed when Java is off, so the user will have an idea of whether he wants to turn Java back on and reload the page. This text can include any valid HTML, so it is possible for the content designer to create a useful alternative to the applet and put it within the applet tag.

Are There Needless or Slow Redirects?

HTML can redirect a browser to a different web page after a programmable delay via the META tag. Here is an example with a two-second delay:

```
<META HTTP-EQUIV = "Refresh" Content = "2;URL=http://www.go here.com">
```

Avoid redirects if at all possible because they waste time. But if you have to use one, at least make it fast by putting in a zero-second delay.

Is Your Web Server Wasting Time on Reverse DNS Lookups?

Web servers are often set by default to take the IP address of the client and do a reverse DNS lookup on it (finding the name associated with the IP address) in order to pass the name to the logging facility or to fill in the REMOTE_HOST CGI environment variable. This is time consuming and not necessary, since a log parsing program can do all the lookups when parsing your log file later.

You might be tempted to turn off logging altogether, but that would not be wise. You really need logs to show how much bandwidth you're using, whether it's increasing, and lots of other valuable performance information. You just don't need to log DNS names. CGIs can also do the reverse lookup themselves if they need it. Every web server has the option to turn off reverse DNS lookups in its configuration files. Refer to your web server's documentation.

Is Your Web Server Retransmitting too Much?

TCP will begin a connection with the assumption that a segment has been lost if it has not been acknowledged within a certain amount of time, typically 200 milliseconds. For some slow Internet connections, this is not long enough. TCP segments may be arriving safely at the browser, only to be counted as lost by the server, which then retransmits them, using up bandwidth. Turning up the TCP retransmit timeout will fix this problem, but it will also reduce performance for fast but lossy connections, where the reliability is poor even if the speed is good. For long-lived TCP connections, TCP will dynamically adapt to the performance of that connection, but most connections to web servers are short, so the initial timeout setting has a big impact.

Are You too Far Away from Your Users?

Internet Protocol data packets must go through a number of forks in the road on the way from the server to the client. Dedicated computers called routers make the decision about which fork to take for every packet. That decision, called a router "hop," takes some small but measurable amount of time, typically a millisecond or two. Servers should be located as few router hops away from the audience as possible.

ISPs usually have their own high-speed network connecting all of their dial-in points of presence (POPs). A web surfer on a particular ISP will probably see better network performance from web servers on that same ISP than from web servers located elsewhere, partly because there are fewer routers between the surfer and the server. National ISPs are near a lot of people. If you know most of your users are on AOL, for example, get one of your servers located inside AOL. The worst situation is to try to serve a population far away, forcing packets to travel long distances and through many routers. A single HTTP transfer from New York to Sydney can be painfully slow to start and simply creep along once it does start, or just stall. The same is true for transfers that cross small distances but too many routers. Another solution is to host your data on one of the many content distribution services, such as Akamai.

Is Your Server Network Connection Overloaded?

The most effective blunt instrument for servers and users alike is a better network connection, with the caveat that it's rather dangerous to spend money on it without doing any analysis. For example, a better network connection won't help an overloaded server in need of a faster disk or more RAM. In fact, it may crash the server because of the additional load from the network.

Is Your Server CPU-Bound?

While server hardware is rarely the bottleneck for serving static HTML, a powerful server is a big help if you are generating a lot of dynamic content or making a lot of database queries. If the CPU usage is at 100 percent, you have found a problem that needs immediate attention.

Whether you will benefit from a CPU upgrade depends entirely on the problem, and the vendor is not likely to tell you don't really need more hardware. You may just have a poorly written application. If you've profiled your application and really need the extra power, it helps to upgrade from PC hardware to Unix boxes from Sun, IBM, or HP. They have much better I/O subsystems and scalability. Monitor your server's hardware utilization to be aware of hardware bottlenecks.

Are You Short of Memory?

On Solaris up to Version 7, run *vmstat* and look at the sr column, which is the scan rate for free memory. If the sr column is consistently above zero, you have a memory shortage. Other indications that you are short of memory are any swapping (swapping activity should be zero at all times) or consistent paging. On Solaris 8 and later, look at free memory.

RAM accesses data thousands of times faster than any disk. So getting more data from RAM rather than from disk can have a huge positive impact on performance. All free memory will automatically be used as filesystem cache in most versions of Unix and in NT, so your machine will perform repetitive file serving faster if you have more RAM. Web servers themselves can make use of available memory for caches. More RAM also gives you more room for network buffers and more room for concurrent CGIs to execute.

You may have plenty of memory, yet find it gets used up over time because a process is leaking (losing references to allocated memory). Simply by looking at the size of individual processes over time with *top*, you should be able to get a feel for which ones are leaking memory. They will have to either be fixed or restarted on a regular basis.

Are Your Disks too Busy?

On Solaris, look at the output from *iostat -x*. Disk access latencies consistently higher than 100 milliseconds are a cause for concern. When buying disks, get those with the lowest seek time, because disks spend most of their time seeking (moving the arm to the correct track) in the kind of random access typical of web serving.

A collection of small disks is often better than a single large disk. 10,000 rpm is better than 7,200 rpm. Bigger disk controller caches are better. SCSI is better than IDE or EIDE. But all of these things cost more money as well.

Could You Benefit from Caching Services?

Use multiple mirrored servers of the same capacity and balance the load between them. There are now many commercial services, such as Akamai, that provide caching servers. Your load will naturally be balanced to some degree if you are running a web site with an audience scattered across time zones or around the world, such as a web site for a multinational corporation.

Are You Suffering from Performance Bugs That Have Already Been Fixed?

Software generally gets faster and better with each revision. At least that's how things are supposed to work. Try the latest version of the operating system and web server and apply all of the non-beta patches, especially the networking and performance-related patches. This rule can sometimes be profitably broken, since old software often takes less memory.

Is cron Killing Performance at Regular Intervals?

If a performance problem happens only at certain intervals, check what *cron* or Autosys jobs the server is running. (Autosys is a commercial version of *cron* from Computer Associates.) These intermittent problems can be infuriating if you notice the slowdown and look for the culprit just as it finishes and goes away. You might just leave *perfmeter* running if you're on Solaris to look for regular CPU spikes. This should illustrate repeating load patterns well. You can disable the *cron* daemon if necessary.

Is Your Web Site Being Crowded by Other Processes?

Don't run anything unnecessary for web service on your web server, middlware, or database machine. In particular, your web server should not be an NFS server, an NNTP server, a mail server, or a DNS server. Find those things other homes. You should run *top* (or *taskmanager* on Windows, or *prstat* on Solaris 8) and figure out which of the processes are using the most CPU and memory. Kill all unnecessary daemons, such as *lpd*.

Don't even run a windowing system on your web server. You don't really need it, and it takes up a lot of RAM. Terminal mode is sufficient for you to administer your web server. On Windows, however, you don't have any choice; Windows always wastes memory and CPU on the GUI because there is no terminal mode.

Are You Wasting Time with SSIs?

Server Side Includes (SSI) are very inefficient. SSI means that the server parses your HTML and looks for commands to run programs and insert content. It is better to dynamically generate the whole page from one CGI or servlet than to run SSIs. CGI is not as bad as it used to be because operating systems have already improved the ability to run many short-lived processes because of demands from the Web.

Is Your Content Unncessarily Dynamic?

You may think that you have to generate content on demand where that's not really the case. You can update static HTML many times a day, giving the impression of dynamic content without incurring nearly the same overhead. It depends on the number of possible inputs from the user. If there are only a few, you can precalculate responses to them all.

Is Your Database Connection Pool too Small?

If you use a middleware server that keeps a database connection pool, beware that growing that pool on demand is very bad for performance. You may be able to start the pool high enough that it will not need to increase. A typical symptom is that performance is fine at low loads, but intermittently slow as the load increases and the pool takes time to grow.

Is Your Database Connection Pool Leaking?

If you are allocating database connections from a pool but not reclaiming them, you may be forcing unnecessary growth of the pool, or even bringing your site to a halt until unused connections time out and are collected. To find such leaks, you can watch the number of connections used under load. Chapter 4 has a script that can screen scrape the Weblogic Admin web page and graph usage. To fix the connection leak, you will have to closely examine your code for overt failures to release connections, and for possible exceptions that can divert code from releasing connections.

Are Your Hubs, Switches, and Routers Overloaded or Misconfigured?

Most network hardware, such as hubs, switches, and routers, are SNMP-compliant, meaning they will give statistics on their load and collision rates to any SNMP-compliant tool. Watch these statistics for signs of overload. Overloaded hubs are especially likely to be offenders, and are easily replaced with better-performing switches. Also beware of Ethernet connections misconfigured such that one side is full duplex while the other side is not.

Do Java Processes Suddenly Stall?

It's probably garbage collection (GC). Since GC is usually single-threaded, you may see one CPU at 100 percent while the others are at 0 percent during the stall. Use *mpstat* on Solaris to see each CPU's load. While increasing the initial and maximum heap sizes helps delay the inevitable GC, they also make it take longer for most VM's. IBM's generational garbage collecting VM may be an exception. Also, set *-verbosegc* when you start the Java VM to clearly see when garbage collection is happening. The latest JDK releases from Sun allow the programmer some control over GC.

Are You Using CORBA, EJBs, or RMI?

Don't. The overhead of serialization of object parameters is very large. Local method calls are many thousands of times faster than remote calls. If at all possible, choose as your client a standard browser displaying HTML for your GUI, not an applet making RMI calls.

Are You Doing Excessive Logging?

Run *strace* on Linux or *truss* on Solaris to see what your server processes are doing. It will quickly become apparent if you are doing too much logging. You will see many small write OS calls, all to the same file descriptor. First, try to buffer the logging, so that it happens in larger increments. Buffered logging is usually an option on most servers. Second, try not to log from Java programs, to avoid the overhead of temporary object creation and conversion between Unicode and ASCII.

Are You Serving Content Directly from a Revision Control System?

Revision control systems are wonderful for tracking changes to HTML and code, but terrible for performance. Copy your production data to your web servers rather than serving directly out of ClearCase or other revision control systems.

The Server Is Not at All Busy, but It's Slow!

Sometimes there's nothing obviously wrong with the server, yet it manages to be very slow. Here are the typical reasons, covered later in this book:

- Expanding a database connection pool
- Reverse DNS lookups
- TCP retransmit timeouts
- Overloaded hubs and switches
- Java doing garbage collection
- Waiting for the return of an RMI or CORBA or EJB call
- Writing massive amounts of data to JDBC logs or other logs in tiny increments
- Accessing production web content directly from revision control systems such as Clearcase
- Too few Apache daemons or Netscape threads

Key Recommendations

- Turn off images on the client.
- Turn off Java on the client.
- Turn off cache validation on the client.
- Put more RAM on the server.
- Put more RAM on the client.
- Buy a better connection to the Internet.
- On a LAN, if you can cache static content in RAM, you can probably serve it at full network speed. If you can't cache content, then your disk is probably the bottleneck.
- On the Internet, the Internet is usually the bottleneck; the next bottlenecks are dynamic content generation and database queries.
- If you have other suggestions for quick checks, please write *p@patrick.net*.

## CHAPTER 2

Web Site Architecture

There are many trade-offs to make in designing a web site, which involve many possible components and configurations. What you need depends on what you're trying to do; one size does not fit all. This chapter goes over the fundamental problems that everyone runs into.

Trade-offs

There are a number of trade-offs to make in designing a web site architecture: state versus scalability, replication versus simplicity, synchronous versus asynchronous, connectionful versus connectionless, speed of development versus planning, and procedural versus object-oriented programming.

State Versus Scalability

Left to its own devices, a web site has no ability to remember individual users from one web transaction to the next. In such "stateless" web sites, users have no particular information that needs to be tracked. The web site has complete amnesia about your previous visits. It delivers the page without considering whether you've asked for it before or what other pages you've viewed.

Web sites that have no user state have no problem with scalability. Stateless web sites are easily replicated for scalability by load balancing across many servers, even if the content is dynamic (for example, a site that serves stock quotes or weather information), as long as the source of that dynamic data can be replicated. Since the web servers are all functionally the same, it does not matter if a user gets the home page from one server, then hits a different server when he clicks on a link on that home page.

This is different for a transactional site where users have state, such as being logged in or out, having items in a shopping cart, or having a balance. User state is the origin of most bottlenecks on transactional sites, limiting scalability by limiting how fast the state can be retrieved or updated, or forcing servers to constantly share state. The "system of record" is the database in which the transactions are legally recorded, and it is inevitably a bottleneck. There are some simple ways to cope with the conflict between state and scalability:

- Keep the state explicit and compact, perhaps in a single cookie so that the state of a transaction is in one convenient package.
- Do not split up state and have it scattered about between the browser, middleware, and database, lest a partial failure leave a huge mess.
- Make state either all committed to your system of record in a single atomic write, or not at all committed.

Keeping state as minimal as possible also greatly improves performance, since less data needs to be retrieved or committed to the database. If you are going to try to scale up a transactional site by keeping state replicated across servers, a small state also helps to facilitate replication.

Spreading a stateful workload over many processors will require intense communication among them to synchronize state, whether the processors are in separate machines in a cluster, or in a single multiprocessing machine. In the former case, we have the issue of networking each pair of machines, while in the latter case we have the issue of synchronizing CPU caches. In either case the number of pairs of machines that need to synchronize goes up exponentially with the number of nodes.

The same thing is true of human workgroups. Too many workers quickly becomes counterproductive because of the communication overhead, i.e., meetings. I remember reading a quote about a CEO in the computer industry who claims that the best way to speed up a bogged-down project is to start removing workers, because a bogged down project is usually overstaffed. He's right.

Replication Versus Simplicity

While you can scale web sites by replicating data to each server each night, scaling a site by replication makes administration more complex, and complexity is the death of web sites. A single authoritative source for data is much simpler.

On the other hand, if you do not replicate, your scalability will be limited by the speed of your central data source, whether it is an NFS server or a relational database. This is particularly true for write access to a central database, because database transactions must satisfy the so-called ACID criteria of Atomicity, Consistency, Isolation, and Durability. To be sure of the self-consistency and durability of the transaction, you must lock the data you are going to operate on before beginning the transaction (isolation). This is so no other process can modify and potentially corrupt the data during the transaction, which either runs to completion or is entirely aborted (atomicity). Because you have a single data set with strict serial access, you will find your transaction rate limited to how fast you can lock, modify, and unlock the data in the database. Locking out others from the database reduces performance. Consistency refers to synchronizing caches with the system of record. Durability means that the data survives reboots.

It is often forgotten that you do not really need complete consistency of a database all the time. You can let the database be inconsistent, i.e., have contradictions, for some period of time without too much risk. Even in the case of a bank that has a central database of account information, suppose each ATM machine has a local data cache and a rule that each account is allowed to withdraw $200 per hour per ATM machine without any immediate database access to the current balance figure. This makes the transaction much quicker for the user. The database can be synchronized within an hour after the transaction takes place, making use of cheaper but slower communication. The bank takes some small risk that the user will go around to many ATM machines and withdraw $200 from all of them in that hour before the database is guaranteed to be consistent, but the risk is rather small relative to the benefits to the user and the bank, particularly if the bank has some minimum balance requirement. The bank officials know exactly how much money was in each account an hour ago, but they can't be exactly sure how much is in each account right this instant. It's a trade-off between wait time for the user, risk for the bank, communication costs, and complexity of programming.

Clustering is becoming more popular. Clustering is getting many machines to act like one bigger machine. Attempts to scale web services by clustering machines are also limited to how fast state can be shared between the members of the cluster. For this reason, some attempts at clustering, such as WebLogic clustering, share state between only two machines in the cluster at any time. This requires that a user be directed to one of those two machines on each hit, increasing complexity. This illustrates James Gosling's truth that solving a problem usually consists of moving the problem to another part of the system.

Replicating slowly changing data is much easier than replicating the state of a particular transaction. Among the many solutions are regular use of the Unix *rdist* and *rsync* commands, caching proxy servers, software products from companies like Marimba, and commercial caching services such as those provided by Akamai and Inktomi.

Synchronous Versus Asynchronous

Synchronous calls block until an answer is returned. Most web pages have you just twiddle your thumbs until the results come back. Asynchronous calls return control to you immediately. Some asynchronous web pages queue your request and immediately send back a message telling you that you'll get an answer later, maybe by email. The question is whether you are willing to wait around for the answer, or whether you would rather move on to other things.

Another example of a synchronous call is a JDBC query to a database, which blocks its Java thread until the database returns the results. This will limit your scalability to the speed of the database. If you get more long-running queries than threads, you will block all your threads and run out of capacity. Asynchronous messaging systems such as Tibco and MQ, on the other hand, let you send a request message and go on to other things.

So why do we use synchronous calls at all? Synchronous calls do have the advantage that you know whether the call succeeded or not before you go on, while asynchronous calls may take more time to report a failure, or may even not report back at all. And synchronous calls are simple to write, while asynchronous calls require you to write both a procedure to make the call and another to handle the result.

Connectionless Versus Connectionful

Connectionless protocols do not require you to maintain a network connection between requests for service. HTTP does use TCP connections, but you are never required to use the same connection for a subsequent request, so we call it connectionless.

Although HTTP is inefficient in that it goes to the trouble of setting up and tearing down a TCP connection for a typically short transfer of data, HTTP happens to be quite scalable exactly because the connections are so short-lived. Connections are unlikely to be concurrent with each other because each is brief. This means that each connection is likely to have good access to the server's resources. For example, you probably won't run out of socket connections, because they're constantly being closed after use.

Since the HTTP protocol is stateless, it is entirely transparent to users if some of their requests are fulfilled by one server and some by another. This makes it easy to add more identical servers on the fly to accommodate larger loads in serving static content and is a fundamental advantage of the Web over, say, client-server systems.

Planning Versus Doing

Some large projects, such as airplanes, bridges, and nuclear power plants, don't work until you're done with them. You can't fly just a piece of a plane. Software is not at all like that. You can rapidly produce a small snippet of software that does something useful, and then get it out there, get some feedback, and improve it incrementally. This is by far the most cost-effective way to write code. There are explanations of why this is true in the book *The Unix Philosophy* by Mike Gancarz (Digital Press), and at the eXtreme Programming web site at *http://www.xprogramming.com/what_is_xp.htm*. The basic idea is that in a rapidly changing environment, such as the Internet, it is not possible to write a lot of code "for the future" because you do not know what the future is going to be like. It's better to keep to a few principles like simplicity and flexibility, which let you quickly cope with the changes as they come along.

Unfortunately, incrementalism and constantly changing requirements do not allow you to tell management exactly what to expect for the money they're spending. They like to have well-defined projects and fixed budgets and schedules, but if you attempt to impose too much order on an inherently chaotic process, you end up bogged down adhering to heavy-weight disciplines like the Rational Unified Process. By the time you deliver something, it will probably be obsolete.

A final example of excessive planning is making a mathematical model of your system to predict exactly how much capacity your new architecture is going to have. Very small changes to code can have dramatic impacts on performance, yet not be accounted for in the model. It is much more effective to simply run load tests against the system as it evolves. Modeling can predict performance for very simple systems, but if you keep your system so simple that you can model it well, then it will probably run so fast that you won't need to model it.

Procedural Versus Object-Oriented

With object-oriented programming (OO) programming, the opportunities to slow down your code expand dramatically. OO is intended to allow the development of reusable components but it rarely works out that way. The overhead of planning "for the future," designing object models, and teaching others the interfaces to your components is usually larger than simply doing a good job coding what you need right now in a procedural language. OO does not lead to more reusable code, or faster development time, or pretty much anything that you couldn't do just as easily in C or Perl. The main reason Java actually does reduce development time is that Java has good portable libraries to which the interfaces are already widely known. Another reason Java is faster to code in is a pointer problem doesn't blow up the whole program—but then you have the expenses of array bounds checking and garbage collection. Neither of these benefits has much to do with OO.

It well known that OO code is slower than procedural code for many reasons. One reason is that OO programs generally have poor locality of reference, breaking many caching schemes. Another is that multiple levels of indirection are usually required to get at parent classes and fields within them.

OO encourages dependencies between classes and that is why it fails at re-use. In fact, OO inevitably results in a spectacular festival of custom interfaces and absolute dependencies between objects. The result is a huge interlinked blob of code, of which no portion can be used without finding and loading all the others. The programs used from the Unix shell are better examples of reusable code than most things written in C++ or Java. Try to use just one class from any Java library the way you can use one small Unix program like *ls*, *cat*, or *wc*. You can't. Yet all of those small Unix programs are reusable and interconnectible in useful pipelines because they all have the same wonderfully simple interface (standard in, standard out, standard error).

However bad OO is, distributed OO is worse. In addition to abysmal performance, distributed OO programs are especially hard to test because there is no simple network protocol like HTTP for communication between objects. Instead, remote methods typically serialize actual objects for sending as parameters across the wire. This means that sending even a single character of data requires the large overhead of first coating the character in an object, serializing that object, and then deserializing it on the other end. Distributed OO is also very fragile because the remote call has to be exactly correct and failures are usually not well planned for. Compare this to the Web, in which you can call a CGI program in a way analogous to a remote object call, but from a myriad of clients without any custom protocol. The Web is much more forgiving.

I don't like OO mostly because I work on performance, but there are cases in which it makes coding much easier. For another point of view, try *http://martinfowler.com/isa/layers.html*.

Elements

In this section, we take a look at the basic elements that make up web site architecture.

Browser

The web browser is a nearly ideal Graphical User Interface (GUI) because it is standard, simple, and ubiquitous. Most of what you need to show users is available: text, graphics, buttons, fill-in boxes, etc. The design of a GUI with HTML is about as easy as it gets. Other GUIs, such as those created with Visual Basic or Java, require much more training to create, and usually interface with the back-end in a non-HTTP way, greatly complicating testing and requiring each user to download a GUI just for that one application. Pretty much every PC in the world now has a browser, and they all read HTML, so it's crazy not to take advantage of that.

It is a particularly bad idea to make any site "Optimized for Internet Explorer" or "Optimized for Netscape." The entire value of the Web lies in its ubiquity and portability. If you start imposing requirements on users that are not strictly necessary, you not only alienate those who do not use your recommended browser, but you also expose yourself to the danger of platform dependence. Once you are dependent on a particular browser, you have given up the freedom of your users as well as your own freedom to look at your content in any other way. Why give up your freedom?

With the emerging Document Object Model (DOM) standard, browsers can do essentially everything you can do with other GUIs, such as column sorting, downloading just data or fractions of HTML pages, and various widgets that would otherwise require a Java applet. DOM is supported by Internet Explorer (IE), Netscape, and Opera, though support for DOM varies in quality and standards compliance. IE and Netscape use different versions of the DOM, and within Netscape, the DOM is different between Versions 4 and 6.

Browsers do run into trouble when downloading or searching very large documents, because browsers are often much larger and slower than necessary. Still, I do not recommend any other GUI for distributed applications because the advantages of browsers are so profound.

Load Balancer

Load balancing is critical to scaling a web site. You may need to balance across different web servers, or to balance requests from web servers across different middleware boxes. Either way, you have many choices between freeware and commercial products.

DNS level

The most common solution is called round robin DNS (RRDNS). The idea is that you set your DNS server to return multiple IP addresses when it is queried with your web server's hostname. Clients choose one of the IP addresses. Note that the Windows clients choose one IP and stick with it, while Unix clients alternate between the given IP addresses. An alternate approach is to set the DNS server to rotate through a set of IP addresses, returning a single one on each query. While round robin DNS does balance load, it may not be exactly what you expect or need for three reasons:

- First, even though the replies are distributed evenly among web servers, round robin DNS makes no attempt to find the closest or most appropriate server for a particular client; it simply points the user to the server next in line, or rather, next in circle. There could be a wide variation in response time if those servers are geographically dispersed or not equivalent.

Round robin DNS is not true load balancing, but it does balance the load in simple cases. True load balancing would be measuring the utilization of servers and assigning connections based on that utilization, so that connections are always assigned to servers with enough spare capacity to handle them. This is very important for, say, a compute-intensive CGI process. You don't want two complex queries going to the same server when another server is lightly loaded with a simple query.

When one server in a round robin set is much slower than the others, a peculiar condition develops called "convoying," in which the users are queued up waiting for the slow servers while the fast servers are unused. If you've ever driven a long way on a narrow mountain road, you've experienced the same thing. No one can go faster than the slowest car. They all catch up to it and remain stuck behind it. True load balancing does not have this problem, because it assigns users to servers based on some usage criteria rather than blind alternation. It lets the cars pass each other.

- Second, RRDNS does not attempt to cope with the failure of a server. Users are still directed to the failed server. True load balancing can improve the availability of your site, since one server can go down and the others will automatically take over its load.
- Third, round robin DNS makes keeping state for a user more difficult. Say a user is trying to use a "shopping cart" application which keeps the user state in memory on a server. If the servers use round robin DNS, then the client may not hit the same server for each HTTP operation, and so may be told that they are not logged in, because their session is on a different machine. "Stickiness" to a particular round robin IP address is not enforceable, because there are many different client implementations of DNS.

In addition, if you want to remove an IP address, you have to contend with the fact that DNS changes propagate slowly and that many users' DNS servers will have the IP cached for that DNS name for a certain length of time. This means that users may attempt to access the wrong IP address and think that your site is down. The Windows operating system will cache DNS mappings, while Unix clients will not. This results in weird reports of errors if, say, one server out of two goes down. Half your Windows-based users will report your site is down, but the other half will report that it is up, while Unix-based users will report your site works for every even or odd numbered hit.

IP level

A more sophisticated solution is offered by Resonate, in a commercial product called Local Director. Local Director works at the IP level, mapping one "virtual" IP address to the real IP addresses of several machines. It does actually measure resource usage on those machines and chooses the most appropriate one, depending on a set of rules you can control. It easily allows you to remove one of the group for maintenance, unlike round robin DNS. Resonate also has a good reputation for reliability.

Round robin DNS records also have a limit of 32 entries per record, so you can't scale past 32 IP addresses per DNS name. Resonate's Global Director uses DNS for load balancing and does not have this limit. See *http://www.resonate.com/*.

Another way to load balance at the IP level is to set up two servers on opposite sides of the country and assign them both the exact same IP address. The nature of the BGP routing protocol ensures that TCP packets don't get confused; the load is automatically balanced across them.

Yet another clever method of using IP for load balancing is to apply multicasting to the problem. Multicast is a publish-and-subscribe mechanism for data at the IP level. Some IP addresses are designated as multicast addresses. The data sent to a multicast IP address is copied to everyone who has expressed an interest in it, but is not copied to anyone else, saving considerable bandwidth over other broadcasting models. Multicasting can be used for web load balancing to subscribe several web servers to the same multicast address, while instructing each server to respond only to requests for a particular class of URL, say a URL from a certain IP address range, or a URL requesting a certain kind of data. Each server should ignore all other requests.

One problem with multicasting is that all of the routers in between the source and destination have to understand the multicast protocol for the transmission to proceed, but currently some routers do not. For more information on multicasting for web load balancing, see *http://gizmo.lut.ac.uk/~martin/wwwcac/wwwcac.html*.

Ethernet level

Dedicated hardware boxes that do load balancing usually work at the Ethernet layer, mapping one IP address to several different Ethernet cards, sharing the load among them. Working at the Ethernet level limits hardware load balancers to one subnet, while software load balancers like Resonate can work across multiple subnets. Another factor to consider is whether a hardware load balancer must be thrown out when it is obsolete, or if the hardware can be kept and used for something else.

Regardless of whether load balancing is at the DNS level, the IP level, or the Ethernet level, it is more efficient if you are balancing across servers of similar capacity.

Web Server

Web servers have become a commodity. My advice is to use the Apache web server because it is free, highly reliable, and high performance. In fact, most sites on the Internet do use Apache.

Internet Information Server (IIS) is to be avoided, primarily because it has been repeatedly afflicted with serious viruses. There is a Gartner Group report on this serious problem with IIS. But there is another reason to be wary of IIS, which is that Microsoft inevitably tries hard to trap your content in their proprietary and undocumented formats. IIS is a serious danger to the portability of your content. Apache runs fine on Windows and has no such danger. There are also few, if any, viruses that affect Apache.

Web server content and logs should be kept separate, each on dedicated disks to keep them from interfering with each other.

Middleware

Any software that interacts with web servers on one side and database on the other side can be considered middleware. CGI was the original middleware, but no one ever called it that. Shortly after CGI became widely used, Netscape and Microsoft both published APIs for generating dynamic content as part of the web server process itself. They were much faster, but not at all portable and prone to crash the server where CGI was not. Following that, Sun came out with the servlet API for Java, which is intermediate in performance between CGI and server APIs, yet safe and portable. Most current middleware servers evolved out of servlet runners. Tuxedo and messaging products like Tibco and MQ can also be used as middleware.

Sun is currently promoting Enterprise JavaBeans™ as a scalable middleware solution, but it has serious performance problems intrinsic to using remote objects. Remote method calls are far slower than local method calls for many reasons. First, there is the physical distance between machines. The speed of light isn't increasing, so the situation will never get better. Another huge penalty is that you have to serialize and unserialize object parameters to RMI calls.

Another problem with EJBs is testing. You won't be able to inspect RMI network traffic easily, the way you can easily snoop HTTP data. And it's hard to write an RMI test client, but easy to write an HTTP test.

It is interesting to compare HTTP POST commands to remote procedure calls, which is actually what they are. The user reads a form, fills in some data, and submits it to a program running on the remote end. The difference is that the form is human-readable, rather than machine-readable, and no one expects any one client browser to call the remote program with anything near the frequency expected of RMI calls. Yet HTTP POSTs are wildly successful, at least for human input to web sites. The reason is that it is a very standardized thing, with arguments and input coded in a universal way. Anyone from any browser can post to any other web server. Simplicity and portability rule.

Database

Database tables should be defined, mirrored, striped, and laid out in such a way as to have maximum parallelism, keeping the flow of data through the database smooth. Database optimization is a huge topic and many books have been written on the subject. A good database administrator (DBA) is very valuable.

Example Web Site Architectures

Now that you know some of the trade-offs and elements of a web site architecture, you need to decide how to put it all together. There are an infinite number of possible arrangements of web site machines and software, but they fall into a few broad categories, which are easily described. Serving of static content is extremely scalable simply by load balancing across more web servers, so that is not very interesting. Instead, I concentrate on transactional web sites or those composed largely of dynamic content.

A number of exact descriptions of architectures are available by reading the details of vendor performance tests. See the Web Bench tests from *http://www.spec.org/* for examples. The following contain some common themes.

One Box

Most small web sites run entirely from one box, typically using Linux, Apache, MySQL, and Perl (from which we have the acronym LAMP). One box means there will be no network traffic between server-side components, and perhaps even the use of extremely fast-shared memory communication rather than loopback network communication. Though the single server will have to context-switch between the various processes, the single box may still have better performance than dedicated boxes connected by Ethernet. It's not clear whether a single box is more reliable, or less.

Larger web sites can also be run from a single box. In fact, Oracle in particular would love it if you ran an Oracle Web Server and executed Java servlets directly in the database. The downside of this approach is scalability: you're limited to the capacity of that one machine, unless you can successfully cluster this approach, which is difficult.

A similar approach is to have exactly two boxes: one for static content such as images, and one for dynamic content generated by servlets or CGI's. This has the advantage that the boxes can be independently optimized. The static content box should have enough memory to hold all the static content, while the dynamic content box should have multiple fast CPUs.

Stacks

Stacked architecture limits state to the database. The rest of the system is simply a set of funnels to the database, so you can scale simply by adding more of them without worrying about load balancing, state "stickiness," or other problems. No caching of any stateful information occurs in any part of the stack, so performance depends entirely on how quickly you can get to the database and how quickly the database responds. The Achilles' heel is, of course, the database.

An example of one stack using leading commercial software would be load balancing across many small Sun web servers. Each of these connects to a single middleware server running a stateless servlet, which uses Tuxedo for transactional integrity, all of which connect to an Oracle database. That is, one web server, sandwiched in a DMZ by firewalls, mapped to one middleware, mapped to the database.* There is a strong dependency on the network between the pieces, so subnets are used to limit traffic on each segment. Also, if any web server goes down, the connected middleware piece is useless, and vice versa.

---

* A "DMZ" is a demilitarized zone, a place on the network halfway between the wild Internet and your secure internal network.

Layers

The theme of a layered architecture is effective resource utilization. Each web server finds the least loaded middleware server, increasing overall performance by increasing utilization over the stack-based approach. This is sometimes called "n to n." Another advantage is any single machine can go down without hurting the utilization of other machines.

A layer of web servers in a DMZ connecting to a layer of middleware servers adds a load distribution requirement between the web servers and middleware. For increased performance, dual home the web servers: make one network card connect to the Internet, and another to the inside middleware or database.

Many small machines, each with one dedicated application, are much faster than fewer larger machines, and more reliable since one can go down without taking out other apps. This is cheaper per MIP, but takes up more space and imposes a higher administration cost, which may negate that. Computer floor space is actually more expensive than the computers in many places, because it has recurring power and cooling costs.[*]

Linux on the Mainframe

The most interesting new architecture proposal I've heard is to run thousands of Linuxes on one OS390 mainframe, though I don't actually know of any site doing this. There is an excellent introduction to Linux on the mainframe at *http://www.4th. com/tech/linux/vmlinux.shtml*. Like other single-box solutions, there are no internal networking problems. Scalability of mainframes is quite good, and over many years the sizing and performance problems have been fairly well worked out in the mainframe world. The downsides are that mainframes are extremely expensive and proprietary.

Real Time

It is possible to write a web system that has latencies and resource consumption that are exactly known in advance of use, though I do not know of any case where this has been done. From knowing the exact resource consumption, we can also know with certainty exactly how many simultaneous users a given amount of hardware can handle. This means that capacity planning becomes a science and load testing becomes only a confirmation of what we already know.

The way to write such a system is with a "real-time" operating system. To date, real-time OS's have been used mostly for embedded systems requiring fixed and known

---

[*] An "MIP" is a million instructions per second—a measure of computing power.

response times, such as in cars, airplanes, and military weapons. But real-time operating systems can also be used for web servers, middleware, and databases. The Internet itself will still have variable latency, but this does not take away from the benefits of known capacity and known latency on the server side.

A company called TimeSys (*http://www.timesys.com/*) has a real-time Linux kernel and real-time Java Virtual Machine. Latencies are known, but are typically slightly larger than in non–real-time systems. Programmer discipline to profile code and make good use of these abilities is also required.

Trends

Though bandwidth is getting steadily better, latencies are not. Packets move at pretty close to the speed of light right now, and that's not going to improve. This means that an exchange of a thousand small packets takes an amount of time proportional to distance. So geography still matters, and always will.

To compensate for the latencies inherent in the Internet, there is a trend toward pushing things out towards users in advance of their requests. Static content has been distributed to servers around the country and the world by companies like Akamai for some time now. A logical next step is to distribute the page-generation applications themselves.

Finally, I can foresee moving dynamic page generation to the browser itself. In fact, this has already happened to some degree, since the latest browsers can cache XSL and images and update and reformat XML data fragments within a single "page" by clever use of the emerging DOM standard for data structures within the browser and JavaScript to modify those structures. It has been possible for some time to request a fragment of a web document with the HTTP Byterange request, which most web servers support. The problem has been getting the browser to integrate that new fragment into a web page already cached in the browser. These things are already possible with applets, but would require a huge amount of custom work. With DOM, it is far easier. This means that a great deal of middleware code can simply go away. It is also conceivable that browsers might just interact directly with relational databases, issuing their own SQL calls to retrieve and update pages.

At this point, you might say, well, if everything else is in the browser, why not a database too? It's always been there. It's called the browser's cache. Caches are not relational, but the basics of storing and looking up data are there. The biggest problem is that the user has no explicit control over the cache. Users cannot directly query the cache, insert things, or update or delete them. If you happen to know how the cache works in your browser, you can modify it, but that's not at all the same as referring to it programmatically from a web page. Once we have that ability, page and application updates can be much smaller and faster.

Another area of potentially huge performance improvements is reducing the number of packets by the use of the Transaction TCP (T/TCP) protocol, which can set up a TCP connection, deliver data, and close the connection all in a single packet. This is about as good as it gets, but requires updating the TCP stack on client machines. See *http://www.kohala.com/start/ttcp.html* for more information on T/TCP.

Connectivity and Server Software at Well-Known Web Sites

There is a list of Internet access providers and server software used for 40 big companies at *http://www.keynote.com/measures/business/business40.html*. You can figure out all of this information for yourself by using *traceroute* and telnetting to port 80 of well-known servers, but Keynote has been kind enough to publish the results of their own research. For the 40 sites they publish data for, the most popular Internet providers are UUNET, BBN, and MCI, and the most popular web servers are Netscape Enterprise and Apache. An even better site for comprehensive web statistics, such as market share for ISPs, web servers, authoring tools, etc., is at *http://www.securityspace.com/*.

Sample Configurations

Now let's examine some sample configurations of web site architectures for low-, medium-, and high-volume sites.

Low Volume

A low-volume site gets one to ten thousand hits per day. Such a site can easily be run out of your home. A typical configuration for this level is good PC hardware ($2,000) running Linux 2.2 (free), Apache 1.3 (free), with connectivity through a cable modem with 100kbps upstream ($100 per month).

For database functionality, you may use flat files, or read all of the elements into a Perl hash table or array in a CGI, and not see any performance problems for a moderate number of users if the database is smaller than, say, a few thousand items. Once you start getting more than one hit per second, or when the database gets bigger than a few thousand items or has multiple tables, you may want to move to the MySQL free relational database.

The database and connectivity are the weak links here. Apache and Linux, on the other hand, are capable of handling large sites.

Medium Volume

A medium volume site gets ten thousand to one million hits per day. A typical configuration for a medium volume site is a Sun Ultra or an Intel Pentium Pro machine with 128 MB for the operating system and filesystem buffer overhead plus 2 to 4 MB per server process. Of course, more memory is better if you can afford it. Such workstation-class machines cost anywhere between $2,000 and $20,000.

You should have separate disks for serving content and for logging hits (and consider a separate disk for swap space), but the size of the content disk really depends on how much content you are serving. Striped disk arrays get better random access performance because multiple seeks can happen in parallel.

You can increase the number of network interfaces to handle the expected number of hits by simply adding more 10BaseT or 100BaseT cards, up to a limit of approximately 45 for some Solaris systems. The Apache web server still works fine for medium volume web sites, but you may want to go to one of the Netscape or other commercial servers either for heavier loads, for formal support, or for particular security or publishing features.

One million hits per day sounds like a lot, but that's only about 12 hits per second if it's spread evenly throughout the day. Even 20 hits per second is within the capacity of most workstations if the site is serving only static HTML and images rather than creating dynamic content. On the other hand, 20 hits per second is a pretty large load from a network capacity point of view. If the average hit is about 10KB, that's $10KB \times 8$ bits/byte $\times 12 = 983,040$ bits/second. You might think that a single T1 line at 1,544,000 bits per second can handle one million hits per day, but remember that web traffic is bursty (because each HTML page results in immediate requests for all embedded images, applets, and so on), so you should expect frequent peaks of three to five times the average. This means you probably cannot effectively serve a million hits per day from a single T1 line, but you should be able to serve one hundred thousand hits per day.

If your site has a large database access component to it, you'll probably want to use one of the high-capacity commercial RDBMS systems like Oracle, Informix, or Sybase, which can have price tags in the $10,000 to $50,000 range. You'll get best performance by keeping database connections open with a connection manager package from the vendor, but you can also write a connection manager yourself or use a TP monitor to manage connections. You probably should not use CGIs at all, but rather servlets, FastCGI, or a server API such as the Apache API, NSAPI, or ISAPI.

High Volume

A high-volume site gets more than one million hits per day. There are many sample configurations submitted to the SPEC organization described at *http://www.spec.org/osg/web99/* under Tuning Descriptions. Another good place to look for sample configurations is *http://www.sun.com/software/solutions/blueprints/*.

What Are the Busiest Sites on the Web?

There is a list of the 100 most trafficed web sites at *http://www.hot100.com*. The data comes largely from analysis of proxy server logs. The site rankings vary over time, but the following sites were the top 10 as of this writing:

- *http://www.yahoo.com/*
- *http://www.microsoft.com/*
- *http://www.lycos.com/*
- *http://www.aol.com/*
- *http://www.go.com/*
- *http://www.google.com/*
- *http://www.altavista.com/*
- *http://www.excite.com/*
- *http://www.chek.com/*
- *http://www.fortunecity.com/*

Key Recommendations

- Be aware of the trade-offs you have to make.
- For every architecture, ask yourself "If I decide I don't like this, can I migrate away from it easily after having implemented it?".
- Plan for future scalability, not just for your immediate needs.

## CHAPTER 3

Capacity Planning

Most processes can be divided into two classes: I/O-bound and CPU-bound. The serving of static HTML is usually I/O-bound. It is limited by the rate at which a file can be retrieved from disk (if not already in memory) and the speed at which the file can be moved out the network interface. Disk and network are I/O devices, far slower than CPU, so CPU power does not play a significant role.

Generation of dynamic HTML is just the opposite. It is usually CPU-bound, meaning that it takes longer to create the page than it does to move the page out the network interface. CPU is critical here, especially if you're using CGI's or Java servlets to create your dynamic pages. Most of that CPU processing is string manipulation. On the other hand, dynamic content depending that depends on database queries is usually limited by the speed of the database, which in turn is usually I/O-bound because it needs to retrieve data from disk. So how to plan for capacity depends entirely on how your site works.

Do the Math . . .

When you evaluate a potential architecture, the most critical part of the job is to compare your required latency and bandwidth to the rated capacity of every link in your proposed configuration. Each component should meet those requirements with an additional margin for component interaction inefficiencies and increasing load over the life of the architecture. You could skip the calculations and forecasting, buy something that satisfies your immediate requirements, and forge ahead, planning to upgrade when necessary—but there are a few reasons why you're well advised to do a little math and think about where you want the system to go in the future.

First of all, management likes to have a good idea of what they're going to get for the money you're spending. If you spend money on a system that cannot deliver because you didn't do a few calculations, you then have the embarrassing task of explaining why you need to spend more. You may not even be able to use what you have already bought if it's not compatible with the higher-performance equipment you need.

Second, unplanned growth has penalties associated with it—for example, unforeseen barriers to scalability, upgrades, or platform changes. You'll probably need more capacity next year than you do this year. If you cannot easily migrate your content and applications to higher-performance equipment, you will suffer.

Third, unplanned systems are more difficult to manage well because they are more difficult to comprehend. Management is inevitably a larger cost than the equipment itself, so whatever you can do to make management easier is worthwhile.

. . . But Trust Your Eyes More than the Math

It is easy, however, to plan too much. Requirements change and new technologies are making older ones obsolete, so you can't know for sure what you'll need in a year or two. It is a good idea to choose a few pieces of flexible, scalable equipment of adequate rated capacity and try them out together, knowing you can add capacity or alter the architecture as you collect real-world data and as new alternatives become available. Choose components that "play nice" with products from other manufacturers, rather than proprietary components. Starting this way has the substantial advantage of giving you continuous feedback on the performance and reliability of live, interacting equipment.

Don't bet the farm on vendor specifications and advertising. They are less reliable sources of information than firsthand experience or the experience of trusted friends. It is shocking, but true, that some vendors have fudged benchmark and scalability tests in their quest for sales. A real system to build on also gives you a gut-level feel for the kind of performance you can expect. You can use this feel to check your analytical model against reality.

Remember that component ratings are the maximum the vendor can plausibly claim, not what you will get in practice. 10Mbps Ethernet will give you a maximum of about 8Mbps of data throughput in practice. Cause a few problems yourself, just to see what's going to happen next year. Better that your server crashes right in front of you, for known reasons, than when you're in bed at 4 a.m. for unknown reasons. Try the load generation tools mentioned in the load testing chapter, but be sure that the load and network match your production environment. Do some tests over 28.8 kbps modems if your customers will be using them.

Generating relevant and complete tests is tricky. For example, no one has tens of thousands of modems just for generating realistic load; you have to use modem-emulation features of load testing software for that. Watch to be sure that latency remains bounded to some reasonable value when you test at very high throughput. Also watch to see what happens when latency does go up. Many applications are sensitive to latency and simply give up if they have to wait too long for a response.

Given that the hardware of your server defines its maximum capabilities, you might be tempted to buy and assemble the biggest components, thinking that this will result in the highest performance server. It ain't necessarily so. For example, small commodity disk drives are less reliable and have lower capacity than more expensive, larger drives. Nonetheless, you will get better availability and performance for the money from a set of small drives working together in a Redundant Array of Inexpensive Disks (RAID) configuration than from a single large drive. Smaller disks often have lower seek times precisely because they are physically smaller. Server vendors add value to components by working out these interactions and encapsulating them for you, giving you the ability to plan at a higher level.

Questions to Ask

The first step in capacity planning is to clarify your requirements and get them down on paper. Here are some questions that will help you pin down what you need.

How Many HTTP Operations per Unit Time Do You Expect?

Unlike the client/server paradigm in which the most important sizing parameter is the number of concurrent users, the relevant parameter for web servers is HTTP operations per second, also referred to as *hits per second*. Few web sites receive more than 25 hits per second.

Web servers do not maintain a dedicated connection to the browser because HTTP 1.0 is a connectionless protocol. The user connects, requests a document, receives it, and disconnects. HTTP was implemented in this way to keep the protocol simple, to conserve bandwidth, and to allow a web page to consist of components from multiple servers. Even though the user has the impression that he or she has been connected during an entire session of reading pages from a web site, from the server's point of view, the user disappears after each request and reappears only when requesting a new page and associated content (such as images).

This loading characteristic of web servers is changing because HTTP 1.1 does allow the user to remain connected for more than one request. Although most hits are very short in duration, the use of HTTP 1.1 persistent connections can make the number of simultaneous connections relevant to your site. Also, Java applets sometimes open a connection back to the web server they came from and can then keep it open.

Because of the simple nature of HTTP, it is easy to make overly simplified assumptions about what "connections per second" actually means. For example, we usually assume that HTTP requests are fulfilled serially and that the connection time is very short. These assumptions are valid if we are serving relatively few users on a fast LAN connection, but not if we have many users on slow modem connections. In the case of many users with slow access, connections are likely to last more than a second. Each connection will require buffer space and processor time, so the server load calculations should measure the load in concurrent users, which is the typical form of client-server load.

So we see that network speed has an important effect on server sizing. Even though HTTP loads are expressed in hits per second rather than number of concurrent users, you have a qualitatively different load if your users are all on Ethernet than if they are on 28.8 kbps modems. The differences are that the Ethernet users will expect lower latency and the server will have fewer concurrent connections for Ethernet. So in one sense, high-speed users place a larger load on the server, since their latency expectations are more demanding. In another sense, they require less of it, because fewer concurrent connections require less memory.

At any speed, HTTP requests tend to cluster because of the need to retrieve embedded images and other such content. The arrival of one connection is a good indication that several others are very likely to arrive soon. If servers were more clever and more powerful, they'd parse HTML as it is served to find embedded images or applets that belong with each HTML page. They could then begin the retrieval of an HTML page's embedded content before the browser even asks for it.

Load on a server is statistically a function of the time of day. Figure 3-1 shows a typical graph of the load on a web server throughout the day. For content with a global audience, the load rises to a gradual peak about noon in California (which is 3 p.m. in New York and 9 p.m. in London). Depending on the market for the content, the shape of this curve will vary over the day and over the week. Stock quote servers will be busiest during working days. Servers advertising specific events can expect a flood of users during the event and relatively few thereafter. Peaks of three to five times the average load are typical during special events. As a general rule, permanent web sites see a continuous rise in load as more people get connected to the Internet, so you must build for this expected growth. The web is not only expanding, but may even be accelerating its growth as it moves to encompass noncomputer devices, DSL, and other technologies give users more network bandwidth.

Keep in mind that even a million hits per day, which until recently would put your site into the top rank of web sites, is not a particularly heavy load per second when averaged smoothly over the day: $1,000,000 / (60 \times 60 \times 24) = 11.6$ hits/second. Given a 10K average transfer size, this load is within the capabilities of even modest machines, but requires a network capable of handling 10240 bytes * 11.6/second * 8 bits/byte * 1.3 for network overhead = 1.2Mbit/second, which is theoretically within range of a T1 connection. It is unlikely that a million hits will be so evenly distributed in time, but the point is that it is within reach of most organizations to run a very substantial web site.

See *Getting Connected* by Kevin Dowd (O'Reilly & Associates) for a worksheet on estimating your Internet bandwidth requirements.

What Is the Purpose of the Web Site?

The purpose of the site will affect the distribution of the load over time. For example, a site used to support a classroom lecture will see a large jump in hits during the

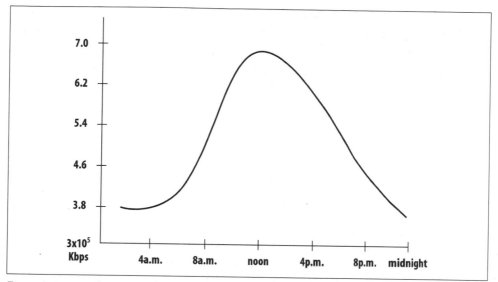

Figure 3-1. Typical Sprint NY NAP usage data from http://www.nlanr.net/

class and possibly synchronized hits during the class hour. Sizing for the average number of hits over the day will result in a system that is inadequate for this class. You may need to size with the assumption that all users will need near-simultaneous access to the same pages. So if there are 30 class members, you may need to provide a server that can handle 30 hits per second, even though this could also be expressed as several million hits per day.

How Tolerant Are Your Users?

Put another way, what are your throughput and latency goals? It is essential to attach numbers and distributions to these goals if you are serious about improving performance. For example, you might establish a goal of satisfying 90 percent of HTTP requests for files under 10K at a rate of 5 seconds or less for each file. Given such a specific goal, you not only have a concrete starting point for planning, but also a clear indication of whether your planning was successful.

User happiness can also be a numerical goal if you decide to measure it. While happiness will vary with the patience of the user and is a "soft" psychology question, surveys give hard numbers, which at least tell you whether satisfaction is rising or falling.

This does not mean that you need only one set of goals. Most sites give all users the same priority, but it is certainly feasible to segment the market. That is, you can provide restricted access to a high-performance server for some users and broader access to a lower-performance server for others. You can even provide differing grades of access to the exact same content if you serve the content from a high-speed NFS server and refer to the same NFS-mounted files from the two web servers of varying capacity. Or you can dual-serve content from a database. In any case, simply restricting the number of users on one web server may define that machine as higher-performance, since it will have a lighter load.

You can also differentiate service on the basis of network speed, server capacity, and many other factors. This differentiation may seem elitist, but there are often practical reasons for it. For example, doctors need immediate access to patient records, while insurance companies can tolerate a longer wait, though both may need access to the same information. So providing a restricted higher-performance service to one group may be a viable solution to complex goals.

Your throughput and latency goals should be checked against the hard limits of your users' network access potential as well as user expectations. A goal of 50 kbps throughput per user is simply unreachable for end users accessing the data through 28.8 kbps modems. Similarly, a latency goal of 10 milliseconds just can't be met for access from Europe to California because that's faster than the speed of light. Expectations vary with network access quality as well. A user with a 28.8 kbps modem might be happy waiting 10 seconds for a static 5K page of HTML text, and may be even more forgiving for images or CGI-calculated output.

Ethernet LAN users accessing an intranet site will have higher expectations, but they may actually see worse throughput during peak loads, because Ethernet performance degrades nonlinearly with throughput. As an Ethernet network approaches its maximum throughput, its latency increases dramatically, to the point where it is no longer usable. In grim Darwinian fashion, when some users give up in frustration, performance gets significantly better for those who remain.

Will You Provide Any Streaming Media?

Streaming media, such as continuous audio or video, needs to be sized separately from the web server, because they are different in nature and may be of indeterminate size. They use up a lot of network bandwidth and have strict latency requirements. A stream can also last minutes. This is far different from the connect time of a standard HTTP transfer, which should last only seconds at most.

Streaming media servers should be sized by the number of simultaneous connections desired, not by connections per second. Some streaming media may use UDP rather than TCP, which decreases system load because is no overhead for maintaining fixed connections. Multicast streaming, where many clients listen to the same data stream, is more efficient for your server as well.

Will the Web Server Spawn Additional Processes?

While serving static HTML and images is rarely enough load to make the server the bottleneck, using CGIs, servlets, or server APIs to dynamically generate HTML or other content can slow your server to a crawl, especially if the content generation requires database access. The load generated by CGIs and databases varies enormously with the application, so it is impossible to make sizing calculations without detailed analysis or experience with the application. When planning a web application, size the server around the content-generation application, because that will be more resource-intensive than serving the results.

Also consider that it is often possible to push some of the processing work onto the client by using Java or JavaScript. Database tuning is a huge field in its own right. Also, see *Oracle Performance Tuning*, by Mark Gurry and Peter Corrigan (O'Reilly & Associates), and see Chapter 20, for hints on how to reduce the impact of CGI.

What Other Processes Need to Run on the Web Server or over the Network?

Don't forget to size for other services that may be running on your web server at the same time. Small companies may be forced by economics to use their web server for additional purposes, such as DNS or NFS services. The load imposed by these other services will reduce the performance of your web server.

A particularly bad additional use for a web server is as a programmer's workstation. I've been the programmer assigned to use a test web server as my work machine, and I found it unacceptable for the usual programming work of coding, compiling, and testing because of large drops in compilation and network performance when the CGI's on the test web server were being hit, even though keyboard response remained good due to the very high priority of keyboard interrupts. Conversely, web server performance suffers from the presence of a programmer on the web server machine.

Also take into account the possible need to share your web server's connection to the Internet with users inside your company who browse the Internet. On a more local scale, if your web server must share a LAN with an NFS server, for example, you need to take into account the bandwidth required by that NFS server in sizing the LAN.

What Sort of Scalability Do You Need?

When you have reached the limits of the current configuration, can you gracefully add more hardware to increase capacity, or will you have to rework everything? Can you upgrade the operating system to handle the new hardware? The ability to gracefully increase the capacity of an architecture is known as scalability. Scalability even has a number associated with it: the ratio of performance increase relative to the hardware you've added, such as RAM, CPU cards, network interface cards, etc. If you get x performance with one CPU and $1.6 x$ performance with 2 CPUs, then your CPU scalability is .6.

Perfect scalability would be getting exactly as much additional performance as additional hardware. Scalability can also be less than zero, meaning that you get worse performance with more hardware! Scalability of less than zero happens because of the overhead in coordinating the activity of all of the components. All systems have negative scalability at some point.

Note the word "gracefully" in the scalability definition. It should not require blood, sweat, or tears to add additional capacity, meaning no major system or database overhauls. It is simple to add more servers next to the first one; the hard part is to add them without turning access to your data into the bottleneck. You might think you can simply replicate or partition your data among machines to provide better access, but replication and partitioning require synchronization and coordination, which are complicated. Some middleware is designed to share load across multiple machines, but that doesn't mean it's easy.

If you haven't planned for it, you don't have scalability. Scalability is the reason why adding CPUs to a single machine is preferred over adding entire mirror machines: it is very quick and simple. Mirror machines may work fine for serving static HTML, but you still have the complexity of keeping them synchronized. Setting up a web-based system for database input or transaction processing always requires real planning for scalability.

It is depressingly typical to build a system that satisfies your immediate needs, only to find that you have to rework it entirely when your needs increase or otherwise change. Given that the Internet is still expanding and new uses are still being found for it, it is certainly advisable to build for growth. The downside is scalable components almost always cost more. Here are a few examples:

- IDE disks and controllers are cheaper, but SCSI scales to much higher throughput.
- A 56K leased line is usually cheaper than the same bandwidth of fractional T1, but the fractional T1 can be upgraded via a computer in the central phone office, while the 56K line cannot be upgraded at all and must be replaced.
- An ordinary PC is limited in the amount of RAM it can take. You may absolutely need more RAM, but find that your machine simply has no extra place to put it, meaning you have to buy not only the RAM, but an entirely new machine.
- It is easier to get started with Windows NT than with Unix, but Unix scales all the way from very cheap 586 hardware (that cannot run NT) up to supercomputers (which also cannot run NT). It also scales sideways across various CPUs.

The scalability of various components is considered in their respective chapters in of this book. The scalability of entire architectures is considered in Chapter 2.

What Is Your Budget?

Money is an important capacity-planning parameter, too. Although how much you can spend defines a hard upper limit on the possible performance of your web site, the range of attainable performance at any given level of spending is huge. You can spend all of your money on equipment that doesn't work together, essentially throwing it away. On the other hand, careful planning and configuration can help you surpass the performance of far more expensive but ill-conceived sites.

It is critical to budget for ongoing maintenance and upgrades when planning your web site. In the long run, these costs will be larger than your initial outlay for equipment. Network connection fees, system administration tasks costs (such as pruning and interpreting log files), and performance monitoring and adjustment costs should all be included in your budget.

How Available Does Your Site Have to Be?

Availability refers to the percentage of time your system is up. Some web sites require 100 percent availability, especially transaction-processing sites, such as banking and brokerage sites. The Internet itself is reasonably reliable because of its built-in ability to route around problems, although it is common for servers providing only static content to be mirrored at several places around the Internet for availability and performance reasons. Transactional sites are generally not mirrored because of the difficulty in coordinating data access across multiple servers. So we must look to individual servers for high availability transaction sites.

The disk drive is by far the hardware component most likely to fail, since it has moving parts. Disk drive unreliability can be overcome, however, by using RAID. See Chapter 16 for a discussion about RAID and disk availability.

Other parts of the server hardware and operating system also have an impact on availability. Commodity PCs are not built for extremely high reliability and occasionally have problems such as thermal shutdown, when connectors disengage due to expansion caused by heat. Workstations are more expensive but have higher quality components and manufacturing. Mainframes are extraordinarily stable but also extraordinarily expensive, so most web sites are run from PC or Unix workstation hardware.

As for operating systems, Windows and Macintosh, though simple, are not stable enough for very important sites. Unix is the most stable operating system for workstations and PCs, sometimes running for years without needing to be rebooted. There are also extremely high-availability operating systems, such as Tandem's line, and hardware failover solutions at additional cost. These are widely used by banks.

Web servers and your web applications themselves have a large impact on your availability. Those that leak memory will slow down your system, and eventually require restarting applications or rebooting. Tools that find memory leaks, such as Purify (*http://www.rational.com/*), can help you fix leaks in your applications, but not leaks in commercial applications like web servers.

All commercial web sites should have uninterruptable power supplies (UPS), both to have a reserve of power in the event of a blackout and to be protected from power surges that can damage equipment. Large commercial web hosting companies often have emergency diesel generators that can be run as long as needed for the power to return.

Finally, consider automatically emailing the pager of your system administrator when performance drops below a certain level. See Chapter 4 for a script that does this. Performance can be monitored from a failover machine or even from somewhere else on the Internet.

Clustering machines (that is, setting up several machines that act as one) can give you better reliability and scalability than is possible with one machine, but have a huge cost and complexity. In a cluster, each machine is equivalent and is monitoring the health of the others. If one machine fails, the others just pick up its load. The machines may share a RAID disk so that they all have access to the same data, yet there is no single point of failure. Note that this is different than a server farm, which is simply a group of distinct machines. Unix machine clustering has been well worked out over the last several years. Windows clustering is also starting to arrive.

Can You Force Suppliers to Compete?

There is a temptation to buy whatever solution is the cheapest or requires the least work to get started. This often means buying everything from a single vendor, which may work just fine for small installations that you know won't grow, but there is a well-known hazard to single-vendor solutions. Once your content or application is tied to some proprietary format, your vendor has you over a barrel. The cost of reworking your content and architecture for some other platform is usually large enough that the vendor can later charge outrageous fees for upgrades or maintenance and you will find it cheaper to simply pay up than to consider switching.

It may in fact cost you more to switch vendors than it cost to implement the solution in the first place. You can't just throw everything out and start over; you have to spend time and money to undo what you've done—for example, to extract your data from some proprietary format or to retrain programmers. Worse, you may find that even though you've paid for repeated upgrades, you still cannot get the scalability, performance, or functionality you need.

One solution to this problem is to use only open standards, by which I mean free, published specifications that have been implemented in fact, not just potentially, by multiple vendors. Open standards include TCP/IP, SVR4 Unix, C, Java, XML, and the standards that have made the web as valuable as it is: HTTP and HTML.

Hey Kid, Want to Try a Browser?

So why does anyone use proprietary platforms? One reason is that proprietary platforms are sometimes given away for free. They are free because vendors can make back an initial loss many times over once users are dependent on a platform. In the web space, Internet Information Server and Internet Explorer are good examples. They are bundled with Windows, so commodity PC hardware includes them. Naive web developers may consider them a good deal regardless of performance because they have not explicitly had to pay for and install them, unlike Netscape's products. Unfortunately, once they write content for any of their proprietary features, such as ISAPI or ActiveX or C#, they no longer have the option of using Netscape servers for that content. Not that Netscape doesn't play a lot of the same games: they have their own web content hooks, such as extensions to JavaScript and extensions to HTML.

At the risk of repeating myself, the lesson is that the free market will fail you in proportion to the difficulty of switching to a competing vendor's products. Only constant competition among vendors using open standards will guarantee improvement and portability. Open-standard monitoring and testing tools will still work even if you change vendors.

The rational motive for using proprietary platforms is they often actually do provide better performance than any implementation of open standards. For example, CGI is an open standard, yet its performance is intrinsically poor. NSAPI and ISAPI are proprietary server API's, which tie your work to one server platform, yet they easily beat CGI in performance. So you have a trade-off to make. Just be aware of what you're getting yourself into. Before you start, ask yourself: "If I don't like this, can I get out easily?"

Other Questions

There are many other requirements to establish before you can complete a web architecture, and these go beyond the performance issues of this book. Among them are the degree of security your web site needs, what programming environment your programmers are used to, and whether you can integrate new and existing equipment.

How Much Bandwidth Do You Need?

Server bandwidth is the single most important factor in the performance of your web site. The math to determine what bandwidth you need is, in essence, very simple:

```
hits/second * average size of a hit in bits = bits/second
```

That is, you need some estimate of the number of hits per second you want to be able to serve. Then you need to know the average size of one of these hits. From this, you know what sort of network bandwidth you need.

Latencies Are More Important than Bandwidth

It has become clear that the number of packets is a more significant determinant of web performance than raw bandwidth once users are beyond ordinary dial-up modems. This is because each packet must be acknowledged, and the speed of light fixed, while bandwidth is increasing. It may take 20 milliseconds to send a 1500-byte packet to a PC on a DSL line, but only 12 milliseconds to get it from the network into the PC. It will take another 20 milliseconds for the acknowledgment to get back to the sender. So the 40 milliseconds latency is more than three times as important as bandwidth in this case, and it will only get more important later.

This is why it is so important to keep the number of individual items on a page to a minimum. Still, because most browsers are multithreaded, some latencies can happen in parallel. It turns out through experimentation that the best number of embedded images on a page is about the same as the number of threads the browser uses. For example, Netscape uses four threads, and you may get best performance by breaking a single large image into four smaller ones, in which acknowledgments can proceed in parallel rather than being strictly serial. But this holds only where the browser uses HTTP persistent connections ("keepalives") to avoid the overhead of setting up a TCP connection for each of the four smaller images.

Here are some numbers to help think about latency. While the latency from CPU to memory is on the order of 100 nanoseconds, LAN latency is usually about 1 millisecond, or 10,000 times slower. Going across a campus with its own network, latencies are about 5 milliseconds. Going across the Internet, latencies range from 10 to 500 milliseconds. Satellite links can take a whole second or more.

Thinking About Bandwidth

You can get some perspective when thinking about bandwidth from the Table 3-1. Note that this chart uses the decimal million (1000000) and not "mega," which is 2^{20} = 1048576.

Table 3-1. Bandwidth comparison

Mode of data transfer	Million bits/second	Comments
Fast typist	0.000035	70 words/min $\times$ 5 chars/word $\times$ 6 bits/char $\times$ M/10^6 $\times$ min/60 seconds.
4800 bps modem	0.004800	4800 bits/sec $\times$ M/10^6. This is also about maximum human reading speed.
POTS sampling rate	0.064000	Voice over plain old telephone service is sampled at 64 kbps.
ISDN, two channels bonded	0.128000	
One million 10000-byte web hits in one day, evenly distributed	0.925925	10^6 hits/day $\times$ 80Kbits/hit $\times$ day/86400 seconds $\times$ M/10^6.
Audio CD	1.411200	44100 samples/second $\times$ 16 bits/sample $\times$ 2 (stereo) $\times$ M/10^6.

Table 3-1. Bandwidth comparison (continued)

Mode of data transfer	Million bits/ second	Comments
T-1 (DS-1 or primary ISDN)	1.544000	Carries 24 POTS channels with 8 kbps overhead.
Ethernet	10.00000	
Token Ring	16.00000	
IDE Hard disk	16.00000	Sustained throughput.
T-3 (DS-3)	44.60000	672 DS-0's, 28 DS-1's, or 7 DS-2's.
FDDI and Fast Ethernet	100.0000	
ISA Bus	128.0000	16 bits @ 8 MHz.
Broadband ISDN	135.0000	
ATM	154.0000	
250 million 10000-byte web hits in one day, evenly distributed	231.4812	About one hit for every U.S. citizen.
EISA bus	264.0000	
Wide Ultra SCSI disk controller	320.0000	
100-nanosecond RAM	320.0000	$32 \text{ bits} / (100 \times 10^{-9}) \text{ seconds} \times M/10^{6}$.
Gigabit Ethernet	1000.000	
PCI Bus	2112.000	64 bits @ 33 MHz.
AT&T Sonet	2400.000	Long-distance fiber trunk.
CPU	3200.000	Hypothetical CPU processing 32-bit instructions at 100Mhz, one per clock cycle.
Human eye-to-brain rate	5600.000	Estimated.
Highest achieved fiber optics	16000.00	Bell Labs.
Theoretical fiber capacity	64000.00	

This chart ignores latency, which varies even from bit to bit, and can be huge, especially upon startup of any component. If you're a bit romantic, you can imagine a blurry picture of virtual reality coming into focus over the years in this chart, from short symbol transmissions twenty years ago, to the limit of human audio perception today, to the limit of visual perception in the coming years.

Estimating Web Server Network Bandwidth

The following chart displays an estimate of the number of hits per second of a given size (y-axis) a given amount of bandwidth (x-axis) can handle with a 30 percent deduction for TCP/IP and other network overhead. Numbers are truncated to integers, so 0 means "less than one per second" rather than truly zero.

Table 3-2. Web server bandwidth requirements

Hit Size	28.8K	56k	ISDN(2)	T1	10bT	T3	100bT Ethernet
1 KB	2	4	10	132	854	3845	8544
2 KB	1	2	5	66	427	1922	4272
4 KB	0	1	2	33	213	961	2136
8 KB	0	0	1	16	106	480	1068
16 KB	0	0	0	8	53	240	534
32 KB	0	0	0	4	26	120	267
64 KB	0	0	0	2	13	60	133
132 KB	0	0	0	1	6	30	66
264 KB	0	0	0	0	3	15	33
512 KB	0	0	0	0	1	7	16
1 MB	0	0	0	0	0	3	8
2 MB	0	0	0	0	0	1	4

You can use the table to estimate, for example, how many 4K files per second your T1 line can handle. The answer is 33. Keep in mind that the table refers just to the network capacity and does not say whether the load was generated by static HTML or CGIs. That is, network capacity says nothing about the capacity of your disk or server CPU, or of a database behind the web server.

In fact, the capacity of a server to fill a network connection is distinctly nonlinear. Smaller packets require a larger overhead in terms of interrupts and packet header processing. This means that sending two packets will require more of the server than combining them into one larger packet.

The table is also a bit deceptive in that you will rarely see a smooth distribution of hits filling your network capacity. Rather, there will be peaks of three to four times the average rate per second and long troughs of no load at all.

To scale any of these connection types, you can add more network cards or modems until you reach the maximum number of cards or modems the server has room for. Then you can move up to the next connection type or to a bigger server. This is the easy way to do things, throwing more hardware into a single server. Scaling across multiple servers is typically more complicated, requiring load balancing strategies.

How Fast a Server Do You Need?

Given a certain network bandwidth, how fast a server do you need? More server disk speed, bus speed, and CPU speed all cost money. From the network bandwidth, you have an upper limit on the HTTP server hardware you need for serving static content such as HTML and images. A 250 MHz Pentium machine serving static files from

Apache is capable of filling a 10 Mbps Ethernet line, because static pages are I/O-bound, not CPU-bound. On the other hand, sites that do a lot of servlets, CGI, or other dynamic content generation, are typically CPU-bound. If you have any dynamic content, you should size your server around that.

Another point to keep in mind is performance serving static files is not a bottleneck for most sites. Server performance is plenty fast enough with pretty much every web server, where "fast enough" means "faster than your outgoing line." Remember that there's no point in buying server hardware that has vastly more throughput capacity than the network it's connected to because you can't use that server's throughput. The web server software and operating system determine how efficiently you can use your server hardware.

The whole connection time for an Internet HTTP transfer is typically 1 to 10 seconds, most of which is usually caused by modem and Internet bandwidth and latency limitations. While this may be frustrating, it does leave quite a bit of breathing room for the server. It makes little sense to insure that a lightly loaded server can generate a response to an HTTP request in one millisecond if the network is going to consume thousands of milliseconds.

This is not to say that web server performance on the Internet is not important; without planning and tuning, a site that performs very well at low volume can degrade dramatically at high volume, overwhelming network considerations, especially if dynamically generated content is involved. But you can easily set up a server and get reasonable performance at light loads without any tuning, giving you some time to figure out what you want to do in the long term for the inevitable increase in load as the web expands.

Symmetric Multi-Processing (SMP) machines have multiple equivalent CPUs. SMP servers scale well because you simply add more CPUs, I/O boards, and storage to get more capacity. SMP machines also have load balancing and redundancy built in. Since most of HTTP's work is done by TCP and since TCP implementations formerly were single-threaded, there was no way to allocate different threads to different CPUs. So, there was no way to take advantage of the multiple CPUs. This changed with Solaris 2.6 as well as with operating systems from other vendors; they now have multithreaded TCP. You may also use SMP to scale multithreaded FastCGI programs or Java programs that use native threads.

Commercial benchmark tests are not useful for forecasting absolute performance because test conditions are very artificial, involving extremely high-speed networks not normally used for surfing the Web. Rather, the use of benchmarks in capacity planning is to get some idea of the relative performance of different components.

CPU power and parallelism are increasing, but for a few years Java and OO techniques were capable of using or wasting all the power you could throw at them. Now that Java is maturing, we should see Java applications get much faster and more efficient. Another big problem is the bloat of applications. Older applications are generally much smaller and quicker, so you can sometimes get much better performance by downgrading software to earlier revisions.

How Much Memory Do You Need?

The answer is "more." It's a rule of thumb that you always need more memory. The worst thing short of total failure that can happen to your server is a memory shortage serious enough to start the swapping of entire processes out to disk. When that happens, performance will quickly drop, and users will wonder if it's worth their time to wait for your content. It is better to refuse the excess connections you cannot handle well than for all of your users to get unacceptable performance.

Servers that run as multiple processes, such as Apache, have a configurable limit to the number of processes and simultaneous connections per process. Multithreaded servers provide limits to the number of active threads. See Chapter 18 for details. You can also limit incoming connections by setting the TCP listen queue small enough so that you are assured of being able to service the users who have connected.

A server that is short of memory may show high CPU utilization because it constantly needs to scan for pages of memory to move out to disk. In such a case, adding CPU power won't help; you need to add more memory or reduce memory usage. Look at the rate of page scanning with *vmstat* under Solaris or with the Performance Monitor under NT. Under Solaris, the sr column of *vmstat* will tell you the scan rate. Sustained scanning for memory is an indication of a memory shortage. Under NT, the clue is that your processor time will be high and almost entirely "privileged" time. This means that the CPU is doing almost no work on behalf of the web server, but only on behalf of the OS itself.

There is a limit to the amount of memory any particular machine physically has room for. Be aware that this is a hard limit on scalability for that machine. When you hit that limit, you will have to replace the machine or offload some of the processing— for example, by running servlets on a middleware box rather than the web server itself.

Memory for the Operating System

First, let's consider the operating system. Linux 2.0 can run well in less than 8 MB, while you should budget 128 MB for Solaris 8 unless you know your configuration requires less. That's just for the operating system, not the web server or applications. Also, it is ironic but true that your OS itself will require slightly more memory when you have more memory. This is because the kernel uses memory to keep tables that track memory usage.

One reason more RAM helps very busy web servers is impolite clients that disconnect abruptly leave open TCP connections, which consume RAM in the kernel until they eventually time out. This often happens because users just switch off their modem or PC with the hardware switch rather than shutting it down via software. The number of such connections can rapidly accumulate on busy web servers. The Unix *netstat* command is an easy way to see how many connections exist at the moment. See the "Keepalive interval" item in the section "TCP" in Chapter 15 for more about the TCP "keepalive" timeout, which clears out the unused connections.

Another reason more RAM helps very busy web servers is many actively used connections can accumulate due to the bandwidth limitations of the Internet. Each connection requires about 50 KB TCP/IP socket buffer memory, whether it's in use or not.

Memory for httpd

Now you should budget for the number of server daemons you have running on top of the memory you have for the OS. Allocate 1 or 2 megabytes per server daemon running as a separate process; you can see memory usage of *httpd* processes with *top* or *ps*. For threaded servers, Adrian Cockcroft, a Sun performance expert, made a rough recommendation of 1M per server process plus 100K per thread, because he measured Netscape 2.0 processes—which can spawn up to 32 threads—and found that they used about 1M when idle and grew to be 3M to 4M when busy, probably due to caching of content. From this it can be assumed that the 32 threads took up 3M, so that's about 100K each. You should also allocate about 50K for each network connection, the number of which will be the same as the number of threads running.

Memory for Content

Of course it is best if you can provide enough RAM to hold all of your static content. Many servers cache recently accessed pages in memory, even though the pages may already be in the filesystem cache. This caching by the server may improve performance slightly over the user of the filesystem cache alone, but it could also double your memory usage. Try turning off the web server's cache and compare performance and memory usage. You may save memory and not lose any performance. Netscape (now iPlanet) servers *mmap* content files, avoiding the double copy.

Memory for CGIs

To budget memory for CGIs, you need to know how many CGIs will be running concurrently. To know the number of concurrent CGIs you'll be running, you need to know the number of CGI requests per second and the time each CGI takes to complete. But that completion time depends on how many CGIs are running! The recursive math quickly gets daunting, but you can get some estimates from running *ps* or *top* to count the number of concurrent CGI's at a sample moment in time.

The safe thing is to budget enough memory to run as many CGI processes as you have server threads or daemons, on the assumption that each thread or daemon may run a CGI concurrently with all the others. CGI processes can easily require more memory than the *httpd* process itself, especially if the CGI is written in an interpreted language (which requires loading the interpreter), or if the CGI accesses a database (which often has large connection libraries that must be loaded before a connection can be made). The use of Transaction Processing (TP) monitors can help performance by managing a pool of open database connections rather than opening a new connection for each CGI. See Chapter 20 for additional hints on how to reduce CGI executable sizes.

It does not take twice as much memory to run two copies of a program, since the text segment can be shared between concurrent instances of the same program, although the heap and stack can not. Use the Unix *size* program to determine the size of the text, data, and bss (uninitialized data) segments of your CGI. The data and bss give you a lower limit for how much additional RAM each instance of the CGI will use. The CGI will use more memory as it runs. Use *ps* and *top* to see how much unshared memory is really being used for a typical copy of the CGI. *pmap -x* is also useful on Solaris. Budget RAM for one copy of the text segment of the CGI, plus RAM for stack, heap, and both initialized and uninitialized data for each concurrent user you expect. Then consider that you need more RAM if users are connecting over 28.8 kbps than over a LAN because the connections are around longer (since the user can't get data out as fast). This means more concurrently running connections and CGIs. A slow CPU will have a similar effect, requiring more RAM.

Key Recommendations

- Write down your requirements.
- Remember that the network constrains the server output.
- Size your server first for the back-end applications, because these are almost always heavier than simple web serving.
- For every architecture, ask yourself "If I decide I don't like this, can I migrate away from it easily after having implemented it?"
- Plan for future scalability, not just for your immediate needs.
- Keep performance records so you know whether your site is meeting expectations.

## CHAPTER 4

Performance Monitoring

The first thing you should do in tuning a web site is to monitor that site so you can see patterns and trends. From this you'll know whether you're helping or not. And as we will see later, the same programs we write for monitoring can also be used for load testing.

In this chapter, we first define some parameters of performance. Then we show how to monitor them with free software from *http://patrick.net/*, without installing anything on production machines.

Parameters of Performance

There are four classic parameters describing the performance of any computer system: latency, throughput, utilization, and efficiency. Tuning a system for performance can be defined as minimizing latency and maximizing the other three parameters. Though the definition is straightforward, the task of tuning itself is not, because the parameters can be traded off against one another and will vary with the time of day, the sort of content served, and many other circumstances. In addition, some performance parameters are more important to an organization's goals than others.

Latency and Throughput

Latency is the time between making a request and beginning to see a result. Some define latency as the time between making a request and the completion of the response, but this definition does not clearly distinguish the psychologically significant time spent waiting, not knowing whether a request has been accepted or understood. You will also see latency defined as the inverse of throughput, but this is not useful because latency would then give you the same information as throughput. Latency is measured in units of time, such as seconds.

Throughput is the number of items processed per unit time, such as bits transmitted per second, HTTP operations per day, or millions of instructions per second (MIPS). It is conventional to use the term "bandwidth" when referring to throughput in bits per second. Throughput is found by adding up the number of items and dividing by the sample interval. This calculation may produce correct but misleading results because it ignores variations in processing speed within the sample interval.

The following examples help clarify the difference between latency and throughput:

- An overnight (24-hour) shipment of 1000 different CDs holding 500 megabytes each has terrific throughput but lousy latency. The throughput is $(500 \times 2^{20} \times 8 \times 1000)$ bits/$(24 \times 60 \times 60)$ seconds = about 49 million bits/second, which is better than a T3's 45 million bits/second. The difference is the overnight shipment bits are delayed for a day and then arrive all at once, but T3 bits begin to arrive immediately, so the T3 has much better latency, even though both methods have approximately the same throughput when considered over the interval of a day. We say that the overnight shipment is bursty traffic. This example was adapted from *Computer Networks* by Andrew S. Tanenbaum (Prentice Hall, 1996).

- Trucks have great throughput because you can carry so much on them, but they are slow to start and stop. Motorcycles have low throughput because you can't carry much on them, but they start and stop more quickly and can weave through traffic so they have better latency.

- Supermarkets would like to achieve maximum throughput per checkout clerk because they can then get by with fewer clerks. One way for them to do this is to increase your latency—that is, to make you wait in line, at least up to the limit of your tolerance. In his book *Configuration and Capacity Planning for Solaris Servers* (Prentice Hall), Brian Wong phrased this dilemma well by saying that throughput is a measure of organizational productivity while latency is a measure of individual productivity. The supermarket may not want to waste your individual time, but it is even more interested in maximizing its own organizational productivity.

- One woman has a throughput of one baby per nine months, barring twins, triplets, etc. Nine women may be able to bear nine babies in nine months, giving the group a throughput of one baby per month, even though the latency cannot be decreased (i.e., even nine women cannot produce one baby in one month). This mildly offensive but unforgettable example is from *The Mythical Man-Month* by Frederick P. Brooks (Addison Wesley).

Although high throughput systems often have low latency, there is no causal link. You've just seen how an overnight shipment can have high throughput with high latency. Large disks tend to have better throughput but worse latency; the disk is physically bigger, so the arm has to seek longer to get to any particular place. The latency of packet network connections also tends to increase with throughput. As you approach your maximum throughput, there are simply more or larger packets to put on the wire, so a packet will have to wait longer for an opening, increasing latency. This is especially true for Ethernet, which allows packets to collide and simply retransmits them if there is a collision, hoping that it retransmitted them into an open slot. It seems obvious that increasing throughput capacity will decrease latency for packet switched networks. However, while latency due to traffic congestion can be reduced, increasing bandwidth will not help in cases in which the latency is imposed by routers or sheer physical distance.

Finally, you can also have low throughput with low latency: a 14.4 kbps modem may get the first of your bits back to you reasonably quickly, but its relatively low throughput means it will still take a tediously long time to get a large graphic to you. With respect to the Internet, the point to remember is that latency can be more significant than throughput. For small HTML files, say under 2K, more of a 28.8 kbps modem user's time is spent between the request and the beginning of a response than waiting for the file to complete its arrival.

A graph of latency versus load is very different from a graph of throughput versus load. Latency will go up exponentially, making a characteristic "backwards L"-shaped graph. Throughput will go up linearly at first, then level out to become nearly flat. Simply by looking at a graph of load test results, you can immediately have a good idea whether it is a latency or throughput graph.

Network Latency

Each step on the network from client to server and back contributes to the latency of an HTTP operation. It is difficult to figure out where in the network most of the latency originates, but there are two commonly available Unix tools that can help. (Note that we're considering network latency here, not application latency, which is the time the applications running on the server itself take to begin to put a result back out on the network.)

If your web server is accessed over the Internet, then much of your latency is probably due to the store-and-forward nature of routers. Each router must accept an incoming packet into a buffer, look at the header information, and make a decision about where to send the packet next. Even once the decision is made, the router will often have to wait for an open slot to send the packet. The latency of your packets will therefore depend strongly on the number of router hops between the web server and the user. Routers themselves will have connections to each other that vary in latency and throughput.

The odd but essential characteristic about the Internet is the path between two endpoints can change automatically to accommodate network trouble, so your latency may vary from packet to packet. Packets can even arrive out of order. You can see the current path your packets are taking and the time between router hops by using the *traceroute* utility that comes with most versions of Unix. (See the *traceroute* manpage for more information.) A number of kind souls have made *traceroute* available from their web servers back to the requesting IP address, so you can look at path and performance to you from another point on the Internet, rather than from you to that point. One page of links to *traceroute* servers is at *http://www.slac.stanford.edu/comp/net/wan-mon/traceroute-srv.html*. Also see *http://www.internetweather.com/* for continuous measurements of ISP latency as measured from one point on the Internet.

Note that by default *traceroute* does a reverse DNS lookup on all intermediate IPs so you can see their names, but this delays the display of results. You can skip the DNS lookup with the *-n* option and you can do fewer measurements per router (the default is three) with the *-q* option. Here's an example of *traceroute* usage:

```
% traceroute -q 2 www.umich.edu
traceroute to www.umich.edu (141.211.144.53), 30 hops max, 40 byte packets
1  router.cableco-op.com (206.24.110.65) 22.779 ms 139.675 ms
2  mv103.mediacity.com (206.24.105.8) 18.714 ms 145.161 ms
3  grfge000.mediacity.com (206.24.105.55) 23.789 ms 141.473 ms
4  bordercore2-hssi0-0.SanFrancisco.mci.net (166.48.15.249) 29.091 ms 39.856 ms
5  bordercore2.WillowSprings.mci.net (166.48.22.1) 63.16 ms 62.75 ms
6  merit.WillowSprings.mci.net (166.48.23.254) 82.212 ms 76.774 ms
7  f-umbin.c-ccb2.umnet.umich.edu (198.108.3.5) 80.474 ms 76.875 ms
8  www.umich.edu (141.211.144.53) 81.611 ms *
```

If you are not concerned with intermediate times and want only to know the current time it takes to get a packet from your machine to another machine on the Internet (or on an intranet) and back to you, you can use the Unix *ping* utility. *ping* sends Internet Control Message Protocol (ICMP) packets to the named host and returns the latency between you and the named host as milliseconds. A latency of 25 milliseconds is pretty good, while 250 milliseconds is not good. See the *ping* manpage for more information. Here's an example of *ping* usage:

```
% ping www.umich.edu
PING www.umich.edu (141.211.144.53): 56 data bytes
64 bytes from 141.211.144.53: icmp_seq=0 ttl=248 time=112.2 ms
64 bytes from 141.211.144.53: icmp_seq=1 ttl=248 time=83.9 ms
64 bytes from 141.211.144.53: icmp_seq=2 ttl=248 time=82.2 ms
64 bytes from 141.211.144.53: icmp_seq=3 ttl=248 time=80.6 ms
64 bytes from 141.211.144.53: icmp_seq=4 ttl=248 time=87.2 ms
64 bytes from 141.211.144.53: icmp_seq=5 ttl=248 time=81.0 ms

--- www.umich.edu ping statistics ---

6 packets transmitted, 6 packets received, 0% packet loss
round-trip min/avg/max = 80.6/87.8/112.2 ms
```

Measuring Network Latency and Throughput

When *ping* measures the latency between you and some remote machine, it sends ICMP messages, which routers handle differently than the TCP segments used to carry HTTP. ICMP packets get lower priority. Routers are sometimes configured to ignore ICMP packets entirely. Furthermore, by default, *ping* sends only a very small amount of information, 56 data bytes, although some versions of *ping* let you send packets of arbitrary size. For these reasons, *ping* is not necessarily accurate in measuring HTTP latency to the remote machine, but it is a good first approximation. Using *telnet* and the Unix *talk* program will give you a manual feel for the latency of a connection.

The simplest ways to measure web latency and throughput are to clear your browser's cache and time how long it takes to get a particular page from your server, have a friend get a page from your server from another point on the Internet, or log in to a remote machine and run: **time lynx -source http://patrick.net/>/dev/null**. This method is sometimes referred to as the *stopwatch* method of web performance monitoring.

Using FTP

Another way to get an idea of network throughput is to use FTP to transfer files to and from a remote system. FTP is like HTTP in that it is carried over TCP. There are some hazards to this approach, but if you are careful, your results should reflect your network conditions.

First, do not put too much stock in the numbers the FTP program reports to you. While the first significant digit or two will probably be correct, the FTP program internally makes some approximations, so the number reported is only approximately accurate.

More importantly, what you do with FTP will determine exactly which part of the system is the bottleneck. To put it another way, what you do with FTP will determine what you're measuring. To insure that you are measuring the throughput of the network and not of the disk of the local or remote system, you want to eliminate any requirements for disk access that could be caused by the FTP transfer. For this reason, you should not FTP a collection of small files in your test; each file creation requires a disk access.

Similarly, you need to limit the size of the file you transfer because a huge file will not fit in the filesystem cache of either the transmitting or receiving machine, again resulting in disk access. To make sure the file is in the cache of the transmitting machine when you start the FTP, you should do the FTP at least twice, throwing away the results from the first iteration. Also, do not write the file on the disk of the receiving machine. You can do this with some versions of FTP by directing the result to */dev/null*. Altogether, we have something like this:

```
ftp> get bigfile /dev/null
```

Try using the FTP *hash* command to get an interactive feel for latency and throughput. The *hash* command prints hash marks (#) after the transfer of a block of data.

The size of the block represented by the hash mark varies with the FTP implementation, but FTP will tell you the size when you turn on hashing:

```
ftp> hash
Hash mark printing on (1024 bytes/hash mark).
ftp> get ers.27may
200 PORT command successful.
150 Opening BINARY mode data connection for ers.27may (362805 bytes).
############################################################################
##
226 Transfer complete.
362805 bytes received in 15 secs (24 Kbytes/sec)
ftp> bye
221 Goodbye.
```

You can use Perl or the Expect scripting language to automatically run an FTP test at regular intervals. Other scripting languages have a difficult time controlling the terminal of a spawned process; if you start FTP from within a shell script, for example, execution of the script halts until FTP returns, so you cannot continue the FTP session. Expect is designed to deal with this exact problem. Expect is well documented in *Exploring Expect*, by Don Libes (O'Reilly & Associates). The *autoexpect* program can be used to automatically record your test.

Other performance measures

You can of course also retrieve content via HTTP from your server to test network performance, but this does not clearly distinguish network performance from server performance.

Here are a few more network testing tools:

ttcp
> *ttcp* is an old C program, circa 1985, for testing TCP connection speed. It makes a connection on port 2000 and transfers zeroed buffers or data copied from STDIN. It is available from *ftp://ftp.arl.mil/pub/ttcp/* and distributed with some Unix systems. Try **which ttcp** and **man ttcp** on your system to see if the binary and documentation are already there.

Nettest
> A more recent tool, circa 1992, is Nettest, available at *ftp://ftp.sgi.com/sgi/src/nettest/*. *nettest* was used to generate some performance statistics for vBNS, the very high-performance backbone network service (see *http://www.vbns.net/*).

bing
> *bing* attempts to measure bandwidth between two points on the Internet. See *http://web.cnam.fr/reseau/bing.html*.

chargen
> The *chargen* service, defined in RFC 864 and implemented by most versions of Unix, simply sends back nonsense characters to the user at the maximum possible rate. This can be used along with some measuring mechanism to determine what that maximum rate is. The TCP form of the service sends a continuous

stream, while the UDP form sends a packet of random size for each packet received. Both run on well-known port 19. *chargen* does not give reliable readings because it cannot distinguish between packets that were dropped on the sending machine from packets dropped at the receiving machine due to buffer overflows.

NetSpec

NetSpec simplifies network testing by allowing users to control processes across multiple hosts using a set of daemons. It can be found at *http://www.tisl.ukans. edu/Projects/AAI/products/netspec.old/*.

Utilization

Utilization is simply the fraction of the capacity of a component that you are actually using. You might think that you want all your components at close to 100 percent utilization in order to get the most bang for your buck, but this is not necessarily how things work. Remember that for disk drives and Ethernet, latency suffers greatly at high utilization. A rule of thumb is many components can run at their best performance up to about 70 percent utilization. The *perfmeter* tool that comes with many versions of Unix is a good graphical way to monitor the utilization of your system.

Efficiency

Efficiency is usually defined as throughput divided by utilization. When comparing two components, if one has a higher throughput at the same level of utilization, it is regarded as more efficient. If both have the same throughput but one has a lower level of utilization, that one is regarded as more efficient. While useful as a basis for comparing components, this definition is otherwise irrelevant, because it is only a division of two other parameters of performance.

A more useful measure of efficiency is performance per unit cost. This is usually called cost efficiency. Performance tuning is the art of increasing cost efficiency: getting more bang for your buck. In fact, the Internet itself owes its popularity to the fact that it is much more cost-efficient than previously existing alternatives for transferring small amounts of information. Email is vastly more cost-efficient than a letter. Both send about the same amount of information, but email has near-zero latency and near-zero incremental cost; it doesn't cost you any more to send two emails rather than one.

Web sites providing product information have lower latency and are cheaper than printed brochures. As the throughput of the Internet increases faster than its cost, entire portions of the economy will be replaced with more cost-efficient alternatives, especially in the business-to-business market, which has little sentimentality for old ways. First, relatively static information such as business paperwork, magazines, books, CDs, and videos will be virtualized. Second, the Internet will become a real-time communications medium.

The cost efficiency of the Internet for real-time communications threatens not only the obvious target of telephone carriers, but also the automobile and airline industries. That is, telecommuting threatens physical commuting. Most of the workforce simply moves bits around, either with computers, on the phone, or in face-to-face conversations (which are, in essence, gigabit–per-second, low-latency video connections). It is only these face-to-face conversations that currently require workers to buy cars for the commute to work. Cars are breathtakingly inefficient, and telecommuting represents an opportunity to save money. Look at the number of cars on an urban highway during rush hour. It's a slow river of metal, fantastically expensive in terms of car purchase, gasoline, driver time, highway construction, insurance, and fatalities. Then consider that most of those cars spend most of the day sitting in a parking lot. Just think of the lost interest on that idle capital. And consider the cost of the parking lot itself, and the office.

As data transmission costs continue to accelerate their fall, car costs cannot fall at the same pace. Gigabit connections between work and home will inevitably be far cheaper than the daily commute, for both the worker and employer. And at gigabit bandwidth, it will feel like you're really there.

Using a Shell Script

You can easily measure web performance yourself by writing scripts that time the retrieval of HTML from a web server—that is, the latency. If you have the text browser Lynx from the University of Kansas, here's a simple way to get an idea of the time to get an answer from any server on the Internet:

```
% time lynx -source http://patrick.net/
0.05user 0.02system 0:00.74elapsed 9%CPU
```

(On some systems the *time* command has been replaced with *timex*). Of course, the startup time for Lynx is included in this, but if you run it twice and throw away the first result, your second result will be fairly accurate and consistent because the Lynx executable won't have to be loaded from disk. Remember that network and server time is included as well. In fact, this includes all the time that is not system or user time: .67 seconds in the example above, which used a cable modem connection to a fast server. So even in the case of very good network connectivity, the Internet can still take most of the time. You can also get basic latency measurements with the free Perl tool *webget* in place of Lynx, or the simple GET program installed with the LWP Perl library.

A great thing about Lynx is that it is runnable via a Telnet session, so if you want to see how the performance or your site looks from elsewhere on the Internet, and you have an account somewhere else on the Internet, you can log in to the remote machine and run the *time lynx* command given earlier. The time given will be the time from the remote point of view. If you'd like to monitor the performance of a web server rather than just measure it once, the following trivial shell script will do just that. Note that we throw out the page we get by redirecting standard output to */dev/null*, because we care only about how long it took. The time measurement will come out on standard error.

```
#!/bin/bash
while true
do
  time lynx -source http://patrick.net/ > /dev/null
  sleep 600
done
```

If you call the above script *mon*, then you can capture the results from standard error (file descriptor 2) to a file called *log* like this in *bash*:

```
$ mon 2>log
```

Using C

Shell scripting is about the least efficient form of programming because a new executable must be forked for almost every line in the script. Here is a tiny C program, modified from the example client in Chapter 11, which prints out the time it takes to retrieve the home page from a web site. It is much more accurate and efficient at runtime, but also much more complex to write. You can download it from *http://patrick. net/software/latency.c*.

```c
#include <stdio.h>
#include <errno.h>
#include <netdb.h>
#include <netinet/in.h>
#include <sys/socket.h>
#include <sys/time.h>

#define PORT 80
#define BUFSIZE 4000

int main(int argc, char *argv[]) {
 int sockfd, count;
 char *request = "GET / HTTP/1.0\n\n";
 char reply[BUFSIZE];
 struct hostent *he;
 struct sockaddr_in target;
 struct timeval *tvs; /* start time */
 struct timeval *tvf; /* finish time */
 struct timezone *tz;

 if ((he=gethostbyname(argv[1])) == NULL) {
        herror("gethostbyname");
        exit(1);
 }

 if ((sockfd = socket(AF_INET, SOCK_STREAM, 0)) == -1) {
        perror("socket");
```

```
        exit(1);
    }

    target.sin_family = AF_INET;
    target.sin_port = htons(PORT);
    target.sin_addr = *((struct in_addr *)he->h_addr);
    bzero(&(target.sin_zero), 8);

    if (connect(sockfd, (struct sockaddr *)&target,
            sizeof(struct sockaddr)) == -1) {
        perror("connect");
        exit(1);
    }

    tvs = (struct timeval *) malloc(sizeof(struct timeval));
    tvf = (struct timeval *) malloc(sizeof(struct timeval));
    tz = (struct timezone *) malloc(sizeof(struct timezone));

    gettimeofday(tvs, tz);
    send(sockfd, request, strlen(request), 0);
    if ((count = recv(sockfd, reply, BUFSIZE, 0)) == -1) {
        perror("recv");
        exit(1);
    }
    gettimeofday(tvf, tz);

    printf("%d bytes received in %d microseconds\n", count,
            (tvf->tv_sec - tvs->tv_sec) * 1000000 +
            (tvf->tv_usec - tvs->tv_usec));
            close(sockfd);
            return 0;
    }
```

Compile it like this:

```
% gcc -o latency latency.c
```

And run it like this:

```
% latency patrick.net
```

Here is sample output:

```
2609 bytes received in 6247 microseconds
```

Using Perl

While the C program does something we want, it is a bit too low-level to be conveniently maintained or updated. Here is a similar program in Perl, which is more efficient than shell scripting, but less efficient than C. We use the LWP::UserAgent library because it is easier than doing direct socket manipulation. We need to use the Time::HiRes library because timings are to whole second resolution by default in Perl.

```
#!/usr/local/bin/perl -w
use LWP::UserAgent;
```

```
use Time::HiRes 'time','sleep';

$ua = LWP::UserAgent->new;
$request = new HTTP::Request('GET', "http://$ARGV[0]/");
$start = time();
$response = $ua->request($request);
$end = time();
$latency = $end - $start;

print length($response->as_string()), " bytes received in $latency seconds\n";
```

Monitoring Web Performance Using Perl

We can easily expand on the earlier Perl example shown previously to create a useful monitoring system. This section shows how I set up an automated system to monitor web performance using Perl and *gnuplot*.

There are some commercial tools that can drive a browser, which are useful in cases, but they have many drawbacks. They usually require you to learn a proprietary scripting language. They are usually Windows-only programs, so they are hard to run from a command line. This also means you generally cannot run them through a firewall, or from a Unix *cron* job. They are hard to scale up to become load tests because they drive individual browsers, meaning you have to load the whole browser on a PC for each test client. Most do not display their results on the Web. Finally, they are very expensive. A Perl and *gnuplot* solution overcomes all these problems.

Perl was chosen over Java partly because of its superior string-handling abilities and partly because of the nifty LWP library, but mostly because there free SSL implementations for Perl exist. When I starting monitoring, there were no free SSL libraries in Java, though at least one free Java implementation is now available.

Plotting Results with Gnuplot

gnuplot, from *http://www.gnuplot.org/* (no relation to the GNU project), was chosen for plotting because you can generate Portable Network Graphics (PNG) images from its command line. The availability of the *http://www.gnuplot.org/* site has been poor recently, but I keep a copy of *gnuplot* for Linux on my web site *http://patrick. net/software/*. There is a mirror of the *gnuplot* web site at *http://www.ucc.ie/gnuplot/*.

At first I used Tom Boutell's GIF library linked to *gnuplot* to generate GIF images, but Tom has withdrawn the GIF library from public circulation, presumably because of an intellectual property dispute with Unisys, which has a patent on the compression scheme used in the GIF format. PNG format works just as well as GIF and has no such problems, though older browsers may not understand the PNG format. The *gd* program, also from Tom Boutell, and its Perl adaptation by Lincoln Stein, are probably just as suitable for generating graphs on the fly as is *gnuplot*, but I haven't tried them.

gnuplot takes commands from standard input, or from a configuration file, and plots in many formats. I show an example *gnuplot* configuration file with the Perl example below. You can start *gnuplot* and just type help for a pretty good explanation of its functions, or just read the *gnuplot* web site at *http://www.gnuplot.org/*. I've also made multiple GIF images into animations using the free *gifsicle* tool. Another easy way to make animations is with the X-based *animate* command. I'm still looking for a portable open source and open-standard way to pop up graph coordinates, select parts of images, zoom, flip, stretch, and edit images directly on a web page; if you hear of such a thing, please write *p@patrick.net*.

An Example Monitoring Script in Perl

It is easy to grab a web page in Perl using the LWP library. The harder parts are dealing with proxies, handling cookies, handling SSL, and handling login forms. The following script can do all of those things. Here's the basic code for getting the home page, logging in, logging out, and graphing all the times. I try to run my monitoring and load testing from a machine that sits on the same LAN as the web server. This way, I know that network latency is not the bottleneck and I have plenty of network capacity to run big load tests.

```
#!/usr/local/bin/perl -w

use LWP::UserAgent;
use Crypt::SSLeay;
use HTTP::Cookies;
use HTTP::Headers;
use HTTP::Request;
use HTTP::Response;
use Time::HiRes 'time','sleep';

# constants:
$DEBUG = 0;
$browser = 'Mozilla/4.04 [en] (X11; I; Patrix 0.0.0 i586)';
$rooturl = 'https://patrick.net';
$user = "pk";
$password = "pw";
$gnuplot = "/usr/local/bin/gnuplot";

# global objects:
$cookie_jar = HTTP::Cookies->new;
$ua = LWP::UserAgent->new;

MAIN: {
 $ua->agent($browser); # This sets browser for all uses of $ua.
 # home page
 $latency = &get("/home.html");
 $latency = -1 unless index "<title>login page</title>" > -1; # verify that we got
the page
 &log("home.log", $latency);
 sleep 2;
```

```perl
    $content = "user=$user&passwd=$password";

    # log in
    $latency = &post("/login.cgi", $content);
    $latency = -1 unless m|<title>welcome</title>|;
    &log("login.log", $latency);
    sleep 2;

    # content page
    $latency = &get("/content.html");
    $latency = -1 unless m|<title>the goodies</title>|;
    &log("content.log", $latency);
    sleep 2;

    # logout
    $latency = &get("/logout.cgi");
    $latency = -1 unless m|<title>bye</title>|;
    &log("logout.log", $latency);

    # plot it all
    `$gnuplot /home/httpd/public_html/demo.gp`;
}

sub get {
 local ($path) = @_;

    $request = new HTTP::Request('GET', "$rooturl$path");

    # If we have a previous response, put its cookies in the new request.
    if ($response) {
        $cookie_jar->extract_cookies($response);
        $cookie_jar->add_cookie_header($request);
    }

    if ($DEBUG) {
        print $request->as_string();
    }

    # Do it.
    $start = time();
    $response = $ua->request($request);
    $end = time();
    $latency = $end - $start;

    if (!$response->is_success) {
        print $request->as_string(), " failed: ", $response->error_as_HTML;
    }

    if ($DEBUG) {
        print "\n############################## Got $path and result was:\n";
        print $response->content;
        print "############################## $path took $latency seconds.\n";
    }
```

```
  $latency;
}

sub post {
 local ($path, $content) = @_;

 $header = new HTTP::Headers;
 $header->content_type('application/x-www-form-urlencoded');
 $header->content_length(length($content));

 $request = new HTTP::Request('POST',
                              "$rooturl$path",
                              $header,
                              $content);

 # If we have a previous response, put its cookies in the new request.
 if ($response) {
     $cookie_jar->extract_cookies($response);
     $cookie_jar->add_cookie_header($request);
 }

 if ($DEBUG) {
     print $request->as_string();
 }

 # Do it.
 $start = time();
 $response = $ua->request($request);
 $end = time();
 $latency = $end - $start;

 if (!$response->is_success) {
     print $request->as_string(), " failed: ", $response->error_as_HTML;
 }

 if ($DEBUG) {
     print "\n################################ Got $path and result was:\n";
     print $response->content;
     print "################################ $path took $latency seconds.\n";
 }

 $latency;
}

# Write log entry in format that gnuplot can use to create an image.
sub log {
 local ($file, $latency) = @_;
 $date = `date +'%Y %m %d %H %M %S'`;
 chop $date;
 # Corresponding to gnuplot command: set timefmt "%y %m %d %H %M %S"
```

```
open(FH, ">>$file") || die "Could not open $file\n";

# Format printing so that we get only 4 decimal places.
printf FH "%s %2.4f\n", $date, $latency;

close(FH);
}
```

This gives us a set of log files with timestamps and latency readings. To generate a graph from that, we need a *gnuplot* configuration file. Here's the *gnuplot* configuration file for plotting the home page times:

```
set term png color
set output "/home/httpd/public_html/demo.png"
set xdata time
set ylabel "latency in seconds"
set bmargin 3
set logscale y
set timefmt "%Y %m %d %H %M %S"
plot "demo.log" using 1:7 title "time to retrieve home page"
```

Note that I set the output to write a PNG image directly into my web server's *public_hml* directory. This way, I merely click on a bookmark in my browser to see the output. Now I just set up a *cron* job to run my script every minute and I have a log of my web page's performance and a constantly updated graph.

Use *crontab -e* to modify your *crontab* file. Here's an example entry in my *crontab* file. (If you're not familiar with Unix *cron* jobs, enter **man crontab** for more information).

```
# MIN   HOUR   DOM    MOY    DOW   Commands
#(0-59) (0-23) (1-31) (1-12) (0-6) (Note: 0=Sun)
*       *      *      *      *     cd /home/httpd/public_html; ./monitor.pl
```

Figure 4-1 shows example output image from a real site I monitored for over a year.

One small problem with this approach is clear if you repeatedly get the same page and look closely at the timings. The first time you get a page it takes about 200 milliseconds longer than each subsequent access using the same Perl process. I attribute this to Perl's need to create the appropriate objects to hold the request and response. Once it has done that, it doesn't need to do it again.

Instead of running from *cron*, you can turn your monitoring script into a functional test by popping up each page in a Netscape browser as you get it, so you can see monitoring as it happens, and also visually verify that pages are correct in addition to checking for a particular string on the page in Perl. For example, from within Perl, you can pop up the *http://patrick.net/* page in Netscape like this:

```
system "netscape -remote 'openURL(http://patrick.net)'";
```

You can redirect the browser display to any Unix machine running the X Window System, or any Microsoft Windows machine using an X Windows server emulator like Exceed. Controlling Netscape from a script is described at *http://home.netscape. com/newsref/std/x-remote.html.*

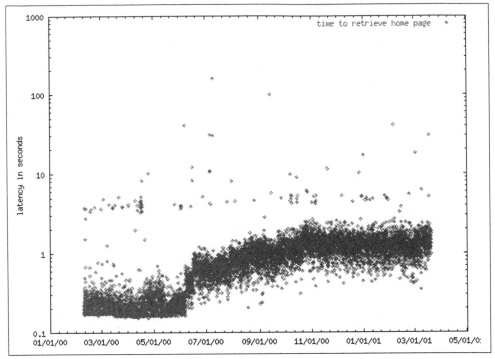

Figure 4-1. Graph of monitored site

The Pieces

Here is a listing of all the pieces you need to use Perl to monitor your web site. It takes work to get and compile each piece, but once you have them, you have enormous power to write many kinds of monitoring and load testing scripts. I know that compiling in the following order works, but some other orders might work as well. Except for *gcc* and Perl, these pieces are all available on my web site at *http://patrick.net/ software/*. Perl is available from *http://www.perl.com/* and *gcc* is available from *ftp:// prep.ai.mit.edu/* as well as many other sites around the world.

```
gcc
perl 5.004_04 or better
openssl-0.9.4
Crypt-SSLeay-0.15
Time-HiRes-01.20
MIME-Base64-2.11
URI-1.03
HTML-Parser-2.23
libnet-1.0606
Digest::MD5-2.07
libwww.perl-5.44
gnuplot
```

Automatically Generating Monitoring Scripts Using Sprocket

Now that you know the basics of how to manually write a performance-monitoring script in Perl, I'm going to tell you that you don't really need to do that. I've modified and added to Randal Schwarz's Perl web proxy server so that it automatically generates monitoring scripts, albeit with some limitations. I call the modified proxy server *sprocket*. The code is Perl that generates Perl, so it may be hard to follow, but you can download it from *http://patrick.net/software/sprocket/sprocket* and use it even if you don't understand exactly how it works.

Here's how to use it:

1. First, you'll need to have the same pieces listed above, all downloadable from *http://patrick.net/software/*.

2. Once you have those things installed, get *sprocket* from *http://patrick.net/ software/sprocket/sprocket*. It is very small and should only take a second or two to download. Put *sprocket* in a directory from which you can view the resulting PNG images. Your web server's *public_html* directory is a good choice.

3. Now set your web browser's proxy to the machine *sprocket* uses by default, port 8008. In Netscape 4, choose Edit → Preferences → Advanced → Proxies → Manual Proxy Configuration → View → HTTP Proxy.

Once your proxy is set, start up *sprocket* with the *-s* option for scripting, redirecting the output to the script your want to create. For example:

```
% sprocket -s > myscript.pl
```

You'll see feedback on standard error as your script is being created. For example:

```
# scripting has started (^C when done)
# set your proxy to <URL:http://localhost:8008/>
# then surf to write a script
# scripted a request
# scripted a request
# scripted a request
```

In this case, we surfed two pages, resulting in three HTTP requests because one of the pages also contained an image. When you have surfed through the pages you want to monitor, enter Ctrl-C to exit *sprocket*. (If you try to start it up again right away, you may see a "port in use" error, but that should go away in a minute or so.)

Now *myscript.pl* contains a script that will duplicate nearly verbatim what you did when you were surfing. The exception is that *sprocket* will not record Set-Cookie responses, because these are unique to the session you had when you were recording the script. The *myscript.pl* you just created will listen for new Set-Cookie responses when you run it, so you will have a new session each time you run the script you made. Here is the example *myscript.pl* file we just created:

```perl
#!/usr/bin/perl
use Socket;
use Time::HiRes 'time','sleep';
$proto = getprotobyname('tcp');



#vvvvvvvvvvvvvvvvvvvvvvvvvvvvvvvvvvvvvvvvvvvvvvvvvvvvvvvv
$host    = "vahe";
$port    = 80;
$request = 'GET / HTTP/1.0
Accept: image/gif, image/x-xbitmap, image/jpeg, image/pjpeg, image/png, */*
Accept-Charset: iso-8859-1,*,utf-8
Accept-Encoding: gzip
Accept-Language: en
Host: vahe
User-Agent: sprocket/0.10
Proxy-Connection: Keep-Alive



';
$proof  = 'HTTP/1.1 200 OK';

$request            =~ s|[\r\n]*$|\r\n|; # strip extra \r\n
foreach(@cookies) {
    $request        .= "Cookie: $_\r\n"; # tack on cookies
}
$request            .= "\r\n";            # terminate request with blank line

socket(SOCK, PF_INET, SOCK_STREAM, $proto);
$start              = time();
$iaddr              = gethostbyname($host);
$paddr              = sockaddr_in($port, $iaddr);
connect(SOCK, $paddr);
$old_fh             = select(SOCK);      # save the old fh
$|                  = 1;                  # turn off buffering
select($old_fh);                          # restore

print SOCK $request;

@response           = <SOCK>;
$end                = time();

$path               = $request;
$path               =~ m|^[A-Z]* (.*) HTTP|;
$path               = $1;
$file               = $path;
$file               =~ s|/|_|g;

open(FILE, ">>$file") || die "cannot create file";
$date = `date +'%m %d %H %M %S %Y'`;
chop $date;
```

```perl
    # validate response here
    if (grep(/$proof/, @response)) {
        print FILE $date, " ", $end - $start, "\n";

    }
    else {
        print FILE $date, " -1\n";
    }

    close FILE;

    $gnuplot_cmd = qq|
        set term png color
        set output "$file.png"
        set xdata time
        set ylabel "latency in seconds"
        set bmargin 3
        set logscale y
        set timefmt "%m %d %H %M %S %Y"
        plot "$file" using 1:7 title "$path" with lines
    |;

    open(GP, "|/usr/local/bin/gnuplot");
    print GP $gnuplot_cmd;
    close(GP);

    foreach (@response) {
        /Set-Cookie: (.*)/ && push(@cookies, $1);
    }

    print;
    close(SOCK);
    #^^^^^^^^^^^^^^^^^^^^^^^^^^^^^^^^^^^^^^^^^^^^^^^^^^^^^^^^^^^^^^^^^^


    #vvvvvvvvvvvvvvvvvvvvvvvvvvvvvvvvvvvvvvvvvvvvvvvvvvvvvvvvvvvvvvvv
    $host    = "vahe";
    $port    = 80;
    $request = 'GET /webpt_sm.gif HTTP/1.0
    Accept: image/gif, image/x-xbitmap, image/jpeg, image/pjpeg, image/png
    Accept-Charset: iso-8859-1,*,utf-8
    Accept-Encoding: gzip
    Accept-Language: en
    Host: vahe
    Referer: http://vahe/
    User-Agent: sprocket/0.10
    Proxy-Connection: Keep-Alive



    ';
    $proof   = 'HTTP/1.1 200 OK';
```

```perl
$request                =~ s|[\r\n]*$|\r\n|; # strip extra \r\n
foreach(@cookies) {
    $request            .= "Cookie: $_\r\n"; # tack on cookies
}
$request                .= "\r\n";              # terminate request with blank line

socket(SOCK, PF_INET, SOCK_STREAM, $proto);
$start                  = time( );
$iaddr                  = gethostbyname($host);
$paddr                  = sockaddr_in($port, $iaddr);
connect(SOCK, $paddr);
$old_fh                 = select(SOCK);     # save the old fh
$|                      = 1;                # turn off buffering
select($old_fh);                             # restore

print SOCK $request;

@response               = <SOCK>;
$end                    = time( );

$path                   = $request;
$path                   =~ m|^[A-Z]* (.*) HTTP|;
$path                   = $1;
$file                   = $path;
$file                   =~ s|/|_|g;

open(FILE, ">>$file") || die "cannot create file";
$date = `date +'%m %d %H %M %S %Y'`;
chop $date;

# validate response here
if (grep(/$proof/, @response)) {
    print FILE $date, " ", $end - $start, "\n";
}
else {
    print FILE $date, " -1\n";
}

close FILE;

$gnuplot_cmd = qq|
    set term png color
    set output "$file.png"
    set xdata time
    set ylabel "latency in seconds"
    set bmargin 3
    set logscale y
    set timefmt "%m %d %H %M %S %Y"
    plot "$file" using 1:7 title "$path" with lines
|;

open(GP, "|/usr/local/bin/gnuplot");
print GP $gnuplot_cmd;
close(GP);
```

```perl
foreach (@response) {
    /Set-Cookie: (.*)/ && push(@cookies, $1);
}

print;
close(SOCK);
#^^^^^^^^^^^^^^^^^^^^^^^^^^^^^^^^^^^^^^^^^^^^^^^^^^^^^^^^^^^^^^^



#vvvvvvvvvvvvvvvvvvvvvvvvvvvvvvvvvvvvvvvvvvvvvvvvvvvvvvvvvvvvvv
$host   = "vahe";
$port   = 80;
$request = 'GET /specs/index.html HTTP/1.0
Accept: image/gif, image/x-xbitmap, image/jpeg, image/pjpeg, image/png, */*
Accept-Charset: iso-8859-1,*,utf-8
Accept-Encoding: gzip
Accept-Language: en
Host: vahe
Referer: http://vahe/
User-Agent: sprocket/0.10
Proxy-Connection: Keep-Alive



';
$proof  = 'HTTP/1.1 200 OK';

$request            =~ s|[\r\n]*$|\r\n|; # strip extra \r\n
foreach(@cookies) {
    $request        .= "Cookie: $_\r\n"; # tack on cookies
}
$request            .= "\r\n";           # terminate request with blank line

socket(SOCK, PF_INET, SOCK_STREAM, $proto);
$start              = time();
$iaddr              = gethostbyname($host);
$paddr              = sockaddr_in($port, $iaddr);
connect(SOCK, $paddr);
$old_fh             = select(SOCK);    # save the old fh
$|                  = 1;               # turn off buffering
select($old_fh);                        # restore

print SOCK $request;

@response           = <SOCK>;
$end                = time();

$path               = $request;
$path               =~ m|^[A-Z]* (.*) HTTP|;
$path               = $1;
$file               = $path;
$file               =~ s|/|_|g;

open(FILE, ">>$file") || die "cannot create file";
```

```
$date = `date +'%m %d %H %M %S %Y'`;
chop $date;

# validate response here
if (grep(/$proof/, @response)) {
    print FILE $date, " ", $end - $start, "\n";
}
else {
    print FILE $date, " -1\n";
}

close FILE;

$gnuplot_cmd = qq|
    set term png color
    set output "$file.png"
    set xdata time
    set ylabel "latency in seconds"
    set bmargin 3
    set logscale y
    set timefmt "%m %d %H %M %S %Y"
    plot "$file" using 1:7 title "$path" with lines
|;

open(GP, "|/usr/local/bin/gnuplot");
print GP $gnuplot_cmd;
close(GP);

foreach (@response) {
    /Set-Cookie: (.*)/ && push(@cookies, $1);
}

print;
close(SOCK);
#^^^^^^^^^^^^^^^^^^^^^^^^^^^^^^^^^^^^^^^^^^^^^^^^^^^^^^^^^^^^^^^
```

You can see that the generated script is low-level and contains no subroutines. It is also very repetitive. But these attributes make it very easy to customize. Note that you cannot record an SSL session (unless the user gives permission), because snooping on an SSL session from a proxy would be proof that SSL doesn't work! But with some effort, you could turn off SSL on your web server, record a session, then modify your generated *myscript.pl* to use SSL.

The monitoring script will log a timestamp and a latency reading for each item it requests, and automatically generate a graph of the results. The log and graph will appear in the directory *sprocket* is in. The name of the log file will be the path of the URL with each slash (/) replaced by an underscore (_). The name of the graph will be the name of the log file, but with *.png* appended.

The first time you run the monitoring script, *gnuplot* will give a warning that you have only one point on each graph so that it does not know how to adjust the axes. You can ignore this warning.

Using a Relational Database to Store and Retrieve Your Monitoring Data

The normal thing to do with your monitoring data is to keep it in a file, but you may want to keep it in a relational database instead. It takes a bit more work to set up, and relational data is not as easily accessible as data in files, but the advantages are huge:

- First, you have all of your data in one place, so you don't have to go hunting for files when you need to find out what happened to the performance of a particular page when a new feature was introduced last month. Of course, having all the data in one place also makes you more vulnerable to losing it all at once.

- You have ease of querying. Rather than manually poking or grepping through a huge file, you can simply make SQL queries for the time range in which you're interested.

- SQL has built-in math functions for relatively easy comparisons and manipulation of the data.

- If you can connect to the database over a network, you have access to the data remotely, which is not necessarily true for flat files.

Storing Data

If you're using Perl for monitoring, you should try the Perl DBI (Database Interface) for storing data. You'll need to download and install the Perl DBI package and a driver for your database. Here's some example Perl code to do the database insertion.

Instead of doing this, as in the previous script:

```
print FILE $date, " ", $end - $start, "\n";
```

You could do the following, assuming that you have a table defined called perfdata, which has fields for a URL, a timestamp, and a latency:

```
use DBI;
$dbh = DBI->connect("dbi:Oracle:perf", "patrick", "passwd")
    or die "Can't connect to Oracle: $DBI::errstr\n";

$sth = $dbh->prepare("insert into perfdata values
    ('$url', to_date('$yyyy $mon $dd $hh $mm $ss', 'YYYY MM DD HH24 MI SS'), $end -
$start)");

$sth->execute();
$dbh->disconnect or warn "Disconnect failed: $DBI::errstr\n";
```

One problem with monitoring data is there is just so much of it, and there is always more. It becomes rather like a memory leak on disk after a while. One way of coping with the volume of data is to simply not log values that are very close to zero. This cuts out most of the data. Another strategy is to roll up daily data into a weekly average after it is a month old, and roll up weekly data into monthly averages after it is a year old, etc. This is the approach taken by the "Big Brother" freeware monitoring tool.

Retrieving Data

Once you have the data in the database, you'll want to use it. Here is an example of how to use it to get today's data out of the database and graph it:

```
#!/usr/local/bin/perl
use DBI;
$dbh = DBI->connect("dbi:Oracle:perf", "patrick", "passwd")
    or die "Can't connect to Oracle: $DBI::errstr\n";

$url = "/home.html";
$sth = $dbh->prepare("select timestamp, latency from latency where
trunc(timestamp)=trunc(sysdate) and url=$url");
$sth->execute();

$gnuplot_cmd = qq|
    set term png color
    set output "$url.png"
    set xdata time
    set ylabel "latency in seconds"
    set bmargin 3
    set logscale y
    set timefmt "%m %d %H %M %S %Y"
    plot "-" using 1:7 title "$path" with lines
|;

while(($timestamp, $latency) = $sth->fetchrow_array) {
    $gp_cmd .= "$timestamp $latency\n";
}

$gp_cmd .= "e\n";

$sth->finish();
$dbh->disconnect or warn "disconnect failed: $DBI::errstr\n";

open(GP, "|/usr/local/bin/gnuplot");
print GP $gp_cmd;
close(GP);
```

Monitoring Machine Utilization with rstat

rstat is an RPC client program I wrote to get and print statistics from any machine running the *rpc.rstatd* daemon, its server-side counterpart. The *rpc.rstad* daemon has been used for many years by tools such as Sun's *perfmeter* and the *rup* command. The *rstat* program is simply a new client for an old daemon. The fact that the *rpc.rstatd* daemon is already installed and running on most Solaris and Linux machines is a huge advantage over other tools that require the installation of custom agents.

My *rstat* client compiles and runs on Solaris and Linux as well and can get statistics from any machine running a current *rpc.rstatd* daemon, such as Solaris, Linux, AIX, and OpenBSD. The *rpc.rstatd* daemon is started from */etc/inetd.conf* on Solaris. I will probably also port the *rstat* client to other platforms. It is similar to *vmstat*, but has some advantages over *vmstat*:

- You can get statistics without logging in to the remote machine, including over the Internet.
- It includes a timestamp.
- The output can be plotted directly by *gnuplot*.

The fact that it runs remotely means that you can use a single central machine to monitor the performance of many remote machines. It also has a disadvantage in that it does not give the useful scan rate measurement of memory shortage, the sr column in *vmstat*. *rstat* will not work across most firewalls because it relies on port 111, the RPC port, which is usually blocked by firewalls.

You can download *rstat* from *http://patrick.net/software/rstat/rstat.html*. As mentioned earlier, Sun's *perfmeter* program is also an *rpc.rstatd* client and can also log remote server statistics to a file. However, I haven't managed to run *perfmeter* without its GUI, though it could perhaps be done using *Xvfb*, the X virtual frame buffer.

To use *rstat*, simply give it the name or IP address of the machine you wish to monitor. Remember that *rpc.rstatd* must be running on that machine. The *rup* command is extremely useful here because with no arguments, it simply prints out a list of all machines on the local network that are running the *rstatd* demon. If a machine is not listed, you may have to start *rstatd* manually. To start *rpc.rstatd* under Red Hat Linux, run **/etc/rc.d/init.d/rstatd start** as *root*. On Solaris, first try running the *rstat* client because *inetd* is often already configured to automatically start *rpc.rstatd* on request. If it the client fails with the error "RPC: Program not registered," make sure you have this line in your */etc/inet/inetd.conf* and *kill -HUP* your *inetd* process to get it to re-read *inetd.conf*, as follows:

```
rstatd/2-4 tli rpc/datagram_v wait root /usr/lib/netsvc/rstat/rpc.rstatd rpc.rstatd
```

Then you can monitor that machine like this:

```
% rstat enkidu
2001 07 10 10 36 08  0   0   0 100   0   27  54   1   0   0  12 0.1
```

This command will give you a one-second average and then it will exit. If you want to continuously monitor, give an interval in seconds on the command line. Here's an example of one line of output every two seconds:

```
% rstat enkidu 2
2001 07 10 10 36 28  0   0   1  98   0   0   7   2   0   0  61 0.0
2001 07 10 10 36 30  0   0   0 100   0   0   0   2   0   0  15 0.0
2001 07 10 10 36 32  0   0   0 100   0   0   0   2   0   0  15 0.0
2001 07 10 10 36 34  0   0   0 100   0   5  10   2   0   0  19 0.0
2001 07 10 10 36 36  0   0   0 100   0   0  46   2   0   0 108 0.0
^C
```

To get a usage message, the output format, the version number, and where to go for updates, just type **rstat** with no parameters:

```
% rstat
usage: rstat machine [interval]
output:
yyyy mm dd hh mm ss usr wio sys idl pgin pgout intr ipkts opkts coll  cs load
docs and src at http://patrick.net/software/rstat/rstat.html
```

Notice that the column headings line up with the output data.

The output may look meaningless to the uninitiated, but it is quite useful and the format was chosen to be easily plotted by the *gnuplot* graphing program. You may download *gnuplot* from *http://www.gnuplot.org/* or *http://patrick.net/software/*. You can ask *gnuplot* to choose any of the fields for plotting. To create a graph of your *rstat* data, redirect or save the *rstat* output data in a file, which I've named *rstat.out* here. Then create the following *gnuplot* configuration file, which we name *enkidu.gp*. Then just run **gnuplot enkidu.gp** and *gnuplot* will create a PNG file called *enkidu.png* that is suitable for display on a web site:

```
set term png color
set output "enkidu.png"
set xdata time
set timefmt "%Y %m %d %H %M %S"
set bmargin 3
set y2label "load"
set ylabel "context switching"
set ytics nomirror
set y2tics nomirror
plot "rstat.out" using 1:17 axes x1y1 title "context switching", \
     "rstat.out" using 1:18 axes x1y2 title "load"
```

Figure 4-2 shows an example GIF depicting context switching and load (the 17th and 18th fields) that I created with *rstat* and *gnuplot*.

Storing rstat Data in a Relational Database

As with latency data, it is good to store *rstat* data in a database for later retrieval and correlation with problems. Here's a SQL command that can be used to create a table for *rstat* data in Oracle:

```
create table rstat (
    machine    varchar2(20),
    timestamp  date not null,
    usr        number(3),
    wio        number(3),
    sys        number(3),
    idl        number(3),
    pgin       number(6),
    pgout      number(6),
    intr       number(6),
    ipkts      number(6),
```

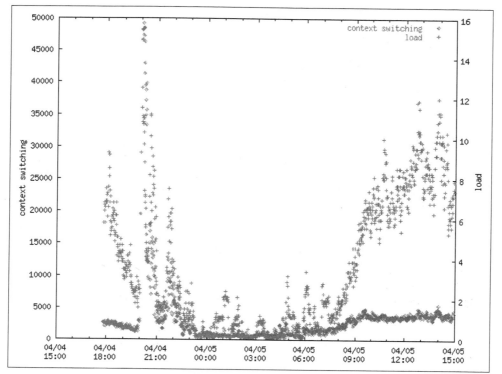

Figure 4-2. Graph of rstat data

```
opkts      number(6),
coll       number(6),
cs         number(8),
load       number(3,1)
)/
```

And here's some example Perl code to run *rstat*, parse out the fields, and perform the
database insertion:

```perl
#!/usr/local/bin/perl
use DBI;
$machine = "vatche";
$interval = 60;
$dbh      = DBI->connect("dbi:Oracle:perf", "patrick", "passwd")
              or die "Can't connect to Oracle: $DBI::errstr\n";

open(RSTAT, "rstat $machine $interval |") || die "could not start rstat";

while(<RSTAT>) {
       ($yyyy, $mon, $dd, $hh, $mm, $ss, $usr, $wio, $sys, $idl, $pgin, $pgout,
$intr,
       $ipkts, $opkts, $coll, $cs, $load) = split(/\s+/);
       $sth = $dbh->prepare("insert into rstat values
               ('$machine', to_date('$yyyy $mon $dd $hh $mm $ss', 'YYYY MM DD HH24
MI SS'),
```

```
                    $usr, $wio, $sys, $idl, $pgin, $pgout, $intr, $ipkts, $opkts, $coll,
    $cs, $load)");
        $sth->execute();
    }

    # If rstat dies, at least we should try to disconnect nicely.
    $dbh->disconnect or warn "Disconnect failed: $DBI::errstr\n";
```

Using rstat Data

Now that you have system data in your database, how do you use it? The answer is
any way that you use any other kind of relational data. Let's say you want to get the
average of the system and user CPU usage for October 8, 2001, between the hours of
9 a.m. and 4 p.m. Here is a query that does this:

```
    select avg(sys + usr) from rstat where timestamp between
    to_date('2001 10 08 09', 'YYYY MM DD HH24') and
    to_date('2001 10 08 16', 'YYYY MM DD HH24') and
    machine='mars';
```

Getting Data from the Database to Standard Output

Often it is useful to be able to *grep*, *sort*, or otherwise process database data on the
Unix command line, but most SQL querying tools are "captive user interfaces" that
do not play nicely with Unix standard in and standard out. Here is a simple Perl
script that will let you do that if you have the DBI module installed and are using
Oracle. It's called *sql.pl* and is available at *http://patrick.net/software/*.

```
    #!/usr/local/bin/perl

    use DBI;

    $ENV{ORACLE_HOME} = "/path/to/ORACLE/product";

    $dbh = DBI->connect("dbi:Oracle:myinstance", "mylogin", "mypassword")
    or die "Can't connect to Oracle: $DBI::errstr\n";

    $sql = $ARGV[0];
    $sth = $dbh->prepare($sql);
    $sth->execute();

    while(@row = $sth->fetchrow_array) {
        print "@row\n";
    }

    $sth->finish();
    $dbh->disconnect or warn "Disconnect failed: $DBI::errstr\n";
```

Generating Graphs Directly from an rstat Database

Getting a single number is interesting, but it is more interesting to see how data varies over time. The following is the HTML for a CGI that will allow anyone to view

graphs of your collected *rstat* data. It will graph a single parameter over time. You will need to alter it to reflect your ORACLE_HOME, your Oracle user and password, and your machine names, but aside from that, it should be ready to run. You can download this script from *http://patrick.net/software/graph.cgi*.

```perl
#!/usr/local/bin/perl
#Author: Patrick Killelea
#Date:  12 April 2001

# You will need to replace "myinstance", "mylogin", and "mypassword" below with
# values for your own environment.

use DBI;

$ENV{ORACLE_HOME} = "/opt/ORACLE/product";

print qq|Content-type: text/html\n\n|;

print qq|<HTML><HEAD><TITLE>generate a graph</TITLE>
<meta http-equiv = "Pragma" Content = "no-cache">
<meta http-equiv = "Expires" Content = "Thu, Jan 1 1970 12:00:00 GMT">
</HEAD><BODY><H1>generate a graph</H1>|;

if ($ENV{'REQUEST_METHOD'} eq 'POST') {
    read(STDIN, $buffer, $ENV{'CONTENT_LENGTH'});
    @pairs = split(/&/, $buffer);
    foreach $pair (@pairs) {
        ($name, $value) = split(/=/, $pair);

        $value =~ tr/+/ /;
        $value =~ s/%([a-fA-F0-9][a-fA-F0-9])/pack("C", hex($1))/eg;
        $contents{$name} = $value;
    }
}

$machine   = $contents{"machine"};
$parameter = $contents{"parameter"};
$daterange = $contents{"daterange"};

if ($machine && $parameter && daterange) {

    `/bin/rm tmp/*.gif`;

    $dbh = DBI->connect("dbi:Oracle:myinstance", "mylogin", "mypassword")
        or die "Can't connect to Oracle: $DBI::errstr\n";

    $sql = "select to_char(timestamp, 'YYYY MM DD HH24 MI'), $parameter from rstat ";

    if ($daterange eq "today") {
        $sql .= "where timestamp between trunc(sysdate) and sysdate and
machine='$machine' ";
    }
```

```perl
    if ($daterange eq "yesterday") {
        $sql .= "where timestamp between trunc(sysdate) - 1 and trunc(sysdate) and
machine='$machine'";
    }

    if ($daterange eq "t-7") {
        $sql .= "where timestamp between trunc(sysdate) - 7 and sysdate and
machine='$machine'";
    }

    if ($daterange eq "t-30") {
        $sql .= "where timestamp between trunc(sysdate) - 30 and sysdate and
machine='$machine'";
    }

    if ($daterange eq "t-365") {
        $sql .= "where timestamp between trunc(sysdate) - 365 and sysdate and
machine='$machine'";
    }

    $sth = $dbh->prepare($sql);
    $sth->execute( ) || print $dbh->errstr;

    ($timestamp, $item) = $sth->fetchrow_array; # get one sample row to be sure we
have data

    if ($timestamp) {

        $date = `date`;
        chop $date;

        open(GP, "|/usr/local/bin/gnuplot");
        print GP $gp_cmd;
        print GP qq|
            set xdata time
            set timefmt "%Y %m %d %H %M"
            set term gif
            set xlabel "graph made on $date"
            set bmargin 4
            set ylabel "$parameter"
            set output "tmp/$$.gif"
            plot '-' using 1:6 title "$parameter on $machine" with lines lt 2
        |;

        while(($timestamp, $item) = $sth->fetchrow_array) {
            print GP "$timestamp $item\n";
        }

        print GP "e\n";
        close(GP);

        $sth->finish( );
        $dbh->disconnect or warn "acsiweba disconnect failed: $DBI::errstr\n";
```

```perl
        print "<p><img src=\"tmp/$$.gif\"><p>";
        print "graph was generated from this query:<p> $sql\n";
    }
    else {
        print "Sorry, I do not have the requested data for that time range for
$machine.";
    }
}

print qq|
<FORM
METHOD="POST" ENCTYPE="application/x-www-form-urlencoded">
<P>select a machine
<SELECT NAME="machine">
<OPTION SELECTED VALUE="venus">venus database
<OPTION VALUE="mars">mars backup database
<OPTION VALUE="pluto">pluto middleware
<OPTION VALUE="saturn">saturn nfs
<OPTION VALUE="earth">earth middleware
</SELECT>
</P>
<P>select a parameter
<SELECT NAME="parameter">
<OPTION SELECTED VALUE="usr">user cpu
<OPTION VALUE="wio">wait io cpu
<OPTION VALUE="sys">system cpu
<OPTION VALUE="idl">idle cpu
<OPTION VALUE="pgin">pgs in per second
<OPTION VALUE="pgout">pgs out per second
<OPTION VALUE="intr">interrupts per second
<OPTION VALUE="ipkts">network in pkts per second
<OPTION VALUE="opkts">network out pkts per second
<OPTION VALUE="coll">collisions per second
<OPTION VALUE="cs">context switches per second
<OPTION VALUE="load">load: procs waiting to run
</SELECT>
</P>
<P>select a date range
<SELECT NAME="daterange">
<OPTION SELECTED VALUE="today">today
<OPTION VALUE="yesterday">yesterday
<OPTION VALUE="t-7">last 7 days
<OPTION VALUE="t-30">last 30 days
<OPTION VALUE="t-365">last 365 days
</SELECT>
</P>
<P>
<INPUT TYPE="submit" NAME="graph" VALUE="graph">
</P><HR><P>|;

print qq|</FORM>Questions? Write
<A HREF="mailto:p\@patrick.net">p\@patrick.net</A>
</BODY></HTML>|;
```

Monitoring Per-Process Statistics

It is very valuable to know which processes are using the most CPU time or other resources on a remote machine. The *rpc.rstatd* daemon, which we used earlier, does not provide per-process information. Commercial software, such as Measureware, requires the installation of potentially buggy remote agents to report per-process information, and keeps its data in a proprietary format. It is often unacceptable to install unknown agents on important production machines, and it is never to your advantage to have your data locked into a proprietary format. Here we look at alternate freeware for collecting the same data—first, at a web server, and second, at *telnet* from a Perl script.

Using CGIs to Run Tools

It is not hard to create a CGI that calls *ps*, *vmstat*, *sar*, *top*, or other system monitoring programs that were intended to be used only by someone logged in to that machine. For example, using Apache, you could copy */bin/ps* to */home/httpd/cgi-bin/ nph-ps* and suddenly you have a version of *ps* that is directly runnable from the Web.

You need to rename it with the *nph-* prefix to tell the Apache web server not to expect or add any headers. If you don't, the web server will expect a Content-Type header from *ps* and give an error because *ps* does not output that header. The *nph-* header tells Apache not to worry about it. ("nph" stands for "nonparsed headers.") What you then get will not be prettily formatted in a browser, but at least will be usable by a script that calls that URL. You could also write a CGI that in turn calls *ps*, then adds the appropriate header, and does any other processing you like, but this adds the overhead of yet another new process every time you call it.

I have used a very tiny web server called *mathopd* from *http://www.mathopd.org/* to run *ps* as a CGI. There is essentially no documentation of this web server, which is distributed as source code, but it is simple enough. It compiles cleanly on Linux, but requires a few tweaks to compile on Solaris, where it also needs the *-lnsl* and *-lsocket* options to *gcc* in the Makefile. *mathopd* has the advantage that it is even smaller than Apache, runs as a single process, and does not allocate any new memory after startup. I am reasonably confident that *mathopd* is free of memory leaks, but it is simple to write a *cron* job that kills and restarts it each night if this is a concern. It is single-process and single-threaded. If you write its log files to */dev/null*, it should not use any disk space. I keep a compiled copy on my web site at *http://patrick.net/ software/*.

Using rstat to Trigger Deeper Analysis

Here is a script that watches CPU usage, and if idle time falls below a certain threshold, it hits the URL to run *ps* as a CGI and mail the result to an administrator, who

---

can determine which of the processes is the offender. It can be run as a *cron* job, or you can make it into a loop and leave a single process going. (I prefer a *cron* job because long-running jobs tend to leak memory or get killed.)

```perl
#!/usr/local/bin/perl
use LWP::UserAgent;

$thresh  = 50;                     # usr CPU threshold, above which we report top 10 procs
$machine = www.patrick.net;
$\       = "\n";                   # automatically append newline to print statements

# grab the cpu usage
$_       = `/opt/bin/rstat $machine`;

($yyyy, $mon, $dd, $hh, $mm, $ss, $usr, $wio, $sys, $idl, $pgin, $pgout, $intr,
$ipkts, $opkts, $coll, $cs, $load) = split(/\s+/);

if ($idl < $thresh) {
    print "$machine is under $thresh\n";
    $ua = LWP::UserAgent->new;

    $request = new HTTP::Request('GET', "http://$machine/nph-ps");
    $response = $ua->request($request);

    if (!$response->is_success) {
        die $request->as_string(), " failed: ", $response->error_as_HTML;
    }

    open (MAIL, '|/bin/mail hostmaster@bigcompany.com');
    print MAIL 'From: hostmistress@bigcompany.com';
    print MAIL 'Reply-To: hostmistress@bigcompany.com';
    print MAIL "Subject: $machine CPU too high";
    print MAIL "";
    print MAIL "CPU idle time is less than $thresh\% on $machine";
    print MAIL "Here are the top 10 processes by CPU on $machine";
    print MAIL $response->content;
    print MAIL "\nThis message generated by cron job /opt/bin/watchcpu.pl";
    close MAIL;
}
```

Using Telnet from Perl

The problem with running a web server to report performance statistics is that it requires the installation of software on your production systems. Installation of extra software on production systems should be avoided for many reasons. Extra software may leak memory or otherwise use up resources, it may open security holes, and it may just be a pain to do. Fortunately, all you really need for a pretty good monitoring system is permission to use tools and interfaces that are probably already there, such as the *rstat* daemon, SQL, SNMP, and Telnet. They will not work through a firewall the way web server–based tools do, but your monitoring system should be on the secure side of your firewall in most cases anyway.

Telnet is the most flexible of these interfaces, because a Telnet session can do any-thing a user can do. Here is an example script that will log in to a machine given on the command line, run *ps*, and dump the results to standard output:

```perl
#!/usr/local/bin/perl

use Net::Telnet;

$host = $ARGV[0];
$user = "patrick";
$password = "passwd";

my $telnet = Net::Telnet->new($host);
$telnet->login($user, $password);
my @lines = $telnet->cmd('/usr/bin/ps -o pid,pmem,pcpu,nlwp,user,args');
print @lines;
$telnet->close;
```

This ability to run a command from Telnet and use the results in a Perl script is incredibly useful, but also easily abused, for example, by running many such scripts every minute from *cron* jobs. Every login will take a tiny bit of disk space (for instance, each will be recorded in */var/run/utmp* on Linux.) Please be cautious about how much monitoring you are doing, lest you become part of your own perfor-mance problem.

To fill out a per-process monitoring system with *telnet* and *ps*, we would like to be able to store our data in a relational database. For that, we need to define a database table. Here's the definition of a table for storing *ps* data in Oracle that I use to store data coming from the Solaris command */usr/bin/ps -o pid,pmem,pcpu,nlwp,user,args*:

```sql
create table ps(
    machine    varchar2(20),
    timestamp  date not null,
    pid        number(6),
    pmem       number(3,1),
    pcpu       number(3,1),
    nlwp       number(5),
    usr        varchar2(8),
    args       varchar2(24)
);
```

And here's a Perl script that can *telnet* to various machines, run *ps*, and store the resulting *ps* data in a database:

```perl
#!/usr/local/bin/perl

$ENV{ORACLE_HOME} = "/opt/ORACLE/product";

use DBI;
use Net::Telnet;

$user     = "patrick";
$pwd      = "telnetpasswd";
```

```
$machine = $ARGV[0];

my $telnet = Net::Telnet->new($machine);
$telnet->timeout(45);
$telnet->login($user,$pwd);
my @lines = $telnet->cmd('/usr/bin/ps -e -o pid,pmem,pcpu,nlwp,user,args');
$telnet->close;

$dbh = DBI->connect("dbi:Oracle:acsiweba", "patrick", "dbpasswd")
    or die "Can't connect to Oracle: $DBI::errstr\n";

foreach (@lines) {
    # Grab the lines with "dummy" in them, and parse out this data:
    #     PID      %MEM      %CPU    NLWP    USER         COMMAND
    #
    # and insert the fields into ps table, which looks like this:
    #
    # Name                                          Null?   Type
    # ---------    -------------------------------------------
    # MACHINE                                               VARCHAR2(20)
    # TIMESTAMP                                     NOT NULL DATE
    # PID                                                   NUMBER(6)
    # PMEM                                                  NUMBER(3,1)
    # PCPU                                                  NUMBER(3,1)
    # NLWP                                                  NUMBER(5)
    # USR                                                   VARCHAR2(8)
    # ARGS                                                  VARCHAR2(24)

    if (/(\d+) +(\d+\.\d) +(\d+\.\d) +(\d+) +(\w+) .*Didentifier=(\w+)/) {

        $sth = $dbh->prepare("insert into ps values ('$machine', sysdate, '$1', '$2',
'$3', '$4', '$5', '$6')");
        $sth->execute();
    }
}

$dbh->disconnect or warn "Disconnect failed: $DBI::errstr\n";
```

Generating Graphs from ps Data

Now that we have all this wonderful *ps* data in a database, what are we going to do
with it? Why, generate graphs of it on request, of course, just like we did with the
rstat data. Here's a sample CGI script that will do just that, and a sample graph generated from it. (To use the CGI script, you have to put it in your web server's *cgi-bin*
directory, and then hit the URL corresponding to the script.)

```
#!/usr/local/bin/perl

use DBI;

$ENV{ORACLE_HOME} = "/opt/ORACLE/product";
```

```perl
print qq|Content-type: text/html\n\n|;

#<meta http-equiv = "Pragma" Content = "no-cache">
#<meta http-equiv = "Expires" Content = "Thu, Jan 1 1970 12:00:00 GMT">

print qq|<HTML><HEAD><TITLE>generate a graph</TITLE>
</HEAD><BODY><H1>generate a graph</H1>|;

if ($ENV{'REQUEST_METHOD'} eq 'POST') {
    read(STDIN, $buffer, $ENV{'CONTENT_LENGTH'});
    @pairs = split(/&/, $buffer);
    foreach $pair (@pairs) {
        ($name, $value) = split(/=/, $pair);

        $value  =~ tr/+/ /;
        $value  =~ s/%([a-fA-F0-9][a-fA-F0-9])/pack("C", hex($1))/eg;
        $contents{$name} = $value;
    }
}

$machine   = $contents{"machine"};
$args      = $contents{"args"};
$daterange = $contents{"daterange"};
$parameter = $contents{"parameter"};

if ($machine && $parameter && daterange) {

    `/bin/rm tmp/*.gif`; # possible removal of someone else's gif before they saw it

    $dbh = DBI->connect("dbi:Oracle:acsiweba", "patrick", "dbpasswd")
        or die "Can't connect to Oracle: $DBI::errstr\n";

    $sql = "select to_char(timestamp, 'YYYY MM DD HH24 MI'), $parameter from patrick.
ps ";

    if ($daterange eq "today") {
        $sql .= "where timestamp between trunc(sysdate) and sysdate and
machine='$machine'";
    }

    if ($daterange eq "yesterday") {
        $sql .= "where timestamp between trunc(sysdate) - 1 and trunc(sysdate) and
machine='$machine'";
    }

    if ($daterange eq "t-7") {
        $sql .= "where timestamp between trunc(sysdate) - 7 and sysdate and
machine='$machine'";
    }

    if ($daterange eq "t-30") {
        $sql .= "where timestamp between trunc(sysdate) - 30 and sysdate and
machine='$machine'";
    }
```

```perl
    if ($daterange eq "t-365") {
        $sql .= "where timestamp between trunc(sysdate) - 365 and sysdate and
machine='$machine'";
    }

    $sql .= " and args='$args'";

    #print "<p>start of query ", `date`;

    $sth = $dbh->prepare($sql);
    $sth->execute() || print $dbh->errstr;

    ($timestamp, $item) = $sth->fetchrow_array; # get one sample row to be sure we
have data
    if ($timestamp) {

        #print "<p>end of query ", `date`;

        $date = `date`;
        chop $date;

        open(GP, "|/usr/local/bin/gnuplot");
        print GP $gp_cmd;
        print GP qq|
            set xdata time
            set timefmt "%Y %m %d %H %M"
            set term gif
            set xlabel "graph made on $date"
            set bmargin 4
            set ylabel "$parameter"
            set output "tmp/$$.gif"
            plot '-' using 1:6 title "$args $parameter on $machine" with lines lt 2
        |;

        while(($timestamp, $item) = $sth->fetchrow_array) {
            print GP "$timestamp $item\n";
        }

        print GP "e\n";
        close(GP);

        $sth->finish();
        $dbh->disconnect or warn "acsiweba disconnect failed: $DBI::errstr\n";

        #print "<p>end of plotting ", `date`;
        print "<p><img src=\"tmp/$$.gif\"><p>";
        print "graph was generated from this query:<p> $sql\n";
    }
    else {
        print "Sorry, I do not have the requested data for that time range for
$machine.";
    }
}
```

```
print qq|
<FORM
METHOD="POST" ENCTYPE="application/x-www-form-urlencoded">
<P>select a machine
<SELECT NAME="machine">
<OPTION SELECTED VALUE="mars">mars middleware
<OPTION VALUE="venus">venus middleware
<OPTION VALUE="mercury">mercury middleware
</SELECT>
</P>
<SELECT NAME="args">
<OPTION SELECTED VALUE="purchase">purchase app
<OPTION VALUE="billing">billing app
<OPTION VALUE="accounting">accounting app
</SELECT>
</P>
<P>select a parameter
<SELECT NAME="parameter">
<OPTION SELECTED VALUE="pmem">pmem
<OPTION          VALUE="pcpu">pcpu
<OPTION          VALUE="nlwp">nwlp
</SELECT>
</P>
<P>select a date range
<SELECT NAME="daterange">
<OPTION SELECTED VALUE="today">today
<OPTION VALUE="yesterday">yesterday
<OPTION VALUE="t-7">last 7 days
<OPTION VALUE="t-30">last 30 days
<OPTION VALUE="t-365">last 365 days
</SELECT>
</P>
<P>
<INPUT TYPE="submit" NAME="graph" VALUE="graph">
</P><HR><P>|;

print qq|</FORM>Questions? Write
<A HREF="mailto:p\@patrick.net">p\@patrick.net</A>
</BODY></HTML>|;
```

Figure 4-3 is an example graph generated from this CGI, showing a memory leak in an application, and restarts on 11/3 and 11/7.

Monitoring Other Things

You can also monitor the contents of the web pages rather than the latency. For example, the Weblogic application server gives a password-protected web page showing the number of database connections used at any given time. The page is intended only for a human reader, but knowing how to automatically grab web pages, we can "screen scrape" the Weblogic monitoring page and keep a log of the number of database connections used over each day and plot this log. We can snoop

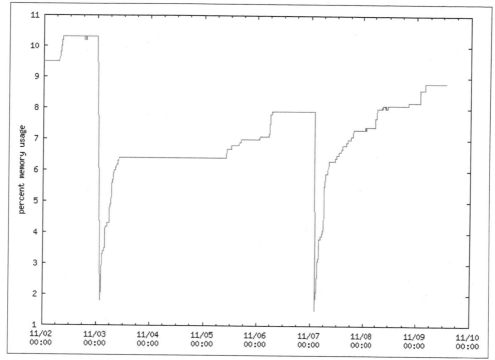

Figure 4-3. Graph of ps data

the header containing the base 64 encoding of the user ID and password and then use that in our script. Here's a simple script that will grab the *Weblogic T3AdminJDBC* page, parse out the number of connections in use, and log that data to a file:

```perl
#!/usr/local/bin/perl

use LWP::UserAgent;
use HTTP::Headers;
use HTTP::Request;
use HTTP::Response;

$gnuplot    = "/usr/local/bin/gnuplot";


MAIN: {
    $ua = LWP::UserAgent->new;
    $ua->timeout(60);              # Set timeout to 60 seconds

    &get("http://$ARGV[0]/T3AdminJDBC");

    s/<.*?>/ /g;                   # remove all the HTML tags
    /cxn_pool +(\d+) +(\d+)/;      # grab the relevant line
    &log("cxn_pool", $1, $2);
```

```
    `$gnuplot *.gp`;
}

sub get {
    local ($url) = @_;

    $request = new HTTP::Request('GET', "$url");

    # This is the base 64 encoding of the weblogic admin login and password.
    $request->push_header("Authorization" => "Basic slkjSLDkf98aljk98797");

    $response = $ua->request($request);

    if (!$response->is_success) {
        #die $request->as_string(), " failed: ", $response->error_as_HTML;
        # HTTP redirections are considered failures by LWP.
    }

    # Put response in default string for easy verification.
    $_ = $response->content;
}

# Write log entry in format that gnuplot can use to create a gif.
sub log {

    local ($file, $connections, $pool) = @_;
    $date = `date +'%Y %m %d %H %M %S'`;
    chop $date;

    # Corresponding to gnuplot command: set timefmt "%Y %m %d %H %M %S";

    open(FH, ">>$file") || die "Could not open $file\n";
    printf FH "$date $connections $pool\n";
    close(FH);
}
```

Once we have our data file, we can plot it using the following *gnuplot* configuration file:

```
set term png color
set output "connections.gif"

set xdata time
set timefmt "%H %M %S"
set xrange ["00 00 00":"24 00 00"]
set xlabel "mountain time"
set format x "%H:%M"
set bmargin 3
set ylabel "connections"
set yrange [0:100]

plot "connections.log" using 4:7 title "connections" w l lt 3
```

And the result is a graph like the one in Figure 4-4.

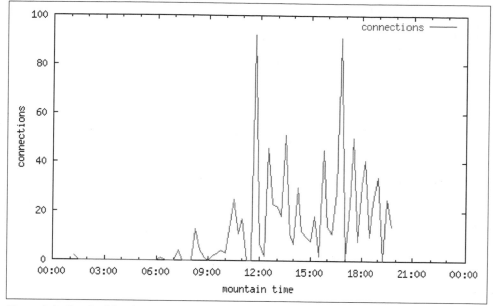

Figure 4-4. Graph of database connections over one day, no leak

We can also easily store this connection data in a database table itself, as we did with the *ps* data. Having done that, we can adapt the dynamic graph generation CGI script above to plot connection data. This is very useful for finding "leaks" in database connections—that is, connections that do not get cleaned up after use. This typically happens because of poor or nonexistent error handling, which leaves an unused database connection in limbo. Figure 4-5 is an example CGI-generated graph over 30 days, showing how the database connections build up between restarts of the Weblogic application server. The server was restarted on 10/13, 10/25, 10/30, and 11/3.

Using Java for Monitoring

Just because I prefer Perl doesn't mean you have to use Perl. Here is an example Java program that monitors the first edition of this book's Amazon sales rank. I wrote a Perl program that does the same thing, and Ian Darwin, the author of O'Reilly's *Java Cookbook*, showed me that it's not much harder in Java. Thanks to Ian for the following example:

```
import java.io.*;
import com.darwinsys.util.FileIO;
import java.net.*;
import java.text.*;
import java.util.*;
import org.apache.regexp.*;
```

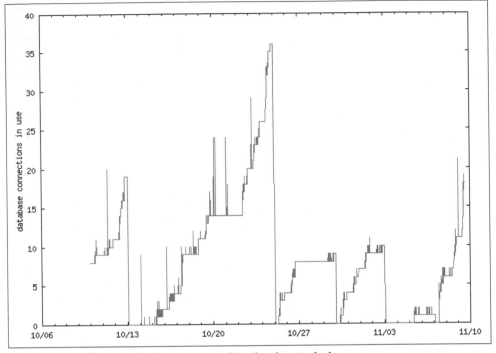

Figure 4-5. Database connections over several weeks, showing leak

```
/** Graph of a book's sales rank on a given bookshop site.
* @author Ian F. Darwin, ian@darwinsys.com, Java Cookbook author,
*       translated fairly literally from Perl into Java.
* @author Patrick Killelea <p@patrick.net>: original Perl version,
*       from the 2nd edition of his book "Web Performance Tuning".
* @version $Id: BookRank.java,v 1.10 2001/04/10 00:28:02 ian Exp $
*/

public class BookRank {
        public final static String ISBN = "0937175307";
        public final static String DATA_FILE = "lint.sales";
        public final static String GRAPH_FILE = "lint.png";
        public final static String TITLE = "Checking C Prog w/ Lint";
        public final static String QUERY = "
                        "http://www.quickbookshops.web/cgi-bin/search?isbn=";

        /** Grab the sales rank off the web page and log it. */
        public static void main(String[] args) throws Exception {

                // Looking for something like this in the input:
                //      <b>QuickBookShop.web Sales Rank: </b>
                //      26,252
                //      </font><br>
                // Patrick Killelea's original RE formulation : match number with
                // comma included, just print minus ",". Loses if fall below 100,000.
                RE r = new RE(" Sales Rank: </b>\\s*(\\d*),*(\\d+)\\s");
```

```
                    // Java: should use "[\d,]+" to extract the number and
                    // NumberFormat.getInstance().parse() to convert to int.

                    // Open the URL and get a Reader from it.
                    BufferedReader is = new BufferedReader(new InputStreamReader(
                            new URL(QUERY + ISBN).openStream()));
                    // Read the URL looking for the rank information, as
                    // a single long string, so can match RE across multi-lines.
                    String input = FileIO.readerToString(is);

                    // If found, append to sales data file.
                    if (r.match(input)) {
                            PrintWriter FH = new PrintWriter(
                                    new FileWriter(DATA_FILE, true));
                            String date = // `date +'%m %d %H %M %S %Y'`;
                                    new SimpleDateFormat("MM dd hh mm ss yyyy ").
                                    format(new Date());
                            // Paren 1 is the optional thousands; paren 2 is low 3 digits.

                            FH.println(date + r.getParen(1) + r.getParen(2));
                            FH.close();
                    }

                    // Whether current data found or not, draw the graph, using
                    // external plotting program against all historical data.
                    // Could use gnuplot, R, any other math/graph program.
                    // Better yet: use one of the Java plotting APIs.

                    String gnuplot_cmd =
                            "set term png color\n" +
                            "set output \"" + GRAPH_FILE + "\"\n" +
                            "set xdata time\n" +
                            "set ylabel \"Book sales rank\"\n" +
                            "set bmargin 3\n" +
                            "set logscale y\n" +
                            "set yrange [1:60000] reverse\n" +
                            "set timefmt \"%Y %m %d %H %M %S\"\n" +
                            "plot \"" + DATA_FILE +
                                    "\" using 1:7 title \"" + TITLE + "\" with lines\n"
                    ;

                    Process p = Runtime.getRuntime().exec("/usr/local/bin/gnuplot");
                    PrintWriter gp = new PrintWriter(p.getOutputStream());
                    gp.print(gnuplot_cmd);
                    gp.close();
            }
    }
```

And here's the original in Perl:

```
#!/usr/local/bin/perl -w

################################
# Set up user agent and proxy. #
```

```
################################

use  LWP::UserAgent;
$ua = LWP::UserAgent->new;
$ua->proxy('http', 'http://httpprox:8080');

#####################################################
# Grab the sales rank off the Amazon page and log it.
#####################################################

$url     = "http://www.amazon.com/exec/obidos/ASIN/1565923790/";
$request = new HTTP::Request('GET', "$url");
$response = $ua->request($request);
$_       = $response->content;
m|Amazon.com Sales Rank: </b>\s*(\d*),*(\d+)\s|s && do {
    open(FH, ">>wpt.sales") || die "Could not open wpt.sales\n";
    $date = `date +'%m %d %H %M %S %Y'`;
    chop $date;
    printf FH "%s %s\n", $date, $1.$2;
    close(FH);
};

##########################
# Regenerate the graph. #
##########################

$gnuplot_cmd = qq|
    set term png color
    set output "sales.png"
    set xdata time
    set ylabel "Amazon sales rank"
    set bmargin 3
    set logscale y
    set yrange [1:30000] reverse
    set timefmt "%m %d %H %M %S %Y"
    plot "wpt.sales" using 1:7 title "web performance tuning" with lines
|;

open(GP, "|/usr/local/bin/gnuplot");
print GP $gnuplot_cmd;
close(GP);
```

Making a System Dashboard Web Page

Once you are updating a few graphs via *cron* jobs, you may want to set up a PC in a public place to show the constantly updated graphs to those who have an interest. Here's a bit of HTML to help you do that. It will make a square table with four images:

```
<html>
<head>
<title>System Dashboard http://patrick.net/graphs.html</title>
```

```
<meta http-equiv = "Refresh" Content = "300">
<meta http-equiv = "Pragma" Content = "no-cache">
<meta http-equiv = "Expires" Content = "Thu, Jan 1 1970 12:00:00 GMT">
</head>
<body bgcolor="#ffffff">
<table cols=2>
   <tr>
      <td><IMG SRC="users.png"></td>
      <td><IMG SRC="purchases.png"></td>
   </tr>
   <tr>
      <td><IMG SRC="cpu.png"></td>
      <td><IMG SRC="disk.png"></td>
   </tr>
</table>
</body>
</html>
```

The 300 is the number of seconds before we refresh the four graph images. The other "meta" tags try to defeat the caching of the browser, which may try to keep the graphs in its cache rather than refresh them from the web server. If you have more than four graphs, it is hard to show them all on a single page, so you may want to alternate between two displays.

```
<META HTTP-EQUIV = "Refresh" Content = "300;URL=http://patrick.net/moregraphs.html">
```

If you don't like the "chrome"—that is, the buttons at the top of the browser— here's another HTML file, containing a JavaScript way to pop up your dashboard window without any of that:

```
<html>
<head>
<title>Dashboard Launcher</title>
</head>
<body bgcolor="#ffffff">

<script language="JavaScript">
<!--
function MM_openBrWindow(theURL,winName,features) { //v2.0
   window.open(theURL,winName,features);
}
//-->
</script>

<a href="index.html"
onclick="MM_openBrWindow('graphs.html',
                         '',
                         'width=640,height=480,resizable=1')">
pop
</body>
</html>
```

Danger! Excessive Monitoring is Hazardous to Your Web Site's Health

Monitoring via your web site is good, but too much of a good thing can be bad.

Keynote is a monitoring service that can end up hitting your heavy dynamic pages from all over the U.S. If each of their agents is set to hit it once per minute, 60 agents will cause hits once per second. Resonate, a load balancing system, could also get those pages every second. And you can easily add to the load as well by inadvertently doing too much monitoring. Keep the capacity usage of monitoring systems to a low percentage of your system capabilities.

SNMP

The Simple Network Management Protocol (SNMP) is a standardized way to track the machines, applications, and bandwidth of your network. It is a valuable tool for performance tuning. SNMP originated in the Unix community, but it is now available on most platforms. There are many SNMP management tools to choose from, such as HP's OpenView and products from IBM, 3Com, Cabletron, Sun, and Cisco.

You can avoid having SNMP traffic add to your production traffic by setting up a separate SNMP management network, although this can be expensive. Each monitored device or application is referred to as an agent and has a Management Information Base (MIB) that defines the information the agent tracks and what sort of remote control of the agent is allowed.

RMON

RMON (Remote MONitoring) is an SNMP MIB definition for Ethernet, defined in RFC 1757 (formerly RFC 1271). RMON II can see HTTP and other kinds of application-level traffic and generate statistics on these. RMON allows monitored devices to be proactive about signalling errors, unlike the traditional polling mechanism used by SNMP. Many commercial systems, such as Tivoli, HP OpenView, and Sun Netmanager understand and use RMON.

ARM

The Application Response Measurement API (ARM) provides a standard way to characterize resource consumption by a particular application, even in a distributed environment. It was developed by Hewlett-Packard and Tivoli Systems. It is a good idea, but it requires that software developers instrument their code using this API. To date, few software vendors have released ARM-compliant code. The ARM working group web site is at *http://www.cmg.org/*.

Other Resources

A few more benchmarking resources on the Web are as follows: the Linpack site, which compares Java to Fortran, at *http://www.netlib.org/benchmark/linpackjava/*; the Netperf site, which has a large database of network performance results found with the free Netperf tool, at *http://www.netperf.org/*; and a Java benchmark page at *http://www.cs.cmu.edu/~jch/java/benchmarks.html*.

Key Recommendations

- Don't put too much stock in benchmarks unless they're very closely related to what you actually intend to do.

- Do monitor your actual web performance, not just the machine-level load, and keep records.

- Do not monitor too much, or you'll become part of the problem.

CHAPTER 5
Load Testing

Load testing your web site is useful for figuring out how much capacity it can handle, but it is more important for shaking out bugs that occur only under heavy load, especially subtle threading issues that can cause deadlock and crash the site. Once the bugs are mostly gone, you should be able to get a nice logarithmic curve that shows throughput level off with increasing load, or, a nice exponential curve that shows that latency goes through the roof as load goes beyond your site's limits.

Load Test Preparation

A good load test requires a lot of difficult preparation:

- Test user accounts need to be set up
- Database tables and content need to be comparable to your production system
- System parameters between the test machines and production machines have to be synchronized
- A realistic set of URLs should be collected for testing
- Client connection speeds should be emulated

Log files give you a good idea of what URLs you are being asked for, but it is usually too much work to create a comprehensive and realistic test starting from log files. In fact, there is not enough data in the log files to reproduce requests because the HTTP POST input data is not recorded in log files, nor is any HTTP header information. Also, note that log file entries record the time that responses were finished, rather than the time requests arrived. This means that log files do not reflect the time distribution of requests to your site.

Emulating the distribution of client connection speeds is also difficult. Some load-testing tools have options to emulate certain modem speeds, but there is no general way to do this. There is also no easy way to tell how fast your users are. In theory, you could check the time between the GET of an HTML file and another GET from the same IP of an image in that HTML file, but this is a coarse measure because log files record whole seconds.

Be sure to set the number of open file descriptors per process on your load generation machine high enough so that you can actually generate the load you need. *ulimit -n 1024* is often all you need. It is a classic mistake to forget this.

First, run a latency test under no load at all, just to get a baseline. Then measure the latency as load goes up to be sure it remains bounded as long as you are within the loads you expect. Run your load test continuously until the response reaches a steady state of some kind. Consider letting it go for a few days as a "soak" test for memory leaks.

Be sure to explicitly test error conditions. Developers usually assume error conditions will be rare and do not put much thought into performance on error. This means that a lot of errors may also be the cause of very poor performance.

Watch Out for Clock Changes

Many Unix systems run *timed* or *xntpd*, which reset their kernel clocks to the correct time every so often from a central source via the network with the `adjtime` or `adjtimex` system call. This is ordinarily a wonderful thing, but if this clock adjustment occurs while you are taking a time measurement, your results will be wrong.

Imagine you get the current time from your system and start a measurement. Then the measured thing finishes and you get the time again. If the system clock has been reset in that interval, then you could potentially see that your end time is earlier than your start time! That has happened to my own tests many times. The only safe thing is to not run *timed* or *xntpd* during your tests and to make sure *cron* isn't running it either.

Why Is Production Performance Different from Test Performance?

It is hard to keep a test system exactly in sync with a production system. There are so many variables. If any of them are even slightly different, performance could be very different between production and the test system. Assuming you are running your servers on Solaris, here are a few things to check:

- First, diff the output from the *prtconf* command to see if memory, disk, or CPU configuration is much different.
- Diff */etc/system* on the two machines.
- Get dumps of the Oracle or other database parameters and diff those.
- Diff *cron* or *autosys* configuration files and diff the output from *ifconfig -a*.
- Diff your network parameters.

Here is a small shell script that will generate a list of *ndd* parameters:

```
for parm in `ndd /dev/tcp \? | cut -f1 -d" " | grep -v _hash | grep -v status | grep
-v \?`
do
    /usr/ucb/echo -n $parm
    /usr/ucb/echo -n " "
    ndd /dev/tcp $parm
done
```

This script is called *dumpndd.sh* and is available at *http://patrick.net/software/*.

Trade-offs with Load Testing Tools

Load testing a web site is not straightforward, unless the site is strictly text. You may want to see how the site will perform when hit by a million browsers, but no one has the hardware to run a million test browsers on individual PCs. So most load tests are done with small programs that emulate browsers. As the realism of the emulation increases to get all the images, use HTTP 1.1, SSL, etc., the emulators approach the size of browsers. The most realistic emulation is finally software that actually controls a browser, but that is not scalable.

Another problem with emulators is that you often have to deeply analyze a web page to write a script that can test it. Pages that post content usually have parameters input by the user, which have to be accounted for in the emulator. You can record a script with my *sprocket* web proxy from Chapter 4, but that will not generalize parameters; it will just record the parameters you used. Many tools can automate the writing of tests simply by surfing, but the tests they generate usually drive a browser, which, as we just noted, is not a scalable way to test. They also leave the problem of parameterizing the tests to the user.

Writing Your Own Load Testing Tools

If you just want to give your server 100 hits, a simple way to do it is with the following shell script. Then take the difference between the start and end times output by the script and divide 100 by that time to get the number of hits per second you delivered to the web server. This script forks a new Lynx browser process for each hit, so the script is not efficient and the total running time is not very accurate, but you can see how easy it is to write a simple load generation tool in a Unix shell language.

```
#!/bin/bash
CNT=0
date
while [ "100" -ne "$CNT" ]
do
    lynx -source http://patrick.net/ > /dev/null &
    CNT=`expr $CNT + 1`
done
date
```

You could also write a similar tool in Java or Perl and get a more accurate reading and heavier generated load by eliminating Lynx startup time.

Here is a simple single-threaded load test script in Perl that hits a page and then sleeps 1/80th of a second, hits it again, sleeps another 1/80th of a second, etc., 100 times. If the page were infinitely fast, this should achieve a result of 80 hits in one second. Then the script does the same thing for 1/79th of a second, and so on, down to one second delays between attempts to get the page. In theory, we should be able to plot a nice load curve for any particular page like this, rising linearly at first, then flattening out as we approach the server's performance limit for serial hits.

```perl
#!/usr/local/bin/perl -w

use LWP::UserAgent;
use Time::HiRes 'time','sleep';

$ua        = LWP::UserAgent->new;
$request    = new HTTP::Request('GET', "http://localhost/index.html");
$hits      = 100;
$hps        = 80;

# Try to do 100 hits at 80 hits per second, then 100 at 79 hits per second, ...

while ($hps) {
    $i     = $hits;
    $start = time();
    while ($i--) {
        $ua->request($request);
        sleep (1/$hps);
    }
    $end     = time();
    print "$hps ", $hits / ($end - $start), "\n";
    $hps--;
}
```

The Timer Problem

When I ran the test, the curve was not at all as smooth as I had hoped. Figure 5-1 shows the result.

You can see the performance level out, but it's a little too level for me. Why do we have such a pronounced stairstep effect? The reason has to do with the timer interrupt. The kernel measures time in multiples of 1/100 of a second. This means that when we try to sleep for 1/80 of a second, it is exactly the same as trying to sleep for 1/79 of a second, so we get the same result. To see why, consider that 1/80 of a second is 0.0125 seconds. And 1/79 of a second is 0.0127 seconds. The difference is 0.0002 seconds, while the smallest difference in time we can distinguish is only 0.01 seconds.

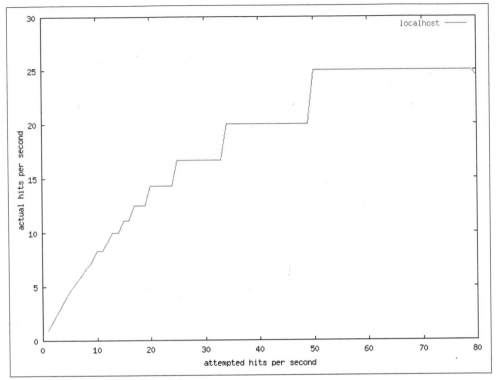

Figure 5-1. Load curve with a timer problem

Fortunately, the timer interrupt is configurable. In Linux for Intel, modify the following line in */usr/include/asm/param.h*:

```
#define HZ 100
```

I modified this to be 1000 and recompiled the Linux kernel, just to see if I could then sleep with a resolution of one millisecond. Modifying the timer interrupt has the unfortunate side effect of breaking device drivers, which depend on fixed timings, but you should simply be able to recompile them if you have the source code—then they are likely to work. In any case, the keyboard worked fine without recompiling its driver. I then tried a more abbreviated version of the test, which measures nothing except the ability to sleep:

```
#!/usr/local/bin/perl -w

$hps        = 80;

while ($hps) {
    $start = time();
    sleep (1/$hps);
    $end   = time();
    print 1/$hps, " ", $end - $start, "\n";
    $hps--;
}
```

Running this with a 100 Hz kernel and again with a 1000 Hz kernel gives the result shown in Figure 5-2.

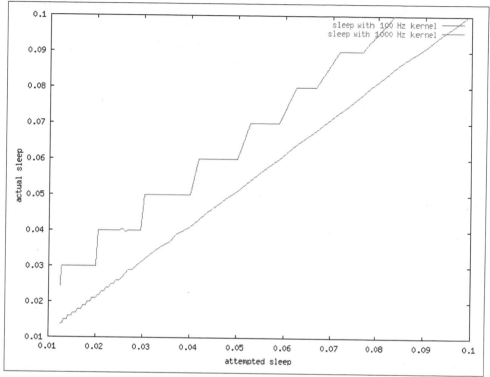

Figure 5-2. A smoother load curve

I was now able to sleep for one millisecond rather than the usual ten milliseconds. Changing process priority doesn't affect the results. Nor does using an alternative way to sleep in Perl, which is the select statement:

```
select undef, undef, undef, (1/$hps);
```

The net result is that your ability to run any load test is limited by the resolution of timing in the kernel. Reducing the interrupt will slow down the system for the reason we have shown, and increasing it too much will also slow down the system because you'll spend too much time handling the timer interrupt. It's probably best to leave it like it is unless you know you need to change it for a particular test.

Load Testing by Excessive Monitoring

In Chapter 4, we discuss how to monitor a web site with Perl by either manually writing a test or using my *sprocket* web proxy to generate a test script by surfing. The great thing about monitoring with a Perl script, or any other method that does not drive a browser, is that you are given a load test for free simply by starting hundreds of monitors at the same time.

Monitoring scripts that drive a browser do not have this advantage. I have found that a Sun E450 with 1 GB can run 300 to 500 copies of a Perl monitoring script at the same time before hitting serious resource limits (usually memory).

While this is not as elegant a way to run a load test as, say, multithreading requests within a single process, the ease of set up overwhelms the disadvantages. Simply create a shell script to run 100 or so monitoring scripts in the background and you have that many virtual users. Each virtual user should write to a file of its own. Otherwise, writes to a single file by multiple processes will result in garbled data. File locking could prevent such garbling, but it would also slow down the load test. Such a test file might look like this:

```
#!/bin/sh
./monitor.pl user001 > results001 &
./monitor.pl user002 > results002 &
./monitor.pl user003 > results003 &
./monitor.pl user004 > results004 &
./monitor.pl user005 > results005 &
...
```

After the test is done, all of the results are easily put into a single file by catting them together:

```
% cat results* > aggregate
```

With a bit more work, you can make a script that runs one virtual user, then two, then three, getting overall latency averages as the workload rises. You should see the classic exponential rise in latency as the number of virtual users rises. That is, response latency should first rise slowly with the number of users, then go up exponentially as you reach your site's capacity. In fact, here is a script that will do just that:

```
#!/bin/bash

# This is a very simple load test relying on process creation rather than
# threads to generate virtual clients. Note that the result files end with only
# one result if you use sh rather than bash. May be a bug in sh.

ulimit -n 1024

# start clean
if [ -f results.1 ]; then /bin/rm results.*; fi
if [ -f averages ];  then /bin/rm averages;  fi

# Run test with RUN=1 user, then 2 users, then 4 users, up to MAX users.
```

```
RUN=1
MAX=1024

while [ "$RUN" -le "$MAX" ]
    do
        USER=1

        # Start up RUN number of users.
        while [ "$USER" -le "$RUN" ]
            do
                echo starting user $USER
                tiny script >> results.$RUN &
                USER=`expr $USER + 1`
            done

        wait    # wait for all the USERs to exit

        sleep 2 # just for good measure

        avg.pl results.$RUN >> averages

        echo  Done running $RUN users.
        RUN=`expr $RUN \* 2`
    done
```

The following is the *gnuplot* config file for graphing the results for a CPU-bound process. Figure 5-3 shows the results.

```
set term gif
set output "load.gif"
set title "results of load test of CPU-bound process"
set ylabel "time in seconds"
set logscale x

plot \
"results.1" using (1):($1/1000000) notitle, \
"results.2" using (2):($1/1000000) notitle, \
"results.4" using (4):($1/1000000) notitle, \
"results.8" using (8):($1/1000000) notitle, \
"results.16" using (16):($1/1000000) notitle, \
"results.32" using (32):($1/1000000) notitle, \
"results.64" using (64):($1/1000000) notitle, \
"results.128" using (128):($1/1000000) notitle, \
"results.256" using (256):($1/1000000) notitle, \
"results.512" using (512):($1/1000000) notitle, \
"results.1024" using (1024):($1/1000000) notitle, \
"averages" using (2**$0):($1/1000000) title "average" with lines
```

Synchronizing a Load Test

If you use many processes to emulate many users, and you want them to all try to do something at the same time, you run into the problem of synchronizing their actions.

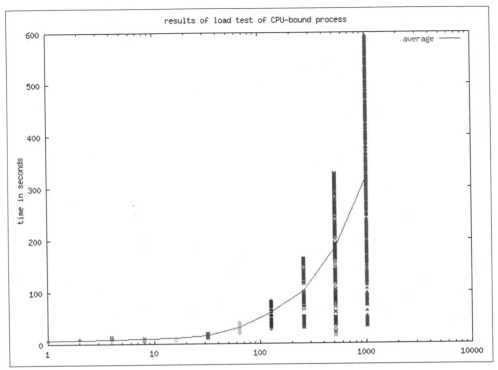

Figure 5-3. Latency averages

A simple way to send them all a signal at about the same time is to create a file. If the processes are all polling for the existence of that file, they will all find that it exists at about the same time. Here's a bit of example Perl code that polls for a file every tenth of a second. The */tmp* filesystem on Solaris is usually in memory, so using */tmp* does not require disk access. Note that you must have the Time::HiRes package installed to sleep for less than a whole number of seconds in Perl.

```
while (! -e "/tmp/go") { sleep 0.1; }
```

If each virtual client script waits at this line, to start the test you can simply **touch /tmp/go**. The file will exist, and each of the waiting processes will continue past that line at about the same time.

A more sophisticated way to synchronize a bunch of processes is to send a signal. If you have set up a signal handler, all the processes will enter it at about the same time.

Randomizing a Load Test

Conversely, you may want your virtual users to emulate the random clicking of human beings reading pages and moving on. You can easily do this in Perl with sleep rand(n) between actions, where n is the maximum number of seconds you want to delay.

Help, I Have to Stop My Load Test!

Sometimes you start a bunch of processes as a load test and need to stop them all. */bin/kill* on Linux (not the same as the *kill* built into the shell) will kill by exact name. So if you have a bunch of processes named *session*, you can kill them all with one command, like this:

```
% /bin/kill session
```

But if your version of *kill* does not kill by name, here's a Perl script that will kill by name. I call it *zap*. You can download this script from *http://patrick.net/software/zap.pl*.

```perl
#!/usr/local/bin/perl

die "Usage: zap <proc name> [-9]\n" unless $ARGV[0];


@procs = `ps -ef`;                            # OS dependent. Customize.

VICTIM:
foreach $proc (@procs) {
    if ($proc =~ /$ARGV[0]/) {

        #($pid) = $proc =~ /^ *(\d*).*/;       # Solaris
        ($pid) = $proc =~ /^[^ ]+ *(\d*).*/;   # Linux

        if ($pid eq $$) { next VICTIM; }       # Don't kill yourself.

        if ($ARGV[1]  =~ /-9/) {
            `kill -9 $pid`;
        }
        else {
            print "$proc";
            print "Kill this one? ";
            $answer = <STDIN>;
            if ($answer =~ /y/) {              # Any answer with a y will kill.
                `kill $pid`;
            }
        }
    }
}
```

Generating Network Load

Sometimes you want to generate a load on your network, rather than on your web service. To generate network load, you have many options. The old *spray* command seems to have fallen out of use and is not distributed with RedHat Linux, but other programs remain, including those in the following list.

ping

The *ping* command has a "flood" option that lets you stress at least a 10 base T Ethernet if you send the maximum size packet of 65,507 bytes. Here's how you would hit IP address 1.2.3.4 with that size packet as fast as possible:

```
% ping -f -s 65507 1.2.3.4
```

Remember that this is essentially a denial of service (DOS) attack, so don't use it on a network others are using.

Netcat

Another similar option is to use the free Netcat program *nc*, by Thomas Weld. I keep a copy of the distribution package on my web site under *http://patrick.net/ software/*. This example will forward the output of the *yes* command to a web server port:

```
% yes AAAAAAAAAAAAAAAAA | nc www.webserver.com 80 > /dev/null
```

chargen

Another fun and easy load generation tool is the *chargen* port. You can *telnet* to it and redirect the output to null to generate quite a network load:

```
% telnet testmachine chargen > /dev/null
```

In this way, I was able to get up to about 86 Mbps on a 100 Mbps Ethernet connection, estimated from looking at *ndd* packet counts.

Benchmark Specifications and Benchmark Tests

We should distinguish between benchmark specifications and benchmark tests. There are several web benchmarks that may be implemented by more than one test since there are implementation details that do not affect the results of the test. For example, a well-specified HTTP load is the same regardless of the hardware and software used to generate the load and regardless of the actual bits in the content. On the other hand, some benchmarks are themselves defined by a test program or suite, so that running the test is the only way to run the benchmark. We will consider both specifications and tests in this section.

The point of a benchmark is to generate performance statistics that can legitimately be used to compare products. To do this, you must try to hold constant all of the conditions around the item under test and then measure performance. If the only thing different between runs is a particular component, then any difference in results must be due to the difference in that component.

Exactly defining the component under test can be a bit tricky. Say you are trying to compare the performance of Solaris and Irix in running Netscape server software. The variable in the tests is not only the operating system but also, by necessity, the hardware. From a benchmark alone, it would be impossible to say which performance characteristics are caused by the operating system and which are caused by the hardware. You would need to undertake a detailed analysis of the OS and the hardware, which is far more difficult.

Another valid way to think of a benchmark test is as the creation of a deliberate bottleneck at the subject of the test. When the subject is definitely the weakest link in the chain, then the throughput and latency of the whole system will reflect those of the subject. The hard part is assuring that the subject is actually the weakest link, because subtle changes in the test can shift the bottleneck from one part of the system to another, as we saw earlier with the FTP test of network capacity. If you're testing server hardware throughput, for example, you want to have far more network throughput than the server could possibly need, otherwise you may get identical results for all hardware (namely, the bandwidth of the network).

One downside of benchmark tests, which measure the maximum throughput of particular components, is it is easy to extrapolate incorrectly—that is, to assume that the performance of a configuration is linear over a wider range of load than it really is. A good example, as mentioned previously, is the server on a very high speed connection. It happens that high speed servers need less RAM for a given rate of HTTP connections, because memory usage for connections and CGI processes is far less likely to be an issue when connections are short-lived. To get, say, one-tenth the server performance over a network that runs at one-tenth of the benchmark speed, you will need more than one-tenth of the RAM in the benchmark server to be assured of sufficient storage for the overhead of concurrent connections and the simultaneously running CGI processes, while still meeting the overhead of the operating system itself.

Your network will make some benchmarks not exactly repeatable, because the number of collisions on an Ethernet network depend on very small differences in time. You may get the same statistical results over several runs of a trial, but you will not get exactly the same results twice.

The moral is that you should find a benchmark that reflects, as much as possible, what you will really be doing. If you will be serving 56 kbps modem users, find a benchmark that calculates the maximum number of 56 kbps users that the server can handle rather than a benchmark that tests the server's ability to fill a T3 line. You should look carefully at the wording of the test before assuming that it has meaning for you. For instance, I regularly benchmark my server hardware for physical speed. It hasn't moved an inch in months, so the speed is zero. Nonetheless, it's pretty good as a web server. Since I don't care whether my server can move, I'm using the wrong benchmark.

How do you determine what your server does in the real world so that you can find a good benchmark test? A good place to start is your log files. They reflect exactly what your server has been up to, at least in terms of HTTP operations and bytes transferred. You could replace your software, OS, or hardware with a trial version of something else, let it run for a while, and then compare the log files. But that may not be accurate, because loads vary over time, and you may be running well under peak capacity in both cases. Log files won't tell you your server's peak capacity; they show only what the server has attained so far. If, however, the log shows that the server was suddenly able to handle a much larger or smaller load when you changed some component, that is probably significant.

Be careful of the fine print in benchmark tests. Consider benchmarks in light of information theory: if you know exactly what's coming, then it isn't information. The point of a computer benchmark is to see how quickly you process information; that is, how quickly you can deal with the real-life uncertainty of what the user wants. If you tune the entire system specifically for the benchmark so there is very little uncertainty left, you've effectively defeated the purpose of the test, and the results have no relevance to real system users. One of the benchmark programs used by the makers of the Zeus web server is rather like that. The test repeatedly requests the same file, so the file is cached in memory after the first request. The benchmark consequently tells you only the rate at which the server can accept connections and dump from a buffer to the connection, not the rate at which it locates the correct file.

This reminds me of a story a friend in a programming class once told me. He had to write a calculator program to work with Roman numerals. He was told exactly which calculations would be asked of the program as a test of its correctness, so rather than writing a useful Roman numeral calculator, which would take a lot of work, he just wrote a hash table that looked up the question and spit out the right answer. You can imagine a naïve web benchmark in which a tester, not realizing there is a file cached in the browser, repeatedly requests it and assumes that the server it originally came from is providing it at an incredible speed.

Similar to hypertuning for the details of a particular test is finding or creating a test that makes you look good, which is like shooting an arrow and then painting the bull's-eye around it. This is known as "benchmarketing," and is the rule rather than the exception for tests from vendors, who count on the fact that most buyers just don't have the time to verify the assumptions and methodology of a test. If you compare the contradictory claims of victory in advertisements from web hardware and software vendors, you'll start to see that exactly what is being measured varies quite a bit or is just so ill-defined that you're not sure what it means. Following are brief reviews of the some standard benchmarks for web performance.

WebStone

The first widely used benchmark of web servers was the WebStone benchmark created by Silicon Graphics. WebStone simulates the activity of many clients making requests of a web server via many client machines each requesting a standard set of files. Each client machine can run multiple instances of a test client. The latest version of WebStone can test CGI and server API performance as well as the serving of plain HTML.

There are some problems with WebStone. The run rules of the test leave many decisions up to the tester, so there is a large opening for benchmarketing, as described previously. The client machines are usually connected to the web server over a 100 Mbps network, but the network speed is not specified by the benchmark. The file set is also small enough that it can be cached, meaning that the test does not necessarily measure disk performance.

Also, WebStone tests only HTTP GETs, not HTTP POSTs. POST is used for sending form information to CGIs.

The WebStone specification is free to the public. A good overview of WebStone is available at *http://www.mindcraft.com/webstone/*. Mindcraft, which acquired WebStone from Silicon Graphics, runs WebStone benchmarks on popular hardware and software web server configurations and publishes the results on the Web.

SPECweb99

A more rigorous test of web server performance is available from the Standard Performance Evaluation Corporation (SPEC). The test specification is not free, but it has significant advantages over other web server benchmarks: there are more detailed run rules, including a required mix of HTTP GET content transfer sizes. The load is modeled on what a typical Internet service provider would experience. More significantly, it is the only web performance benchmark that did not originate with a vendor of web server hardware or software, so it is presumably free of deliberate bias toward one vendor.

See *http://www.specbench.org/osg/web99/*. Also see *http://open.specbench.org/osg/web/results/* for some benchmark results. Spec also publishes a benchmark for Java; see *http://www.spec.org/*.

TPC-C and TPC-D

The same Internet infrastructure that lets a user request a particular HTML document can also be used to let the user request that the server perform transaction processing tasks, such as transferring money from one account to another. Transaction processing has stricter requirements than ordinary web services, such as insuring that a transaction either completes correctly or is rolled back, meaning that it is invalidated and discarded. There can be no ambiguity about whether you paid a bill or not, for example.

Transaction processing is fundamentally different from serving HTML in both protocols and complexity. There are benchmarks specifically for transaction processing that existed long before the Web. The standard transaction processing benchmarks are currently TPC-C and TPC-D, created by the Transaction Processing Council. The earliest widespread transaction processing benchmark was known as debit-credit, and simulated withdrawals and deposits into a bank account. However, it was found to be fundamentally flawed because it was poorly specified, allowing a number of ways to get whatever results were desired—for example, by caching the entire data set in memory. Debit-credit was replaced by the well-specified benchmarks TPC-A and TPC-B, but these are now obsolete. TPC-C and TPC-D results are audited, and include not only raw performance, but also scalability and the total cost of ownership.

For a more detailed description of transaction benchmarking, see Jim Gray's *The Benchmark Handbook for Database and Transaction Processing Systems* (Morgan Kaufmann), or the TPC web site at *http://www.tpc.org/*.

Proxy Benchmarks

Wisconsin Proxy Benchmark uses only HTTP/1.0 and no persistent connections; see *http://www.cs.wisc.edu/~cao/wpb1.0.html*.

The Squid people developed their own proxy benchmarking suite; see *http://www.ircache.net/Polygraph/*.

Vendor-Standard Benchmarks

For widespread but proprietary applications, such as SAP and Oracle Financials, you may find that the only option is to use benchmark tests and results from the product vendors themselves.

CaffeineMark

The CaffeineMark benchmark for Java is identical to the testing tool: the score is simply how well it runs the tool. It has been called unreliable because it does not test method calls, allocation, synchronization, or runtime facilities. It is possible to customize Java applications to get arbitrary results on the CaffeineMark test. The CaffeineMark was created by Pendragon.

Other Resources

A few more benchmarking resources on the Web are the Linpack site (which compares Java to Fortran) at *http://www.netlib.org/benchmark/linpackjava/*, and a Java benchmark page at *http://www.cs.cmu.edu/~jch/java/benchmarks.html*.

Some kinds of attacks you might want to look up for load testing purposes are Syn attacks, Ping of Death attacks, Land Attacks, and Smurf attacks. There is much free hacking software that can generate enormous loads of various kinds, most of which is designed to confuse and overwhelm web servers.

Key Recommendations

- Don't put too much stock in benchmarks unless they're very closely related to what you actually intend to do.
- Remember to increase the `ulimit` on the load generation client.

## CHAPTER 6

Performance Analysis

The most important thing to know about your system is if you can't understand it easily, you can't fix it easily. Complex systems are dependent on the few people who do understand it. If they leave, you have a big problem. A similar issue is that the number of problems rises much faster than the number of interdependent "features." More features equal many more problems. Fortunately, all web sites have to obey standards to some degree or they would not be usable with a wide variety of browsers. Because of this standardization, there are a number of standard steps you can take to pin down your problem.

Using analysis.cgi to Find a Bottleneck

A simple first step in diagnosing a performance problem is to break down performance into five categories: DNS lookup time, connection setup time, server silence, transmission time, and connection close time. These steps always happen in this order. I've written a tool to automatically time each of these five steps and to generate a graph of the results and some advice. I call it *analysis.cgi* and it can be run from my home page, *http://patrick.net/*. Simply enter a URL and it will try to graph the breakdown of these components for that URL. Figure 6-1 shows an example output graph for my own home page. Here is the advice:

```
advice for http://patrick.net/

DNS

I spent a cumulative 0.4052 seconds resolving hostnames. No problem with DNS.
network

It took a cumulative total of 0.0650 seconds to set up the connections to download
your content. The average time to connect was 0.0325 seconds. The latency to make a
connection to your site was OK. I spent 0.0012 seconds closing the socket.
server
```

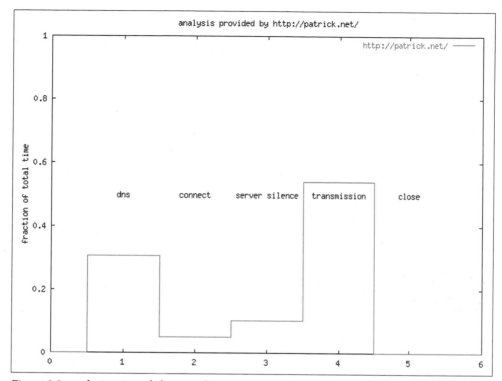

Figure 6-1. analysis.cgi graph for patrick.net

There was a cumulative 0.1334 seconds of server silence. The average period of server silence was 0.0667 seconds. Your server is using HTTP 1.1, which has better performance than HTTP 1.0. Good.

content

Your content was a total of 4984 bytes, including headers. It would take at least 0. 7120 seconds to download the content over a 56 Kbps modem. It would take at least 0. 0791 seconds to download the content over a 500 Kbps DSL line. Your content size is well suited for surfing with a 56K modem: less than 3 seconds. Here are URLs of the 2 elements on the page, with server response headers:

```
http://patrick.net:80/webpt_sm.gif

HTTP/1.1 200 OK
Date: Mon, 23 Apr 2001 19:14:29 GMT
Server: Apache/1.3.9 (Unix)
Last-Modified: Tue, 07 Nov 2000 05:56:29 GMT
ETag: "11aaa93-865-3a07998d"
Accept-Ranges: bytes
Content-Length: 2149
Connection: close
Content-Type: image/gif
http://patrick.net/
```

```
HTTP/1.1 200 OK
Date: Mon, 23 Apr 2001 19:14:29 GMT
Server: Apache/1.3.9 (Unix)
Last-Modified: Sat, 03 Mar 2001 22:56:46 GMT
ETag: "11aaa81-929-3aa176ae"
Accept-Ranges: bytes
Content-Length: 2345
Connection: close
Content-Type: text/html
```

Multiple copies of the same element are counted only once, on the assumption that the
browser is smart enough to reuse them.
summary

The total is 1.3168 seconds.
The bottleneck was transmission.

From this we can see that the bottleneck was transmission time. The best way to make this page faster is to get it from a faster connection. A total content size of 4,984 bytes is already small, so there's not much room for improvement. There is little point in making the servers faster in this case because the potential gain from increased server speed is so small.

Here are some general guidelines for the five possible bottlenecks:

- If DNS is the bottleneck, then either my *analysis.cgi* client needs to point to a faster DNS server, or your web site's name needs to be more aggressively propagated to DNS servers around the Internet, where it will be cached. It's ironic, but a more popular site will be a bit faster because the DNS to IP mapping will already be cached in so many DNS servers.

- If connection time is the bottleneck, then there is certainly a network problem. Perhaps a packet was lost during connection set up because of an overloaded hub. Routers, interfaces, and cable should be examined for errors.

- If server silence is the bottleneck, then the server is overloaded in some way and could probably benefit from better hardware or a more highly optimized server application or database.

- If transmission time is the bottleneck, then client connection speed is too small or the content you are trying to push down it is too large.

- If connection close is the bottleneck, we again have a network problem.

Snooping HTTP with Sprocket

It is often instructive to watch HTTP traffic while getting a web page, so you can correlate network activity with what you see in the browser. One way to do this is with a web proxy configured to print out HTTP requests and responses as it sees them. I have such a proxy at *http://patrick.net/software/sprocket/sprocket* that you can download for free. You need only start it up with the *-d* option (for "dump") to see everything going on at the HTTP level.

Of course this does not work with SSL connections, because snooping SSL content would be a proof that SSL does not work. You might be able to get some idea of the request an SSL browser is making by using a system call tracer like *truss* on Solaris or *strace* on Linux, or by running a browser under a debugger, if you have the source code. You can get the source code for the Mozilla browser from *http://www.mozilla.org/*.

Here is an example of snooping HTTP traffic with *sprocket*. Start up *sprocket* in the following manner:

```
% sprocket -d
```

It will give you a message like this:

```
set your proxy to <URL:http://localhost:8008/>
```

Use that information to set your proxy. Then get a web page, and observe output like this:

```
GET http://vahe/ HTTP/1.0
Accept: image/gif, image/x-xbitmap, image/jpeg, image/pjpeg, image/png, */*
Accept-Charset: iso-8859-1,*,utf-8
Accept-Encoding: gzip
Accept-Language: en
Host: vahe
User-Agent: sprocket/0.10
Proxy-Connection: Keep-Alive

HTTP/1.1 200 OK
Connection: close
Date: Mon, 23 Apr 2001 21:07:13 GMT
Accept-Ranges: bytes
Server: Apache/1.3.9 (Unix)  (Red Hat/Linux)
Content-Length: 2345
Content-Type: text/html
Content-Type: text/html; charset=iso-8859-1
ETag: "54802-929-3a967bd6"
Last-Modified: Fri, 23 Feb 2001 15:03:50 GMT
Client-Date: Mon, 23 Apr 2001 21:07:13 GMT
Client-Peer: 127.0.0.1:80
Title: welcome to patrick.net
X-Meta-DESCRIPTION: advice on increasing the performance of your web site
X-Meta-KEYWORDS: web, performance, tuning, book

<!DOCTYPE HTML PUBLIC "-//W3C//DTD HTML 3.2//EN">
<HTML>
<HEAD>
<TITLE>welcome to patrick.net</TITLE>
...
```

And so on. In general you can get enough information like this to have a good idea of what is going over the wire. From this information, you may be able to figure out ways to reduce your content size.

Look at Connections

Another good way to understand what is happening in your site is to look at connections as they are created and dropped. One good way to do this is to run *netstat* in a loop on your web server or middleware or database. On NT, just run *netstat* with some number of seconds to delay between loops. On Linux, run *netstat -c* to see connections once per second.

Databases often have hundreds of open connections. A good way to see just the new connections is to turn on the Oracle listener log and run *tail -f <logfile>*. Only new connections will appear in the log.

Log File Analysis

In a sense, all web servers come with a performance monitoring tool, the logging facility of the server. This leaves the webmaster the problem of interpreting the logged data. The one-line-per-transfer format is difficult to analyze by directly reading it.

The need to extract as much useful information as possible from log files has given rise to a small industry of log parsing and graphing packages like Interse, the freeware analog tool net.Analysis (*http://www.netgen.com/*), and the Netscape servers' built-in *analyze* command. These tools are useful, but you can also simply import log files into a spreadsheet program and use the spreadsheet to plot the results in various ways. A good spreadsheet program will have graphing ability similar to dedicated log graphing packages, and the added advantage is that you may already own one.

To provide additional information, some web servers use extended log formats, including details such as how long the transfer actually took to complete. Your log file can also tell you where your users are by logging IP addresses or machine names. Are they across the whole Internet? In a 50-location extranet? All in one building? If you can figure this out from the IP addresses, you might be able to improve performance by locating your servers close to the largest concentrations of users.

How can you know the number and distribution of connections to expect over each day? If your web server is already live, then you have an excellent source of information about the sort of load you should tune for, because your web server logs can tell you how much bandwidth you are currently using, whether it's increasing or decreasing, and how quickly. Of course, the log may merely reflect a bottleneck in your system and not the system's potential capacity or the potential demand from users. Web server log files are almost always in Common Log Format (CLF), as one line per HTTP operation, giving the following information in this order:

1. The domain name or IP address of the requesting machine
2. Username

3. Password if supplied for access-controlled files, dashes otherwise

4. Parsed date

5. Request issued by client

6. The HTTP response code

7. Number of bytes transferred

See *mod_log_config.html* in the Apache distribution for more information on the format and on custom modifications you can make.

Apache will let you record the duration of a connection, but Netscape Enterprise will not. If you use any of Netscape's custom log options, it will not use its cache of static files, which will hurt performance. Neither Netscape nor Apache include the HTTP headers in the count of bytes transferred, so your throughput calculation result will be slightly low if you just use the log file to calculate total bytes transferred.

For example, here is a log file line from the NCSA server:

```
client8.isp.com - - [21/Aug/1997:16:56:57 -0500] "GET /recipe.html HTTP/1.0" 200 217
```

You can calculate the number of completed HTTP operations per second by looking at the number of lines in any time interval and dividing by that interval. Similarly, you can figure out your throughput in bytes per second by adding up the bytes transferred over some interval and dividing it by that interval. Again, most servers do not include the header data in the recorded number of bytes transferred. In the example log file line above, *recipe.html* is exactly 217 bytes long, yet the server also transmitted HTTP headers back to the client but didn't record them in the log file. Those headers look like this:

```
HTTP/1.0 200 Document follows
Date: Sat, 30 Aug 1997 04:31:18 GMT
Server: NCSA/1.4.2
Content-type: text/html
Last-modified: Mon, 16 Dec 1996 04:51:12 GMT
Content-length: 217
```

This header itself is 174 bytes, which is 45 percent of your server's output in this case. Header size has been creeping up as more capabilities are added to web servers, and can be a significant burden if many long cookies are added for surfing a particular site.

Your log file can give you a feel for how hard your server is being hit right now via the Unix *tail -f* command. Find your server access log file (e.g., *access_log*) and try this:

```
% tail -f access_log
```

The *tail* command shows the last few lines of a file, while the *-f* option tells the *tail* command that the file isn't yet complete and that it should continue to print new lines as they are added to the file. You'll see new lines in the log file as they are added when users hit the site, or perhaps after a short delay if log file buffering is turned on to increase performance.

While useful for giving you a picture of the current state of affairs, log files are limited as a performance diagnosis tool. For example, your log file will not tell you if the user tried to contact your server but was unable to, although errors are logged for connections that get through. A lightly loaded server could be an indication of performance problems rather than an indication of unused capacity; maybe your site is unpopular because the performance is poor.

Average Transfer Size

The typical size for an HTTP transfer is about 10K. Text tends to be smaller, at around 5K per page. Images tend to be larger, say 15K. If you have a document tree of static HTML text and GIF images, it's quite simple to calculate the average size of a file. Here's a little script I wrote that will do it for you (you may need to change the path to perl and make sure the *find* command is in your PATH environment variable):

```
#!/usr/local/bin/perl

# Finds the average size in bytes of all .html and .gif files below
# the given directory, or the current directory if none given.

$ARGV[0] = "." unless $ARGV[0];

@files = `find $ARGV[0]`;
chop @files;

foreach (@files) {
    if (/\.html$/ || /\.gif$/) {
        $count++;
        $sum += -s;
        # print -s, "\n"; # Uncomment to see all file sizes.
    }
}

$avg = int($sum/$count);

print "Average size is $avg bytes.\n";
```

Run this script by giving it the name of your *public_html* directory:

```
% avgsize.pl /home/patrick/public_html
Average size is 12038 bytes.
```

Although this script is an easy way to get an idea of the average size of your static content, it is just a starting point because it tells you only the size of the average file available to the user, not the average size of files actually sent, which is the total bytes transferred during some time interval divided by the number of files. Your log file will give you a better picture of your true average transfer size because it will have a record of the actual content transfer sizes, including CGI-generated content. Here's a modified version of the previous script that looks at the transfer size, which is the last number of each line in a common log format log file, and prints the average size transferred, excluding headers. Lines ending in a dash (-) indicate something other than a successful transfer and will be added in as a 0-byte transfer by this script:

```perl
#!/usr/local/bin/perl

# Finds the average size in bytes of all file transfers recorded by a CLF
# log file.

while (<>) {
    / (\d*)$/;
    $count++;
    $sum += $1;
}

$avg = int($sum/$count);

print "Average size is $avg bytes.\n";
```

Run this script by giving it the name of your log file:

```
% avgsize.pl /opt/apache_1.2.4/logs/access_log
Average size is 5515 bytes.
```

The average size actually transferred in a web transaction was less than half the average size of my content, because most transfers were my home page, which is very small and mostly text.

Log files themselves are not completely accurate because, as we've seen, they do not include the size of header information and have no mechanism for recording the load created by other non-HTTP activity, such as socket connections created by Java applets or nonparsed-header files.

The distribution of transfer sizes can be more important than the average size. Implicit in most discussions of web planning is the assumption that the distribution of transfer sizes falls into a classic bell curve. It may not be that way. You may find that 95 percent of your transfers are around 10K, but that your average is skewed upwards to 50K because 5 percent of your transfers are downloads of large files like executable software, high-resolution images, music files, or video. This is more a bi-modal distribution than a bell curve and is quite common. A more useful script than the one already shown would give you the distribution of file sizes. Such a script is given next.

The distribution in time of these large transfers can also be irregular. For example, if you happen to be distributing software from your site, you can expect a surge in downloads of large software files when you post new versions. If your web site supports operators in a call center by providing them applets for database access, you can expect many large transfers when work starts in the morning and users need to load the applets. A good architecture for these kinds of problems is to have two web servers: one for the average of many small transfers and one that serves the few large files. HTTP is perfectly suited for transparently distributing hits among servers. There is no requirement that a JPEG embedded in a page must be served from the same server that provides the surrounding HTML. There may be a slight penalty to this in the form of an additional DNS lookup for the JPEG—or not, if you use an IP address in the embedded JPEG link rather than a machine name.

Response Size Distribution

It is important to have some idea of the distribution of your servers' response sizes. With this information, you can decide whether it makes sense for you to have multiple servers, each targeted at a different response size. Fortunately, most web server access log files have the same format, the Common Log Format (CLF). Many middleware servers, such as BEA's Weblogic, also use this format. The last item on each line of a CLF file is the number of bytes served, excluding HTTP headers. This makes it trivial to write a Perl script to extract the size distribution and to write a *gnuplot* configuration file to plot it. Here is a Perl script that will generate the distribution data. You can download it from *http://patrick.net/software/rsd.pl*.

```perl
#!/usr/local/bin/perl

$\ = "\n";

while(<>) {
    if (/\s(\d+)\s*$/) {
        $bucket{$1}++;
    }
}

foreach $key (sort keys %bucket) {
    print $key, " ", $bucket{$key};
}
```

And here is a *gnuplot* configuration file to plot the resulting output. You can download it from *http://patrick.net/software/rsd.gp*.

```
set term png color
set output "distribution.gif"

set logscale x
set logscale y
set xlabel "size of response"
set ylabel "number of responses"

plot "out" title "response size distribution"
```

Figure 6-2 shows an example bimodal distribution graph from a web site that serves lots of dynamically generated graphs. You can see a clear break between the sizes of the HTML (1,000 to 10,000 bytes) and the images (10,000 to 100,000 bytes). Note that it's rare for this site to generate many responses that are exactly the same size.

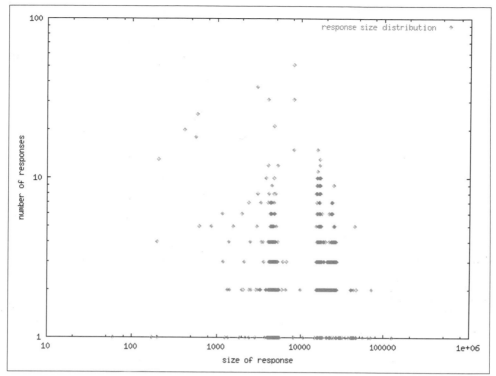

Figure 6-2. Bimodal distribution graph

Hits per Second

Here is a little Perl script you can run against your log file to generate a hits per second distribution over the day. You can download it from *http://patrick.net/software/ hps.pl*. Be aware that response times get recorded when the response finishes, not when it starts, so the hits per second you see are responses completed in that second, not how many simultaneous requests you received.

```
#!/usr/local/bin/perl

$\ = "\n";

while(<>) {
    /(:\d\d:\d\d:\d\d)/;  # hour min second
    #/(:\d\d:\d\d):\d\d/; # or use this match for hits per minute

    $key = $1;

    $key =~ s/:/ /g;       # remove ":" so gnuplot can digest output

    $bucket{$key}++;       # add a hit to the bucket for that second
}
```

```
foreach $key (sort keys %bucket) {
    print $key, " ", $bucket{$key};
}
```

Once you have the output from that, say in a file called *out*, you can plot it with the following *gnuplot* configuration file. You can download it from *http://patrick.net/software/hps.gp*.

```
set term png color
set output "hps.gif"
set xdata time
set timefmt "%H %M %S"
set xrange ["00:00":"23:59"]
set ylabel "hits per second"
plot "out" using 1:4 notitle with lines
```

Figure 6-3 contains some example output.

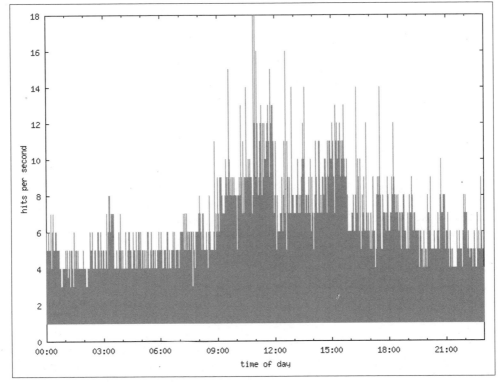

Figure 6-3. Hits per second throughout the day

Variable Load and Queue Length

A sudden burst of activity can cause a large backup in your processing. To see why, consider a system that is receiving one request per second and takes one second to handle each. There is no backup. But what if we suddenly receive no request in one second, and two requests in the next? We now have a queue of one, and if requests continue to arrive at one per second after that, we will forever have an extra second to wait to get to the front of the queue.

Let's take a more realistic example. What if each request takes only a tenth of a second, and we have an average arrival rate of four per second? We're doing fine, because we take only four tenths of each second. There is no queue. Suddenly we get a burst of 25 hits per second for three seconds, then it drops back down to four. During each of those three seconds, the backlog grows at a rate of 25 − 10 = 15 per second, so we come out of it with 45 hits to work off. How long will it take? We have a net rate of 10 − 4 = 6 per second decrease in the queue. So the queue will take 45 / 6 = 7.5 seconds to work off, during which response time will be much worse than the usual tenth of a second. Figure 6-4 contains a graph to make it clearer.

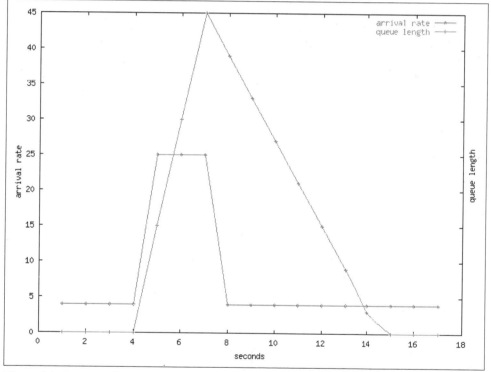

Figure 6-4. Queue peak

The poor guy who arrives at the peak queue length of 45 is going to have to wait 4.5 seconds for his response. The guy who arrives when the queue is 39 is going to wait 3.9 seconds, and so on. The 4.5 seconds is 45 times worse than the usual tenth of a second. Large transient loads cause response time to get bad very quickly, and they take a long time to work off.

It may seem that a tenth of a second is fast enough for most sites, but this is actually not true for a site with even moderate spikes in activity. The latency of an unloaded system is important and should be as low as possible, or parallel processing should be used to spread the load over many CPUs or many servers.

When Exactly Are Hits Logged?

Unfortunately, almost all web servers and application servers log only in integral seconds, not milliseconds, and do not tell you whether the time recorded is the beginning of the request, middle of processing, or end of the response. If you think about it, you'll realize that the logging must be at the end of the response, because the success of the response and response size is recorded.

I set up a test in which 94 users hit the same dynamic page within the same second, and recorded both the beginning of each request and the end of the corresponding response, down to the millisecond, for each of the 94 users. Then I compared that to what was recorded in the log file. The results are in Figure 6-5. The lefthand vertical axis shows the number of hits in the log file each second. The righthand vertical axis is just an arbitrary "user number" to help keep track of the start and stop times of the 94 users.

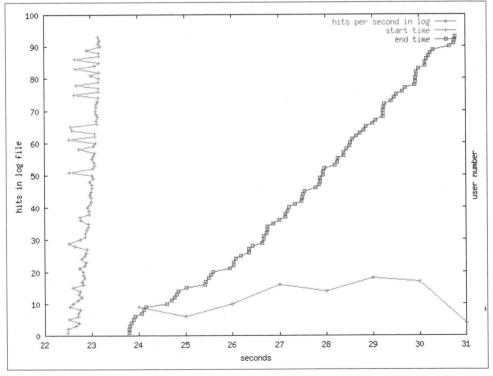

Figure 6-5. Log timestamps lagging

You can see that 94 incoming requests per second, all arriving between second 22 and second 23, do not get recorded as 94 hits per second in the log. Rather they are logged after they finish as having happened in the preceding second. So the first 9 responses are recorded at second 24. A few of them seem to have ended just after second 24, but I attribute that to the delay inherent in my Perl script printing the result. The thing to note is that 94 requests per second ended up recorded in the log files as hit rates below 20 per second for several seconds. So you don't actually know your incoming request rate from your logs.

Another point to keep in mind is even though the logging is delayed, the response is not. So your client machine may see responses far in advance of when the response is logged on the server side. This is especially true if your log file process is slow because of reverse DNS lookups, for example.

Finally, also note that every web server and middleware server log I have seen writes results only in whole second increments, and only when the response is complete. It would be valuable to log both the start of the request and the end of the response down to millisecond resolution.

Who Is the Most Common User?

It is trivial under Unix to look at your *access.log* files and figure out the most common user IP. For example, to get a listing of hit count per IP address, try this:

```
% sort log* | awk '{print $1}' | uniq -c | sort -n
```

The result will look something like the following, with hits in the first column, and IP address in the second column:

```
12 39.203.39.11
13 2.39 48.111
13 39.34.10.22
...
```

Which Process Is Mine?

If you are going to monitor the resource usage of a particular process, you have to know its process ID, or *pid* for short. This is harder than it sounds. Big Unix servers often run hundreds of processes, and may need to be rebooted occasionally. When they get rebooted, all the pids change.

One straightforward way to identify processes is to create a user ID for each process you intend to run. Then you can find your target pid simply by doing a *ps -u <username>*. The downside to this is that you have to create a new user each time you want to install another program. Another issue is that some programs like webservers automatically spawn multiple copies of themselves, so you still would not be able to uniquely identify any one process.

You can *grep* your *ps* output for the name of your program, but you'd be surprised how frequently they change. In fact, most programs can themselves change what *ps* writes by overwriting argv[0], for the C programmers out there. You can add an identifying but unused command-line option like *-MYPROC* when the process gets started and restarted, but those strings often get truncated by the limited length of ps output lines.

It can be easier to identify your process by the port it is using than to identify it by *ps* output. If you know what port your process is listening on, you can identify it on Solaris by using *lsof -i:<port>*. For example, to find the process id of the web server listening on port 80, you can use *lsof -i:80*. See *http://patrick.net/software/* for a downloadable copy of *lsof* for Solaris.

identd is another tool that provides similar ability to look up the process that owns a particular TCP/IP connection and runs on many varieties of Unix.

A third very useful tool is *fuser*. On Linux, *fuser 80/tcp* tells what process ID's are using port 80. You may instead need to say *fuser -n tcp 80* depending on your kernel and version of *fuser*. Finally, note that *netstat -p* will tell which process ID is using a certain port on Linux.

Who Is Using That File?

fuser is also useful for figuring out who is using a particular file on Linux and Solaris. If you give *fuser* a filename, it can report the PID of all processes using that file. On Linux, *fuser* can also report the process ID for TCP and UDP ports. Use *man fuser* for more information.

What Files Are My Process Using?

If you are using an operating system call tracer, such as *strace* on Linux or *truss* on Solaris, you may see thousands of writes to a particular file descriptor, yet not know which file that refers to. Since writing to files is a potential bottleneck, it is important to know which files these are. Fortunately, it is easy to find out. Simply find the process ID of your process, then look under */proc* for that number. Under there, you will find a directory named *fd*, and in that, each file descriptor will be a symbolic link to the actual file. For example, if your web server PID is 480:

```
# ls -l /proc/480/fd
total 0
lr-x------  1 root     root           64 Mar 29 09:30 0 -> /dev/null
l-wx------  1 root     root           64 Mar 29 09:30 1 -> /dev/null
l-wx------  1 root     root           64 Mar 29 09:30 15 -> /var/log/httpd/error_log
lrwx------  1 root     root           64 Mar 29 09:30 16 -> socket:[475]
l-wx------  1 root     root           64 Mar 29 09:30 17 -> /var/log/httpd/access_
log
l-wx------  1 root     root           64 Mar 29 09:30 18 -> /var/run/httpd.lock.473
(deleted)
l-wx------  1 root     root           64 Mar 29 09:30 2 -> /var/log/httpd/error_log
```

```
l-wx------    1 root     root        64 Mar 29 09:30 21 -> pipe:[466]
lr-x------    1 root     root        64 Mar 29 09:30 3 -> /etc/initlog.conf
lr-x------    1 root     root        64 Mar 29 09:30 8 -> pipe:[466]
```

What Happens if the Database Is Hung?

It is instructive to simply lock a critical table in your database and see what happens to your web site. For example, you can lock a table in Oracle and unlock it with a rollback like this:

```
lock table user_data in exclusive mode;
rollback;
```

One reason you might do this is to see how many user requests get queued up at the database for a given number of user clicks on the web site. Or you might want to use this to simulate a too-busy database and see what breaks. Or you can find out if any particular page has database dependencies. Here is a PL/SQL script from database guru Bosco Albuquerque that lists how many SQL requests were pending. Put this in a file called *waiting*, and run it from the > sqlplus prompt with an @ sign like this:

```
> @waiting;
```

Here is the script:

```
col sid      format       9999    heading "Sess|ID"
col event    format        a30    heading "Wait Event" wrap
col state    format        a10    heading "Wait State" trunc
col siw      format 999999999     heading "Waited So|Far (cs) "
col wt       format 999999999     heading "Time|Waited (cs)"
col p1       format 999999999     heading "p1"
col p2       format 999999999     heading "p2"
col p3       format 999999999     heading "p3"

set lines 132 pages 100
select sid , event , state, seconds_in_wait siw,
  wait_time wt, p1, p2, p3
  from v$session_wait
  where event NOT IN ('SQL*Net message from client',
                      'Null event',
                      'rdbms ipc message',
                      'rdbms ipc reply',
                      'pmon timer')
  order by sid
  ;
```

A Few More Tips

- Get a good topology diagram with all servers and connections clearly marked.
- Consider changing the highest levels first (that is, the architecture) and identify steps or machines that could possibly be eliminated. Low-level tuning should be saved for much later, because the gains are smaller, and any work you put into low-level tuning may be wiped out by architecture changes.

- The most likely suspects for performance problems are home-grown applications, high-level architecture, databases, the Internet, and hard disks.
- Try running a load test when no other users or processes are on the system, perhaps late at night, to find out what the best possible performance of the current configuration is. This helps clarify the difference between bad applications and excessive load on the system. If performance is bad for a single user with no network load, then the problem probably lies in the application. If performance is only intermittently bad, look for low-efficiency error handling by the application.
- Look for memory leaks by monitoring process size.
- Look at the server log files for errors.
- Check physical cable connections and look for kinks or sources of interference such as proximity to fluorescent lights or radio transmitters.

Remember that performance problems always come down to unhappy people somewhere, and that success means making them happy rather than resolving all technical issues.

Key Recommendations

- Learn what tools are available for mapping activity to PIDs.
- Don't assume logs files are more accurate than they really are.
- Remember that log file times are when the response finished, not when it started.

## CHAPTER 7

Reliability

It seems there are an infinite number of ways for a web site to break, making it difficult to systematically check all of them. The longer I work on web sites, the more surprised I am at the creativity of complex systems in finding ways to fail.

Typical Failures

I cannot make an exhaustive list here, so I'll concentrate on the most common problems capable of crashing a web site. If you guard against these routine problems, the problems that eventually get you will be worthy opponents. If you find patterns of failure not mentioned here, please write *p@patrick.net*. I would be interested to hear about them.

Disk Full

The most likely cause of a system failure is a full disk. A good system administrator will watch disk usage closely and offload to backup storage, such as tape, at regular intervals.

Log files use up disk space quickly. Web server log files, SQL*Net log files, JDBC log files, and application server log files are all the disk equivalents of memory leaks. One good preventative measure is to keep log files on a different filesystem from the operating system. The web server may still hang when the log filesystem is full, but the machine itself is less likely to hang.

Process Out of File Descriptors

If a web server or other critical process needs more file descriptors than are allotted to it, it will hang or give an error until it gets what it needs. File descriptors are used to keep track of open files and open sockets, both of which are critical for web servers, whose job is to copy files to network connections. The default for most shells is

64 file descriptors, meaning every process started from that shell will be able to open only 64 simultaneous files and network connections. Most shells have a built-in *ulimit* command to increase this. For example, *ulimit -n 1024* will cause all processes started from the shell to be allocated 1,024 file descriptors.

If you want to see how many descriptors are in use and the contents of the files they point to, you can look in */proc/<pid>/fd/* and see them directly on Solaris and Linux.

C Pointer Error

Programs written in C or C++, such as web server API modules, are susceptible to crashing because a single error in de-referencing a pointer (i.e., accessing the memory pointed to) causes the operating system to kill them. Experienced C programmers know this and are careful in their use of pointers.

The Java analog of using a bad C pointer is accessing a null object reference. Null references in Java do not usually result in the immediate exit of the JVM, but give the programmer a chance to handle the mistake gracefully, with an exception handling method. Java does not require as much caution in this regard, but there is a performance penalty associated with using Java to gain this extra measure of reliability.

Memory Leaks

C/C++ programs are also prone to another pointer problem: losing references to allocated memory. This typically happens when memory is allocated in a subroutine and the program returns from the subroutine without freeing the memory. The reference to the allocated memory is then lost, yet the memory is in use by that process as far as the operating system is concerned. The result is a program that uses ever more memory, degrading performance until the machine finally halts, entirely out of RAM and swap space.

One solution is to carefully analyze your own code with code profiling tools, such as Purify, to find potential leaks. But this will not find leaks in libraries created by others, for which source code is not available. Another solution is simply to kill and restart processes at regular intervals. The Apache web server creates and kills child processes for this reason.

According to the `malloc` manpage on Linux, newer versions of `malloc` have some protections against poiner errors and memory leaks at the expense of performance:

> Recent versions of Linux *libc* (later than 5.4.23) and GNU *libc* (2.x) include a `malloc` implementation which is tunable via environment variables. When MALLOC_ CHECK_ is set, a special (less efficient) implementation is used which is designed to be tolerant against simple errors, such as double calls of free( ) with the same argument, or overruns of a single byte (off-by-one bugs). Not all such errors can be protected against, however, and memory leaks can result.

In spite of the fact that Java has no pointers per se, Java programs are generally worse than C programs in their use of memory. Objects are created very frequently in Java and the garbage collector will not free the memory unless all references to the object are gone. Even when the garbage collector runs, it only gives memory back to the VM, not the operating system. The result is Java programs tend to use all of the heap given to them, and never shrink. They can also grow to be several times the size of the maximum heap size because of stores of code created by "Just In Time" (JIT) compilers.

A similar problem is allocating a database connection from a pool and failing to return the connection to the pool in all circumstances. Some pools have activity timers that release database connections after a period of inactivity, but this may not be sufficient to save your site in the case of very poor code that leaks database connections quickly.

Thread Deadlock

The performance improvements afforded by multithreading all come at the expense of reliability, primarily because of potential thread deadlocks, in which one thread is waiting for a second to release a resource, but the second is waiting for the first to release it. Consider trying to pass someone on the sidewalk, and you both step the same way to avoid each other, then the other way, blocking each other at every step. Imagine that going on forever, and you understand thread deadlock.

There is no easy cure for deadlocks, especially since the cases that bring them about are subtle and often seen only at very high loads. Most software testing does not create enough load to fully shake out all threading bugs. Thread deadlock is a problem in every language with threads. Because thread programming in Java is much easier than in C, more programmers are using threads, and deadlocks are becoming more common. Deadlocks can be reduced by increasing the use of the synchronized keyword in Java code, but then you pay a performance penalty. Databases can also deadlock internally under heavy load.

Dead Process Holding Lock

If your program uses persistent locks, such as a lock file, and the program dies without cleaning up the lock, then it may not be possible for any other process using that kind of lock to run or to remove the lock. This causes further failures. In this case, the lock must be manually removed.

Server Overloaded

Netscape web servers use one thread per connection. When Netscape Enterprise web server runs out of threads, it hangs, not even servicing existing connections. If you have a load distribution mechanism that detects that the server is not responding, its load will be distributed to other web servers, perhaps causing them to run out of threads in turn. In this way, an entire server farm can be hung. New connections may still be accepted at the operating system level, but the application (the web server) never gets around to servicing them. The user sees "connected" in the browser status bar, but nothing happens after that.

One cure for this problem is to set the *obj.conf* parameter RqThrottle below the number of threads, so new connections beyond that RqThrottle number will not be accepted. The server will seem to be down to those who cannot connect, and response time may be poor for those who are connected, but at least the server will not hang. File descriptors should also be set at least to the number of threads, or file descriptors will be a bottleneck.

Say for example you decide on 4 *httpd* processes and a RqThrottle of 1,000. Then you may potentially have 4,000 concurrent threads on that machine. File descriptors should be set to at least 1,024 per process. Note that you may see many more than 4,000 open sockets with *netstat* or another OS-level tool because the connection is opened before the application accepts it.

If you set a per-*httpd*-process memory limit, say 32 MB, then you will get errors in the log file. such as "Fatal, cannot allocate memory," when you hit that limit. It will require some experimentation to see whether you hit that limit before hitting the RqThrottle limit.

Load Balancer Fails to Detect Dead Machine

Round robin DNS works as a simple kind of load balancing, but it cannot detect that a particular server is down or re-route traffic to a different server. The effect of a single server failure on a Round Robin pair of servers varies with client operating systems. Windows machines seem to cache one of the IP addresses and always use that. So the web site either seems entirely down, or entirely up, depending on which IP address was cached by the Windows client machine. Unix client machines perform the DNS name lookup every time you hit the site, so the site seems to alternate between down and up as the name server gives the different responses.

Resonate and other load balancers that work at the IP level do not have this problem because they do not depend on the client. They redirect traffic according to the health of the servers.

Subnet Flooded

For various reasons a specific network segment can become overloaded. Put redundant boxes on different subnets so that excessive traffic on one subnet will not affect the other.

Out of ptys

For applications like Telnet, which get a pseudo-terminal (pty) on the server, if sessions exceed the available terminals in *dev/pty**, additional sessions will not be accepted. The solution is to create more ptys. How you do this depends on your operating system.

Database Out of Cursors

Many databases run with a fixed number of cursors, which are memory areas holding the results of a query. They are released after all the data is read, but a large number of simultaneous queries may run up against this limit. At this point, further queries will be queued and not actually happen until a cursor is freed up for them.

This is another problem that is not apparent to developers but shows up under a load test. It may well be obvious to your database administrator (DBA) though.

Similar problems are insufficient tablespace settings and low sequence number constraints resulting in table overflow errors. Such problems illustrate the importance of getting a good DBA to review production database settings and performance periodically. Also, most database vendors have monitoring and modelling tools to help with such issues.

Bad Device Driver

While Unix is very reliable in handling user-level programs such as web servers, application servers, and databases, kernel-level code can easily crash the whole system because it has the power to do anything. The only time you normally add new kernel code is when a device driver is loaded—for example, to handle a particular brand of Ethernet card. Load such kernel modules with extreme caution in production environments. There is no cure except well-coded device drivers.

Hardware Failures

Disks, as the moving parts on servers, are the most likely part to fail, but memory chips and even CPU's can also fail, typically because of overheating. Extremely high-availability hardware is available, but for an extremely high price. The next best solution is redundancy of cheaper parts: mirrored disks, multiple CPU's, clusters, and load balancing across machines with tools such as Resonate.

Power Outage

Most business sites run on Uninterruptable Power Supplies (UPSs) but basic power problems still happen. Power cords should be out of the way, preferably under a raised floor. It is very easy to trip over them, pulling them out of the wall. Children should not be allowed in the same room with critical computers. Small children love big red switches and feel compelled to do the obvious thing with them.

Administrator on Wrong Server

An eternally recurring problem is rebooting or reconfiguring the wrong server. When you *telnet* from one machine to the next, it is hard to remember just what machine you're talking to at any given moment, especially when all you can see is the minimal *root* prompt (#). Some precautions you can take include requiring all *root* prompts to be prefixed by the machine name (machinename#), disallowing remote login as *root*, and mounting / and */usr* as read-only filesystems. No one but the true administrator should have *root* or *sudo* privileges on production servers.

Wildcards Including Wrong File

Another classic mistake is to include too many files in a wildcard expression. For example, *gnuplot *.gp* will cause all files ending in *.gp* to be used as input for plotting, but it's not obvious is that only one instance of *gnuplot* will run. This means configuration parameters set in one file will continue to be set for plotting all subsequent files. When you go back to the specific configuration file for a graph that has an unexpected appearance, you will not see anything wrong, because it was the configuration of a previous file that carried over and caused the problem.

A more subtle case of this is when the operating system itself uses wildcards. For example, if a boot-time Netscape server startup script called *S98.netscape* in */etc/rc.d/rc3.d* is backed up to *S98.netscape.original* and then left in that directory, it will be run immediately after *S98.netscape*! The operating system will run anything beginning with an "S" and two digits.

Permissions Problems

An experience all CGI programmers go through is to write a correct CGI script, only to see it fail the first time it is run from the production web server. The reason is most production web servers are configured to run as *nobody*, who is a user with very restricted permissions, but the developer probably tested with a web server running as himself. The CGI is often owned by the developer, and execute permission does not include the world. Once the CGI is given world execute permission, it often fails again because it needs to write to a file or directory that does not allow world write access.

Path Problems

Similar to permissions problems, path problems often result when a program is developed as one user and run as another, or under a different environment. For example, *cron* jobs run with a truly minimal PATH, and so they cannot access the same executable programs a developer usually can. The developer writes a *cron* job, thinks it fine, but when the time comes for the *cron* daemon to run it, it fails. A good precaution is to use absolute pathnames in all *cron* jobs.

Patch Problems

You can avoid many reliability problems by having the proper system patches on a system. The system administrator should periodically check and install the appropriate patches on running systems. On Solaris, *showrev -p* will show the installed patches. Which patches are appropriate depends on the applications you are running. Your operating system vendor should know which patches are critical for the reliability of your system.

Cascade of Overloads

When one component of a system depends on another, a chain reaction of bad effects can occur. If a middleware server needs information from a database, and the database slows down, then the middleware may end up with all its threads waiting for the database. When the middleware does not respond to a query from a monitoring system, it may be failed over to a backup, even though it is still functional.

Monitoring Causing Failures

Monitoring systems designed to watch for failures may cause failures themselves. Programs such as FirstWatch and Tivoli, which are given the power to restart servers, also have the power to bring down healthy systems. For example, a database reaches the maximum connections allowed, then FirstWatch thinks it's down because it cannot make a new connection and reboots it, killing all of the open connections even though they were all functioning correctly. Another example is the Keynote monitors scattered around the U.S., each hitting a compute-intensive web page, can be a much heavier load than expected from actual users. Resonate agents that check the health of a web site continuously are also a significant source of load. One solution is to have Resonate watch something like log file or *truss* output rather than hitting your web site over and over.

Retries Cause Further Failures

Badly coded error handling, which retries a connection or retries to start a process over and over without any delay between tries, can itself swamp a system. Worse, while the error-handling code is swamping the system, it may be nearly impossible to kill because it is so busy.

Critical Tables Locked by Accident

Don't let everyone have the ability to lock critical database tables or rows. They can stop the web site simply by forgetting to commit a change before they go to lunch. Tables or rows are locked when changes are made, and unlocked only when the changes are committed.

Using a Database Where Files Will Do

Databases are very valuable for certain kinds of problems, but using them to store small amounts of information that could just as easily be stored in files is begging for problems, just because databases are so much more complex than files.

Program Fails to Reconnect to Database After Failure

Make sure database connection pools can automatically recover after database failures. Actually test when the database suddenly reboots and check to see that your entire system recovers. In the past, Weblogic's database pools have had some trouble in this regard.

Program Fails to Restart After Reboot

Make sure all critical programs are in */etc/rc.d* startup scripts so that they will automatically be run upon reboot. Some Unix machines are up for months or even years without a failure. When they finally need to be rebooted, it may be only then that you realize that an application like the web server itself was manually started, but never added to the startup scripts. Short-running jobs can be run from *cron* and will gain a similar ability to survive reboots because the *cron* daemon, *crond*, is automatically restarted on reboot.

Split-Brain Syndrome

Redundant boxes can cause their own reliability problems in addition to solving reliability problems. Say you have a backup database, and the primary database slows down. Depending on timing issues, the primary may recover and think it is still the primary while the backup is activated and also thinks it is the primary. Careful configuration of failover schemes is required to avoid such "split-brain" scenarios.

Firewall "Cleanup" Blocks Essential Service

Firewalls are intended to prevent the functioning of bad programs, and only allow the good. They do this primarily by blocking all ports except those essential to running the web site. Unfortunately, it isn't always clear that a port is essential until it has been turned off. A similar problem happens when security people remove lines from */etc/inetd.conf* or */etc/services*.

Screen Scraping Fails Because of Design Change

You'd be surprised how much data transfer is done by "screen scraping", i.e., programs picking data out of displays intended for human consumption. The hazard here is that someone will change the display, breaking the program that depends on finding certain data at a certain point on the screen. Screen scraping is never an acceptable long-term strategy, but it can be used short-term if this risk is taken into account.

Dependencies

Every failure has its origin in a dependency. To minimize failures, minimize dependencies.

On the other hand, there is often a good economic reason for a dependency. For example, a program that uses shared libraries is dependent on those libraries; it will not run without them. A change to the system libraries, or to the path used to look for them (LD_LIBRARY_PATH), may break the program. But in return for this dependency, you get an executable that is smaller. The alternative is to use a statically linked program, which is larger because it includes the libraries, but cannot be broken by a change in the system libraries or the library path.

Another good example is how many applications you should run per box. If you run dozens of applications on one machine, each can affect the other. Worse, it is not easy to figure out which one is misbehaving at any point. If you run each application on its own box, they cannot affect each other directly and you can instantly tell which one is misbehaving, but it's much more expensive to have that extra hardware. Computer room floor space can cost more than the computers that sit on it, so having more physical machines is expensive for both reasons.

Here are other dependencies to watch out for:

- Dependencies between software modules you write
- Dependencies on features specific to only one browser
- Dependencies on only one operating system
- Dependencies on manual reconnection to database after failure
- Dependencies on a networked filesystem

Smoothing Outages

Sometimes you have to bring your site down, or you have to figure out how to bring it up again after it has crashed. There are some things you can do ahead of time to ease the pain:

- First of all, reduce complexity to the bare minimum. Fewer moving parts are always better. Be very critical of new features that add flash but little substance. Everything should be what it seems to be. Once you think your web site is as simple as possible, make it even simpler.

- Documentation should paradoxically be very sparse and thorough. Use big pictures to show all networks, IP addresses, machines, and applications. No one has time to read more than a few lines during outage emergencies.

- Make sure there is a well-known "out-of-service" web page that can be put on the site at a moment's notice. If you have regular subscribers, consider an instant messaging system to inform them of outages and estimated time until the site will be back up.

- Use Resonate or another system that can easily remove one server for a backout of bad software while the others continue to function in a limited way.

Key Recommendations

- Code and configure with possible failures in mind.
- Minimize dependencies.

## CHAPTER 8

Security

Web site security usually comes at the cost of performance, but not always. Some security changes can also increase performance. For example, keeping a site simple and avoiding Java and JavaScript means fewer points of weakness. Also, avoiding Microsoft's IIS web server will likely improve performance while eliminating vulnerability to a large number of viruses that can infect only IIS.

In this chapter, I cover a few security points only as they relate to performance. If you are looking for pure security information, try *Practical Unix and Internet Security*, by Simpson Garfinkel and Gene Spafford (O'Reilly & Associates).

HTTPS and SSL

Secure HTTP (HTTPS) uses ordinary HTTP over the Secure Socket Layer (SSL) protocol on port 443 by default. SSL encrypts all traffic, so you can be confident that your content will not be intelligible to anyone snooping Internet packets. In fact, even the HTTP headers and all images will be encrypted. You might think that you can save some server CPU power by not encrypting images (that is, putting links to a non-SSL image server). However, browsers do not allow unencrypted images on SSL protected pages.

HTTPS uses public-key encryption just long enough to exchange keys, and then it switches to private-key encryption for better performance. The private keys will be cached by both the client and server so that additional connections to the same site will be faster, at least until the entry expires from the connection cache. Netscape Enterprise web server allows the number of entries in the SSL connection cache to be configured with the `SSLCacheEntires` parameter in *magnus.conf*. It defaults to 10,000.

HTTPS has a significant performance penalty associated with it that can be as high as tenfold for small transmissions. The problem is the public-key cryptography "key-pair generation" at the beginning of the secure connection rather than the overhead of encrypting and decrypting the data sent across the wire. In fact, I ran some load tests using 40-bit data encryption versus 128-bit data encryption and found no difference at all because the encryption itself is so quick. Again, the slow part is setting up the SSL connection rather than actually using the SSL connection.

If your site uses SSL, consider using a cryptographic accelerator card. This is a board that plugs into your server and does the key-pair generation for SSL connection setup in hardware. The two dominant cards seem to be nCipher (*http://www.ncipher.com/*) and Rainbow (*http://www.rainbow.com/*). An interesting interaction between SSL and SMP is that SSL key generation in the Netscape Enterprise servers uses many malloc( ) calls. malloc( ) is single-threaded by default in most operating systems, so only one CPU will be able to do the work of key generation at a time unless multithreaded malloc is specifically enabled.

I ran some tests of response time and throughput under load with and without an nCipher card. The test machine was running Netscape Enterprise 3.6 web server on Solaris 2.6 on a 4-CPU Sun E450. For a small (1 KB) static file served via SSL on a server under no load, the card brought server response time down from about 75 milliseconds to about 25 milliseconds. Though it is three times faster, the 50 millisecond increase won't make any difference to a human observer. I also tested a very large (15MB) file. There was no measurable difference between using the card and not using it. This makes sense, because the card accelerates the SSL connection setup, not the exchange of SSL-encrypted data. So when there are relatively few new connections per second, the card doesn't seem to make much difference.

On the other hand, the card makes a large difference in throughput when the server needs to make new SSL connections at a high rate. I used the following script to generate load. The script simply retrieves a small static image file over and over, at increasing rates. A single running copy of the script does not generate the maximum possible load because the requests are all strictly serial, but if you run enough copies of it simultaneously, you should be able to generate any desired load.

```perl
#!/usr/bin/perl

use LWP::UserAgent;
use Crypt::SSLeay;
use HTTP::Headers;
use HTTP::Request;
use HTTP::Response;
use Time::HiRes 'time','sleep';

$\          = "\n";              # Add newlines to output print statements.
$rooturl    = 'https://1.2.3.4'; # IP address of HTTPS server goes here
$path       = '/images/test.gif'; # get a static image file

MAIN: {
    $ua         = LWP::UserAgent->new;
    $request    = new HTTP::Request('GET', "$rooturl$path");
    $max        = 80;
    $hps        = 1;
```

```
while ($hps <= $max) {
    $i     = $hps;
    $start = time( );
    while ($i--) {
        $response = $ua->request($request);
        if (!$response->is_success) { die $response->error_as_HTML; }
        sleep (1/$hps);
    }
    $end   = time( );
    print "$hps ", $hps / ($end - $start);
    $hps++;
    sleep 1;
}
```

I restarted the web server three times for three different cases. First, I entered "security off" in Netscape's *magnus.conf*; second, I enabled security and turned on the nCipher card by uncommenting its configuration lines in Netscape's *obj.conf*; third, I left security on and commented out the nCiper configuration lines. I ran each test three times and averaged the results to smooth them out. Figure 8-1 is a graph of the results.

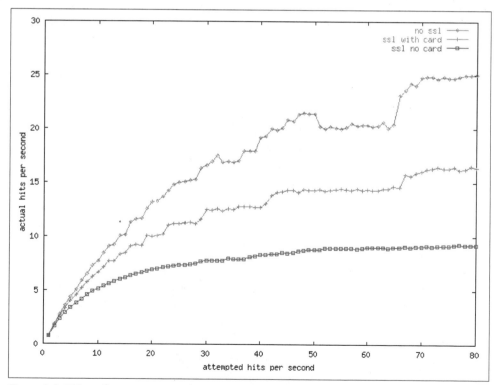

Figure 8-1. SSL performance comparison

You can clearly see that it is best for performance not to use SSL at all, that it is second best to use SSL with a cryptographic accelerator card, and worst to use SSL without a card. The difference is throughput of 25 hits per second with no SSL compared to 17 hits per second with SSL and a card compared to 9 hits per second with SSL and no card. Also note that at low attempted throughputs, say below 5 hits per second, it really doesn't matter whether you use an SSL accelerator card. Remember that this was just a relative test, not an absolute measure of the capacity of the server. In fact, I ran 16 copies of the load script and that seemed to max out my test client, while the server was serving about 70 SSL hits per second with no accelerator card.

SSL 3.0 allows caching of SSL sessions, so that new TCP connections from the same browser to the same server can use existing sessions. This means that servers do not have to slog through public-key generation for every connection, but rather can use the same private keys for multiple HTTP transactions. In Netscape Enterprise 4.0/ iPlanet Web Server, the `SSL3SessionTimeout` directive in *magnus.conf* controls SSL3 session caching by specifying the number of seconds until a cached SSL3 session becomes invalid. The default is 86,400, which is 24 hours. `SSLCacheEntries` specifies the number of SSL sessions that can be cached.

Another point to remember with SSL is that the encrypted data it generates will not be compressible, which stops modems from using their built-in compression schemes, further slowing down data transfer. For example, ASCII is normally compressible by a factor of two, but would not be at all compressible if served with SSL encryption. On the other hand, many servers can be configured to serve *gzip*-compressed data to browsers than can decompress such data (the latest Netscape and IE can). Using this *gzip* compression with SSL can restore or even improve upon the performance gain of modem data compression.

There is an open source implementation of SSL by Eric A. Young, called SSLeay. If you want to get some idea of your server's SSL performance, you can use the benchmark called "speed" that comes with the SSLeay implementation of SSL.

Firewalls

Firewalls are routers which are usually configured to block all traffic except that on specific ports, usually the web service ports 80 and 443. This may insulate your intranet from the Internet, but at the cost of increased difficulty of maintenance because it will be impossible to *telnet* in from the outside and impossible to redirect the display of GUI's.

There is almost no performance impact from a properly configured hardware firewall that simply blocks most ports, but firewalls that also encrypt all traffic can increase latency dramatically, easily taking twice as long to make a transfer. A couple of rules for reducing the impact of firewalls are to use dedicated firewall hardware doing nothing but firewall duty, and to put the most used rules at the top of your rules list so they are read first. Multiple firewall machines may be able to work in parallel. See *Building Internet Firewalls*, by Brent Chapman and Elizabeth Zwicky (O'Reilly & Associates).

Bastion Hosts

Bastion hosts are more complicated than Firewalls. Bastion host software is often run on ordinary PC or workstation hardware and is essentially a proxy server for requests coming from outside your organization, so bastion hosts are sometimes called reverse proxies.

Bastion hosts actually look inside packets for suspicious patterns. Each packet needs to be examined and then routed out to another interface. The examination may be several protocols deep, unlike a normal router that simply looks at the IP headers for the port number. While firewalls do not break a TCP connection, bastion hosts do terminate the connection and then make a new connection into your internal network so that the outside world cannot see your internal IP addresses. It is common to put the bastion host and web servers between two firewalls in a "DMZ"; this will slow access from inside the organization still further.

chroot

Many web servers are run via the *chroot* command to provide an added measure of security by defining a certain directory as the new document root, but this has two problems. First, it is a pain because all system libraries and commands the web server may need must be in this directory. Nothing outside of this directory will be visible to a process started under *chroot*. Second, it is a performance hit every time your web server accesses the filesystem, because ever file access is filtered through the *chroot* command.

Key Recomendation

- Consider using an SSL accelerator card if you need SSL.

## CHAPTER 9

Case Studies

In this chapter, we present some real-life situations. Each of the following cases is true, though some names and circumstances may have been changed to protect the guilty.

Database Table Growing Without Limit

The home page of a particular newspaper web site typically takes about one second to be dynamically generated from a database query. A new "personalization" feature is added to the web page at the end of January. Every time the home page is hit, a database is now queried for news that fits the user's preferences. This feature is well received, but monitoring shows a jump in latency when the feature was added. Worse, monitoring also shows that the time to retrieve that customized page is continuously increasing (see Figure 9-1).

It is determined that the database table of all news stories is being fully scanned for relevant news on each login, and that table continuously grows in size. The solution to this problem is that a new index is added to the table, mapping each story to the relevant users when it is added to the database, and latency falls back to as good as it was before the feature was added. The creation of the index is a simple SQL statement that looks like this:

```
create index news_index on news_story(user, story_age, already_read);
```

Reverse DNS Lookups Slows Logging

Brian Robinson of Harvard University kindly allowed me to include his account here. Using Netscape Server on Unix, static pages tended not to have any noticeable problem until the thread count maxed out, then had huge delays in the 2-minute range. Server-Side Include (SSI) pages had problems whenever the busy thread count was rising (about a 10-second response time) and were very bad when the thread count maxed out. Response times then seemed to correspond with how long the threads were maxed out—in one case over 15 minutes.

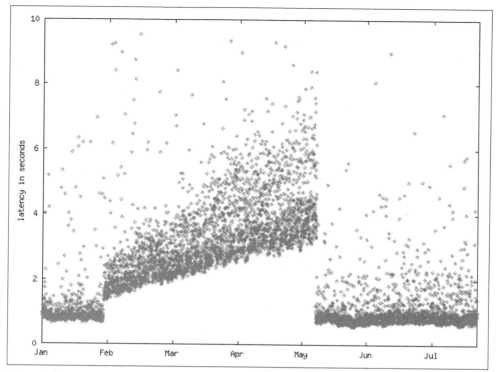

Figure 9-1. Latency increase with new customization page

During a bad period, he could see a gradual clogging of Netscape busy threads followed by dramatic clearing from a relatively constant load. The performance of SSI pages was most impacted, and poor performance corresponded closely to the number of busy threads reaching the configured maximum. Performance was also poor when Netscape was allocating more active threads, which it does in chunks. SSI pages normally responded in about 250 ms, but took about 10 seconds when busy thread counts were rising (see Figure 9-2). The performance of static HTML pages was poor only when busy thread count maxed out.

A critical clue was that the Netscape log was indicating spikes of up to 350 hits per second when a test was certainly generating only 5 to 10 hits per second. From that, it became clear that there were delays between the time a page arrived back to the client and the time it was stamped and entered in the log. This meant there were delays in the logging process, of which DNS is one of the steps.

So the delay between the time the page is received at the browser and the time it appeared in the log file was charted, and this matched up almost exactly to the busy thread graph, confirming that logging was the problem. Reverse DNS lookups were disabled and all of the delays disappeared (see Figure 9-3).

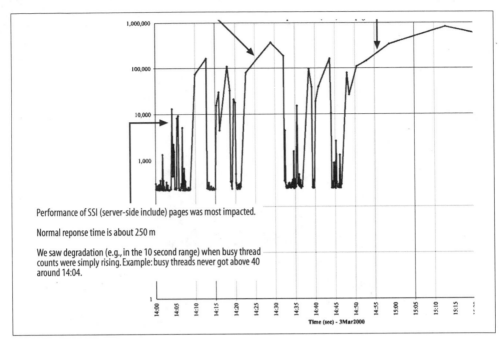

Performance of SSI (server-side include) pages was most impacted.

Normal reponse time is about 250 m

We saw degradation (e.g., in the 10 second range) when busy thread counts were simply rising. Example: busy threads never got above 40 around 14:04.

Figure 9-2. SSI response rates

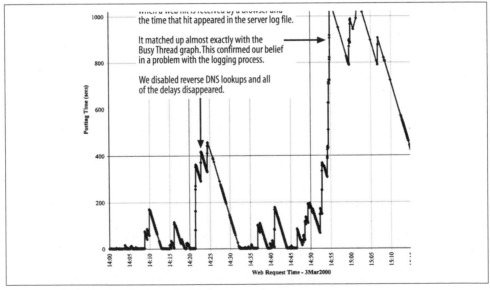

the time that hit appeared in the server log file.

It matched up almost exactly with the Busy Thread graph. This confirmed our belief in a problem with the logging process.

We disabled reverse DNS lookups and all of the delays disappeared.

Figure 9-3. Reverse DNS lookups disabled

Kinked Cable

Monitoring of a web site from the same LAN reveals that static pages are either served instantly, or after a fixed delay. The monitoring graph in Figure 9-4 has horizontal striations as a result.

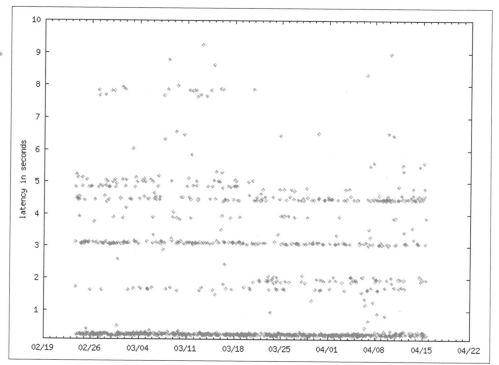

Figure 9-4. Some pages delivered with a fixed delay

Since the web server is on a Solaris machine, we use the *snoop* command to see what is going on at a packet level while hitting the web server. We use the *-t d* option to print time differentials between packets. The open source *tcpdump* command would also work here.

    # **snoop -t d server port 80**

Here is a shell script that grabs a page with the Perl LWP library's GET command and simply redirects standard output to */dev/null*, instead of printing out the time it took to get the page. Note that */bin/time* writes to standard error.

```
#!/bin/bash
while true
    do
    /bin/time GET http://server/file.html 1>/dev/null
    sleep 1
done
```

We ran this and just watched the page latency for a while. When we noticed that a particular response was slow, we examined the trace for that request. You have to know a little bit about TCP to make sense of these traces, but the basic idea is that each line of the trace shows one packet. Here is an example trace, with seconds between packets as the first column:

```
0.65715   client -> server    TCP D=80   S=64474 Syn Seq=3316330059 Len=0 Win=8760
0.00007   server -> client    TCP D=64474    S=80 Syn Ack=3316330060 Seq=956551078
Len=0 Win=8760
3.09232   server -> client    TCP D=64474    S=80 Syn Ack=3316330060 Seq=956551078
Len=0 Win=8760
0.00234   client -> server    TCP D=80   S=64474     Ack=956551079 Seq=3316330060
Len=0 Win=8760
0.00210   client -> server    TCP D=80   S=64474     Ack=956551079 Seq=3316330060
Len=79 Win=8760
0.00018   server -> client    TCP D=64474    S=80     Ack=3316330139 Seq=956551079
Len=0 Win=8760
0.00170   server -> client    TCP D=64474    S=80     Ack=3316330139 Seq=956551079
Len=788 Win=8760
0.00048   server -> client    TCP D=64474    S=80 Fin Ack=3316330139 Seq=956551867
Len=0 Win=8760
0.00105   client -> server    TCP D=80   S=64474     Ack=956551867 Seq=3316330139
Len=0 Win=8760
0.00006   client -> server    TCP D=80   S=64474     Ack=956551868 Seq=3316330139
Len=0 Win=8760
0.00356   client -> server    TCP D=80   S=64474 Fin Ack=956551868 Seq=3316330139
Len=0 Win=8760
0.00157   server -> client    TCP D=64474    S=80     Ack=3316330140 Seq=956551868
Len=0 Win=8760
```

We can see in the third line that we sent out a duplicate Syn packet after waiting 3.09232 seconds in vain for an Ack. We look some more and find another slow response and look at its trace as well:

```
0.66140   client -> server    TCP D=80   S=63644 Syn Seq=3123165939 Len=0 Win=8760
0.00118   server -> client    TCP D=63644    S=80 Syn Ack=3123165940 Seq=666055481
Len=0 Win=8760
0.00112   client -> server    TCP D=80   S=63644     Ack=666055482 Seq=3123165940
Len=0 Win=8760
0.00182   client -> server    TCP D=80   S=63644     Ack=666055482 Seq=3123165940
Len=79 Win=8760
0.00032   server -> client    TCP D=63644    S=80     Ack=3123166019 Seq=666055482
Len=0 Win=8760
0.00188   server -> client    TCP D=63644    S=80     Ack=3123166019 Seq=666055482
Len=788 Win=8760
0.00069   server -> client    TCP D=63644    S=80 Fin Ack=3123166019 Seq=666056270
Len=0 Win=8760
3.09849   server -> client    TCP D=63644    S=80 Fin Ack=3123166019 Seq=666055482
Len=788 Win=8760
```

```
4.59986   server -> client    TCP D=63644   S=80 Fin Ack=3123166019 Seq=666055482
Len=788 Win=8760
0.00191   client -> server    TCP D=80   S=63644    Ack=666056271 Seq=3123166019
Len=0 Win=8760
0.00410   client -> server    TCP D=80   S=63644 Fin Ack=666056271 Seq=3123166019
Len=0 Win=8760
0.00128   server -> client    TCP D=63644   S=80    Ack=3123166020 Seq=666056271
Len=0 Win=8760
```

We see that the server sent the same Fin to the client three times. The first one was lost and the second was sent after waiting 3.09849 seconds. The second one was also lost, so a third was sent after another 4.59986 seconds. That one was acknowledged, but in the mean-time, the client was waiting an extra 10 seconds.

Knowing that packets were being dropped intermittently leads to the suspicion that the hub connecting the server to the LAN is overloaded, but replacing the hub with a switch does not solve the problem. Finally, a cable under the floor is found to be kinked, probably because the installer just threw the cable loops under the flooring and pulled on the other end. When it is straightened out the striations no longer appear from the graph. So packets were being dropped because of the electrical interference caused by the kink.

Database Connection Pool Growth Limits Performance

Delays in web site response seem to correlate with periods of growth in the JDBC connection pool. To prove a causal relationship between delays and pool growth, two load tests are done. First, the connection pool is set to 10 connections. The web site is hit with 94 web test clients all within about 1 second. The start and stop times of all 94 clients are recorded, as is the growth of the connection pool over time. Figure 9-5 shows the results. The connection pool size is on the lefthand vertical axis and the web test client number is on the righthand vertical axis. Time in seconds is on the horizontal axis, but starts at about 628 rather than 0 because of the way the times were recorded in the test clients.

The wavy vertical line at about second number 633 shows the start times of the incoming hits on the web site. The hits begin to finish at about second number 658 and the connection pool size stabilizes. The size of this JDBC connection pool was "screen scraped" at intervals from the Weblogic JDBCAdmin web page, which provides this data. The average response time is about 27 seconds. We set the pool up to 70 connections, and re-run the test (see Figure 9-6). Now the average response time is down to 7 seconds.

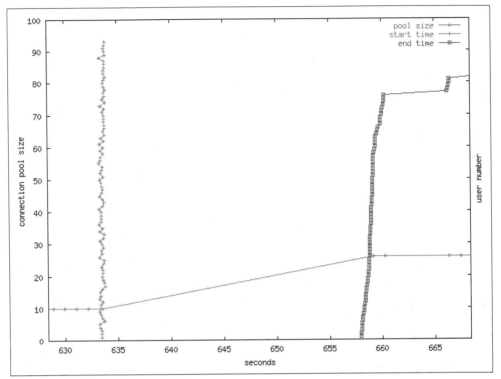

Figure 9-5. Connection pool growth

Clearly it is much better to have a larger connection pool if the database can support it, because the web site cannot respond until the database connection pool is grown enough to accommodate the current queries.

But there are other complicating factors to note. First, performance also increases as we reduce the number of Weblogic "execute threads," but this may limit capacity because each JDBC query occupies a thread. Second, it is discovered that database connections are not being released after use because of a programming oversight, so they remain "in use" for four more minutes because that is the connection idle time-out in the "middlware" server. A change to the code to return connections to the pool immediately after use neatly fixes the problem.

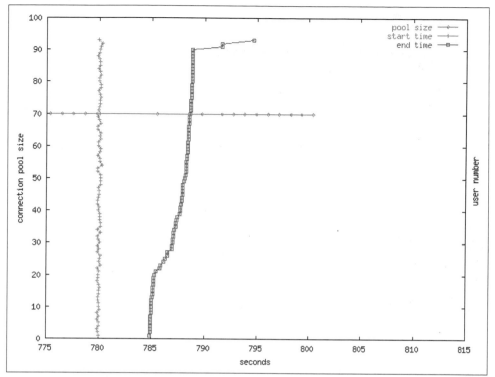

Figure 9-6. Larger connection pool

Key Recommendation

- Read about problems others have had to see if the solutions may apply to your own web site. Please write *p@patrick.net* with examples of problems and solutions on your own web site.

## CHAPTER 10

Principles and Patterns

There are some principles of performance tuning that apply in the general case and some patterns that unify the specific solutions. In this chapter, I try to summarize these principles and patterns.

Principles of Performance Tuning

The following sections cover some general principles of performance tuning.

Sometimes You Lose

You don't know whether you can improve the performance of a system until you study it, but you risk wasting your time just figuring out that there's nothing you can do, particularly when you are under tight budget or time constraints. You have to weigh the probable difficulty of the analysis against the potential gains. If the gains could be very large, it is a good bet to try to improve performance, but otherwise it's not worth your time.

To Measure Something Is to Change It

The physicist Werner Heisenberg pointed out that measuring anything changes it, if only slightly, so there is some uncertainty to all measurements. This is called the uncertainty principle, and is definitely true when measuring computer performance.

The classic example is running *ps* to see which processes are running on your server, and noticing that the only thing you ever see in the run state is *ps* itself. This must be so because *ps* has to be the running process in order to check which process is currently running. Similarly, when you take performance measurements on a machine doing some work, you are necessarily measuring not only the load of the work, but also the load caused by measurement.

Do not let this lead to disturbing recursive thoughts. The uncertainty is negligible if the measurement itself was small and quick. So keep your measurements small and quick.

Reading Is Fundamental

When you walk through a room in the dark, you can bruise your shins. When you turn on the lights, it gets much easier. The light gives you knowledge that lets you optimize your path. It's exactly the same for performance tuning. The better your mental model of the problem, the easier it is to solve. Your guiding lights are the manuals that come with your workstation, software, and routers, so do the right thing and RTFM.

Manuals are not at all dull when they hold the keys to lessening your pain. It's okay to experiment with settings and measure performance, but it's better to know why settings make a difference and how they interact with other settings and subsystems. This knowledge is in the manuals. A performance increase in one place may come at the expense of a loss in another place. If you don't know what you paid, you don't know whether the change was worthwhile.

There Is No Free Lunch

While the point of performance tuning is to get more without necessarily spending more, you will have to pay something for every increase in performance, if only the effort you put into understanding the problem and the solution. In some cases, you will have to buy new hardware, re-architect your system, or perhaps lose on portability, maintainability, security, reliability, or developer time. You can overclock the system bus for better server performance, but then the system is more likely to crash. You can remove your firewall and any encryption for better performance, but then you are exposed to attack. You can write all of your web software in optimized assembly or build web-specific chips, but the maintenance difficulties or size of investment relative to the performance gain would almost certainly mean that you made a very bad business decision. It is also unfortunate but true that optimizations for known usage patterns will inevitably hurt under some different usage patterns.

The trick is not to spend too much for what you get. Maybe there's no free lunch, but a cheap lunch is possible.

Returns Diminish

Costs also tell you when you have finished tuning the hardware you've got. When you begin tuning a system, it is usually easy to find "low hanging fruit" problems and fix them. As the system is tuned, additional performance gains become harder to find and more dependent on the particular configuration and usage pattern. When the investment is not worth the return, tuning is finished. Worth is subjective, but here are some clues that you're finished, at least for the moment:

- Your users no longer notice improvements.
- Your violations of good programming style in the quest for performance make the code unportable and unmaintainable.
- You are considering writing in assembly language.
- Your total cost per page view is greater than hiring someone to staff a telephone and fax the information on demand.
- You are getting very annoyed.

Perfect tuning is a moving target, because your configuration, usage patterns, and available components are also constantly moving, making it impossible to get and keep that last bit of optimal performance. You'll do better in the long run to tune to standard protocols and APIs rather than using proprietary solutions or inventing your own. Then your tuning efforts will pay you back in portability across multiple generations of systems, for a much greater long-term return on investment.

Portability Will Reduce Performance

There is a conflict between performance and portability. The best performance is achieved by optimizing for one specific set of circumstances, but portability is defined as identical functionality under many different circumstances. You cannot optimize for all circumstances, so you have to choose just where to trade performance against portability.

Completely optimized software is tied to a particular platform because it must take advantage of every available performance feature of that platform, such as the use of special CPU registers or system calls. Portable software, on the other hand, cannot take advantage of features that are specific to just one platform. If it did, it would not be portable. At another level, there can be dependence in optimizations that assume a particular usage pattern. These optimizations are likely to hurt rather than help performance in other situations. The trade-offs are endless.

Loss of software portability to optimizations would not matter much if not for the fact that portable software, in particular, is a very valuable commodity. Portability at the source code level means code does not have to be rewritten to run on another platform, just recompiled. This saves development costs and provides larger markets. Portability at the object code level, for example Java and Smalltalk, is a worthy goal for developers and users alike. Developers can concentrate on writing rather than porting, while users are free to choose whichever platform they like. There is never any benefit to the user in being tied to a platform.

A different kind of portability is possible by following open networking standards, so software that may not be portable itself can at least communicate easily with other computers. The rise of the Web is directly due to the portability of the HTTP protocol. HTTP may not give optimal performance on any particular machine, but since it has been implemented on so many different machines, its value for sharing content is more important. Any server on the Web can be accessed by any browser, because they all speak the same language. The lesson here is that you can trade portability for performance, but it's a Faustian bargain. There will be a very high cost to pay eventually.

Increasing Abstraction Will Reduce Performance

Programming at "higher" levels of abstraction, where more of the details are taken care of for you, will give you only the most generic performance, never the best performance. Whether programming in a high-level language or automatically generating SQL, letting a program deal with the details of optimizing your system gives away understanding and control in return for simplicity. Sometimes it's a good deal, and sometimes it isn't.

Security Will Reduce Performance

Security is another constraint you place on your system and all constraints reduce your freedom to optimize performance. SSL connection setup takes time, firewalls slow down packets, and entering passwords slows down the user. Security is necessary, but its impact on performance is usually significant.

Memory Is Hierarchical

The Web can be thought of as simply the slowest and cheapest form of memory on your computer. Even though the Web is not really on your computer and it's mostly read-only, it fits in well with the rest of the memory hierarchy (see Figure 10-1).

Each level of the memory hierarchy makes a different trade-off between cost and performance, with cost always directly related to access speed. Recently used data from each level is usually cached by the next faster level. The goal of caching is to maximize performance by using the fastest memory the most. This can also be stated as minimizing the number of cache misses. Of course, cache reads must eventually miss, or you wouldn't need all the slower levels. A cache miss is expensive because of the relatively larger access time of the next slower level.

It is often said that the Web makes distance irrelevant, but that's not quite true. You pay just once for your local disk and you can use it for a long time, if not forever. You have to pay over and over to send and receive data over the Internet. So in the case of the Web, caching not only helps performance, but also reduces cost. If you are going to use data many times, it is cheaper to store the data in a cache than to transmit it any significant distance.

Storing information is just transmitting it through time rather than space. To move a bit from now to later in some storage medium is analogous to moving a bit from here

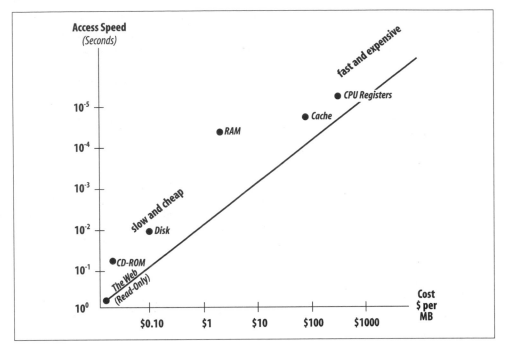

Figure 10-1. The memory hierarchy

to there over some transmission medium. In both cases you are concerned with assuring that the bits are not changed along the way. The same error-correction schemes work for both cases.

Caches Depend on Locality of Reference

If memory access were completely random, caching would not help performance much. Your cache would be constantly overwritten with new data from random parts of memory, so it would be unlikely that you would access the same data twice in an interval short enough to find it still in the cache.

Fortunately, there is a pattern to memory access. Memory locations that were accessed recently are likely to be accessed again soon, as are nearby memory locations. This pattern is referred to as locality of reference. That is, memory accesses tend to cluster in address space and in time. This is why algorithms that cache the contents of recently accessed memory and nearby locations do in fact significantly help performance. This works quite well for the Unix filesystem buffer and for web browser caches, for example.

I/O Is Slow

I/O stands for Input and Output, the processes by which information enters or leaves your computer. I/O can also refer to input and output between components within the computer.

I/O is not what computers do best. Computers are much better at calculating than at outputting the results of calculation. Unfortunately, I/O is what the Web is all about: network access, disk access to content and log files, and screen rendering. This is why CPU speed is not nearly as important as bus speed and network speed for browsers or servers.

Mechanical devices are the worst I/O offenders. Anything with moving parts just can't keep up with the purely electronic speeds in the rest of the computer. This means the hard disk is the slowest part of your web server. How slow? Compare 50 ns (10^{-9}) RAM to 10 ms (10^{-3}) disk. That's on the order of 10^5 (or 100,000) times slower. You clearly want to minimize disk access if you can access RAM instead.

Network I/O has historically been much slower than bus speeds, but recent LAN I/O cards and networking equipment, such as gigabit Ethernet, are quite capable of saturating both the bus and the CPU of most computers. If this trend continues out to the WAN level and latency issues are resolved by clever use of caching, it will be possible to build a truly distributed computer, with processing power and storage scattered around the Internet. But for now, the Internet rivals your disk for last place in web component performance.

Information Is Relative

Information theory defines information as that which reduces uncertainty. When a computer is listening to a network connection, it is uncertain whether the next bit is going to be a one or a zero. When a bit of information arrives, that uncertainty is gone. Information tells us what we did not know. So whether or not bits are information depends on what we do know.

It follows that a server can reduce the number of bits transmitted simply by using what the client already knows. Caching mechanisms take advantage of this. When the client doesn't know whether its cached data is up to date or fresh, it sends a request to the server describing the information it has. The server tells it whether the information is fresh. This is exactly how If-modified-since headers work in HTTP. It saves quite a bit of Internet bandwidth and improves performance.

Here are some rules of thumb for applying what your client already knows to web performance problems:

- First, send only the difference, or delta, when updating information. An example is the repeated use of a stock price query applet rather than a CGI. The CGI sends the entire HTML page and graphics with every result, wasting bandwidth and slowing performance. A stock query applet can receive and display just the stock price, a much smaller amount of information, avoiding retransmission of the graphics and HTML.

- Second, optimize using what you know about the pattern of requests that you'll get. You don't have to be ready for anything if only a limited number of things are likely to happen. For example, file access in HTTP servers is not random: the HTML text file contains links to other files, such as those containing the page's embedded graphics, which will definitely be requested immediately after the HTML file. To optimize for this, you could place the HTML file first on disk, followed immediately by the other files, reducing disk seek time. This might not help at all for heavily loaded servers with continuous requests for different pages, but you get the idea.

As another example, if you knew the users were all going to ask for a certain page at a certain time, you could optimize for that, moving it from disk to filesystem cache or server cache in advance. Log files are a good source of information on usage patterns. In some ways, performance tuning for the Web is easier than general computer performance tuning, because you can learn a lot about the usage patterns of the HTTP server and client.

- Third, optimize using what you know about the data set. Bits are bits, but you can tune for a particular kind of data. For example, some data sets have a characteristic distribution of file sizes. A web site providing downloads of large files will get better filesystem performance by increasing the amount of data a single inode can refer to, and it will get better network performance by ensuring that the maximum transmission unit (MTU) is as large as the smallest MTU along the route.

- Fourth, optimize using what you know about the user. What sort of compression does his or her browser understand? Does the browser understand the performance improvements of HTTP 1.1 or Java 1.2? What sort of latency and throughput does the user expect? Each of these things can help you to meet the user's expectations.

An interesting aside about compression and information is any compression scheme requires agreement between sender and receiver on an algorithm describing how to reconstitute the data. The agreement could be a simple mechanism for reducing redundancy, but the agreement could also contain a data set itself.

Some kinds of speech compression for police and fire radio systems work this way. Human beings produce a limited number of kinds of sounds. You can get good performance over low-bandwidth links by keeping a "codebook" of these basic sounds and simply transmitting an index pointing to the sound you want, along with some modification parameters to make it flow with the surrounding speech and sound more natural. The compression is what gives some police radio signals their characteristic sound.

There have been some proprietary attempts to make the Web work better through a similar scheme to send all users of a service a CD with images and sounds on it, so that surfing the proprietary site would be simply the retrieval of text along with pointers to images and sounds on the CD. It never caught on, because a single CD is so tiny and inflexible compared with the vast ocean of always changing information on the Web.

Hardware Is Cheap, Software Is Expensive

I should qualify that. Hardware is not all that cheap, and mass-market software can be pretty cheap. But if you have to fix a performance problem quickly, throwing more or better hardware at it is often the most economical solution.

Software, on the other hand, is expensive to write or debug, and you cannot amortize the cost of custom software over a large number of users. Software can take a long time to write, and good programmers charge a lot of money. And unlike hardware performance, programmer performance is not improving exponentially, because programmers are only human.

The Goal of Tuning Is Simultaneous Failure

A web system is considered to be in tune when there are no bottlenecks. This definition says nothing about the total throughput of the system—a very low throughput system can technically be in tune. The goal of tuning is to waste no capacity at all; in other words, every component should reach its limits at the same time. This is not a new idea: Henry Ford supposedly commissioned someone to study cars in junkyards in order to find out which Ford parts wore out last. Then he reduced the quality of those parts in order to save money. It didn't make sense to have some parts of a system that lasted much longer than other parts.

I'm not recommending that you downgrade pieces of your system until all are equally bad. Ford was trying to cut costs on an assembly line; you are probably not churning out web systems for profit, but instead have a single system to improve. You'll want to do the opposite: find the weakest link and improve that.

It is also interesting to observe that a poorly tuned system is the easiest to tune. When one component is taking almost all of the time (most likely fat content moving over a slow modem), it is clear that you should concentrate on that. As you fix one problem after another, the cycle time will decrease until all components are equally the problem. Then you're done tuning.

Since web systems are usually dynamic, with new pieces constantly being introduced, finding the weakest link at any moment in time may be nearly impossible. Rather than spending all your time chasing the elusive bottleneck just to be in tune, it makes sense to specify a certain performance as good enough for the moment, even if a few components are underused. It is a problem, though, when most of the components are underused.

Better Is Relative

You should be monitoring performance and keeping performance records, which provide a baseline for evaluating changes as well as clues as to where bottlenecks might be lurking. Your log files contain valuable information that should be kept for years or forever, if you have the storage. The ultimate measure of performance is user satisfaction, so keep organized records of performance complaints. Think of complaints as free performance monitoring data.

Bits Are Cost

In the U.S. Postal Service, the size of the package doesn't affect its transit time much. On the Web, the smaller the package, the more quickly it arrives. No matter how tuned your system, excessively large content can crush your performance. Keep your content light and small. Don't throw everything into every page just because you can. It goes the other way, too. Don't accept arbitrarily large input from users; cut them off at some reasonable point.

Internet Performance Degrades Nonlinearly

Internet services tend to degrade ungracefully and quickly past a certain point, like hitting a wall, rather than just gradually getting slower with increasing load. This is mostly due to the fact that the Internet is a shared medium, just like a road, and therefore subject to traffic jams, just like a road.

Tuning at the Highest Level Gives the Biggest Gains

You hardly ever get a performance tuning home run by tweaking some parameters. You get them by wiping out whole sections of your architecture or eliminating processing steps. To get the biggest gains, analyze your architecture at the highest level first. There is also less risk of wasting your work this way; if you tune some fine level of detail, you may waste your effort when you later realize that you can eliminate that entire step of processing.

Whatever Occurs Once Is Likely to Happen Again Soon

Weird but true. I think this is because the conditions that led to the first event are probably still in place a few moments later. When someone calls on the phone, they are more likely to call again right away because they forgot to say something than they are to call at some other time. Caching works because you are likely to request something again before it gets pushed out of the cache by other material. If that were not true, caches would be counterproductive, taking the time to store information that never gets recalled.

The 80/20 Rule

80 percent of time will be spent running in 20 percent of the code. It just always seems to work out that way. That's why optimizing the "hot spots" is a good investment. It seems to be that the 80/20 rule applies to many other things as well. The

economist Pareto noticed that 80 percent of wealth is usually concentrated in the upper 20 percent of any given population.

It's Not What You Know, It's Whom You Know

Whom you know is still more important than what you know. The details of web services and performance are changing so fast that it is impossible for any one person to keep up with it all. Your own trade secrets about how to improve your web site's performance are not going to help you nearly as much as a large set of friends in a similar situation who will share their experiences with you. To get their trust, you have to help them out. You can meet a lot of web people on *comp.infosystems. www.servers.* and *comp.infosystems.www.misc.*

As George Bernard Shaw once said, "If you have an apple and I have an apple and we exchange apples, then you and I will each have one apple. But if you have an idea and I have an idea and we exchange these ideas, then each of us will have two ideas."

Patterns of Performance Improvement

Performance improvements can be grouped into patterns of the way things tend to work rather than concrete advice. The following sections discuss some patterns that unify performance improvement techniques.

Amortization

Performance improvements often involve amortizing overhead among many transactions for an economy of scale:

- HTTP 1.1 allows a single TCP connection to be reused for multiple file downloads. This feature is known as *persistent connections*. The overhead of setting up and tearing down a TCP connection is spread among several files rather than reincurred for each file.

- Java *.jar* files work in a similar way, grouping Java *.class* files together into a package that can be downloaded in one TCP connection rather than setting up a separate TCP connection for each class. The downside here is that *.jar* files may include classes you never use.

- A composite imagemap is another example. Rather than sending multiple small images to the user, send a single large image. If the original individual images were clickable, you can maintain the same functionality by making the large image a clickable imagemap.

Caching

Caching is the most important and widely used performance technique. The idea is simple: keep frequently accessed data close at hand. Caching helps only if some data is in fact more frequently accessed than other data, but this is usually the case.

- You can often trade storage space for more performance by running the most popular inputs to your CGI programs offline and caching all the results. Users can then rapidly access static HTML rather than forcing the generation of dynamic HTML.
- More memory will reduce the need for your servers to go to disk for content, increasing access time. Unix will cache frequently accessed files in physical memory rather than go to disk for them, if there is enough memory.
- Web proxy servers reduce the load on an organization's Internet access point as well as providing better access time for popular web pages by caching those popular pages.

Profiling

Profiling is looking at usage patterns, either to find bottlenecks in your code or to optimize for real-world usage. You want to follow "Amdahl's advice" to make the common case fast:

- Code profilers find the code that is most frequently accessed so that it can be most optimized, perhaps by rewriting it in assembly language. The HotSpot Java VM dynamically calculates which code is most heavily used and compiles it on the fly to native code.
- You can profile your users and use that information to put your web site closer to them. For example, if most of your users happen to be in Japan, you'll probably give them better performance by putting your web server in Japan.
- It is possible to profile the download times of your customers and make assumptions about what sort of access throughput they have. Adjust your content to something reasonable for their access type.

Parallel Processing

Many problems in web serving benefit from letting more than one entity work on the problem at the same time:

- Netscape and some other browsers will open several simultaneous connections to the server and make multiple requests in parallel, hoping that the server can then figure out the most efficient order to serve the requests rather than letting the client make the requests in a random order.
- Java programs benefit from multithreading, which allows some threads to continue execution while others are blocked. For example, the user of a Java application may need to fill in a login screen. This is an opportunity to download additional class files in the background in a different thread. Do not serialize tasks unless there is really a dependence on the sequence.
- Symmetric multiprocessing (SMP) hardware is capable of mapping multiple threads to multiple CPUs and executing code in parallel.

Using What You Know

Don't underestimate the value of even the most tr

- You know the next hit is likely to be for an in servers could, in theory, parse HTML and pre-fe
- When a connection gets used once, it's likely t HTTP 1.1 has persistent connections.
- If your web server can recognize a particular user mize for them, perhaps by preparing content it wo ate dynamically.

Simplicity

Many gains come just from keeping things simple and minim

- Internal modems have no cable between the modem and therefore not only faster but also cheaper. It is also impos cable for them simply because there isn't any cable.
- Making HTML content small and simple with no frames images can have a dramatic improvement on download time. like this.
- Using only static content and no CGIs at all greatly improves s expense of flexibility.

Finally, remember that the fastest way to do anything is not to do it a you can eliminate part of your system, you should. One way is simply dancy and remove it, but a better way is to think outside the box en your users can run their own web servers. Maybe you don't even need your particular business. Then web performance problems just go away.

Key Recommendations

- RTFM.
- KISS: keep it simple, stupid.
- Minimize I/O.
- Send only deltas (where possible).
- Cache what you can.
- You're much better off sharing tips than hiding them.

Tuning in Depth

## CHAPTER 11

Browsers

The idea of a hypertext browser is not new. Many word processing packages, such as FrameMaker, and formats, such as PDF, generate or incorporate hyperlinks. The idea of basing a hypertext browser on common standards, such as ASCII text and Unix sockets, was an advance first made by the Gopher client and server from the University of Minnesota.

Gopher proved to be extremely light and quick, but the links were presented in a menu separate from the text, and Gopher did not have the ability to automatically load images. The first drawback was solved by the invention of HTML, and the second was solved in the first graphical HTML browser, Mosaic, produced in 1993 at the University of Illinois National Center for Supercomputing Applications (NCSA). Many of the original students who developed Mosaic were among the founders of Netscape the following year.

An effort by the University of Illinois to commercialize Mosaic led to the founding of Spyglass, which licensed its code to Microsoft for the creation of Internet Explorer. Netscape and IE have been at the forefront of browser advances in the last few years, but the core function of the browser, to retrieve and display hypertext and images, has remained the same.

How Browsers Work

The basic function of a browser is extremely simple. Any programmer with a good knowledge of Perl or Java can write a minimal but functional text-only browser in one day. The browser makes a TCP socket connection to a web server, usually on port 80, and requests a document using HTTP syntax. The browser receives an HTML document over the connection and then parses and displays it, indicating in some way that parts of the text are links to other documents or images. When the user selects one of the links, perhaps by clicking on it, the process starts all over again, with the browser requesting another document. In spite of the advances in HTML, HTTP, and Java, the basic functionality is exactly the same for all web browsers.

In fact, here is the minimal C code you need in order to request the home page from any web server. I started with a tiny example of how to connect to servers in general from the excellent page on Internet socket programming at *http://www.ecst.csuchico.edu/~beej/guide/net/* and modified it to request a web page. The following code is very similar to the guts of every Unix client program. You can download it from *http://patrick.net/software/tiny.c*.

```c
#include <stdio.h>
#include <errno.h>
#include <netdb.h>
#include <netinet/in.h>
#include <sys/socket.h>

#define PORT      80
#define BUFSIZE 4000

int main(int argc, char *argv[]) {
    int                sockfd, count;
    char               *request = "GET / HTTP/1.0\n\n";
    char               reply[BUFSIZE];
    struct hostent     *he;
    struct sockaddr_in  target;

    if ((he=gethostbyname(argv[1])) == NULL) {
        herror("gethostbyname");
        exit(1);
    }

    if ((sockfd = socket(AF_INET, SOCK_STREAM, 0)) == -1) {
        perror("socket");
        exit(1);
    }

    target.sin_family  = AF_INET;
    target.sin_port    = htons(PORT);
    target.sin_addr    = *((struct in_addr *)he->h_addr);
    bzero(&(target.sin_zero), 8);

    if (connect(sockfd, (struct sockaddr *)&target,
        sizeof(struct sockaddr)) == -1) {
        perror("connect");
        exit(1);
    }

    send(sockfd, request, strlen(request), 0);

    if ((count = recv(sockfd, reply, BUFSIZE, 0)) == -1) {
        perror("recv");
        exit(1);
    }

    reply[count] = '\0';
```

```
            printf("%s", reply);

            close(sockfd);
            return 0;
    }
```

If you compile the program like this:

```
% gcc -o tiny tiny.c
```

then you can use it in the following manner:

```
% tiny patrick.net
```

and it will dump the home page from the server you name to standard output.

Let's take a look at the functionality of recent browsers in more detail, noting performance issues. To get the ball rolling, the browser first has to parse the URL you've typed into the "Location:" box or recognize the link you've clicked on. This should be extremely quick. The browser then checks its cache to see if it has that page. The page is found through a quick hashed database mapping URLs to cache locations. Dynamic content should not be cached, but if the provider of the content did not specify an immediate timeout in the HTTP header or if the browser is not clever enough to recognize CGI output from URLs, then dynamic content will be cached as well.

If the page requested is in the cache and the user has requested (via a preference setting) that the browser check for updated versions of pages, then a good browser will try to save time by making only an HTTP HEAD request to the server with an If-modified-since line to check whether the cached page is out of date. If the reply is that the cached page is still current, the browser simply displays the page from the cache. If the desired web page is not in the cache, or is in the cache but is stale, then the browser needs to request the current version of the page from the server.

In order to connect to a web server, the client machine needs to know the server's four-byte IP address (e.g., 198.137.240.92). But the browser usually has only the fully-qualified server name (e.g., *www.whitehouse.gov*) from the user's manual request or from the HTML of a previous page. The client machine must figure out which IP address is associated with the DNS name of a web server. It does this via the distributed database of domain name to IP mappings—that is, DNS, or Domain Name Service. The client machine makes a request of its local name server, which either knows the answer or queries a higher-level server for the answer. If an IP answer is found, the client can then make a request directly to the server by using that IP address. If no answer is found, the request cannot proceed and the browser will display "No DNS Entry" or some other cryptic message to the user.

The performance problem here is that DNS lookups are usually implemented with blocking system calls, meaning that nothing else can happen in the browser until the DNS lookup succeeds or fails. If your local DNS server is overloaded, the browser will simply hang until some rather long operating system timeout expires, perhaps one minute.

DNS services, like most other Internet services, tend to get exponentially slower under heavy load. The only guaranteed way to avoid the performance penalty associated with DNS is not to use it. You can simply embed IP addresses in HTML or type them in by hand. This is hard on the user, because DNS names are much easier to remember than IP addresses, and because it is confusing to see an IP address appear in the "Location:" box of the browser. Under good conditions, DNS lookup takes only a few tenths of a second. Under bad conditions, it can be intolerably slow.

The client-side implementation of DNS is known as the *resolver*. The resolver is usually just a set of library calls rather than a distinct program. Under Unix, for example, the resolver is part of the *libc* library that most C programmers use for their applications. Some DNS resolvers cache recently requested DNS names, so subsequent lookups are much faster than the first, but Unix does not.

Once a browser client has the IP address of the desired server, it generates the HTTP request describing its abilities and what it wants, and hands off the request to the OS for transmission. In generating the HTTP request, the browser will check for previously received cookies associated with the desired page or DNS domain and send those along with the request so that the web server can easily identify repeat customers. The whole request is small, a few hundred bytes. The OS attempts to establish a TCP connection to the server and to give the server the browser's request. The browser then simply waits for the answer or a timeout. If no reply is forthcoming, the reason could be that the server is overloaded and cannot accept a new connection, the server crashed, or the server's network connection is down.

When the response from the server arrives, the OS gives it to the browser, which then checks the header for a valid HTTP response code and a new cookie. If the response is OK, the browser stores any cookie, parses the HTML content or image, and starts to calculate how to display it. Parsing is very CPU-intensive. You can feel how fast your CPU is when you load a big HTML page, say 100K or more, from cache or over a very fast network connection. Remember that parsing text is a step distinct from laying out and displaying it. Netscape, in particular, will delay the display of parsed text until the size of every embedded image is known. If the image sizes are not included in the HTML <IMG> tag, this means that the browser must request every image and receive a response before the user sees anything on the page.

The order in which an HTML page is laid out is up to the particular browser. In Netscape 4.x, web pages were rendered in the following order, once all the image sizes were known:

1. The text of the page is laid out. Links in the text are checked against a history database, and if found, are shown in a different color to indicate that the user has already clicked on them.

2. The boundary boxes for images are displayed with any ALT text for the image and with the image icon.

3. Images are displayed, perhaps with progressive rendering, where the image gains in definition as data arrives rather than simply filling in from top to bottom.

4. Subsidiary frames are loaded starting over at step 1.

A browser may open multiple connections to the server. You can clearly see this by running *netstat -c* to poll network activity on a Linux client, and then using Netscape to request a page with multiple embedded images. You'll probably see four connections open, indicated by the word ESTABLISHED in the state column.

The number of simultaneous connections is a tunable option in some browsers, but Netscape seems to use no more than four connections. Clients with fast Internet access will benefit from simultaneous connections. Clients with slow Internet access may see no improvement from simultaneous connections if they are already using all of their bandwidth. Each of the multiple connections may also be using HTTP 1.1's persistent connections to retrieve several pages in sequence.

Future versions of HTTP will have pipelining within each persistent connection. Pipelining means starting another request before the previous request has returned a complete response, so the requests and responses will be interleaved and the browser must sort them out. HTTP 1.1 will be used automatically if your browser and the contacted server support it.

You can see the progress of the various downloads in the Netscape footer messages: every flash of a URL is an HTTP connection for an HTML page, an image, or a Java *.class* or *.jar* file. It is usually too confusing to try to figure out which connection being shown in the footer corresponds to an image on the page.

If the user hits the browser's Stop button, a TCP reset, also called an abortive release, is sent to the server immediately. See *TCP/IP Illustrated, Volume 1*, by Richard Stevens (Addison Wesley), for the TCP details of a reset. If the server is calculating CGI output when the Stop button is hit, the CGI process will not hear about it until it completes and tries to send the output back to the web server for forwarding to the client. Under Unix, the CGI process will get a SIGPIPE signal because the socket to the web server is no longer valid.

Types of Browsers

There are a lot of browsers, but only a few are widely used. See *http://www.boutell.com/openfaq/browsers/* for a comprehensive list and *http://www.cen.uiuc.edu/bstats/latest.html* for statistics on market share. The following browsers are distinguished either by their market share or their features.

Netscape

Netscape Navigator, usually just called "Netscape," was the first commercial browser, but it has been losing ground to Internet Explorer. Netscape 4 was a major overhaul of Netscape 3, and Netscape 6 has a complete rewrite of Netscape 4, incorporating the new "Gecko" rendering engine. Netscape 1.0 and later versions all have persistent connection ability, but use it via a Connection:Keep-Alive header rather than as part of a full implementation of HTTP 1.1. See Chapter 15 for more about HTTP. Netscape exists as native code for Linux, Solaris, Macintosh, Windows, and many other platforms.

There is an annoying bug in the Netscape 4 implementation for Windows that causes Netscape to reload the current page when the browser or window is resized. It's a performance problem if the page is noncacheable, because the user may get a page, resize the window to read it better, and then find he has to wait to get it again.

Netscape 6 has better performance than Netscape 4 and is smaller. Netscape 6 includes support for the Document Object Model (DOM), which allows many new kinds of dynamic content. Netscape 6 does not include Java as part of the standard installation, but Java is in the "full" installation.

Netscape has made the source code for their browser available on the Web at *http://www.mozilla.org/*. This opens the door to performance improvements by the Internet community as a whole. I'm personally hoping that someone will write a filter that eliminates blinking GIF advertisements.

Internet Explorer

Internet Explorer (IE) is bundled with every copy of Windows and Windows NT. Because Windows has a monopoly on commercial PC operating systems, Internet Explorer is already installed on nearly every PC desktop. This fact, combined with the similarity of the two browsers, removes the incentive to even take the time to install any other browser. Whether Microsoft may continue to bundle IE with Windows is still in the courts as of this writing because the bundling looks very much like an abuse of monopoly power.

That said, Internet Explorer does have a few performance features to recommend it. First, it outputs document requests with the HTTP 1.1 header, implying that it has full HTTP 1.1 support. Beyond keepalives, HTTP 1.1 has support for byte-range downloading, the continuation of interrupted transfers, and other features that improve performance under certain conditions. IE also seems always to display the text of a page first, before any images, so that you can start to read immediately and decide whether you want to stop the download. Current versions of IE support DOM, but not exactly the same way Netscape 6 supports it, leading to the need to write different content for different browsers. IE exists for Windows, the Mac, and Solaris, although the non-Windows versions have less functionality.

Appendix C of *Professional Web Site Optimization*, by Scott Ware et al. (Wrox Press) shows that Netscape 3.0 is about twice as fast at loading and displaying web pages than Internet Explorer 3.0. The difference is attributed to IE's need to support the COM threading model. I haven't tested Netscape 4.x or 6.x.

IE's progress bar keeps incrementing once a connection has been made. This gives the unfortunate illusion that something is happening even if the remote server went down and is no longer sending anything.

IE 6 does not have Java support. To get Java applet support in IE 6 requires the installation of Sun's "Java Plug-In," available from *http://java.sun.com/*.

Opera

The Opera browser from *http://www.opera.com/* is very small (less than 2 MB) yet complete. It is free if you are willing to tolerate an advertising header, but you can also pay to get a version with no advertising. It has some excellent features to recommend it, such as speed, the ability to turn off all animated GIF's, and to zoom in or out of a page. It supports DOM and JavaScript, and supports Java with an add-in that greatly increases the size of the browser. It is available for Windows, Mac, and Linux. I have not run any tests on it, but it feels very quick in comparison with Netscape and IE.

Neoplanet

Neoplanet supports JavaScript, and it is small (less than 5 MB) but very flashy. The current version is 5. It had a number of annoying bugs that prevented me from wanting to using it as my primary browser. It's available at *http://www.neoplanet.com/*.

WebTV

WebTV is a hardware box that turns a TV into a web browser. The WebTV browser is built in to that box. It has many limitations and nothing in particular to recommend it other than the fact that it works with a TV. I believe it runs only on the WebTV box. It supports some JavaScript. The current version is 2.0.

Cello

The current version of Cello is 1.0. Development seems to have been discontinued in 1994 but the browser is still available from *http://www.law.cornell.edu/cello/cellotop.html*.

Mosaic

The original web browser developed by Marc Andreessen and others at the University of Illinois at Urbana-Champaign is NCSA Mosaic and can still be downloaded from *http://www.ncsa.uiuc.edu/SDG/Software/mosaic-w/*. The feature that used to distinguish Mosaic is support for *gzip* decompression, but this is now also supported by

Netscape's browsers and IE. You can configure Apache to report that a file is *gzip* compressed by adding the following lines to Apache's *srm.conf*:

```
# AddEncoding allows you to have certain browsers (Mosaic/X 2.1+) uncompress
# information on the fly. Note: Not all browsers support this.
AddEncoding x-compress Z
AddEncoding x-gzip gz
```

This is useful for large text files, in which *gzip* can decrease the size by more than half, but is not worth the trouble for very small files, or files that do not compress well, because the download difference will not be noticeable and you will still have the overhead of running *gunzip*. Another reason content compression may not give you dramatic gains is that modems often already use compression themselves.

Mosaic runs on Unix, Windows, and Macintosh. It has the additional advantage that it is available at no cost along with its source code, but development has been discontinued at Version 3.0.

Lynx

Lynx is a text-only web browser available from *http://lynx.browser.org/*. It was originally developed at the University of Kansas. It is capable of displaying images via helper applications. Advantages of Lynx are it is free along with its source code, you can run it over shell accounts as well as directly via PPP, it has a *-source* option that is convenient for scripting the retrieval of data, and it is very fast. We saw a use of the *-source* option in Chapter 5. Another very useful feature is the ability to link-check an entire site: *lynx -traversal -crawl <URL>*. Lynx supports SSL through a set of source code patches, but the ability to link-check seems to break when you add SSL. The current version as of this writing is 2.8.1.

Amaya

Amaya is a free open source browser from the W3C, available at *http://www.w3.org/Amaya/*. It is not particularly high performance or robust, but has the interesting feature that the browser is also an HTML editor. After you get a page, you can immediately modify it just by typing into the browser. I think this is a useful feature that all browsers should have.

Tango

Tango is a browser, email client, and HTML composition tool specifically designed to work with over 90 languages including Arabic, Chinese, and Thai. It supports frames, SSL, and cookies, so should be usable with most web sites. See *http://atzl.com/tango.htm*. This is sometimes confused with the Tango Web development tools from WithEnerprise (*http://www.witango.com/*).

The Perfect Browser

My ideal browser would have a number of unusual features:

- It would give the user the power to explicitly override no-cache directives in HTTP headers so that you could force caching of certain pages.
- If desired, it would cache completely parsed pages so that hitting the Back button would cause instant redisplay of the previous page, rather than re-retrieval of nonparsed HTML from disk—or worse, from the network.
- It would disable all animation in GIFs with a single button.
- It would optionally display all HTTP traffic, including traffic before encryption with SSL. This would be especially useful for seeing just what data is being sent with an HTTP POST.
- HTML source and HTTP headers for every downloaded page would be optionally visible in the editor of your choice and edited content would be redisplayed, including dynamically generated pages.
- GET and POST request data and headers would be also optionally editable before being sent.
- It would show a breakdown of the time spent in connecting, DNS, server silence, and data transfer.
- It would have a command-line option to run without a GUI.
- It would be easily scriptable to generate various tests. The scripts should be generated by clicking around on the GUI version, but would be output in Perl for easy modification.
- It would be able to choose the best proxy server from a list by actual performance.
- It would not support Java applets at all.
- It would support HTTP 1.1 "Byte-range" downloads to download just the fraction of the page that has changed since the last download.

Browser Speed

The web browser is probably not going to be your bottleneck simply because the average performance of a point-to-point TCP connection on the Internet is only about 50K bytes per second, while most browsers are able to parse and display data faster than that. See *http://www.keynote.com/measures/top10.html* and *http://www. orckit.com/* for Internet performance statistics. My own seat-of-the-pants benchmark is that Netscape 4 running on an old 166 MHz Pentium laptop under Linux 2.0 can parse a large HTML file from memory cache or from a 10 Mbps LAN connection at a rate of about 100 KB per second.

For a different test, I served an old 69 MB file to Internet Explorer 5.5 on a Windows NT 4.0 machine with 128 MB of RAM. It took about 23 minutes to load the page, which came out to about 47 KB per second. The browser froze when I tried to scroll down, so it wasn't much use. Opera 3.62 had similar performance on the 69 MB file. The text-only Lynx browser took just one minute on Solaris to load the 69 MB file, and scrolled nicely.

Netscape 4.51 on Linux 2.2 with 256 MB of RAM and 500 MHz CPU loaded half of the file in 5 minutes with CPU at about 15 percent, but then the browser size in memory was over 200 MB and the machine swapped terribly, making it useless. Still it did load at about 230 KB per second while it worked.

One might think that browsers would store cached documents in a parsed format for quicker display when recovered from cache, but an examination of the cache shows that this is not the case. This raises the interesting possibility of preparsing HTML on the server and storing it in parsed format. There is no standard format for parsed HTML, so the performance gain would be at the expense of portability and human readability. In any case, it is unusual for the Internet to return enough data in HTTP replies to overwhelm the parsing capability of the browser. What this means for capacity planning is that performance is not currently a factor in choosing web browsers, although this may change as Internet infrastructure is upgraded.

In the outbound direction, web browsers do not need to make sustained HTTP requests any faster than a human can digest the replies. Web browsers are generally capable of about 20 HTTP connections per second. Even a person ready to click away furiously could not click on 20 distinct links in one second, but it is possible for a multithreaded browser to reach this rate when parsing HTML pages with many embedded images or applets. Even a burst of 20 requests in a second from one browser is no particular problem for most servers. A typical average rate for requests from a browser is less than 1 HTTP operation per second.

Browser Tuning Tips

The browser may not typically be a bottleneck, but you probably want to get the best performance out of it that you can. Here are some suggestions, both general and specific to certain browsers.

General Tips

The following sections provide some general tips for getting the most out of your browser.

Upgrade

Try to get the latest nonbeta version of your browser. Newer versions usually include new features like HTTP 1.1 persistent connections to improve performance.

That said, there are some things to be said for the older versions. First of all, beta versions of new browsers often have bugs and performance problems associated with them, while the older nonbeta versions are more stable. Netscape 4.0 beta ran Java especially slowly, but this was fixed in the version that was officially released. You may want to wait until a browser is officially released before trying it.

Second, browsers have been getting fatter very fast. Netscape 3 for Linux takes about 5M of memory when you first start it up, Netscape 4 takes about 8M, and the latest browsers can take 20M or more. As you use them, they both grow through the loading of features and through memory leaks. If you're memory-constrained, you will get better performance with the older version, especially if it makes the difference between swapping to disk or not.

Do less

You can change your browser's settings so that the browser does only the minimum necessary to get and show you a page:

- First, turn off the automatic loading of images, since they take up most of your bandwidth, and each requires a separate connection unless both your browser and server understand persistent connections. You'll see placeholders for unloaded images that you can click on individually for loading, or you can load them all at once through a menu option.

- Similarly, you should probably turn Java off if you are bandwidth- or memory-constrained.

- To get the browser to start a little more quickly, set it to load only a blank page on startup.

- Load as few plug-ins as possible, because they add to your startup time.

- On a Macintosh, load fewer fonts.

- To prevent any network access when you have a page in the cache, set the verify option to "never." This risks your viewing out-of-date pages, but it is a significant performance boost if you do have the page in cache.

- You can clear your history cache for another slight performance boost, but you will no longer see visited links in a different color. In Netscape 4.0, clear the history cache like this: Edit → Preferences → Navigator → Clear History button. If you find this is a significant help, you can set your history of links visited to always expire immediately so that you never spend time recognizing and colorizing visited links. This does not affect your browser's cache.

- Not accepting or sending cookies will give another slight gain in performance and a large gain in privacy, but this will break many web sites that depend on cookies for their functionality, such as sites that personalize content for you.

- Save frequently accessed pages, such as search engine home pages, to a local file on your hard disk with File → Save As, and bookmark where you saved them.

The next time you go to one of these saved pages, you won't have any network traffic, and it won't expire from the browser's cache. You may have to modify the HTML in the saved file so that all links are absolute (that is, so they include the server name), because relative links are now relative to the filesystem on your own machine rather than to the document root of the original web server. The easiest way to do this is to add a <BASE> tag to the HTML head, like this:

```
<html>
<head>
<base href="http://www.search.engine.com/">
</head>
...
```

This is also an opportunity to eliminate the lines of HTML that put in the blinking GIF ads so you won't have to see the ads right away. Here's a bit of Perl that just wipes out all images from an HTML file:

```
% perl -pi.bak -e 's/<img*?>//gi' index.html
```

You may have to edit further, removing references to stylesheets, for example. Once you get a page back from the original server—for instance, by submitting a search request—the HTML you'll get back will be new, and you'll have ads again.

- You can cache whole sites in a similar way by choosing a new cache location with Netscape's Preferences, then simply browsing the site you want to cache. The new cache will contain the site, and you can keep it there permanently by setting the cache location back to the cache used for most of your browsing. In Navigator 4, you change the cache location with Edit → Preferences → Advanced → Change Cache Folder.

Finally, make good use of the Stop button. Stop page downloading if you know you don't want the rest, and stop animated GIFs if you are CPU-constrained. Infinitely looping animated GIFs can easily waste 10 percent of your CPU capacity and will continue to do so until you stop them. This is an issue if you are running the browser and some other CPU-intensive applications at the same time. Some Java applets may also consume CPU time even when you're not using them, or even after you've left that web page. This happens because the applet programmer did not override the applet's stop() method, for whatever reason. Applets cannot be stopped with the Stop button, but you can turn off Java to stop them. In Netscape 4, to turn off Java, select Edit → Preferences → Advanced and deselect "Enable Java."

Use shortcuts

A number of shortcuts can improve the user's performance in handling the browser (rather than improving the browser's performance itself):

- First of all, you don't always have to type in complete URLs. Most browsers will fill in the rest of a URL with the default "http://www." and ".com" if you just type in the domain name. So, for example, you can type "sun" instead of "http://www.sun.com".

However, beware that this may actually slow performance or not work at all in some cases. For example, if you are in an organization named Patrick Net, Inc., that has set up its DNS to assume that incomplete URLs should end in your organization's domain name, "patrick.net," then simply entering "sun" in your browser will cause a lookup of *http://sun.patrick.net/*. If there is no local machine named "sun," your DNS may or may not redirect the browser to *http://www.sun.com/*, depending on how DNS was configured.

If the web server machine name is something other than "www," you can still leave off the "http://" part. So if the server is named "web" at *patrick.net*, you can type in "web.patrick.net" instead of "http://web.patrick.net."

- Second, use keyboard shortcuts when they are available, like the Escape key for Stop. On Linux, Alt-left arrow moves back, Alt-right arrow moves forward, and Alt-r reloads the current page. You'll find that you can type the keys for Stop, Back, Forward, Open, etc., much faster than you can move the mouse to select them. You have to know what they are, but once you get used to them, you'll never go back. This is also why Unix command-line users tend to disdain GUIs: it's much faster to type a command than to move the mouse. If you have to use a GUI menu or set of buttons, note that Tab or Alt-Tab will sometimes change which one is currently selected, but in this case, it may be quicker to use the mouse than to tab around in a GUI.

- Third, use the Go menu to select a page from your history of recently viewed pages rather than hitting the Back button repeatedly. It's much faster. IE has a nice feature that automatically tries to complete the URL you are typing with recently viewed URLs.

Increase caches

Pump up the memory and disk cache in your browser if you can afford it. Clearing your browser's memory and disk cache may help a little if you are hitting new sites, since the browser will have less to check, but it will hurt a lot if you are hitting sites you've seen before, since all the data must be downloaded again. As a rule, you want to set the cache to be as big as your machine can handle.

Reboot

It is unfortunate but true that Netscape and Internet Explorer both tend to take memory from you and not give it back. This can be due to inadvertent memory leaks or to the accumulation of features loaded into memory as you use the browser. If you notice that your browser runs much faster after you quit and restart it or after you reboot your machine, it's an indication that your browser is hogging memory. There's not much you can do in that case but restart the browser regularly or not load features like Java or the email client.

Multitask

If a page is taking a long time to load, you can open a new browser window and continue browsing in the new window while the old one churns away. In Netscape, use File → New → Navigator Window, or even better, Alt-N.

Stop it

The Stop button can actually speed things up. Hitting Stop will cause Netscape to stop loading and to display what it's got so far, which may be all you need. If you hit Stop and it turns out nothing was loaded, hit Reload and you may find that the server responds much more quickly the second time around. It is possible that the packet containing your request was lost somewhere on the Internet. A major flaw with browsers is the fact that you cannot stop Java from starting once you've begun to download an applet, and you can't do anything else until Java is fully initialized.

Use Java plug-in

There is an ActiveX control and Netscape plug-in called Activator that will download a current and correct Virtual Machine (VM) from JavaSoft. Not only does the plug-in insure that you will consistently have the latest and fully functional VM, but it also solves some performance problems with other implementations of the VM. Netscape has been known to download and instantiate Java classes several times more slowly than IE, but this problem goes away with Activator. See *http://www.javasoft.com/products/activator/*.

Browse in a new window

You can click on a link with both buttons, or perhaps the middle button if you have one, to open the link in a new window. Instead of hitting the Back button, you can then use Alt-W or similar to get the window to instantly go away. This is much faster than hitting the Back button because you need not reparse the previous page, as would happen with the Back button. Also, many pages refuse to be cached even if you tell the browser not to verify document freshness, so actually go back to the server side when you hit the Back button. All of this is avoided by opening links in new windows.

Internet Explorer Tips

The following sections provide tips specific to Microsoft Internet Explorer.

Don't redraw while scrolling

If your machine doesn't have enough spare CPU cycles to keep the images smooth when you scroll in IE, you can turn off smooth scrolling with Tools → Internet Options → Advanced → Use Smooth Scrolling. You will be spared the ugly image of your machine struggling to keep up, and scrolling will feel snappy.

Browse in a new process

If hitting the Back button on IE causes a long delay and always gets the page via modem regardless of whether you told it to get pages from cache, try setting Tools → Internet Options → Advanced → Browse In A New Process. This will start new copies of IE that do not share system resources. The idea behind the option is to isolate IE from your system in case IE crashes, but it may have the side effect of making the Back button work quickly and correctly. Another thing to try is to make sure that Tools → Internet Options → Settings is not set to "Every visit to the page."

Netscape Tips

The following sections present tips that apply only to the Netscape Navigator browser.

Prestart Java

Rather than get stuck watching the Java VM start up the first time you hit an applet, you can ask Communicator to initialize Java with the browser itself by using the command line *netscape.exe -start_java*. This option is not available for the Unix versions of Netscape.

Use fewer colors

If you don't really care about accurate colors in Netscape on a PC, you can use approximate colors for a significant speed gain. On Communicator 3.0, select General Preferences → Images → Substitute Colors. On Communicator 4, select Edit Preferences → Appearance → Colors and check "Always Use My Colors." This doesn't work on the Macintosh or on Unix.

Make smaller buttons

You can save a little bit of valuable screen real estate by showing the buttons as text only. In Netscape, Edit → Preferences → Appearance → Show Toolbars As Text Only. Or, you can eliminate them altogether if you know all the keystroke shortcuts.

Non-Browser Web Clients

Given the simplicity of programming basic web functionality, it is entirely practical to write your own HTTP clients for specific uses. Currently, the most popular non-browser web clients are robots that index the Web for search engines and link checkers that find broken links, but there are an infinite number of possible client programs and devices. See *Web Client Programming with Perl*, by Clinton Wong (O'Reilly & Associates) for examples of Perl scripts that access the Web.

In fact, here is a one-line shell script I use now and then to grab web pages from within other shell scripts:

```
% (/usr/bin/echo "GET /index.html HTTP/1.0\r\n\r"; sleep 5) | telnet patrick.net 80
```

The trick to this script is it sleeps for five seconds, keeping *telnet* around long enough to get a response. If you don't sleep, then the request gets piped into *telnet*, which makes the request, and then exits instantly because its input pipe closed. It exits so fast that it never gets a chance to display the output. Another trick here is that the *echo* command itself will add the last newline (\n) character. Different versions of *echo* do different things, so you may have to study the manpage for your version of *echo* to get this to work. For example, an *echo* on Linux requires the *-e* switch to interpret \r and \n.

Another similar way to get a web page, but requiring a software installation, is to use Stevens' *sock* utility:

```
% echo -ne "GET /index.html  HTTP/1.0\r\n\r\n" | sock -h patrick.net 80
```

sock -h won't work if half-closed connections are not supported.

Yet another way to grab a web page, or even perform an HTTP POST from a shell script, is to use the example GET and POST commands that are installed in */usr/local/bin* with the LWP package. If you have SSL libraries installed, it will automatically use them.

```
% /usr/local/bin/GET http://patrick.net/
```

Then there is *curl*, a small C program that directly grabs web pages and is capable of working with SSL. See *http://curl.haxx.se/*:

```
% curl http://patrick.net
```

Finally, you can also use *netcat*, which requires no timeout and will itself keep the connection open until the entire result comes back. See *http://patrick.net/software/* for a copy of *netcat*.

If you want to strip out all the HTML from a web page you retrieved, here's a line of Perl that does it. The deletion is applied to tags contained in the $_ variable. Note that the key is that we do a "nongreedy" match with the ? character, so that we don't delete the opening bracket of one tag and then everything to the end of the last tag we find, which is the default pattern matching behavior in Perl.

```
s/<.*?>//;
```

The *appletviewer* program that ships with Sun's Java Development Kit loads applets much faster than Netscape or other browsers do, probably because it has no cache to check for previously loaded classes. The *appletviewer* works well with Java *.jar* files.

Gnutella and Peer to Peer

Web clients that use the gnutella protocol are both web clients and web servers, in that gnutella uses the HTTP protocol to retrieve files. When you use a gnutella program, you connect to others who are also using gnutella programs. When you look for a file, your query goes to your closest neighbors, and from them to their neighbors and so on. Once the file is found, you can download it, and then you are a server for that file. The search capability is integrated with the protocol, so there are no search engines that index sites. Sites themselves are transient, so there would be little point in including them in an index. It's a fantastic idea, and has been going by the name "peer-to-peer networking." It won't replace the Web, but compliments it in a way that cannot be easily controlled by corporations or governments. Much of the advice in this book—for example, about operating systems and network protocols—is just as applicable to serving files over gnutella as it is to more conventional web sites.

Another interesting scheme is to let browsers share what is in their cache with other nearby users, avoiding trips to the server side. A company called eMikolo is trying out this idea. Sun is also promoting a Java framework for peer-to-peer sharing called JXTA.

Key Recommendations

- Set the browser to check cache only once per session, or never.
- Increase the memory and disk cache as much as possible.
- Use the latest browser version for HTTP 1.1 and other advantages. Set the browser to load a blank page upon startup.

CHAPTER 12

Client Operating System

The browser doesn't live in a vacuum. The operating system it runs on might have its own inefficiencies that affect the browser's performance. As volumes have been written about optimizing desktop systems, I'm going to touch on only a few points that directly relate to your web browsing performance. A good source for more detailed client performance information is *http://www.speedguide.net/*.

Microsoft Windows

The most effective way to improve the performance of PC hardware running Windows is to erase Windows and install a version of Unix for Intel, such as Linux, Solaris x86, FreeBSD, BSDI, or SCO Unix. Unfortunately, this is not an option for most people because of the complexity of installing an operating system and the need to run applications that run only on Windows. If you have to live with Windows, there are some things you can do to improve browser performance.

System Clutter

Back up your system files, then remove utilities you don't use from your *win.ini* and *system.ini* files. As with eliminating unused Mac extensions, the utilities that are left will run faster.

Specific Video Drivers

A device driver written specifically for your video card should give you better performance and stability than the default VGA driver. Here are some indications that you need a better video driver:

- Changing Control Panel → Display settings causes crashes if you are using particular screen sizes or number of colors but not otherwise.

- Setting Control Panel → System → Performance → Graphics → Maximum Hardware Acceleration causes the machine to crash.

- The browser consistently bombs at certain web sites. This could also be due to a Windows or JavaScript security problem.

You can usually download the correct driver from your video card manufacturer's web site, or from the web site of the manufacturer of the chip on your video card.

Newer versions of device drivers usually give better performance than older versions. Also check to see that you have the latest Windows service packs and TCP/IP stack, called Winsock under Windows. The book *Core Java Web Server* by Taylor and Kimmet (Prentice Hall) includes a bit of sample code in Chapter 2 that you can compile and run to tell you the version of your Winsock. BIOS should also be upgraded every other year or so for BIOS improvements, but your PC will probably be obsolete in two years anyway.

Memory and Disk

Windows disk caching schemes can help or hurt you. On one hand, the disk cache will make most writes to disk appear to be much faster, because the data is not being written out to disk synchronously with the write command, but instead queued up to be written some time later. This is known as "write-behind caching." This was the function of the *smartdrv.exe* line in your *AUTOEXEC.BAT* file under Windows 3.1. Disk cache can also be used to read ahead, anticipating that you will probably want more data from the disk after the current read completes. This is known as *read-ahead* caching and can be turned on in Windows 95 like this: Control Panel → System → Performance → File System → Read Ahead Optimization Max.

On the other hand, some older hard disk drivers delay lower-priority interrupts while synchronizing disk with disk cache. This would be okay, except that low-priority COM port interrupts must be handled before the UART buffer overflows. If the disk has the COM port locked out and data is lost, the data must be retransmitted, slowing perceived network performance. The best solution is to get an updated driver for your disk, but you could also turn off the disk cache for a quick fix of network performance at the expense of disk performance.

Being short on disk space will hurt Netscape performance, as it will have to search around for enough open space to write its cache and work files. Defragmenting your disk regularly with the *defrag* or *scandisk* utilities will help disk performance. You can defragment under Windows 98 and NT like this: My Computer → Hard Drive → Properties → Tools → Defragment Now.

On NT, you can see how much memory you're using by starting the *taskmanager* tool with Ctrl-Alt-Del.

System Monitor

Windows 98 has a useful System Monitor tool that you can use to help pinpoint bottlenecks. To use it: Start → Run → enter "sysmon". Add all of the options, but especially these:

- Memory Manager: Swapfile in Use
- Memory Manager: Free Memory
- Dial-Up Network Adapter: Buffer Overruns

You don't want to see any network buffer overruns. If there are overruns, you are not retrieving data from the UART as fast as it is filling up. This could be due to COM interrupts being starved for attention, an old UART (not likely on anything better than a 386), or the buffer being too small. You can change the buffer size under Windows 98 like this: Start Settings → Control Panel → System → Device Manager → Modem Connection Port Settings → use slider to increase capacity of Receive Buffer. You do want to see a bit of headroom in Free Memory and not too much swapfile in use.

You can detect whether there is noise on your line by looking for Cyclic Redundancy Check (CRC) errors with *sysmon*: Start → Run → enter sysmon → Edit → Add Item → Dial-Up Networking Adapter → CRC errors. You shouldn't see any errors on a reasonably good line.

If your CPU is shown to be overloaded, the solutions are to upgrade to a faster CPU or reduce the number or kind of applications you are running.

Network Utilities

There are a few Unix network utilities available for Windows. Windows 98 and NT have versions of *ping* and *traceroute*. To run *ping*, choose Start → Run → type ping www.someserver.com. *traceroute* is called *tracert* under Windows; run it just like *ping*. There is also a third-party version of *traceroute* for Windows called QuickRoute, from Starfish's Internet Utilities (*http://www.starfishsoftware.com/*). On the Macintosh, use *whatroute*.

MTU

There are programs to adjust your Maximum Transmission Unit available from many places on the Web—for example, *http://www.speedguide.net/Cable_modems/cable_registry.shtml*.

Your optimum MTU is the maximum that can be sent to your ISP without getting a reply that the packet is too big and needs to be fragmented. To figure this out on Windows, you can open a DOS prompt and type this:

```
C\> ping -f -l 1500 www.myISP.com
```

Of course, put in your own ISP. A value of 1,500 bytes will most likely get you an error such as "Packet needs to be fragmented, but DF set." Keep reducing the value until the ping works. Now you know the optimum value for your MTU.

If you are on a LAN, leave your MTU at the default of 1,500 bytes. If you're dialing up and dealing with the Internet, try setting the MTU to 576 bytes. You may see some increased performance due to reduced fragmentation, as described previously in the Macintosh section. See *http://www.sysopt.com/maxmtu.html* for additional information on MTUs under Windows.

Macintosh

Mac users have their own idiosyncrasies to deal with, as the following sections describe.

68K Emulation

Apple's change of CPU from Motorola's 68000 series to the PowerPC increased Mac performance in one way, but hurt it in another. Performance is helped because the PowerPC is a much faster, more modern CPU. Performance is hurt because most of the software available for the Mac was written for the 68K chip and runs on the PowerPC chip only in emulation. Not only the applications but also parts of the Mac OS themselves were left in 68K binary format. There are a few things you can do to minimize the impact of emulation on your performance:

- First, always try to get a native PowerMac version of your browser in preference to a 68K version.
- Second, try replacing the emulator that ships with the OS with Speed Doubler from Connectix, *http://www.connectix.com/*. Connectix also makes a well regarded RAM Doubler product.
- Finally, upgrade to Mac OSX, which has more native PowerPC code and faster and more robust TCP/IP.

Networking

For the best networking performance on a Macintosh, make sure you're using a recent native-binary Open Transport TCP/IP stack. See Open Transport Mac tips at *http://www.go2mac.com/*. Macintosh PPP programs can usually be configured to automatically dial the modem and start PPP when an application such as a browser needs network connectivity. This makes startup a little easier on the user.

Use the Mac TCP Monitor to check whether TCP packets are timing out and retransmitting—that is, if they're being reported as lost when they're really just pokey. Retransmits can happen if you are on a slow connection or if there are errors in the data received. If the TCP Monitor shows retransmits, you may want to set the TCP retransmit timeout higher and see if that helps. If the retransmits are happening because of errors instead of a high-latency connection, increasing the timeout will actually hurt performance.

Another network parameter you can modify is the Maximum Transmission Unit (MTU), which is the largest IP packet your machine will send. You want to limit this to the size of the largest MTU allowed along the route to any particular web server. If you hit a router with an MTU smaller than yours, then your IP packets may be fragmented from that router on, which will slow them down. Try changing MTU in PPP from 1,500 to 576, which is the largest MTU size guaranteed not to fragment. Again, be careful to check performance before and after because this will definitely slow down performance if fragmentation was not your problem.

The MacOS networking code seems to have a threading problem, which can cause a hang when the browser is trying to use HTTP 1.1's persistent connections (also called "keepalives"). There also seems to be a keepalive bug that hangs Netscape Versions 3.04 and 3.05. This is very unfortunate, because it causes some sites to turn off keepalives and give up a large performance improvement.

Memory and Disk

If you've used Netscape on a Mac after using it on Windows or Unix, you may have noticed that the Mac seems to be missing a memory cache in the Netscape configuration options. There is a memory cache for Netscape, but it isn't handled from the Netscape preferences. Rather, it is handled from the Control Panel as a general disk cache, in the sense of caching disk data in memory rather than in the sense of explicitly caching web pages on disk. You want to have a disk cache large enough to improve performance by avoiding a significant number of disk accesses, but not so large that you starve applications of memory and hurt their performance. A rule of thumb is to have about 32K of cache for every 1M of RAM in the computer; so, for example, a 24M computer should have 768K of disk cache. To change the disk cache setting, select Control Panel → Memory → Disk Cache.

Under System 9, Macintosh applications cannot dynamically take memory as they need it as they can under other operating systems; you have to specifically allocate more memory to an application if needed. To find out how much memory is allocated to Netscape and to change it, first make sure Netscape is not running, then select the Netscape icon and click on File → Get Info…. You'll see two values: the minimum size (what Netscape minimally needs to run), and the preferred size (the most Netscape is allowed to have). You can't do much about the minimum size, but if you give a larger preferred size, Netscape may run a little faster. 16 MB is a reasonable value for Netscape 4.0. Mac OS X is faster and more reliable, so you should upgrade to it if you haven't already.

Extensions

Extensions consume system resources, so removing all unnecessary extensions will improve overall performance as well as making boot time shorter. You can turn off all extensions by holding down the Shift key when the Macintosh is booting, but this will also turn off extensions that help performance, such as the Symantec JIT. When you use Netscape to browse a Java-enabled page, Java will start more quickly if you move the Symantec JIT, labelled "Java Accelerator for the Power PC," out of the Netscape folder and into the Extensions folder. This ensures that it will be loaded on startup. Make sure you move it and don't just copy it.

Unix

Any Unix workstation can run a web client, but it is probably overkill to dedicate workstation hardware to web browsing when Macintosh or PC hardware will do just fine. Linux is the most popular version of Unix for commodity PC hardware, partly because it is free along with all of the source code, though Linux is not Unix in a legal sense.

Given identical PC hardware, you can get much better performance from Linux than from Windows, but until recently there has been little commercial software available for Linux because of its origins in the hobby world. Linux does have sufficient software to be a good web client because there is Netscape for Linux and a good Java Virtual Machine as well as all the usual Unix tools that make it relatively easy to figure out exactly what's going on in the system and the network: *top*, *vmstat*, *strace*, *traceroute*, *ping*, etc. Linux is a boon for anyone interested in operating systems.

Here are a few of the things you can do to figure out exactly what is going on in your Linux web client:

- Start *top* and use M to sort all processes by memory usage. Leave it running. You'll probably see that Netscape is your single largest process and that it keeps growing as you use more of its features.

- Leave *netstat -c* running and you can see Netscape open connections as you retrieve web pages. Connections are open when *netstat* says they are in the ESTABLISHED state. The connections should all eventually be closed, except perhaps for connections such as the one to your POP mail server that polls for new mail.

- You can run Netscape with the *strace* command to see all system calls as they are made and understand a bit more of what Netscape is doing. Netscape's performance will probably be unbearably slow while you're tracing it, but it is instructive. You can also get the Netscape source code from *http://www.mozilla.org/*, if you want to try to modify the code to improve the browser's performance yourself.

- You can use *ping* to see what the latency to any given web server is. Most web servers are configured to respond to *ping*. If you *ping* yourself and the latency is significantly over 1 ms, this indicates that you have a poor implementation of IP. Pinging a web server on the same LAN should have a latency under 10 ms. If not, you may have an overloaded LAN or a very poor implementation of IP. If you're pinging a web server across the Internet, anything under 50 ms is good, but latency up to 200 ms is quite normal. When latency gets close to one second, you have a poor connection to that server. The *traceroute* command can tell you at exactly which router things start to slow down. This is useful for detecting the quality of an ISP.

If a server is not responding at all, try using *nslookup* or *dig* on the web server name. It may just be that you can't resolve the name, not that the web server itself is actually down. DNS service, like most Internet services, does not degrade linearly but instead hits a wall at a certain load. You can use *nslookup* with DNS servers outside your own organization, find the correct IP for a site, and then browse by using the IP address in place of the web server's name in the URL. You can even point your machine to the other DNS server permanently if your ISP's DNS server is not satisfactory, but this is rather rude unless you have some explicit agreement with the owner of the other DNS server.

Consider running a DNS server on your own machine. A private DNS server will cache your frequent queries and provide much better response time for those queries. See *DNS and BIND*, by Paul Albitz and Cricket Liu (O'Reilly & Associates) for instructions on setting up your own DNS server.

Use the latest Linux kernel for the latest TCP/IP fixes and speed improvements, but don't feel the need to upgrade more than once or twice a year. Compile in only the drivers you need, and no others. For example, you don't need floating-point emulation on most modern chips, because a floating-point unit is now standard. Compile in the TCP retransmit interval to be one second, if it isn't already. Change the */etc/rc.d/* * files to run as few daemons as necessary.

You can modify your MTU on Linux with the following:

```
# /sbin/ifconfig eth0 mtu 1500
```

Key Recommendations

- Use your OS's tools to tell you if you're running out of RAM or mistransmitting or misreceiving packets, and if the server is up and responding.
- Increase receive buffer size if possible.
- Use the latest and best implementation of drivers and TCP/IP.

## CHAPTER 13

Client Hardware

The client hardware for the Web is mostly standard PC hardware these days. Although there are a significant number of Macintoshes, cell phones, and PDA's, such as the Palm Pilot used for web browsing, the PC is by far the most commonly used hardware platform.

In this chapter, I will concentrate on the components of PC client hardware, because the components differentiate the packages. There is still a great deal of standardization and interchangeability of components at this level, resulting in healthy competition and many price versus performance options.

CPU

The most important thing to remember about web client CPUs is that they're not very important. Web surfing is an I/O-bound activity, not a CPU-bound activity. In any case, PC hardware is almost always overendowed with CPU relative to bus. That is, an extremely fast CPU will probably spend most of its time waiting for the bus to catch up with it. Nonetheless, the CPU frequency and model is what sells the machine, so manufacturers are forced to supply the latest and fastest CPU even if the previous generation of CPU would do just fine for most people. Web access speed is influenced much more by disk and network I/O than by CPU or even bus speed.

That said, there are some reasons to have a good CPU on your web browsing machine. For one thing, HTML and image rendering does take some CPU power. If you use a performance monitor and watch your CPU load while parsing a large HTML page, you'll see that parsing creates a significant CPU load. To prove the load is from parsing and not network access or something else, you can see that the CPU is again heavily loaded when you hit the back button to go back to a large page in memory cache, not touching the network. On the other hand, most web pages are small, so you often don't even notice the time it takes to parse them.

A better reason to buy a client machine with a fast CPU is to be able to run emulated programs as quickly as possible. Your machine has value in proportion to the number of useful programs it can run. In principle, any machine can emulate any other machine, but emulation is costly in terms of CPU cycles because there is rarely a one-to-one mapping of system calls between operating systems, or of machine code instructions between CPUs. If you have a Sparcstation and want to run MS Office, you have to do it in emulation (with SoftPC, for example), and this will slow you down. You can run Mac programs on your Linux machine with Executor. And note that the Power Macintosh runs all old 68K Mac programs in emulation.

As CPUs increase in power, emulation becomes a more realistic alternative to being locked in to any one platform by your applications. The most important sort of emulation for a web client is emulation of the Java virtual machine. Java, by its nature, does not produce native code for any existing CPU, so it requires emulation. The need for this kind of emulation in the future is justification for a faster CPU, even if your native code applications are fast enough for you now. Finally, your graphics performance will be better if you have a faster CPU. VRML, in particular, requires intense calculation in order to run smoothly.

Two clues that you need a faster CPU are silent delays during your work (when you cannot hear disk activity) and a consistently high reading on your CPU monitor program.

Here are some of the things you should look for when buying a faster CPU:

- More on-chip cache, also known as level 1 (L1) cache, helps because L1 cache is directly in the CPU and so has excellent access time.

- A higher CPU clock is invariably better within the same generation of chip, but not necessarily between different kinds of chips. For example, a 800 MHz Pentium II should be faster than a 600 MHz Pentium II, but you can't say right off whether it will be faster than a 600 MHz version of a chip from another generation or another manufacturer.

- Pipelining, when several instructions are simultaneously in various stages of execution, helps because instruction addresses are sequential most of the time. Sequential flow is faster than branching, which takes a cycle and breaks the pipeline, though some CPUs try to do branch prediction so as not to break the pipeline.

- Floating-point units are not particularly important for web clients, but they are included on most CPUs these days anyway.

- Reduced Instruction Set Chip (RISC) CPUs such as the PowerPC or SPARC are generally faster than Complex Instruction Set (CISC) CPUs such as the Intel x86 family, because there are fewer instructions and they are all the same length in bits. This means the RISC CPU design can be streamlined in ways the CISC CPU cannot. The trade-off is that you need more RISC instructions to do what one CISC instruction can do, so RISC executables are slightly bigger, and you need more memory and disk space.

A 64-bit CPU won't necessarily help if all of your software is written for a 32-bit CPU, as most software currently is. 64 bits can refer to a number of things: the size of CPU registers, the width of busses, and the address space size. For the C programmers out there, the address space size is the size of a pointer. CPUs with 64-bit registers can do arithmetic operations directly on 64-bit operands.

Low-voltage CPUs, such as those found in laptops, run more slowly than the same CPU models running at a higher voltage. This is because each transistor on a CPU has a certain capacitance determined by the size of the wires on the CPU. At a higher voltage, the wires fill with electricity and flip the state of the transistor more quickly, just as a garden hose fills with water more quickly if you turn the spigot further. You sometimes hear the phrase "submicron technology," which refers to the size of the wires etched on the chip. At the same voltage, a smaller chip with thinner wires runs more quickly, partly because the sheer physical distances on the chip are smaller, but also because of capacitance. Laptops often use the exact same chip as desktop machines, but at a slower clock speed to save power. All of this also holds for other chips, like memory. The point to remember is performance fights power conservation for a given generation of chip.

The bizarre thing about the semiconductor industry is a given number of transistors in each new generation of chips are not only denser, but also use less power and are faster because of their increased density. They are also cheaper per transistor, because more transistors can be etched into a single silicon wafer.

RAM

More RAM is almost always better, so that you can support a bigger cache and bigger browser binaries; but more RAM won't necessarily help performance if the problem is elsewhere. Use your system's monitoring tools to tell you if you're using all your RAM. If you browse a very large web page on a machine without much RAM, you may crash the browser. This is particularly easy to do on old Windows 3.1 machines with 16M RAM.

RAM in PC hardware usually sits on a fast system bus connected directly to the CPU, not on the EISA or PCI bus. The RAM is arranged in a bank that has as many chips as there are data lines on the bus. During a memory access, one bit is retrieved in parallel from each RAM chip in the bank.

The two principle flavors of RAM are dynamic (DRAM) and static (SRAM), with DRAM being the most common. DRAM must constantly be refreshed, because each bit storage location is, in effect, a tiny capacitor that is always leaking charge. SRAM does not need to be refreshed constantly by some external logic, because each bit storage location is an arrangement of five or so transistors called a flip-flop, which is self-refreshing. DRAM is denser and cheaper because of its simplicity. SRAM is more expensive, but much faster. DRAM multiplexes the row and column address onto the same set of wires, so addresses are asserted in two phases: first row, then column. An SRAM address is asserted in one phase, which is one reason it is faster.

DRAM comes in various permutations. Note that DRAM chips can contain quite a bit of logic in addition to the raw storage. The advertised speed of RAM is how fast the bits are provided to the chip's internal controller logic. It can take as long again to set up the address internally and prepare for a new cycle once the current access cycle is over, so the speed the chip claims is not exactly what your memory bus will see. Each bit is referred to by a row address and a column address. Fast Page RAM allows the controller to start setting up a new row address before the current cycle is over. Extended Data Output (EDO) RAM allows the controller to start setting up new row and column addresses before the current cycle is over. You need a specific kind of motherboard for each kind of RAM. See *http://www.dataram.com/bytes/edo.htm*.

Synchronous DRAM (called SDRAM) is synchronized with the memory bus, is faster than EDO RAM, and is currently the most common kind of memory.

Cache

Note that RAM typically runs at about 70 nanoseconds and can provide data at about 30 Mhz (33 nanoseconds), while all new CPUs run faster than this. Level 2 (L2) cache (which is off the CPU, as opposed to L1 cache, which is on the CPU) is used to bridge the difference, but the utility of L2 cache decreases with multitasking machines like Unix servers, since different areas of memory will be accessed and there will be more cache misses. L2 cache is usually SRAM, which runs much faster (3 to 8 nanoseconds), but is bigger (less dense), hotter, and about 10 times more expensive than DRAM.

Bus

PCs originally had memory on the same bus as everything else, but recent hardware all has a distinct memory bus for increasing memory access speed. Workstations and high-end PCs often have additional busses for I/O.

The memory bus, also known as the external CPU bus, would run best in exactly two cycles: assert address, then read/write data. Unfortunately most RAM is slower than the memory bus, so several wait states, or unused bus cycles, are inserted to give the RAM time to get at its data. Five wait states is quite common.

The ISA and EISA system bus clock frequency can often be increased with a CMOS, or BIOS, setting to some integer fraction (1/8 or 1/10, for example) of the CPU clock speed. If you increase the system bus clock too much, data on the bus will be corrupted and the system will crash, but a moderate increase helps the performance of all cards connected to the bus, such as the disk controller, video controller, and network interface cards.

PCI is now the standard bus in new PCs. It has very good bandwidth and the added advantage of being a cross-platform standard—Apple, SGI, Sun, and DEC all use it, making the resulting card market much bigger. PCI runs at 66 MHz and 132 MHz and is available in 32-bit and 64-bit versions. PCI motherboards often come with legacy EISA slots that allow you to continue using your old cards. See Chapter 16 for more information.

If you're surfing from a local network, the bus can bottleneck your receiving speed. If you're on the Internet, the Internet is your bottleneck.

Disk

The two most important parameters for a client disk are the maximum seek time and the rotation speed. Maximum seek time is the time it takes for the disk arm to move from the edge to the center of the disk surface. This puts an upper bound on how long it will take you to get any piece of data. A maximum seek time of 12 milliseconds is pretty good. Do not confuse maximum seek time with access time, average seek time, or any of the other terms used by disk manufacturers.

The other important parameter is rotational speed. Typical IDE PC disk rotational speed is 4,500 rpm, but SCSI disks run at 7,200 and 10,000 rpm. Maximum seek time is more important for random access patterns, and rotational speed is more important for sequential reads and writes.

IDE

The Integrated Drive Electronics (IDE) interface is a hard disk standard that specifies the connection between the disk and the system bus. It is also known as the AT bus Attachment (ATA) standard. The interface is 16 bits wide and was originally intended for use with the ISA bus. There are now adapter cards that let you use IDE drives on a PCI bus. IDE drives are currently the cheapest and most common option. As of this writing, IDE drives have a transfer rate ranging from 1 MB per second to 20 MB per second and sizes ranging up to 60 GB.

Though IDE has control circuits integrated with the drive itself, a separate IDE controller card is still required. One controller card can handle one or two drives, but if there are two drives, they do not operate independently—only one can be active at any time. If you would like to use multiple IDE drives in parallel for performance, you can do so by installing multiple controller cards, though you would probably be better advised to upgrade to SCSI disks.

There have been many extensions to IDE, such as EIDE and Ultra ATA. Ultra ATA is a standard developed by Quantum and Intel that specifies a faster rotation rate and faster transfers between disk and memory than EIDE.

SCSI

The Small Computer System Interface (SCSI) is a general standard for connecting peripherals to computers. Disks that use the SCSI standard are more expensive and higher performance than IDE disks. IDE disks are inexpensive and have good enough performance to make them a reasonable choice for most client hardware, but you will want SCSI disks for servers. See Chapter 16 for more information on SCSI.

Fragmentation

When the disk gets very full, new files must often be written into whatever open space the disk can find. A file will probably have to be split up, with pieces stored in several places on the disk, making access slow because multiple seeks must be done to read one file. Defragmentation utilities rearrange the files on your disk to be contiguous wherever possible, thus increasing access speed.

Video

Your display monitor is not as important as your video card for performance. Laptop displays are slower than the standard Cathode Ray Tube (CRT), but both are much faster than the video cards that drive them. You want a card with enough video RAM (VRAM), sometimes called Windows RAM (WRAM), to hold your entire display at its full color depth. Your video speed will increase with additional video RAM only up to this point. 2 MB is usually enough, but you can get up to 32 MB.

You can get a feel for your graphics performance by noting how quickly and smoothly you can scroll or drag around a window, or flip between different open windows. Some high-performance video cards currently on the market (for example, the 64-bit Matrox MGA Millennium II and Intergraph's Intense3D) are Accelerated Graphics Port (AGP) cards. Some motherboards have a video controller built in, which makes the computer a little cheaper, but also more difficult to upgrade.

MMX

Intel's MMX CPU instruction extensions do help graphics and video performance, but the software that can take advantage of them is not portable to other CPUs, with the exception of AMD CPUs. MMX's primary mechanism for speeding performance is an on-chip 16K cache for graphics. A good video card will give you a similar or even larger graphics performance boost.

Colors and Resolution

Video card manufacturers like to brag that their cards can display millions of colors, but they're ignoring the fact that the human eye cannot distinguish that many and the calculations to display the colors are a drag on performance.

Eight-bit color (256 colors) is satisfactory for most web browsing, but doesn't display photographs well. For a high-quality display, you need 16- or 24-bit color. If you run multiple applications simultaneously and have only 8-bit color, you may run out of video card buffer space for your color map. This may force one application or the other to use nonoptimal colors, or to give up its color map when it is inactive, causing a flashing effect.

Resolution, the number of pixels on your screen, is more important than colors. Computer screen resolution is nowhere near the level of the human eye, so improvements are very noticeable. You may get better performance with lower resolution, but the speed is usually not worth the loss of image quality. At this point, 800×600 pixels is a minimum standard for web browsing.

Manufacturers often quote screen size in diagonal inches rather than pixel density. This is misleading: size is nice, but a larger display of a low-resolution image does not make it any more pleasant to look at.

You can change the number of colors and sometimes the video resolution with your computer's configuration utilities. Sometimes this also requires you to move jumpers on the motherboard. Jumpers are little links between two pins that can be moved around to configure the machine.

Drivers

As with disk drive drivers, the latest video drivers are recommended. Some video cards from S3 and other vendors will gain graphics performance by interrupting your CPU and using spare CPU cycles while you're not busy. However, this can keep your CPU from servicing COM interrupts and can result in overrun buffers, lost packets, and ultimately, worse network performance. Good video drivers, such as those from Number Nine, will give you the option to turn off cycle-stealing.

3D and Video Clips

You rarely need a 2D or 3D video accelerator card for surfing the Web. The exceptions are when you're trying to play interactive games via the Web, browsing VRML, or using a video conferencing application. This may change if Internet bandwidth increases enough to make heavy visual content practical. AGP cards provide a faster and wider data path for graphics applications like these.

Video Card Benchmarks

Some popular video card benchmarks include Cbench, Wintach 1.2, VidSpeed 4.0, SpeedMark, and Xbench for Xfree86. Cbench (short for ChrisBench), is intended to measure the speed of DOS games.

I/O Port

The I/O capacity of PC hardware is small relative to that of dedicated server hardware, but sufficient for web browsing. When a web browser makes a request, it simply asks the OS to forward the request to the remote server. The communications part of the OS—Winsock or your TCP/IP—stack, makes a connection to your serial (COM) port if you're using a modem, or to your network card. The chip that controls your serial port is called a Universal Asynchronous Receiver and Transmitter (UART).

The UART

The UART is a buffer with some logic for talking between the (usually RS-232) modem connection on the one hand and the system bus on the other. To continue forwarding a web server query, the OS signals the UART to listen to the bus, then forwards data. The UART reads the data off the bus and signals the modem that it has data to send. The modem accepts that data and eventually is ready with a reply from the web server. It begins to write this into the UART, which generates an interrupt request (IRQ) asking for the OS to come and get the data.

So far, so good, but a problem arises: some older PCs have UARTs like the 8250 or 16450, which accept only one byte before demanding service through an IRQ. The CPU may be busy dealing with a higher-priority interrupt, while the modem continues to accept and pass on data at whatever rate you've set for the serial port. The result of an IRQ service delay is UART buffer gets overwritten before the CPU has a chance to read it. The network routines in the OS find that the data does not match the associated checksum of the link layer (probably PPP or SLIP) and ask for the data to be retransmitted. This slows down your perceived network access speed. One-byte UARTs can handle up to ISDN speeds if your OS is doing very little else, as in the case of DOS, but a Windows machine with a one-byte UART will probably find itself limited to 14.4 kbps or lower.

One solution to serial port overruns is to slow down the serial port setting—the rate at which the machine tells the modem it can accept data. This may give you better data integrity and fewer retransmits, but faster network access is our goal here. A better solution is to use a machine with a newer UART, like the 16550A. The 16550A can hold 8 to 16 bytes in its buffer, giving the OS more time to deal with the IRQ. A PC with a 16550A or better should be able to handle even 500 kbps if the OS's network code is efficient. It is difficult to upgrade the UART on a motherboard because it is usually soldered in place, but you can use an internal modem for a similar performance boost, because internal modems come with a UART on the modem card itself.

BIOS

The Basic Input Output System (BIOS) is the lowest level of software on your PC. It is also called the CMOS, after the kind of chip that stores the BIOS settings (Complementary Metal Oxide Semiconductor).

Hardware Compression Can Increase Overruns

Remember that modems often use hardware data compression by default unless you tell them otherwise. The modems think they're helping you out, but an old UART may be overwhelmed because it is reading two or three bytes of compressible data, such as text, for every compressed byte transmitted by the modem. This may be confusing if you think you've set the serial port rate low enough for your UART. Again, the best solutions are to upgrade the UART or to use a newer PC with a better UART.

The BIOS is the first thing that starts when you turn on the computer. It consists of three main parts: the Power On Self Test (POST), the interrupt handlers, and the system options. The POST is run immediately when you switch on the computer, and it checks that the CPU has access to memory and that the video card, disk drive, and other components are installed correctly. It also installs some basic interrupt handlers, such as one for the keyboard. If the right key combination is pressed, the BIOS will run a program that allows you to change system options. This key combination is different for different BIOSes, such as Phoenix BIOS and AMI BIOS. On my laptop, I can get into Phoenix BIOS by pressing a special key. With AMI BIOS, hold down the Delete key while booting; with some other machines, press Ctrl-Alt-Insert. See your computer's documentation and the web site of the BIOS maker.

There are some things you can do with your BIOS to get better performance. Set CPU speed to "fast" if that's an option. Enable the floating-point unit (FPU) and all caches. Lower the number of wait states for memory or bus to speed memory access. You probably wonder why these settings are not enabled by default; the answer is stability. If you push your machine harder with all of these settings, it may crash more frequently because you've crossed the hardware's physical limits of performance. Since these settings are in the BIOS, you are assured that you can at least boot far enough to change them back if they are a problem. If your BIOS doesn't have many options, you can install utilities that will give you more. See *http://www. sysopt.com/bios.html*.

Another useful BIOS option is Resume mode, especially on laptops. Resume mode usually dumps the state of RAM to the hard disk and then restores it on power-up, saving a great deal of boot time. Also note that using BIOS to configure the hard disk to spin down after a period of inactivity will give you longer battery life, but will insert annoying delays if the disk is off and you try to run or save something that requires the disk. On the Macintosh PowerBook, you can control many of these things through the control panels. For example, Control Panels → Powerbook → Better Performance will cause the disk to wait longer before spinning down.

Key Recommendations

- Don't worry about getting the latest CPU.
- Buy PCI bus rather than ISA or EISA.
- Buy enough RAM that you rarely need to swap.
- Buy a SCSI disk rather than IDE.
- Use a PC or modem card with a 16550A UART or better.

## CHAPTER 14

Lines and Terminators

In this chapter, I'll cover the various kinds of lines and terminators at each link in the chain between client and server, pointing out when higher-speed connections are worth the investment, and suggesting how you can get connections to work better.

A line is a connection between two points. Every connection segment on the Internet is composed of a physical line made of metal, optical fiber, or simply space, as well as a pair of terminators, one at each end-point. The physical properties of the line put theoretical bounds on the performance of the line, but the terminators determine the low-level line protocol and, ultimately, how close you can get to that theoretical maximum performance. The copper telephone line most people use to connect to their Internet Service Provider (ISP) is bounded by two modems, although there is a telco switch in the middle. At the ISP, there are probably two Ethernet cards connecting a modem bank and a router. The router feeds a T1 bounded by two CSU/DSUs. And so on.

Millions of web surfers curse their local lines and modems because of slow access, but their wrath is, in part, misdirected. Even with infinite throughput to their local ISP, web surfing would not be incredibly fast. The bottleneck would simply move to the ISP's access point; if you could defeat that bottleneck, it would move to the closest Network Access Point (NAP), which is where ISPs exchange packets. The Internet as a whole, on average, gets a point-to-point throughput of only about 50 KB per second. And remember that most servers are not connected to a backbone, but dangle off an ISP several layers down the tree of connectivity.

You can see the law of diminishing returns in action if you upgrade web client access from 28.8 kbps to ISDN and then to cable modem. The 28.8 kbps to 128 kbps ISDN increase is impressive, but the 128K ISDN to 500K cable modem increase is not as noticeable, though much larger in absolute terms.

Forwarding and Latency

Every physical line has at least the latency imposed by the speed of light, but most latency on the Internet is caused by the number of terminators and connection points, such as routers, that the bits must pass through. The fewer the termination and decision points, the lower the latency. In particular, you want few connection points where the medium or speed is different between the two sides of the connection.

The interface between lines of two different speeds or protocol types is a choke point. A packet on a slow line cannot instantly be forwarded bit by bit onto a faster line, because the data is always kept in packets in which all bits are adjacent to one another in time. A packet must be received in its entirety before it can be forwarded onto the higher-speed interface. This adds latency. The same story is true for converting protocol types, such as Ethernet to token ring. The moral is to have as few connection points as possible, and to use as few protocols and as few different speeds as possible. The lowest latency comes from a direct connection between the browser and the server, but this is rarely possible.

Your Modem, the Information Driveway

Analog modems convert a stream of digital data into an audio-band analog format that can be sent over Plain Old Telephone Service (POTS) to another analog modem. (The telephone network is also sometimes referred to as the Public Switched Telephone Network, or PSTN.) The increases in modem performance of the last few years have come as modem makers learn to cope better with the difficulties imposed by sending digital data over a quirky analog system.

POTS was built and optimized for voice traffic. There are filters in the phone system that amplify the portion of the audio spectrum humans hear best (300 Hz to 3300 Hz), at the expense of other frequencies. There are also filters for echo cancellation. Many phone lines have poor quality. The analog data is sampled at 64 kbps, losing some information, and is sent in digital form to the remote phone switch, where it is reconstructed into analog form (see Figure 14-1). All of these voice-oriented characteristics of the phone system present problems to modem manufacturers, but modem performance has risen to near the theoretical maximum of 64 kbps imposed by the switches with the current generation of 56 kbps modems. For speeds beyond 64 kbps, the data signal must bypass the phone switch analog-digital-analog conversion or bypass the phone switches altogether, which is how DSL works.

Modems usually send bits by altering the state of a carrier signal of a given frequency. The carrier's signal state varies by combinations of phase and amplitude. Note that the actual rate at which distinct states can be transmitted (the baud rate) has not increased appreciably from earlier modems, but clever encoding schemes have increased the number of possible states so that more bits can be encoded in each baud. For example, V.32 modems send one of 64 distinct states with each state change, so each state encodes 6 bits ($2^6 = 64$). V.32 modems run at 2,400 baud, so $2,400 \times 6 = 14,400$ bits/second can be sent. V.34 modems run at 3,200 baud, but send 512 distinct states, so each state encodes 9 bits ($2^9 = 512$). V.34 modems can therefore send $3,200 \times 9 = 28,800$ bits/second.

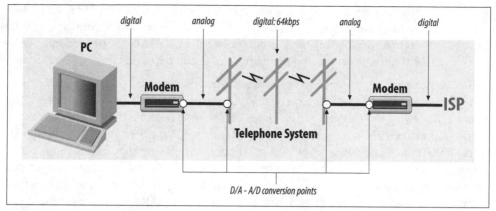

Figure 14-1. Signal conversions with modem use

There is often confusion between baud and bits per second, because in early modems they were the same number. That is, early modems, up to 2,400 bits per second, transmitted only one of two possible states at any moment, corresponding to a single bit.

Latency and Throughput, Modem to Modem

Modem latency is high relative to the latency of a purely digital Internet connection, even an Internet connection through several routers. I made a simple test to confirm this. A *ping* between two machines directly connected by modems in the same city took 160 milliseconds, while a *ping* between two machines connected via digital links from one coast of the U.S. to the other took 120 milliseconds, even though it went through eight routers. The latency is distributed between the phone system, the transport encoding, and the modem itself, but the point is that any use of a modem imposes a small, but noticeable, latency penalty.

Make sure your modem's throughput is the same or better than your ISP's modems' throughput. Most modems can interoperate with lower-speed modems, so you can buy a modem better than your ISP's modems, use it now, and be ready when your ISP upgrades. There is a catch: 56K modems are not all mutually compatible, so you may buy a 56K modem and not be able to get 56K even after your ISP upgrades. Even if the modem is compatible with your ISP's modems, you may still only get about 45 kbps because of poor line quality. However, 33.6 kbps modems run at the rated speed more reliably.

Getting Synchronous

Modem bandwidth is limited not only by the protocols and line quality, but also because the connection is asynchronous, so transmission can begin whenever there is data to send. To give the other side a demarcation of valid data, modems by default send an extra 2 bits per byte to mark the start and stop bits for that byte, so 10 bits are transmitted for every byte of data. A 14.4 kbps modem's maximum throughput of data is therefore 1,400 bytes per second, rather than 1,800 bytes per second. Analogously, a 28.8 kbps modem has a throughput of 2,800 bytes per second, and so on.

This overhead of 20 percent can be avoided through the use of Link Access Procedure for Modems (LAP-M) or one of the Microcom Network Protocols (MNP). By using LAP-M or MNP, an entire PPP frame can be sent continuously, with no start or stop bits between the bytes. Of course, the modems at both ends of the phone call must understand and agree on which protocol to use. Note that LAP-M and MNP happen in the modem, so the serial port will actually see the rated modem speed without any 20 percent penalty. This means that turning on one of these options will increase the load on the serial port, and could result in UART buffer overruns if the computer was only marginally able to handle the load before.

Hardware Compression

Another commonly available modem option is hardware compression. This is compression done by your modem hardware rather than by software in your computer prior to sending the data to the modem. Hardware compression is most useful for large transfers and for text, which is highly compressible. Remember that not all files are compressible, so there is no guarantee you'll see any benefit from turning on hardware compression. Hardware compression is usually part of one of the MNP options.

Error Correction

Modems are now clever enough to deal with noise on the telephone line by slowing down the baud rate and/or using simpler state encoding symbols, rather than repeatedly asking for retransmission of damaged data or giving up altogether and ending the call. They are also clever enough to increase the transmission rate when the phone line gets cleaner.

Remember that modems know only that they are sending blocks of raw data to each other. The fact that you are sending an HTTP request wrapped in a TCP segment wrapped in an IP packet wrapped in a PPP frame is unknown to the modem. PPP frames are checked for errors once the data percolates up into the IP socket connection, but this takes a relatively long time to happen, and PPP's only option on error is to ask for the whole frame to be retransmitted. It is much faster to have the modem correct an error, if it can.

V.42 modems have built-in error correction that should be left on. If you turn it off, you'll have more PPP frame check errors. On a good phone line, you may not notice that it's off, but on a noisy line, this may be enough to cause the modem to hang up.

Disable Xon/Xoff flow control, also known as software handshaking, because it uses characters in the data stream itself to start and stop transmission. This is the cause of many situations in which transfer stops, for no apparent reason, because a flow control character happens to be in a binary data stream. Enable RTS/CTS flow control, or hardware handshaking, if your ISP supports it. This happens faster and does not offer the opportunity to confuse data with flow control instructions.

Line Quality

You can sometimes tell that you have a noise problem on your phone line by listening to what ought to be silence during a phone call. If it's clearly not silence, you may have a problem. You might have some luck getting your local telephone company to improve it if you complain; then again, you might not. Local phone companies are, after all, still monopolies for now. (Other performance tuning tips: pay attention to the FCC rules, and write your congress person asking for more competition.) Of course, the problem could also be the wire in your house, which you have to pay to repair. Hanging up and redialing—that is, rebooting the phone—often helps.

You may see a CONNECT 14,400 message when you have a 28.8 kbps modem—for example, if you are connecting over a noisy line. The rate can vary as the modem adapts to the line noise. Your modem control program should have an option to tell you exactly what throughput you're really getting and whether there are Cyclic Redundancy Check (CRC) errors. CRC errors imply line noise. A strange number (not one of the standard speeds, 14.4, 28.8, etc.) below your modem's rated speed also implies that you are dealing with noise. If you are getting a lower number than what is one of the usual modem speeds, then your modem may have dropped to a lower rate to compensate for noise, or you may have simply dialed in to a lower-speed modem.

If you have an external modem, it is connected to your machine via an RS-232 modem cable. Modem cable is not all alike. Capacitance makes some RS-232 cables suitable for high-speed modems, and some less so. If you are using a 14.4 kbps modem or better, you need a high-speed cable. If you use a slow cable, you will see many errors and retransmits.

Internal Modems Are Faster

Internal modems have several performance advantages if you are willing to go to the trouble to open up your computer and install one. There is no RS-232 cable involved, so you can't pick the wrong cable. The modem will have its own UART or will emulate one, so you don't have to worry about having an obsolete UART. Finally, internal modems are directly on the bus, so there is less latency in moving bits between the modem and the computer.

There are also parallel port modems that connect to your printer port. You need to install a software driver to use them, but they also have less latency than an external serial port modem.

UART Buffer Overruns

The UART chip that controls your machine's serial port has a FIFO buffer of probably eight bytes, which must be cleared before the UART can accept any new data. If your machine does not clear the UART data in the time it has told the serial port it would, data will be overwritten and lost, resulting in PPP frame check errors and costly retransmits. The modem's error correction can't help you here—it's already done its job in delivering data to the UART.

The cause of UART overruns is the failure of the computer to get the data from the UART's buffer in time. How long does the computer have? The UART assembles a byte as the bits arrive, then pushes the byte into the FIFO buffer. Say that you have a 28.8 kbps modem. It therefore takes 1 sec/28,800 bits $\times$ 8 bits = .28 milliseconds to receive one byte. This sounds like a very short time, but remember that a 33 MHz bus could go through 33 million $\times$ .28 $\times$ 10^{-3} = 9240 bus cycles in that period, and it should take only one bus cycle to move a byte from the UART to the bus. Starting from an empty buffer, your computer has eight bytes worth of time (2.2 milliseconds) to come and get at least one byte before an eight-byte buffer wraps and begins to overwrite data. So it's not much of a challenge for a lightly loaded PC to retrieve data from the UART.

The ultimate origin of UART overruns is usually an interrupt request (IRQ) from a poorly written disk drive driver or video driver that monopolizes the CPU. The trick is to know when your communication problem is due to an overrun and not to line noise. If it is a driver problem, you probably need a new driver. Fortunately, the UART itself knows when an overrun has occurred, because it can detect when data is unloaded from the buffer. In the case of an overrun, a flag will be set in the UART's status register, which can be read by your Winsock or other networking software. The networking software, in turn, should have a mechanism for notifying you of overruns. If you see a PPP frame check error and no overrun, the problem is likely to be line noise. If you see a PPP frame check error with an overrun, the problem is likely to be a poor device driver or even poor networking code, which can be fixed only by upgrading the drivers or the operating system.

AT Commands and Dialing Time

If you use a Hayes-compatible modem, try setting the S11 register lower than the default value of 70 milliseconds. 35 milliseconds often works just fine, and cuts the dialing time in half; that may not be a huge improvement, but it is noticeable. Use the modem AT command ATS11=35. Similarly, you may be able to get away with starting to dial after only 1 second of waiting for a dial tone, rather than the default of 2 seconds; use ATS6=1. Neither of these options is guaranteed to work with any particular modem or local phone line.

Bonding Channels

You cannot do much about the latency inherent in using modems, but it is possible to get better than 56K throughput by using multiple analog lines in parallel. This is called bonding channels and requires that both ends have multiple modems and the correct bonding software. Diamond Multimedia (*http://www.diamondmm.com/*) sells its Shotgun product, which bonds two 56K analog modems to 112K. Ramp Networks' WebRamp M3t lets you multiplex three modems. Of course, you then need three phone lines, but this may still be cheaper and more reliable than ISDN.

ISDN

Integrated Service Digital Network (ISDN) provides an entirely digital connection between your home and the phone company switch, so there is no loss of data in an analog-to-digital conversion. This allows you to get the full 64 kbps that the phone system uses internally for transmitting voice data.

An ISDN modem looks and acts quite a bit like an analog modem, but dials and connects very quickly (often in under 1 second) and makes no noise. It is possible to run a web server from ISDN and save connection fees by having your ISP dial your modem and set up a connection to a web server at your home when anyone surfs to a web page at your IP address. This adds a noticeable delay for the surfer, however, and is nontrivial to set up. ISDN is customarily provided as two "B" channels of 64 kbps each that can be bonded into one 128 kbps channel. There is no loss of start and stop bits because the connection is synchronous, so the actual throughput can be 16,000 bytes per second. Some telcos provide only 56 kbps B channels because they use one bit out of eight for error correction or synchronization.

A direct ISDN connection from home to your LAN at work does provide enough bandwidth that it feels distinctly better than any analog modem. Video conferencing, for example, is much more reasonable over ISDN than over analog modem. If you can make a local toll-free ISDN call to the same ISP that your employer uses, and your company allows Internet access to the LAN (perhaps with a password), you should also get very good throughput and latency because your packets will remain within your ISP's private network rather than being routed over random points on the Internet. It takes a bit of detective work to find out your company's ISP (use *traceroute*), whether the ISP has a local dial-in number near you (use the ISP's web page), and whether an ISDN call to that number is a local toll-free call (use the front of your phone book).

A significant disadvantage to ISDN is that it is still not available everywhere and is not well supported. In fact, even if your local telco offers ISDN, their service representatives may know nothing about it. This happened to me: I called the information number and asked if ISDN was available. The service representative had never heard of ISDN, and asked me to spell it. Hmmm. I spelled it. Then I was asked what it stood for. I said, "I Still Don't kNow." The representative seemed satisfied with that, and asked for some time to find someone who had heard of it. I eventually got a call back and was told the service was available.

The setup was very hard because only certain brands of ISDN modems work with the particular kind of switch your telco has in its local office. Furthermore, once you have found out what kind of switch your telco has—for example, a 5ESS—and you've found a modem that is supposed to be compatible with it, you still need to configure many parameters on the modem. Worse, the telco switch also has to be configured for the service, and you need the help of someone at the phone company central office switch to do that. Once it was finally configured correctly, the ISDN performance was good, but I would not recommend ISDN where any other option for high-speed access is available.

Cable Modems

High-speed access over the same coaxial cable that brings you cable TV is a good alternative to ISDN. Installation is usually simple: your cable company provides you with the cable modem, and will probably install it. It's a very simple box that takes a coaxial connection in one side and provides you with an Ethernet connection on the other side. There are no user-configurable parameters. Most cable modems use the same Rockwell chip set, so if you have to buy one, it may be portable to other cable modem service areas. You need to configure your computer to use the IP address the cable company gives you, but you have to do that with most ISPs, anyway.

The downstream bandwidth is usually better than 384 kbps, which is excellent, and especially nice if you are getting data from a fast server close to you in router hops. You'll be ahead of the average speed of the Internet; you will still hit bottlenecks, but now the bottlenecks will not be at your connection. Upstream bandwidth is usually around 100 kbps, which is sufficient for a small web server. There are no connect-time charges, and there is not even an on/off switch on the modem. It is always on when plugged in.

A disadvantage is that your connection is shared with your local neighborhood. An area with many busy users will give you lower performance. There is also nothing to stop your neighbors from snooping on your IP packets, if they are so inclined, since you are all effectively on the same LAN. Finally, cable modem is available only in a few areas as of this writing, but services such as @Home (*http://www.home.com/*) are expanding rapidly, after a long period of indecision on the part of the cable companies. Pricing is inconsistent, and you may pay anywhere from $30 per month to $100 per month for the exact same service.

xDSL

The physical characteristics of the copper lines that run into your home are not what limit the speeds you can achieve via analog modem. The limiting factor is the conversion into a 64 kbps stream at the telephone company switch. What if you could bypass the telephone switch and hook directly into a digital line at the telco office? ISDN does this, but it connects to a 64 kbps digital line, which is not a vast improvement over 56 kbps modems. A direct connection to a digital line into the Internet from the other end of the pair of copper wires in your home sets apart Asymmetric Digital Subscriber Line (ADSL) and its cousins, grouped as xDSL.

xDSL speeds vary, but 1.5 Mbps downstream and 128 kbps upstream are common numbers. This is faster than cable modem. xDSL is now widely available. You may have to get two accounts to use it: one with your telco, and one with the ISP that has an agreement with your telco to place its xDSL equipment at the telco's local Central Office (CO).

You can get an idea of your actual DSL bandwidth by using the online tests at *http://www.dslreports.com/stest*.

Higher Capacity Lines

Here is a brief overview of the high-speed connectivity options for web servers, each with its own kind of router or switch and termination hardware. These options are all overkill for a simple web surfing client. See *Getting Connected*, by Kevin Dowd (O'Reilly & Associates), for a detailed explanation of these kinds of lines.

56K, T1, and T3

You can get a direct digital connection between your home or organization and your ISP through special services provided by your local telco. These direct digital lines typically come in speeds of 56 kbps, T1 (1.544 Mbps), and T3 (45 Mbps). You can also get a fraction of a T1 or T3 and upgrade it later via a software switch in the Central Office.

A 56K dedicated digital line might seem useless since there are 56K analog modems, but remember that the 56K line is more reliable, less subject to noise, and synchronous, so there is less overhead per packet.

T1 and T3 are synchronous serial lines, so no overhead is wasted on start bits. Actual throughput can be very high, better than 90 percent of the rated capacity, and latency is very low. The downside to these lines is they are expensive. It is common for a T1 connection from you to an ISP in the same city to cost $1,000 per month. Long-distance T1 connections cost much more.

Frame Relay

Frame Relay is a packet switched wide area networking protocol. It provides a virtual point-to-point connection called a permanent virtual circuit (PVC). Frame Relay is a far more cost-effective option than a long-distance T1 line, because with Frame Relay, the long-distance hardware of cable is shared among many customers, though customers see only their own packets. Customers thus have virtual circuits to themselves.

Frame Relay is an unreliable protocol, meaning there is no guarantee that packets will arrive on time, or that they will arrive at all. It is up to higher layers of software to ask for retransmits of missing packets. This is transparent to the user in a well-managed ISP.

Frame Relay has built-in prioritization of Committed Information Rate (CIR) packets. Frame Relay generally has good price per performance, especially for the long haul between the U.S. and abroad, but that's often because it's under utilized. When a carrier fills up their capacity, performance drops. Judge Frame Relay service on the packet drop rate, regardless of the CIR, because a high drop rate will make the CIR irrelevant.

ATM

Asynchronous Transfer Mode (ATM) is a packet switched protocol with quality of service (QOS) guarantees. Actually, ATM does not switch packets per se, but rather fixed-length (53-byte) cells. ATM routing equipment does not have to calculate the length of the cell, and the cells are short; both factors contribute to ATM's very low latency capability. Voice and video services can be provided over ATM links without fear that some data will be arbitrarily delayed.

ATM is often run over copper at 16 Mbps and is also used over optical fiber. Common fiber speeds are Optical Carrier 3 (OC3), which runs at 155 Mbps, and OC12, which runs at 622 Mbps. These options are expensive, but they have the advantage that you can buy a fraction of what you need and quickly get more bandwidth from your provider when you need it without waiting for additional lines to be installed. It often takes weeks to get a T1 line installed, but only minutes to get an equivalent increase from your ATM provider.

Satellite

There are various services available via satellite. Asymmetric web client services require a modem connection to request pages, which are then received via a satellite dish at 1 Mbps or so. Symmetrical services are expensive, but may be cheaper than dealing with government phone monopolies in poor countries.

Satellite services always involve considerable latency because of the sheer distances involved, but low earth orbit (LEO) satellites can have one-tenth the latency of the much higher orbit geosynchronous satellites. The disadvantage to LEO satellites is that they regularly move out of range, so there must be provisions for handing off the signal to another satellite in the group. Geosynchronous satellites remain positioned over one spot on the earth. See *http://www.intelsat.int/* for more information on symmetrical satellite services.

Intranets

An intranet is a TCP/IP network within an organization. Intranet planners have the luxury of having much more control over the network and client software than is possible on the Internet. This control makes it possible to guarantee a better quality of service and to use available bandwidth more efficiently, so that time-critical applications like streaming audio or video run smoothly.

Partitioning

You can't randomly expand an intranet forever without overloading some parts. You will start to need a hierarchy in your network. The general rule is to keep the machines that frequently talk to one another close together in the network, preferably on the same IP subnet, where communications will be fastest. See Chapter 12 in *Managing NFS and NIS* by Hal Stern (O'Reilly & Associates) for more details on partitioning networks.

When deciding where to place a web server on your intranet, consider whether it will be accessed by the outside world as well as from inside your organization, and who has priority. If you have two distinct sets of web content, one internal and one external, you should run at least two web servers, perhaps two virtual servers on the same machine.

Web servers that talk to the Internet should have their best connection be to the Internet, but if internal users are also sharing that connection for email and Usenet traffic, for example, then outside web surfers may be starved for network bandwidth. A full duplex connection to your ISP helps to mitigate this, since your internal users have mostly inbound traffic, while external users have mostly outbound traffic. If you have many internal Internet users, or plan to provide essential services to the Internet community via your web server, you should consider a dedicated Internet connection for the web server, even if it is lower in bandwidth than the connection your organization uses for outbound access. Place the web server outside your firewall and try to minimize traffic (such as database access) across the firewall. Two gateways to the Internet often work better than one gateway with twice the nominal capacity.

If you're forced to share one connection for an important web server with other traffic, or if external access to your web server is swamping an internal LAN, the four Ps for dealing with the problem are policy, prioritization, proxies, and partitioning:

- Tell users what sort of traffic is acceptable by policy.
- Use one of the traffic management products below to prioritize packets so the most important ones get through.
- Set up a proxy web server where the connection comes into your organization.
- Be sure to place the internal web server on a segment that does not have much broadcast traffic or NFS traffic.

Hardware for Partitioning

The hardware boxes that break up your LAN into segments and connect you to the Internet all add latency to traffic, so don't use them gratuitously. Here's a quick summary:

Repeaters
Repeaters extend the effective length of a cable and do not partition at all. They repeat whatever you put on them, with bits sharpened and amplified.

Bridges
Bridges contain a table of local MAC-layer addresses such as Ethernet addresses, and they forward packets that don't belong to any local machine to the next network over. This allows easy segmentation of Ethernet traffic, but bridges aren't suitable for large-scale networks because they use broadcasts for all dynamic configuration, which would flood a large network with configuration packets.

Hubs
Hubs also repeat, but they repeat out to multiple machines, creating a network structure that looks like the hub and spokes of a wheel. The network interface card of every machine attached to the hub will see all of the traffic. This can be a security problem, because any host on the hub can snoop all of the traffic. Hubs are intrinsically half-duplex, meaning that they cannot send and receive at exactly the same time.

Switches
Switches are like hubs, but make a momentary connection between exactly two machines. They can do this simultaneously between multiple pairs of machines, so they can achieve much higher throughput. Switches have much better security than hubs because other machines cannot snoop conversations. Switches are also smarter than hubs, often running Cisco's IOS operating system, while hubs usually have no operating system or statistics available. Switches that give access to control and statistics remotely are called "manageable" switches. Switches can be full duplex, transmitting and receiving simultaneously.

Routers

    Routers divide networks by IP network number, the next higher level of protocol. You can put multiple NIC cards in a machine and force it into router duty with the appropriate software, but you'll get better throughput and latency from purpose-built routers.

There is some information about routers later in this chapter, but a detailed analysis of performance issues for all these network devices is beyond the scope of this book. See *Managing IP Networks with Cisco Routers* by Scott Ballew (O'Reilly & Associates) for more information.

One critical issue with network devices is matching IP Maximum Transmission Units (MTUs) between different protocols. For example, if you are routing from Ethernet to token ring, FDDI, or ATM, you will deliver IP packets more efficiently if they do not need to be fragmented at this boundary—that is, if the MTUs match. FDDI has a larger default MTU than Ethernet (4,500 bytes rather than 1,500 bytes), so packets originating on FDDI may get fragmented when they hit Ethernet. Any protocol conversion has some overhead, so you should avoid conversions that you don't absolutely need. See "IP" in Chapter 15 for more information about MTUs.

Ethernet

Ethernet is currently the dominant LAN medium. Most installed Ethernet is 10baseT Ethernet, which runs at 10 Mbps—but 100 Mbps Ethernet is increasing rapidly. The general Unix *ifconfig -a* command will usually show 10 Mbps Ethernet as interface le0 and 100 Mbps Ethernet cards as hme0 or be0. Under NT, use *ipconfig*.

Ethernet cards are now cheap commodity items, and Ethernet is easy to set up, but it has a significant drawback. Because Ethernet is a shared medium, multiple machines can begin to transmit at the same time, resulting in collisions. The algorithm Ethernet uses for retransmits is to back off for a random amount of time on the first collision, but for an exponentially larger, but still random, amount of time with each subsequent collision that occurs when trying to send the same packet. This works quite well for light loads, but causes throughput to degrade dramatically above 70 percent utilization (see Figure 14-2), so you should consider 10 Mbps Ethernet to have a maximum throughput of 7 Mbps. You can monitor Ethernet collisions under Linux, Solaris, and some other versions of Unix with the *netstat -i* command.

The minimum packet length, or more properly, frame length, for Ethernet is 72 bytes, so there is quite a bit of overhead for interactive sessions, in which individual characters are sent with 71 bytes of overhead as they are typed. This is not a problem with web transmissions, in which data is returned in relatively large chunks that can fill the default frame size of 1,500 bytes.

On the other hand, Ethernet frames are always 1,500 bytes. If you send anything out of a webserver on Ethernet, it will be put into a 1,500-byte frame. And if you're

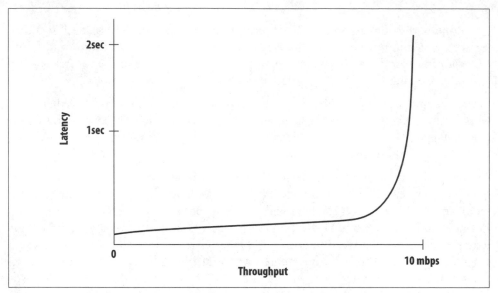

Figure 14-2. Ethernet latency versus throughput

receiving something from on Ethernet, say from the router to you, again it will always be put into a 1,500-byte frame. This is very different from PPP on a modem, in which the lower limit is 1 byte.

The 1,500-byte fixed Ethernet frame size lets you easily use *rstat* to calculate how much of your Ethernet you're using. Ignoring the interframe gap, on a 10 Mbps network, the highest Ethernet frame count per second you could ever see is 833. On 100 Mbps Ethernet, it's 8,333 packets per second.

Note that 10 Mbps Ethernet is normally half-duplex, meaning traffic can flow in only one direction at a time, while 100 Mbps hme0 cards can autodetect the speed of the card on the other end and do anything from half-duplex 10 Mbps to full-duplex at 100 Mbps. It is quite common to find that one side of an Ethernet connection is configured for half-duplex, while the other side is configured for full-duplex. The result is poor performance, though the connection works. Most 100 Mbit Ethernet cards seem to be configured for half-duplex by default.

To configure full-duplex Ethernet in */etc/system* on Solaris you would enter these settings and reboot:

```
set hme:hme_adv_100fdx_cap=1
set hme:hme_adv_100hdx_cap=0
```

Packet Snooping

An Ethernet card will, by default, discard packets that are not addressed to its globally unique MAC address. There is also a "promiscuous" mode, however, which looks at all packets on the LAN, regardless of destination. Solaris comes bundled with the *snoop* tool, which is very useful for placing an Ethernet card into promiscuous mode and unwinding the layers of protocols around packets. You must be *root* to run *snoop*. It lets you see that the Ethernet holds an IP packet and that the IP packet holds a TCP segment, and will even show you the data contents of the packet. Here's an example *snoop* of a browser's HTTP request going to a proxy server:

```
# snoop -v -x 0
ETHER: ----- Ether Header -----
ETHER:
ETHER: Packet 4 arrived at 11:33:12.22
ETHER: Packet size = 337 bytes
ETHER: Destination = 0:60:5c:f3:71:57,
ETHER: Source = 8:0:20:7b:87:4c, Sun
ETHER: Ethertype = 0800 (IP)
ETHER:
IP: ----- IP Header -----
IP:
IP: Version = 4
IP: Header length = 20 bytes
IP: Type of service = 0x00
IP: xxx. .... = 0 (precedence)
IP: ...0 .... = normal delay
IP: .... 0... = normal throughput
IP: .... .0.. = normal reliability
IP: Total length = 323 bytes
IP: Identification = 27865
IP: Flags = 0x4
IP: .1.. .... = do not fragment
IP: ..0. .... = last fragment
IP: Fragment offset = 0 bytes
IP: Time to live = 255 seconds/hops
IP: Protocol = 6 (TCP)
IP: Header checksum = 450d
IP: Source address = 10.15.6.126, guest
IP: Destination address = 10.15.19.32, webcache.patrick.net
IP: No options
IP:
TCP: ----- TCP Header -----
TCP:
TCP: Source port = 38685
TCP: Destination port = 8080 (HTTP (proxy))
TCP: Sequence number = 1844000715
TCP: Acknowledgement number = 1830043605
TCP: Data offset = 20 bytes
TCP: Flags = 0x18
TCP: ..0. .... = No urgent pointer
TCP: ...1 .... = Acknowledgement
TCP: .... 1... = Push
TCP: .... .0.. = No reset
TCP: .... ..0. = No Syn
TCP: .... ...0 = No Fin
TCP: Window = 8760
```

```
TCP: Checksum = 0xe027
TCP: Urgent pointer = 0
TCP: No options
TCP:
HTTP: ----- HyperText Transfer Protocol -----
HTTP:
HTTP: GET http://patrick.net/ HTTP/1.0
HTTP: Proxy-Connection: Keep-Alive
HTTP: User-Agent: Mozilla/4.02 [en] (X11; U; SunOS 5.6 sun4u)
HTTP: Pragma: no-cache
HTTP: Host: patrick.net
HTTP: Accept: image/gif, image/x-xbitmap, image/jpeg, image/pjpeg, */*
HTTP: Accept-Language: en
HTTP: Accept-Charset: iso-8859-1,*,utf-8
HTTP:
  0: 0060 5cf3 7157 0800 207b 874c 0800 4500    .`\.qW.. {.L..E.
 16: 0143 6cd9 4000 ff06 450d 8199 067e 8196    .Cl.@...E....~..
 32: bf20 971d 1f90 6de9 37cb 6d14 3fd5 5018    . ....m.7.m.?.P.
 48: 2238 e027 0000 4745 5420 6874 7470 3a2f    "8.'..GET http:/
 64: 2f70 6174 7269 636b 2e6e 6574 2f20 4854    /patrick.net/ HT
 80: 5450 2f31 2e30 0d0a 5072 6f78 792d 436f    TP/1.0..Proxy-Co
 96: 6e6e 6563 7469 6f6e 3a20 4b65 6570 2d41    nnection: Keep-A
112: 6c69 7665 0d0a 5573 6572 2d41 6765 6e74    live..User-Agent
128: 3a20 4d6f 7a69 6c6c 612f 342e 3032 205b    : Mozilla/4.02 [
144: 656e 5d20 2858 3131 3b20 553b 2053 756e    en] (X11; U; Sun
160: 4f53 2035 2e36 2073 756e 3475 290d 0a50    OS 5.6 sun4u)..P
176: 7261 676d 613a 206e 6f2d 6361 6368 650d    ragma: no-cache.
192: 0a48 6f73 743a 2070 6174 7269 636b 2e6e    .Host: patrick.n
208: 6574 0d0a 4163 6365 7074 3a20 696d 6167    et..Accept: imag
224: 652f 6769 662c 2069 6d61 6765 2f78 2d78    e/gif, image/x-x
240: 6269 746d 6170 2c20 696d 6167 652f 6a70    bitmap, image/jp
256: 6567 2c20 696d 6167 652f 706a 7065 672c    eg, image/pjpeg,
272: 202a 2f2a 0d0a 4163 6365 7074 2d4c 616e    */*..Accept-Lan
288: 6775 6167 653a 2065 6e0d 0a41 6363 6570    guage: en..Accep
304: 742d 4368 6172 7365 743a 2069 736f 2d38    t-Charset: iso-8
320: 3835 392d 312c 2a2c 7574 662d 380d 0a0d    859-1,*,utf-8...
336: 0a
```

While this is interesting and may show you some unexpected kinds of load on your LAN, you can also send the output to */dev/audio* (turn down the volume first) for continuous feedback on the activity of your LAN. *snoop -a* will do this, or you can simply redirect *snoop* output to */dev/audio* using your shell. It's kind of fun to leave it on and hear the patterns of various kinds of activity.

snoop is good for looking at, capturing, or listening to collections of packets, but it can drown you in data. *snoop* does not give statistical output or characterize your traffic patterns, such as excessive retransmits. For this, you need to use network sniffing hardware (Sniffer is a trademark of Network General) or one of the many LAN analyzer software packages such as Sun's traffic program. Solaris' *netstat -s* provides summary data: look at the number of bytes retransmitted relative to the total number of bytes sent. SNMP tools also characterize network traffic.

Do not snoop from the machine that is also being snooped, or you will see your recursive output explode as your own snoop output gets snooped as well!

The freely available *tcpdump* program does many of the same things as *snoop* but does not seem to unwind packets.

NIC Buffers

Like serial port cards, Ethernet Network Interface Cards (NICs) have limited buffer sizes. Ethernet cards have far larger buffers, because they are accumulating data at a much faster rate. 8-bit cards tend to have 8 KB buffers, and 16-bit cards tend to have 16 KB buffers. Ethernet is serial, so bits enter the buffer one at a time. Whether a card is 8-bit or 16-bit refers to how many bits it can transfer from its buffer to the system bus in one bus cycle. This is much less important than buffer size because the bus can empty the NIC buffer very quickly.

At 10 Mbps, Ethernet can fill an 8 KB buffer in (1 sec / 10×10^6 bits) $\times 8 \times 1024 \times 8$ bits/byte = 6.6 milliseconds. This is a bit more leeway than the 2.2 milliseconds that we calculated it takes to fill an 8-byte buffer from a 28.8 kbps modem. Remember that Ethernet packets are 1,500 bytes by default, so an 8 KB buffer can hold only 5 complete packets.

Your OS may reserve a part of your NIC buffer for outgoing data, leaving you a smaller buffer for receiving data. As with modems, problems arise because the computer may not be able to get the data from the card's buffer before more data arrives, resulting in costly retransmissions. Your alternatives for eliminating this problem are better device drivers, a faster machine, better TCP/IP implementation, or simply a NIC card with bigger buffers.

See *http://www.spade.com/* for more information on NIC buffer sizes.

Fast Ethernet

Fast Ethernet is the same technology as Ethernet, only 10 times faster, or 100 Mbps. This alone reduces collisions, and improves performance under heavy loads. Gigabit Ethernet, which runs at 1 Gbps, 10 times the rate of fast Ethernet, has now appeared (see *http://www.yago.com/*). FDDI is an alternative that is very similar in performance to fast Ethernet.

A web server showing greater than 20 percent Ethernet collisions should be connected to its router to the Internet via fast Ethernet. But the downside to fast and gigabit Ethernet is cost. You have to upgrade both NICs and hubs.

Switched Ethernet

An Ethernet switch is a lot like a hub, only better (and more expensive). With switched Ethernet, all packets are held in a buffer at the switch until the connection to the destination is open. The time waited is usually very small, and the time saved in avoiding a collision is relatively large. The destination may try to send a packet back out to the switch at the same time the switch is forwarding a packet on to that destination, resulting in a collision, but it is at least guaranteed that there will be no inbound collisions to any destination on the LAN. For this reason, switched Ethernet gives large performance gains over ordinary Ethernet segments connected via a hub. Another reason for improved performance is that multiple machines on the same segment can simultaneously talk to one another, which is not possible on a hub.

Allowing 20 percent for packet overhead, assuming each transfer is 10 KB and ignoring switch latency, a switched Ethernet connection between a client and web server has a theoretical potential of $.8 \times 1$ HTTP transfer/10,240 bytes $\times$ 1,250,000 bytes/second = $\sim$100 HTTP transfers/second.

One problem here is that multiple clients on the switch may be contending for the same web server. If the web server is on the same speed segment as several clients simultaneously trying to get at it, most of the performance advantages of a switch are lost. The solution here is to put the web server on a 100 Mbps segment if the clients are all on 10 Mbps segments. Many switches can handle having some segments at higher speeds than others.

Ethernet switching is often called "layer 2 switching" because Ethernet corresponds to layer 2 of the OSI network model. Layer 3 switching is really just fast routing at the IP level, often with special route lookup hardware rather than the traditional software lookup. See *Computer Networks* by Andrew Tannenbaum (Prentice Hall) for more information on the OSI network layers.

Ethernet Cabling

Keep in mind that electrical cables effectively transmit signals up to only a certain cable length because of capacitance, which is essentially the rate at which the cable fills with electricity. If your cable is too long, a high-frequency signal will smear, and you'll lose packets. You can use repeaters to get around cable-length limitations to some degree. For Ethernet, you can use only four repeaters between any two nodes; more may increase the transit time beyond the maximum time of the packet to live.

Category 5 (Cat 5) unshielded twisted pair (UTP) works well up to 100BaseT Ethernet. Cat 5 has more twists per foot than Cat 3 cable. UTP performance is slightly better if you use the pair that are twisted together as a send/receive pair. Ethernet can act like an antenna and send or receive signals inadvertently. Gigabit Ethernet may not work well over Cat 5 cable, because it uses all four pairs of wires in the cable rather than two pairs, leading to more electrical cross-talk. Because of this problem, the first specification for gigabit Ethernet is for optical fiber. Another hazard is connectors that have a lower rating than your cable and therefore generate a high number of errors. The coaxial "thicknet" variety of Ethernet cable is now obsolete.

Check to see that Ethernet connections are matched up—for example, full-duplex 100 to full-duplex 100. Mismatches may work, but at low performance.

Noise

Improper termination of Ethernet lines will cause reflection noise that will hurt throughput. Other causes of reflections are kinks or sharp bends.

It is also easy to destroy LAN performance by running the Ethernet cable in drop ceilings next to fluorescent lights, which generate a lot of radio-frequency noise. If you have a walkman and know of a store with a neon sign, turn on the walkman and get near the neon light. You'll hear a loud hum, because the sign is acting like a radio transmitter. I once met a system administrator who inadvertently clipped Ethernet cable to the antenna line of a dispatch radio system in the office. While anyone was transmitting by radio, Ethernet performance would drop to zero. Avoid large power cables for the same reason; if your computer monitor is showing a distorted image in one part of the office but is okay in another part, you may have a power cable running in the wall or through a pillar.

Noise not only garbles valid messages, but can also cause spurious interrupts that the computer assumes are signal data. When the computer tries to get the message, it hears only nonsense.

Network Modeling Tools

You can play out various intranet configuration scenarios with network modeling software to see if your proposed web server location will have a significant impact on your LAN traffic. Three such network modeling products are Cisco's NETSYS (*http://www.netsystech.com/*), Mil3's OPNET (*http://www.mil3.com/*), and Optimal Networks' Optimal Application Expert (*http://www.optimal.com/*).

The Internet

The Internet is intrinsically less predictable than well-characterized private networks because it was built by a heterogeneous group with many different motives, budgets, and technical skills. This is not to say you can't make some good assumptions about the throughput and latency of the Internet based on physics, the behavior of the components, and past experience.

While the latency of the Internet can be arbitrarily high, it has a fixed lower boundary given by the speed of light. The minimum latency for any information to travel 2,000 miles, for example, is (1 second / 186,000 miles) × 2,000 miles = 10.8 milliseconds. So even under the best possible circumstances, say a direct 2,000-mile ATM link over optical fiber, you're going to have at least 10.8 ms of latency. Remember that you'll have to send a request before getting a response, so the latency between the start of the request and the start of the response will be double that, even with infinitely fast processing time at the server. The amazing thing is that a *ping* across the country shows that the Internet is operating fairly close to the theoretical maximum, frequently only 30 ms or so from one coast to the other.

If you want to get a feel for the latency of your connection, run a Telnet session over a long distance. Be sure the Telnet server puts the session in character mode rather than line mode. In character-mode sessions, each keystroke is echoed across the link. In line mode, the client data is sent only when the client hits the Return key. Line mode, of course, has a much better feel to it, but it limits you to sending and receiving entire lines so you cannot use applications such as *vi*, which react to individual keystrokes. Line mode is also more efficient: the minimum IP overhead per packet is 42 bytes, so you're going to send 41 times as much overhead as data when sending single characters across a character-mode line.

In addition to the latency imposed by the speed of light, each router also injects several milliseconds of latency because it has to receive your data to a buffer before it can decide what to do with it. So the fewer routers you go through, the better. In addition, small cells impose less latency, because they can be received in their entirety and forwarded in a shorter amount of time. This is one reason why all of the national ISPs backbone connections are switched ATM, which uses 53-byte cells, rather than routed IP using variable-length packets. If you know where your customers are, you can reduce the number of routers on the path by choosing a close ISP, as described later in this chapter. One millisecond of router savings is worth about 200 physical miles of distance. Packets pick up the performance characteristics of the worst link in the chain from source to destination; if you have fewer links, you have less chance of producing delinquent packets.

Keynote Systems is in the business of measuring actual Internet performance from many different points and has published very interesting findings on its web site (*http://www.keynote.com/*). They have found that on the average, the Internet delivers web data at about 50,000 characters per second, or 400,000 bits per second for any single point-to-point TCP connection. Remember that this is only an average, and furthermore, this average is dragged down by the large number of users on slow (that is, modem) connections. You will still see a client-side performance improvement from a 500 kbps cable modem because web sites close to you, or on high-bandwidth connections to you, will have better throughput than the 400,000 bps average. Cities served by poor Internet infrastructure have slower access, as expected. Keynote reports that some of these cities (as of January, 1998) are Phoenix, Dallas, Houston, Kansas City, and Miami. CompuServe, CWIX, and SAVVIS offer the best backbone performance because they are relatively obscure and uncrowded national providers. Internet performance improves on holidays, when most people are not surfing. Packet loss in the Internet itself (not losses caused by an inadequate TCP retransmit timeout) is about 10 percent. You can check this with *ping*, which reports packet loss statistics.

There are some attempts to document the overall state of the Internet in graphical form at *http://www.mids.org/weather/* and *http://www.internetweather.com/*. They are Internet "weather" reports documenting latency in a graphical way or over many different ISPs. There are also statistics on routing performance and latency at *http://www.merit.edu/ipma/*. Note that the IETF is working on standards for measuring performance of the Internet itself. See *http://io.advanced.org/IPPM/* (though ironically the availability of this URL is spotty). Merit has some analysis of Internet performance statistics at *http://www.merit.edu/ipma/analysis/*.

Bypassing the Internet

The joys and pains of packet switching are displayed on the Internet. On one hand, the Internet is very cheap relative to a circuit-switched call, for which you're charged in whole-minute increments but latency and throughput are guaranteed. On the other hand, you have to share the bandwidth, so your packet has to wait its turn. Low cost and shared bandwidth lead inexorably to a wait. What happens when an ice cream shop is giving away samples on the street? A big crowd forms and you have to wait a long time to get it, even if it's free.

The Internet is not the ideal solution to all communication needs. If the uncertainty and delays of the Internet are not acceptable, and you control both ends of the connection, you still have the option of renting a private dedicated line, or simply making a phone call. A 56 kbps modem connection back to the office LAN is acceptable for many uses. You can also buy long-distance, dedicated TCP/IP service, but this is expensive.

NAPs

Network Access Points (NAPs) are points where large ISPs exchange traffic with one another. NAP is a poor acronym, because the "network access" part sounds like a place where ISPs get access to something larger, when in reality, it is simply a place where each ISP exchanges traffic with its peers, though some peers are better connected than others. NAPs put the "Inter" in Internet: without exchange of traffic between ISP's private networks, you have, well, private networks.

Note that the backbone lines and routers of the Internet are all owned by individual ISPs. NAPs interconnect the ISPs with one another via high-speed Ethernet and FDDI switches, and help them maintain routing tables. Other Three-Letter Acronyms (TLAs) for NAP are MAE (now Metropolitan Area Exchange, originally Metropolitan Area Ethernet) and FIX (Federal Internet Exchange). The MAEs are all run by Worldcom, which recently merged with UUNet. Here are the major NAPs:

- CIX, the Commercial Internet Exchange.
- FIX West at NASA's Ames Research Center in Mountain View. FIX West is directly connected to MAE West.

- Genuity's NAP in Arizona.
- MAE Chicago.
- MAE Dallas.
- MAE Los Angeles.
- MAE New York.
- MAE East in Washington, D.C. (also handles incoming European connections).
- MAE West in San Jose (also handles incoming Pacific Rim connections).
- PacBell NAP in San Francisco.
- Sprint's NAP in Pennsauken, NJ.

Where do NAPs come from? In the early 1990s, WorldCom and a few ISPs like Metropolitan Fiber Systems (MFS) arranged to exchange traffic for their mutual benefit. In 1993, the National Science Foundation paid to have its NSFNet connected to this hub in Washington, D.C. This was the beginning of MAE East.

Because NAPs are very crowded and busy, they tend to lose packets and to introduce delays. By some estimates, they lose about a third of all packets at peak times. This is one reason that communication within a single ISP is usually faster than communication that crosses ISPs, even if the two ISPs are in the same city. ISPs have no control over how NAPs are run or what hardware and software they use, and they have to pay a large fee for interconnection privileges.

Most traffic may go through NAPs, but there is no law that says it has to. Any ISP can set up a peering agreement and hardware to connect to any other ISP or other private network. This gives both parties independence from the NAPs' and the major ISPs' backbone lines. If almost all of your users are on AOL, for example, get a direct connection into AOL. Some ISPs, such as InterNex, have aggressively pursued redundant connections. InterNex connects to 6 major carriers and 90 other ISPs at the time of this writing.

ISPs

Choosing an ISP carefully can make a huge difference in performance. You might consider the location of the ISP and also several other factors that determine whether the ISP can deliver adequate performance for your needs.

Placement

If you're running a web site, your principal weapon in dealing with network hardware owned by someone else is deciding where to position your servers on the Internet. You want two things from a position: proximity (topological and physical) to your customers and big available bandwidth.

Being topologically close to your customers means that there are relatively few routing hops between you and them. Remember that the Internet is a tree; you want as few branch points as possible between you and the target for minimum latency.

If you have customers or telecommuters who are using the Internet for access to your server, you definitely want them to be on your ISP, if possible. If your ISP has no local access points near your users, the next best thing is to find them an ISP that connects to the same upstream ISP or NAP as your ISP. Or, of course, you can move your server to their ISP. You can do a *traceroute* to yourself to find out how many routers separate any two points and what sort of latency they are introducing.

If your users are scattered nationally, you will probably do best with a national ISP like Netcom, MCI, or Sprint. See *http://nitrous.digex.net/* for cool lists of who's connected to which NAP. Figure 14-3 shows a map of ISPs and their connections to the Internet backbone.

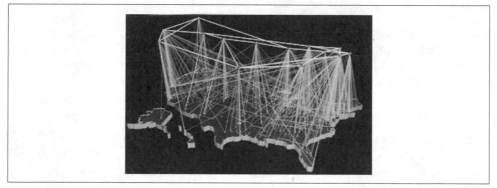

Figure 14-3. ISP connections to Internet backbone

There is an occasional hazard associated with being on the same ISP as your customers, though. Sometimes your ISP will be overloaded, and the fastest possible route will be to use another ISP for a few hops. This is sort of like taking side streets to get around a traffic jam. Unfortunately, routing packets manually, or *source routing*, is not allowed for security reasons, and the ISP's equipment will not even think of routing your packets elsewhere if it sees that both origin and destination are on its network. This means you will get stuck using a slow route sometimes. That's the way things work right now.

ISP performance

The economics of the Internet, where ISPs buy lines and higher-level access at a flat rate and then sell flat-rate access, means that ISPs have an incentive to oversell their services, at least until the point where customers are so unhappy with the performance that they begin to leave. At peak times, in particular, access may be very poor.

Before you blame the ISP, consider that ISPs are forced to oversell; otherwise, they could not offer rates competitive with other ISPs that also oversell. Airlines overbook flights for the same reason. Furthermore, an ISP can comfortably oversell by a large margin before customers begin to notice. Your ISP may have a single T1 to its upstream provider and turn around and sell 15 or so T1s to customers, yet still provide them all with satisfactory bandwidth. This is because most users need access only for short and randomly scattered periods of time. The ISP is providing a service by aggregating packets. You will get much better throughput by sharing a T1 to a major backbone than by having a dedicated connection with one-fifteenth of the bandwidth.

If you really want guarantees of performance, you have to pay for them. The ISP can guarantee only the performance of its own network, but this may be good enough if your audience is on the same ISP. If you're very serious about performance and have a lot of money, you can get a direct, unshared connection to a major ISP or even a NAP.

There are no good, comprehensive statistics on ISP performance. There are only scattered statistics as users publish them. Even if comprehensive statistics were available, they would have to be constantly updated, because usage patterns shift and ISPs upgrade hardware and connections.

Choosing an ISP

So how should you choose an ISP? There are many things to look for. First of all, ask the ISP how they're doing. Asking for the statistics lets them know that you're paying attention and they should be able to provide you with the information. How big is the provider's network backbone? How many users are there, and how many times oversold is the upstream connection? Exactly what is their connectivity to an upstream provider or NAP? Can you get statistics from that provider? How many packets do their routers drop, and what percentage is this? Be sure to cover both incoming and outgoing lines. Also look for outage reporting. See Chapter 3 of *Getting Connected*, by Kevin Dowd (O'Reilly & Associates), for a numerical method of evaluating your ISP. Also see Appendix B of that book.

You would ideally like a first-tier ISP to have ATM backbones and redundant connections to the NAPs. Be aware that an ISP's claim of FDDI to the local NAP really doesn't mean much to you if the ISP's network backbones are much smaller than that. You'd like a second-tier ISP to have peering agreements with several other ISPs, or multiple connections to first-tier providers. A good proxy cache is also a plus, because it reduces the load on your server. (AOL has a proxy that caches frequently requested pages and gives those pages priority over pages not in the cache. This is good for popular pages, but bad for pages that are rarely hit. You can "seed" the proxy simply by getting an AOL account and spidering your way across your site from the account.)

You can get some feel for the performance of your current ISP by looking in your modem program or TCP/IP tools for timeouts and retransmits. If there are a lot of timeouts, you'll also notice that Netscape itself will time out frequently and give you an error message when you try to connect.

One questionable thing ISPs may do to save money is have many dial-in POPs (Points of Presence), which are really just forwarded lines that get around tolls by keeping each forward distance within a local toll-free limit. The end result is that your call may be bounced through several switches before getting to a computer that's actually connected to the Internet, increasing latency and reducing the quality of the line, and therefore of throughput.

The performance of other ISPs can affect you even if you don't use them at all. If AOL's mail system crashes, so many messages for AOL users may back up on your ISP's servers that they crash too, cutting off your access. No ISP is an island.

Co-location and mirroring

Many companies now provide server-hosting facilities. The cost can be steep, but the benefits are also large. You can offload all the worry of keeping the server and connection up, and concentrate on content. These co-location companies usually have excellent connectivity to the local NAP, redundant connections, and backup power, and also provide mirroring to other parts of the country or the world.

For example, GlobalCenter (*http://www.globalcenter.net/*) has a 100 Mbps connection to the NAP in San Jose and mirroring locations on the East Coast and in London. It hosts Yahoo!, Playboy, and part of the Netscape site on racks of Sun and SGI servers. It has a diesel generator on-site for backup power.

Routers

Every router injects latency into the path a packet takes, because a packet must be received and its destination address examined before it can be routed on its way. Fast routers may add only 1 or 2 milliseconds, but slow routers can add 10 milliseconds or more. Router latency can easily be more significant than the latency imposed by sheer distance.

Old workstations used as routers may have fine bandwidth, but they will have much worse latency than purpose-built routers. Not only should you have purpose-built hardware routers, but you should also get the fastest routers you can afford. Hardware routers don't have to deal with most of the tasks of regular OSs, such as managing multiple users and tasks, so they can be optimized for the one thing they do. Hardware routers have better buffering, more efficient interrupt handling, and busses specialized for moving data from one interface to another. For most routers, the bottleneck is not CPU power, but the bus traversal when copying data between the different interfaces. Even though hardware routers are expensive, as hardware goes, they are actually quite cheap per port if you buy a router with many ports.

You can prioritize some kinds of traffic (like Telnet traffic) at the router level. This is a kind of traffic shaping like that done by the dedicated boxes described in the "IP Traffic Management Products" section in the Appendix. Cisco Systems Internetwork Operating System (IOS) 11.1 for its routers explicitly gives the ability to tag certain IP packets as higher priority than other packets, helping to give some sessions better quality of service and leaving the remaining sessions whatever bandwidth is left over. Some routers also have useful tracing features that help you optimize router use.

IP switching (layer 3 switching) has recently become popular. The name is a little misleading: IP switching isn't really switching at all in the sense of setting up a temporary dedicated connection. IP switches still produce packets that share the line with other packets. IP switching is basically route table lookups in hardware using special-purpose chips rather than software. IP switches are 2 to 3 times faster than conventional routing. See *http://www.ipsilon.com/* for more information.

Link-level compression in routers does not necessarily bring any advantage, because the compression is usually done in software, putting an additional burden on the router's CPU. For heavily loaded routers, this compression load may decrease performance more than the compression increases it. You'll have to experiment to see if it works for you.

Packet size has a very big influence on the CPU power needed for routing. According to Craig Partridge, in his book *Gigabit Networking* (Addison Wesley), a 486 PC can usually route 1 Gbps of 1 KB packets, but it cannot route the same bandwidth of 128-byte packets. This is because the CPU is primarily occupied in determining where to send the packet, not in the actual sending. Large packets amortize the processing time over more data.

Check out the freeware Multi Router Traffic Grapher by Tobias Oetiker at *http://www.mrtg.org/*. It uses SNMP and freeware plotting to generate real-time graphs of router traffic viewable over the Web.

Placing Blame

It is possible to figure out more or less who's to blame for slow external network performance. If network performance varies considerably between day and night, the problem is likely to be the greater congestion of the Internet as a whole during the day. Remember that different parts of the U.S. and the world vary in Internet infrastructure, so you will see different performance depending on where you are. See *http://www.keynote.com/measures/business/business40.html*.

There's a very cool trick for figuring out whether the problem is with your ISP or with a remote web server's ISP. Say you're getting poor download speed from a remote web server. Try simultaneously loading another remote web site in another copy of the browser. If your modem control program or network tool tells you that you're getting better total throughput when you simultaneously load from a different remote web server, then it's clear that your ISP had some room on the wire to send more packets to you, and the bottleneck is not in your ISP but in the over-loaded remote web server or router along the path. If simultaneously loading from another remote web site makes no difference in throughput, then your ISP is at fault and you should complain (or you've reached the maximum throughput of your local connection). Be careful to start the experiment with empty caches.

If *traceroute* is not available, *ping -sRv <host>* on Solaris (or *ping -Rv <host>* on Linux) will report the route to and from the machine in question.

The Future of the Internet

There are at least two alternative Internets being built right now to try to correct some of the deficiencies in the current system. Merit, at *http://www.merit.edu/*, has a lot of information on the latest happenings.

Internet2

Internet2 is a consortium of educational institutions that are building a network to include definable and measurable qualities of service, including latency and jitter specifications, bandwidth interrogation and reservation capabilities, and packet delivery guarantees. See *http://www.internet2.edu/*.

NGI

The U.S. government's Next Generation Internet (NGI) will also have very specific goals for service quality. The NGI will connect research institutions with high-speed networks that are one hundred to one thousand times faster than today's Internet and use the latest networking technologies.

PTTs

In some parts of the world, the phone company is a national monopoly called the PTT (Post, Telephone, Telegraph). Don't expect much from a PTT. Dealing with a PTT in some countries, both poor and rich, is like going back in time. There may be only rotary service, or even operators with patch cords. It may take many months, or even years, to get an ordinary phone line, and it is likely to be more expensive than in the U.S. It's ironic, but you can get a high-performance PC almost anywhere on earth, though more than half the world population does not have access to a tele-phone and has never made a telephone call. The situation is changing, as cellular infrastructure is being installed in many poor countries because it is cheaper and more flexible than installing land lines.

Key Recommendations

- Use the best modem that matches your ISP's modem.
- If on an Ethernet LAN, buy a card with 16K buffers or bigger.
- Use an ISP close in hops to your most-visited sites, like work.
- Use your employer's ISP if you will be accessing the employer's web site frequently, or dial in directly to the office LAN.
- Buy a real router rather than pressing an old workstation into service.
- Dedicate an Internet connection to your server. Don't use the connection for browsing, system management transmissions, or system administration traffic.
- Remember that you must have good data integrity to get good bandwidth.

## CHAPTER 15

Network Protocols

Power and Protocols

Let's take a minute to consider the politics of protocols, because politics are more likely than performance to determine which protocols are actually used and which remain only theoretical.

Protocols have value in proportion to the number of users: a widely used protocol gives you the desirable ability to communicate with a large number of people. So when a protocol has enough users, it tends to attract even more users. Let's call this the snowball effect, because a simple snowball thrown down the side of a mountain can grow to be an avalanche. The snowball effect doesn't take into account whether the communications protocol is high performance. Just being able to communicate at all with huge numbers of people is valuable. This is exactly what happened with HTTP. It's not a particularly efficient protocol, but it has provided great value through its ubiquity.

Open protocols are at the core of the Internet and the Web. TCP/IP, HTTP, HTML, Java, and CORBA are all open protocols. There are many competing definitions of "open" that serve the needs of the parties doing the defining. I say a protocol is open if the complete specification is publicly available for use or implementation at no cost. Open protocols tend to spread faster than closed protocols because they add nothing to the price of software that uses them. Open protocols were essential to the development of the free Internet software that gave rise to the Web. Paying even a small price for software is always a barrier to acceptance, if only because of the overhead involved in making the payment.

Open protocols also tend to benefit the end user more than closed protocols do, because multiple compatible implementations of the protocol compete in quality, performance, and cost. For example, because no one owns the HTTP protocol, there are many different web servers and clients, which vary in both price and performance; the efficiency of these implementations has been increasing. Another critical factor in the success of HTTP is its simplicity. The most common cause of death among open protocols is sheer bloat and complexity. All of these protocols, with the exception of CORBA, are relatively simple and have excellent prospects for the future.

If open protocols benefit users, why do we still have closed protocols? One reason is that businesses are motivated not by user benefit, but by money. There is a huge monetary incentive to be the sole person to implement a successful closed protocol, while it is much harder, though not impossible, to make money from an open protocol. Many open protocols come out of government research projects because these projects are not usually profit-oriented. The incentive to remain closed comes from the possibility that the closed protocol may snowball into a worldwide de facto standard. If this happens, the sheer ubiquity of the protocol will force users to purchase the implementation to communicate, increasing the company's market domination still further. Eventually, everyone will have to purchase the implementation, regardless of its quality. This is not good for users, but it is great for business.

Still, closed protocols are not all bad: centralized control assures that the protocol will not fragment into incompatible dialects. If you consider that operating system APIs are actually protocols for communication between applications and operating systems, then you can see that this fragmentation is exactly what happened with Unix. Unix has better performance than Windows, but Unix vendors tried to distinguish themselves with proprietary features that made it impossible for any one application to run on all versions of Unix. That is, it became impossible for Unix applications to communicate with other Unix operating systems, although the situation has improved with the widespread use of the Posix standard. Windows became a monolithic success partly because there was exactly one API; however, that has now changed with the introduction of the various flavors of Windows.

Java is an interesting twist on this situation. The Java specification (except for J2EE) is publicly available at no charge, and others are free to reimplement it from this specification, yet the specification remains the property of Sun Microsystems. Customers can be assured that the Java specification will not fragment, but they don't have to worry that they will be trapped into using only one implementation. On the other hand, Sun retains quite a bit of power because it can extend Java in ways favorable to itself. This seems to be a good compromise between open and closed protocols.

In the larger sense, the story of communication protocols is really nothing new. The English language is an example of how an open protocol can benefit its originators. The British imposed English as the official language in their colonies around the world. Now that English is the most widespread business language, it continues to snowball in market share because it is valuable for communication. The British (and Americans) still benefit from this, as they can travel and do business widely without learning another language. What's new with the Internet is the speed with which protocols can propagate.

Factors Affecting Network Protocol Performance

Network protocols have a combination of properties that affect their performance. Most of the properties are discussed in Andrew Tannenbaum's book, *Computer Networks* (Prentice Hall) and are discussed in the following sections.

Fixed- Versus Variable-Sized Packets/Cells/Frames

You can build more efficient hardware for fixed-length packets (usually called cells), such as ATM cells because you know, for example, the exact buffer sizes needed for a given performance. You also know that you can use the very efficient cross-bar switch, where each input is directly connected to each output.

Piggybacking

Some protocols allow you to send an acknowledgment of the previous packet attached to the current packet for greater efficiency. TCP supports piggybacking with delayed ACK, where an acknowledgment is delayed for a moment, allowing the acknowledging application to send a data reply along with the ACK. See RFC 1122 for details.

Pipelining Versus ACK-ing Each Packet

The window is the number of packets that you send without getting an acknowledgment. The optimum window size depends on the length of the cable in bits—that is, the maximum number of bits in transit on the cable at any moment. For a longer or more reliable cable, a larger window is more efficient. See Tannenbaum's book for a detailed explanation.

Full/half duplex

Full-duplex protocols can transmit in both directions simultaneously. Half-duplex protocols transmit in both directions, but not at the same time.

Errors

The optimum packet size depends on the error rate. If no errors are possible, bigger packets amortize the header overhead and network interrupt handling time better. If there is a high likelihood of errors, small packets make retransmissions less costly.

Number of Hops

If there are a large number of hops between you and a particular destination, you can take advantage of parallelism with smaller packets. You can't move data from one router to the next until the entire packet is received, so if you have large packets, the bits spend a longer time within one router before beginning to move on to the next. If you have small packets, then many of them can be in transit between the end-points at the same time. It's like using trucks versus small cars for carrying goods: it's inefficient to carry freight in lots of small cars on a highway, but in a town with many stop lights, the cars will start up faster than the trucks and get the goods through more quickly, even though they have more overhead.

Layers

Remember that networking is built on layers of protocols: HTTP runs on TCP, which runs on IP, which usually runs on Ethernet. Tuning a high layer will not help if the layers below are the problem. Start with the physical layer and work your way up when looking for network inefficiencies.

The Protocols of the Web

Following are descriptions of the most important network protocols for the Web with performance information on each. Lower layers are presented first.

ARP

The Address Resolution Protocol (ARP) is what translates IP addresses to Ethernet's hardware addresses, also known as Media Access Control (MAC) addresses. A host needing to get an IP packet to a final destination on the same LAN as itself sends out an ARP broadcast asking if anyone knows the MAC address assigned to the desired IP. The machine with the target IP should answer the ARP request. ARP is cached for a timeout period, and is generally quite efficient. But it does take a moment, so lightly used web servers will have a slight delay the first time they are used after a period of non-use.

ARP can be a problem, however, if it is used in place of true routing. Clients should be configured to send packets directly to the local router if no one on the LAN claims them. It may seem clever to have the router send an ARP reply for all addresses (called proxy ARP), rather than just the addresses that are not on the local subnet, but this puts a big load on the router and network because all packets then have to be examined by the router. See *Managing IP Networks with Cisco Routers*, by Scott Ballew (O'Reilly & Associates).

PPP

PPP is a link-level protocol for carrying any network-layer protocol, unlike SLIP, which carries only IP. If you are using a modem to connect to the Internet directly, chances are you're using PPP. PPP frames use checksums to flag errors in transmission; a frame with an invalid checksum is retransmitted, slowing perceived speed. A

PPP frame is often 1,500 bytes because that size allows it to carry one Ethernet packet, but the size of the frame is negotiated by the copies of PPP at both ends of the link. PPP generally drops the connection of a line that has too many checksum errors.

Routing Protocols

Routing protocols, such as RIP, OSPF, and BGP, are beyond the scope of this book. See the aforementioned *Managing IP Networks with Cisco Routers*, by Scott Ballew, for a good explanation of router configuration. *TCP/IP Illustrated, Volume 1*, by Richard Stevens (Addison Wesley), also has good explanations of routing protocols.

IP

The Internet Protocol (IP) is the network-layer protocol of the Internet. HTTP runs on TCP, which runs on IP. See *TCP/IP Illustrated* for an in-depth explanation of IP. The basic facts you need to know for performance tuning are that DNS names are mapped to four-byte IP addresses, and that IP packets find their destinations through routers, which make decisions at Internet branch points about where the packet should go next. Both of these facts are sources of latency: names have to be resolved and route decisions have to be made for each HTTP request.

In spite of all the hype about the Internet making distance irrelevant, distance—at least distance as measured in terms of router hops—still matters, since each hop adds latency. For this reason, it is important to look at your server logs for customer distribution and try to locate servers near your customers.

Keep in mind that IP was designed to use dynamic routing to bypass down or slow routers, so the route between two hosts on the Internet may change from one moment to the next. It is possible for the sending host to request an exact path through the Internet to another host. This is known as *source routing*, but it works only if all the routers along the way agree to it. They generally don't, for security reasons; a user could use source routing to make a packet appear to come from somewhere it didn't. On an intranet, where you have control over the routers, you can set up static routing tables rather than letting the tables dynamically update, depending on conditions. This has a performance hazard: an error in the static routing table can cause a time-consuming ICMP redirect message to be generated for every packet sent to an incorrect gateway, even if the redirect message lets the packets find their correct destination.

The maximum theoretical IP packet size is 64 kilobytes with a minimum of 42 bytes of overhead per packet, so most HTTP transfers could fit easily in a single packet. In reality, the Maximum Transmission Unit (MTU) is typically 536 bytes. The MTU is set to the minimum of the value given when an interface is brought up or the Maximum Segment Size (MSS) value given by the remote peer. Use *ifconfig -a* to see your interfaces and their MTUs. If the remote peer does not give an MSS value, 536 bytes is assumed.

In addition, IP packets are subject to fragmentation into smaller pieces to fit routers along the path with a smaller Maximum Transmission Unit. The IP header and TCP header are both 20 bytes, so the maximum TCP data segment (the MSS) can be only the MTU minus 40 bytes without fragmentation. Fragmentation slows down a transfer, because the fragments have to be reassembled into a coherent whole by TCP. A well-tuned intranet will have the same MTU from end to end, but there is not much you can do about small MTUs on the Internet as a whole.

Your interface's MRU setting is the size of the largest IP packet you will accept from the network. It should be set to your ISP's MTU; there is no point in setting it larger, because you will never get a packet larger than the ISP's MTU. There is also no point in setting it smaller, because you don't need to worry about fragmentation once a packet has reached you. MRU and MTU are usually the same. If you are using PPP, the MTU will be 1,500 by default. This is a reasonable value because it is also the maximum Ethernet packet size and most ISPs use Ethernet internally.

When a packet size exceeds the MTU of any router along the path, it must be broken up. It can be broken up at the router that cannot accept it and reassembled at the destination, or, if the "don't fragment" bit is set in the IP header, the entire packet will be discarded and an ICMP error message "fragmentation needed" will be sent back to the client. This "don't fragment" message is the basis for Path MTU Discovery, which is a mechanism that determines the largest MTU that works for the whole path. I'm not convinced that the overhead of Path MTU Discovery is worthwhile for HTTP, because connections are so short-lived. You can turn it off by setting the *ndd* parameter ip_path_mtu_discovery to 0.

Here's a little script I wrote to *ping* my ISP's router with packets ranging in size from 64 bytes to 4,000 bytes and to save the output to a file that is easily plottable with *gnuplot*:

```
#!/usr/local/bin/perl -w
$| = 1; # Don't buffer so we can interrupt and not lose data.
open(OUT, ">out");
print OUT "# Latency vs ICMP ping packet size.\n";
LOOP: for ($i=64; $i<4000; $i++) {
    $_ = `ping -c1 -n -s$i 1.2.3.4`;
    m!100% packet loss! && next LOOP;
    m!(\d+) data bytes.*= (.*)/(.*)/(.*) ms!s;
    print OUT "$1 $3\n";
}
```

Figure 15-1 shows the results. The MTU of my machine was 1,500, but perhaps the MRU of the receiving machine was less, accounting for the displacement of discontinuity from multiples of 1,500. The overhead for IP is at least 20 bytes, overhead for ICMP is 8 bytes, and there is also a struct timeval that should be simply 2 ints of 4 bytes each. So the overhead in the packet cannot account for the fact that fragmentation seems to be occurring at about 1,250 bytes.

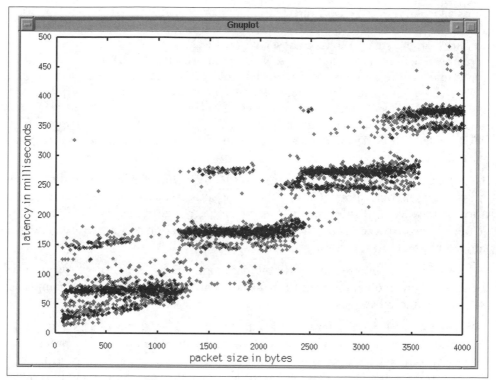

Figure 15-1. Packet fragmentation

You can get the source code for a version of *traceroute* that finds MTUs along the route from the code associated with Stevens, *TCP/IP Illustrated, Volume 1*, which is at *ftp://ftp.uu.net/published/books/stevens/tcpipiv1.tar.Z*. Also note that Solaris 2.*x* includes MTU discovery in the kernel. There is now a standard for MTU discovery, specified in RFC 1191. MTU discovery works by a machine's sending out a large IP packet with the Don't Fragment (DF) option set in the IP header. When the packet hits a router or bridge with a lower MTU, the router will generate an ICMP "Can't Fragment" reply. The sending machine will get the reply and then try a smaller MTU. This continues until an MTU that works along the entire route is discovered.

DNS and Trivial FTP (TFTP) use packets of only 512 bytes maximum because fragmentation is guaranteed not to occur for packets of less than 576 bytes. So you could say that 576 is the minimum maximum transmission unit. On an Ethernet LAN, the MTU is generally set to 1,500 bytes; this is the default configuration for many clients, such as Windows. However, on the Internet it is sometimes a better idea to set the MTU to 576. You can use the modified *traceroute* program mentioned earlier to find out about the MTU between yourself and points you commonly visit.

IP can carry messages intended to control the IP flow itself. These are appropriately called Internet Control Message Protocol (ICMP) packets. Some of the possible messages are the packet could not be sent, the packet exceeded the number of router hops allowed, the packet was directed to an incorrect gateway, or the remote host is reachable. This last kind of ICMP message is the basis of the Unix *ping* program used to check on the status of remote hosts. *ping* is disabled on many ISPs because it has often been abused; it is simple to use *ping* to send so many ICMP status check messages that the ISP's servers' performance is ruined. This can also be done with TCP SYN packets asking to initiate a connection. These abuses are known as *ping flooding* and *SYN flooding*, which are instances of denial of service (DOS) attacks. It is possible to track down the origin of *ping* and SYN flooding: there is a free tool from MCI called DOS Tracker that helps you do so at *ftp://ftp.mci.net/outgoing/dostrack742812.tar*.

Note that the *traceroute* command also uses ICMP to find the latency of the various hops between routers, but ICMP is the lowest priority, so *traceroute* will generally show results worse than normal traffic, which has a higher priority. NTP (Network Time Protocol) packets have the highest priority, which makes sense, because they are used to set clocks, so timing is critical.

See Chapter 3 for information on IP multicasting, which is an effective way to save bandwidth on information sent to many users at a specific time—for example, in real-time audio broadcasts.

Note that TCP/IP implementations vary in efficiency. The latency of a TCP/IP implementation is proportional to how much buffering is done before the user process can receive incoming data, and to how long the CPU takes to process each segment. A big IP packet will monopolize the line until it gets through, potentially blocking a smaller but more time-critical packet, like a packet of real-time voice data.

Van Jacobson compression reduces IP header size by using the fact that the headers in a group of sequential IP packets are mostly the same. It compresses only the headers, not the data being sent, and is most useful for large transfers.

TCP

Transmission Control Protocol (TCP) was designed to create a reliable connection on top of unreliable media by breaking up a transmission into IP packets, assigning them numbers, and retransmitting packets that are not acknowledged as received within a certain time interval. It also takes into account that the packets may not be received in the same order as they were transmitted, and automatically rearranges them.

TCP was designed with certain assumptions in mind—for example, that connections would be relatively infrequent, that the amount of data transferred would be relatively large, and that correctness and completeness were much more important than performance. These assumptions fit FTP, but not HTTP, which typically requires many very short-lived connections in rapid sequence, each transferring only a few kilobytes. The importance of absolute correctness and completeness for HTTP transfers is debatable.

To set up or shut down a TCP connection requires several exchanges of packets between client and server, which is considerable overhead on a typical HTTP data transfer of 10 KB. Since we need to send or receive three packets to set up the connection, a minimum of two packets to send a request and get a reply, and two packets to tear down a TCP connection, a minimum of seven IP packets must go across the network for even the smallest request.

Use latest TCP patches

You cannot change the fact that web servers use HTTP, so what can you do about the performance hit associated with the use of TCP? Since implementations of HTTP and TCP are becoming more aware of each other, one thing you should do is use the most recent implementations of both web servers and TCP stacks. TCP is built into the Unix kernel and is upgradable with patches. You should install all TCP patches. Solaris versions after 2.6, in particular, are aware of HTTP's needs. As for HTTP, use a web server that understands HTTP 1.1, which has the ability to use one TCP connection for many file transfers, a process known as persistent connections, or less formally, keepalives. See Chapter 18 for information on which servers use HTTP 1.1.

TCP has intrinsic performance limits, but these should not be any real obstacle. One limit is the potential for older TCP byte–sequence numbers to overflow and then wrap around on a very fast connection, but this is not a problem on more recent implementations incorporating Protection Against Wrapped Sequence Numbers (PAWS). See *TCP/IP Illustrated Vol. 1* for details. Another potential limitation is that TCP allows only one full "window" of data to be outstanding on the network at any time. This window was traditionally limited to 64K, but with the window scale option in recent TCP implementations, the window can be up to 1 Gbyte. If you assume a 20 millisecond round-trip time between two points more than a thousand miles apart, then the maximum throughput we could get is 10^9 bytes / 20 * $10{-3}$ seconds = 200 Gbytes / second, which should be sufficient for any use of the Internet I can imagine today.

TCP parameters

TCP has many parameters that can be adjusted to affect network performance. A primary concern is avoiding retransmission of packets that are received intact but are delayed because of the latency inherent in the Internet. The default settings may work fine on a low-latency LAN, but then may wind up causing unneeded retransmission on the Internet. Under Solaris, many TCP/IP parameters can be changed in a running kernel with the *ndd* command. This is a vast improvement over the previous situation, which required a reboot. The *ndd* timing parameters are in milliseconds. You can see *ndd* parameters, even if you are not *root*, by using the command *ndd / dev/tcp \?*, but you cannot change anything with *ndd* unless you are *root*. Even if you change things, your *ndd* changes can sometimes be overridden by applications that explicitly set parameters when establishing a socket.

A common problem is comparing the TCP settings on two different machines—for example, to compare your test machine to your production machine. Here is a shell script that will dump your configurable *ndd* parameters on Solaris. You can run this on both machines and then use *diff* to see the differences clearly. It is available from *http://patrick.net/software/dumpndd.sh*.

```
#!/bin/sh
for parm in `ndd /dev/tcp \? | cut -f1 -d" " | grep -v _hash | grep -v status | grep
-v \?`
do
/usr/ucb/echo -n $parm
/usr/ucb/echo -n " "
ndd /dev/tcp $parm
done
```

Listen queues

A common explanation of the listen queue is to compare it to a customer service center to which you dial in and are put on hold while waiting for the "next available representative." The number of people simultaneously on hold is analogous to the TCP listen queue. Your call has been acknowledged, but no one is doing anything to service your request.

There are actually two listen queues. The kernel establishes a TCP connection in stages, first placing requests in an incomplete connection queue, then moving them to a completed connection queue once they are established. Being in the incomplete listen queue is analogous to having your call picked up, but not yet being put on hold. These are also called the incomplete handshake queue and the completed handshake queue. Sometimes the word "backlog" is used instead of "queue." The idea of having two queues is to protect against SYN flooding attacks, in which millions of SYN packets are sent to a server just to keep it from doing any useful work. (As mentioned earlier, this kind of attack is also known as a Denial Of Service (DOS) attack.)

These listen queues exist for each server process that is listening for incoming connections. If the incomplete listen queue gets full, clients get back no response at all, so the site appears dead. When this happens, the client will typically time out and resend a SYN, though the user will see no indication this is happening. If the user makes it into the completed connection queue, the browser will show "Site contacted, waiting for reply..." Once the connection is established, *netstat* will show the connection as ESTABLISHED, whether or not the application has accepted the connection. At this point, the browser may send the request, which should be buffered by the socket if the application has not yet accepted the connection.

The completed connection queue length can set in the listen( ) system call in the server, up to the maximum the OS allows. The OS maximum can be set with *ndd* on Solaris. The length requested by the server in listen( ) may either be hardcoded, thus not changeable unless you have the source and can recompile, or it may be read in from a web server configuration file. Stevens showed that completed connection queues are usually empty, meaning you don't particularly need to waste memory on them unless your server is really busy. Incomplete connection queues need to be a little larger.

The incomplete connection queue does not use up file descriptors, I believe, so can be set very large to protect against SYN flood attacks. For example:

```
# /usr/sbin/ndd -set /dev/tcp tcp_conn_req_max_q0 10000
```

The completed queue length should be at least as large as the listen queue configured for the web server software, but note that a larger queue will consume more RAM. There is no point in configuring the completed connection queue to be larger than the number of file descriptors available to the process, because the server won't be able to make more connections than file descriptors. The Netscape Commerce server defaults to a 128-entry listen queue, for example, so the OS-level queue should also be adjusted to 128. I like to set the listenQ in Netscape's *magnus.conf* to 1024 and therefore the Solaris per-process listen queue to the same 1024, though it is rare to need this large a queue. You can adjust the Solaris completed handshake listen queue size like this:

```
# /usr/sbin/ndd -set /dev/tcp tcp_conn_req_max_q 1024
```

You can monitor the listen queues in Solaris like this:

```
# /usr/sbin/ndd -get /dev/tcp tcp_listen_hash
```

You can also use *netstat -s* to see the number of connections dropped due to an insufficient listen queue, called tcpListenDrop.

Under Linux 2.0, you can change the (single) listen queue by changing SOMAX-CONN in the *include/linux/socket.h* file from its default of 128 and recompiling the kernel. Under BSD, the incomplete connection queue is so_q0len and the completed connection queue is so_qlen. The kernel has to be recompiled to change them.

Retransmission delay

If TCP does not receive a segment acknowledgment within a certain interval of time, it considers the segment lost and sends another copy. A fixed timeout for each connection is used at first, then the timeout is dynamically recalculated depending on the performance of that connection. You can help by changing settings to correspond to what you know about your clients. The trade-off with retransmission delay is that a too-high timeout will make a lossy connection run more slowly than it would otherwise, because you will wait longer for each missing packet to be replaced. A too-low timeout will cause many packets to be unnecessarily retransmitted, because they will be counted as lost when they were really just slow. A good way to monitor the number of retransmissions under Solaris is to use the command:

```
% netstat -s
```

In the output from the command, compare `tcpOutDataSegs` to `tcpRetransSegs` and `tcpOutDataBytes` to `tcpRetransBytes`. If you are retransmitting more than 20 percent of the segments or bytes, try setting the retransmission interval higher and reexamine the *netstat* output. The Mac TCP Monitor tool is a good way to see retransmissions on the client side if your clients are Macs. The retransmission delay parameter is known as `RTOmax` on Windows.

The amount of time waited before the first retransmit on a connection is set on Solaris with `tcp_rexmit_interval_initial`. This default initial timeout is 200 milliseconds, which is fine on a LAN, but inadequate for the much larger latencies of the Internet. A good value for the Internet as a whole is one second (1,000 milliseconds).

```
# /usr/sbin/ndd -set /dev/tcp tcp_rexmit_interval_initial 1000
```

You can also set the minimum and maximum retransmission delays, in milliseconds:

```
# /usr/sbin/ndd -set /dev/tcp tcp_rexmit_interval_min    1000
# /usr/sbin/ndd -set /dev/tcp tcp_rexmit_interval_max    10000
```

The maximum is the maximum amount of time to wait between retransmissions. The retransmission algorithm will vary your retransmit timeout for a particular connection between the minimum and maximum depending on how things are going. Given that most HTTP connections are very short, it doesn't make much sense to set any retransmit intervals very high. The user will most likely give up if he has to wait ten seconds or more.

TIME_WAIT interval

A TIME_WAIT interval is how long a socket will be unavailable for reuse by another client after it has been closed. If it is set too low, you may reuse the socket and get garbled data if a TCP segment that actually belonged to the last connection arrives late. If it is set too high, you may run out of TCP connections because they are all in the TIME_WAIT state. Ideally, you should set it to wait just long enough that no valid TCP segments for that socket could still be in transit. Sixty seconds is a good starting point, and this is what BSD uses for a default. For an explanation of the trade-offs, see Chapter 18 of *TCP/IP Illustrated*.

```
# /usr/sbin/ndd -set /dev/tcp tcp_close_wait_interval 60000
```

Abort interval

This is how long retransmissions will be attempted before giving up on a network connection. Once the sending side gives up, it sends a final reset. The default on Solaris is 7,200,000 ms, which is two hours, as recommended by rfc1122. For busy web servers, this is far too long, since clients often disappear without notice and you don't want to hold resources for them. 60,000 ms (one minute) is much more reasonable.

```
# /usr/sbin/ndd -set /dev/tcp tcp_ip_abort_interval 60000
```

Maximum segment lifetime and maximum connection rate

The TCP parameter of Maximum Segment Lifetime (MSL) happens to limit the number of new connections per second that can be made to a server. For example with an MSL of 120 seconds, we cannot make a new connection between the same two port and IP pairs for 120 seconds. There are 65,536 ports, but 1024 are reserved for use by root. This means we can make a maximum of (65,536 – 1024 ports)/120 sec = 538 connections per second as the maximum sustainable connection rate, if the server is doing the active close. What pitch is that? Middle-A is 440 cycles per second, so maybe that's about a C-sharp. You could get an unsustainable rate of up to 64,512 for one second though.

Keepalive interval

TCP has a keepalive option that is not related to the HTTP 1.1 keepalive (persistent connection) option. TCP connections do not carry any traffic at all unless one side needs to send data to the other, so there is no polling or other network overhead on an idle connection. This means that one side of a connection can go down and the other side won't know about it until it tries to contact the other side, if ever. This is not a particular problem for web clients, but it can be a resource-sapping hazard for servers maintaining buffers in memory for network connections that no longer exist. Clients frequently disappear without properly shutting down the connection because users shut off the modem or computer; eventually, the server would run out of memory if there were not some way to detect a connection that won't be used again.

It may be the proper responsibility of the web server to check these connections, but there is a TCP keepalive option in most TCP implementations to check the other end at regular intervals. The default interval is typically two to eight hours, but for a busy web server it should be reduced to the maximum amount of time a user might reasonably have an idle connection open. If set too low, it can make maintenance more difficult by closing *telnet* connections that are not constantly in use.

If *netstat* shows you a large number of connections in the FIN_WAIT_2 state, it means that clients are not properly shutting down TCP connections. Try reducing the keepalive interval to fix this. See *http://www.apache.org/* for a discussion of the FIN_WAIT_2 problem. It seems that clients disconnected for exceeding the HTTP 1.1 KeepAliveTimeout may not be shutting down the connection correctly. Five minutes (300000 ms) is reasonable for a busy server.

```
# /usr/sbin/ndd -set /dev/tcp tcp_keepalive_interval 300000
```

Receive window

The TCP receive window is also known as the Receive WINdow (RWIN) or Rx Window. It is the amount of data allowed to be outstanding on the Internet without acknowledgment at any one time. This window is advertised by the receiver to the sender. This window limits the number of TCP segments the sender can push out at any one time, and so it limits your maximum transmission rate to the window size divided by the round-trip time. You can transmit faster by increasing the window size or decreasing the round-trip time.

A typical receive window is 32 KB, so a server could send at most 32 KB without getting an ACK that data was received. This is how a slow TCP receiver such as a web client deals with a fast TCP sender such as a web server; it is a flow control mechanism. With every acknowledgment, the TCP receiver also includes in the reply header the amount of data it can still accept at the moment. This amount is known as the offered window, and is the receive window less the amount of data the receiver still has to drain from its socket receive buffer. The offered window is necessarily less than or equal to the receive window. See Section 20.3 of *TCP/IP Illustrated* for a detailed explanation. The socket receive buffer will be as large as the receive window size so that the client can accept any data in flight (one full pipe) even if the application is busy and can't drain the data from the receive buffer.

You want a receive window large enough to keep the pipeline as full as the receiver can handle. A full pipe is easily calculated as the bandwidth-delay product. For example, if the round trip delay for your 56K modem is 200 milliseconds, one full pipe is (56000 bits per second / 10 bits per byte with start and stop bits) * 200 milliseconds = 1120 bytes. So you would want a receive window of 1,120 bytes. If the round trip delay for your 10 Mbps ethernet is 5 milliseconds, one full pipe is 6,250 bytes and you would want a receive window of 6,250 bytes.

Too large a window could have negative effects. ISPs may allocate only a fixed-size buffer on their routers per dial-in port. If you advertise a window larger than this, the sender could fill the router's buffer before you can drain it over the dial-in connection. Any additional data would be dropped and have to be retransmitted.

It is a good idea to set the receive window size to be an integer multiple of the TCP Maximum Segment Size (MSS) so that a large data stream can efficiently fill the receive window without fragmentation. Try setting your receive window at four or eight times your MSS. The receive window is limited by your socket buffer size. Applications may ask for larger socket buffers with setsockopt( ), but there is no guarantee that the OS will give it to them. The OS may have a hard limit on socket buffer size written into it.

If you browse and download primarily from one ISP, use that ISP's MTU setting for maximum efficiency.

An interesting flaw in TCP is that a sufficiently long and fast connection will cause the 31-bit TCP sequence numbers to wrap around back to 0 before the receiving end can ACK the first segment. All ACKs will then be ambiguous; they could refer to an earlier or later scan through all the sequence numbers. This is solved by the PAWS algorithm (Protection Against Wrapped Sequence Numbers), but not all TCP implementations use PAWS.

Delayed ACK

Some TCP implementations optionally delay sending an ACK because a delay gives the application a chance so generate and send response data along with the ACK. For example, an ACK of an HTTP request might be delayed to give the web server a chance to put the HTTP response in the packet as well. While this would reduce the number of packets sent out by the server, it might also slow down the responses. I would leave it at its default of 50 milliseconds on Solaris. The *ndd* parameter is tcp_defered_ack_interval.

Slow start

Some recommend disabling TCP slow start, which is flow control from the TCP sender's point of view. Using slow start, the sender will put only one TCP segment (and therefore only one IP packet) out onto the network, and wait until it is acknowledged. If the first packet is successfully acknowledged, the sender will send two segments and wait for their ACKs, then four, and so on, up to the congestion window maximum of the sender, which specifies the maximum amount of unacknowledged data that can be in transit at any point. In this way, the amount of data put onto the network is guaranteed to be within the capacity of the receiver to absorb it. See *TCP/IP Illustrated* or RFC 2001 for more about slow start.

One problem with slow start on the Web is that new TCP connections are very frequent and very short-lived. Slow start tends to waste time figuring out an optimum transmission rate for a connection that is about to be closed anyway, although it may indeed be useful for large web transmissions over slow links.

A more serious problem with slow start is that Windows clients have a TCP/IP stack that expects a server to send out two packets to begin a slow start, rather than one packet. This is not correct behavior, but most Unix servers have adapted to it. The exception was Solaris 2.6, which by default sent out only one packet and then waited for an ACK. Windows clients of such servers received the first packet from the server and silently waited for the second one, which would never arrive. The client timed out, then sent the ACK for the first packet, so there would be a timeout delay for the default configuration of a Solaris server and a Windows client. This delay happened for each TCP connection, that is, for each image and other component of a web page, unless HTTP 1.1 persistent connections were being used. The repeated client timeouts can more than double the time it takes for a client to get a page. The solution here is to tell Solaris 2.6 (or Solaris 2.5.1 with TCP patches loaded) to start TCP transmissions with two packets instead of one:

```
# /usr/sbin/ndd -set /dev/tcp tcp_slow_start_initial 2
```

BSD and Windows servers send two unacknowledged packets by default, so they don't need any modification. Solaris 7 and later also now start with two, and the TCP specification itself was modified to allow two.

Another problem with slow start is that the congestion window is limited to 64 KB in most implementations of TCP. It is quite easy to exceed this on a 100 Mbps Ethernet LAN. If a 100 Mbps LAN has a latency of 10 milliseconds, you could have 1 Mbit (= 125 KB) in transit. The RFC 1323 TCP Large Window Extensions allows you to expand the congestion window for these cases, and this is implemented as of Solaris 2.6. You can set the maximum congestion window on Solaris like this:

```
# /usr/sbin/ndd -set /dev/tcp tcp_cwnd_max 100000
```

Maximum Segment Size

The Maximum Segment Size (MSS) is the largest TCP segment that a connection will accept. It is announced by the TCP requester when the connection is established. The sender can use any smaller segment size but may not exceed the MSS. The trade-off here is to make the MSS small enough to avoid IP-level fragmentation, yet large enough so that the overhead of the IP and TCP headers is a relatively small fraction of the entire IP packet. Many TCP implementations have a default of 536 bytes, which is a reasonable value for web services. The Solaris default is to use per-route MTU discovery. You can see your default value like this:

```
# ndd -get /dev/tcp tcp_mss_def
```

You can also query or set `tcp_mss_max` and `tcp_mss_min`.

Please see Jens-S. Voeckler's excellent web page at *http://www.rvs.uni-hannover.de/people/voeckler/tune/EN/tune.html* for a much more detailed treatment of Solaris TCP parameters.

Monitoring TCP

Volumes have been written about network monitoring, so I'm not going to try to duplicate that content here. Regardless of exactly which tools you use to monitor TCP, there are a few patterns to look for. Input errors have many causes. For example, your cable may be too long, damaged, or just the wrong kind. You may have NIC connector problems. Errors may mean network problems or just that the network device driver has buffer overflows. Output errors may imply that the NIC connector is damaged or that the network is simply not responding.

You can figure out if you're retransmitting due to timeouts. Compare output segments to segment retransmissions or output bytes to bytes retransmitted. If you're retransmitting more than 20 percent, try increasing the TCP retransmit interval. If you're not replying in time for the server, it will retransmit to you, resulting in unacceptable TCP segments or TCP resynchronization pauses. Look for dropped packets, which imply that you have buffer overflows that could be solved with bigger buffers. Here are several of the better known network monitoring programs:

netstat

> *netstat* is a standard Unix program for monitoring network connections. Type *man netstat* on almost all Unix systems for more information. *netstat* is usually available to all users, not just *root*. *netstat -a* shows you all the current connections on your machine. *netstat* gives statistics on network performance such as buffer overruns and packet drops. Under Linux, you can simply look at */proc/net/dev* for much of the same information. Windows NT has an imitation of *netstat*, also called *netstat*.

snoop

> *snoop* is a Solaris utility that puts the Ethernet card into promiscuous mode, meaning that it can see every packet on the local Ethernet segment. You must be *root* to have permission to use this. It is extremely useful for seeing the contents of network data packets, but it tends to produce a flood of data by default. *snoop* has many options for filtering and displaying data. Chapter 14 has an example of *snoop* output.

tcpdump

> *tcpdump* is another Unix utility using the promiscuous mode of Ethernet cards, but unlike *snoop* does not show the actual contents of each packet. It comes bundled with Red Hat Linux in */usr/sbin/tcpdump*, but is not bundled with Solaris. For more information, see *TCP/IP Illustrated* and the associated *tcpdump* source code.

Here's a slightly modified example of *tcpdump* output. I hit a web page that was already in the browser's cache, and the server said the page was not modified.

```
# tcpdump
Kernel filter, protocol ALL, datagram packet socket
tcpdump: listening on all devices
08:36:12.195549  browser.1026 > server.www: S 3311753430:3311753430(0) win 31072
<mss 3884,sackOK,timestamp 2712118 0,nop,wscale 0> (DF)
08:36:12.195681  browser.www > server.1026: S 3305435973:3305435973(0) ack
3311753431 win 31072 <mss 3884,sackOK,timestamp 2712118 2712118,nop,wscale 0> (
DF)
08:36:12.195738  browser.1026 > server.www: . 1:1(0) ack 1 win 31072 <nop,nop,tim
estamp 2712118 2712118> (DF)
08:36:12.217507  browser.1026 > server.www: P 1:342(341) ack 1 win 31072 <nop,nop
,timestamp 2712120 2712118> (DF)
08:36:12.217604  browser.www > server.1026: . 1:1(0) ack 342 win 30731 <nop,nop,t
imestamp 2712120 2712120> (DF)
08:36:12.220354  browser.www > server.1026: P 1:198(197) ack 342 win 31072 <nop,n
op,timestamp 2712120 2712120> (DF)
08:36:12.220431  browser.1026 > server.www: . 342:342(0) ack 198 win 30875 <nop,n
op,timestamp 2712120 2712120> (DF)
08:36:28.893523  browser.www > server.1026: F 198:198(0) ack 342 win 31072 <nop,n
op,timestamp 2713788 2712120> (DF)
08:36:28.893637  browser.1026 > server.www: . 342:342(0) ack 199 win 31072 <nop,n
op,timestamp 2713788 2713788> (DF)
```

Some interesting things to notice here are the timestamp at the beginning of each line, the high random port the browser uses (1026) to connect to the standard port the server uses (80, called *www* here), the three-way handshake setting up the TCP connection, and the 16-second delay before the HTTP 1.1 persistent connection is closed.

There are similar freeware tools, such as *aps*, the advanced packet sniffer, that will display the contents of packets on Linux.

T/TCP

In the future, bandwidth will improve, but latency will not because the speed of light is fixed. We are already near the minimum possible latencies. You can prove it for yourself: do a *ping* to a server in a faraway place and compare the time it takes to the time it would take light to travel that distance.

Since long-distance latency is a fixed barrier, it is important to decrease the number of round trips in the TCP-connection setup. That is the goal of the Transaction TCP, or T/TCP, protocol. The setup of the connection and first segment of data are all put into one packet. This can make a significant difference in the time it takes to get a web page.

The catch is that not all servers and even fewer web clients understand the T/TCP protocol. Some clients may get so confused by seeing both connection setup and data in the same packet that they crash. Another consideration is that there may be no effective defense against denial of service attacks for servers accepting T/TCP. The servers at *http://www.yahoo.com/* supposedly can use T/TCP, but I haven't been able to prove this yet. There was a sample implementation of T/TCP in BSD Unix.

UDP

The User Datagram Protocol (UDP) is a transport layer protocol on top of IP, like TCP, but connectionless and unreliable, unlike TCP. UDP, however, has better performance than TCP because it does so little. It is very useful for situations in which the application can handle reliability (that is, it can request retransmission of missing packets) and not every packet is needed but speed is very important—for example, when sending streaming audio or video over the Internet. DNS, NFS, and the RealAudio protocol all use UDP.

DNS

Domain Name Service (DNS) is a UDP-based service that resolves fully qualified names (FQNs), such as *www.umich.edu.* to IP addresses, such as 141.211.144.53. This is critical for the Web, because most sites are referred to by FQN both when typed in by hand and when used as links in a web page.

A little-known fact is that the root domain is simply a dot (.) so all FQN's technically must end in a dot. In practice, the dot is implied and not written, except in DSN configuration files. One DNS performance tip is that you don't have to use DNS. If DNS is very slow for you, use IP addresses rather than domain names in your HTML so that the browser does not have to take time to find the IP address. It is a bit confusing for users to see an IP address appear in their browsers' "Location:" field, but the title of the web page should be able to orient them well enough. And note that graphics do not show their URL to the user, except in the HTML source.

A hazard in using IP addresses is that cookies are usually associated with a specific domain, and will not be sent by the browser back to your server except for that specific domain. If you are using IP addresses, cookies may not work at all.

DNS is a hierarchical distributed database. If your local DNS server doesn't have the IP address you're looking for, it knows whom to ask next in the hierarchy. Looking up an uncommon name may take a few seconds because the request may get bumped up the hierarchy several times.

Unix users can also use FQNs entirely without a DNS server by resorting to the primitive original method for mapping FQNs to IP addresses: simply add an entry to your /etc/hosts file. This makes for very fast lookup, but is not dynamically updated like DNS servers and is considered very bad form in system administration. You can rely on /etc/hosts only for addresses you control, but you do have complete control, unlike DNS. Here is an example /etc/hosts file from a Linux machine:

```
# hosts This file describes a number of hostname-to-address
# mappings for the TCP/IP subsystem. It is mostly
# used at boot time, when no name servers are running.
# On small systems, this file can be used instead of a
# "named" name server. Just add the names, addresses
# and any aliases to this file...
127.0.0.1 localhost
141.211.144.53 www.umich.edu
```

Unix users can easily set up a DNS server on their own client machines. The advantage here is that DNS servers cache entries they've looked up, making subsequent access much faster. Netscape Navigator's DNS helper also caches DNS entries automatically for you.

Although DNS servers generally don't see a very large load, try to be sure that your DNS server and web server are not competing for bandwidth on your Internet connection. This may mean placing a DNS server inside your organization rather than relying on your ISP's DNS server. Note that DNS servers, like most Internet servers, tend to degrade in a nonlinear way, with performance dropping off rapidly after a certain load.

Unix and Windows clients handle round robin DNS very differently. Unix does a lookup every time, while DOS/Windows does a lookup once, and caches one IP for that name. This means that test results can be different when one machine in a round robin pair is down. Windows machines will give you the misleading impression that both are up or both are down, while Unix clients will show intermittent up and down results depending on each lookup.

Solaris includes a generic Name Service Cache Daemon for all name services. Use *nscd -g* to get statistics from it. You can control the Time To Live (TTL) of each cache and also configure negative caching.

NFS

The Network File System (NFS) from Sun Microsystems is a method of making a set of files on a remote system appear to be on the disk of local computer. "Remote" can mean across a WAN, but NFS is much more commonly used on LANs because its performance over WANs is usually not good. NFS is a stateless protocol. NFS Version 2 runs over UDP, and Version 3 runs over TCP (by default, but UDP is still allowed).

A well-tuned NFS server has much better throughput than most web servers, given the same hardware. This means it is feasible to use an NFS server to help scale web services, particularly if you are serving static content. You can set up multiple web servers and provide the content to each server from the same central NFS server to keep the content synchronized across all servers.

There is a filesystem caching mechanism for NFS, called *cachefs*, which keeps a local copy of files served by NFS and greatly improves read performance for subsequent access. Write performance is much lower than read performance for NFS because writes must be committed to a nonvolatile medium such as disk, according to the NFS protocol. Note that each directory requires an NFS lookup, so looking up a path with many directories over NFS results in a big performance loss the first time you do it. See *Managing NFS and NIS*, by Hal Stern (O'Reilly & Associates).

Poor NFS usage can hurt web server performance a lot. For example, you don't want your web server log file NFS-mounted, because a block of the log will have to be appended and copied back to the NFS server for each hit. In fact, I had a similar problem when appending mail messages to my mbox. The *mbox* file was on the NFS server because it was in my home directory, which was NFS-mounted. I noticed that as the *mbox* grew bigger, appending new messages to it became slower. A quick use of *snoop* showed that a large piece of my *mbox* was being copied to my machine, appended, and copied back to the NFS server. The answer for me (there are many) was to simply make the *mbox* in my home directory a link to */opt/mbox*, which was actually on my local disk. The performance problem went away, but the local disk is not backed up by my system administrator, as the NFS server is.

HTTP

HyperText Transfer Protocol (HTTP) is the protocol at the core of the Web. It was created at the CERN research institute in Switzerland by Tim Berners-Lee, originally as a way for scientists to share research papers. It was designed to be simple and extensible, but it was also designed for delivering static content, which is the origin of its inefficiency as a protocol for transaction processing.

HTTP certainly is simple: the client requests a document, the server returns it, and the connection is closed. That's all there was to it, at first. Although there's a significant amount of overhead involved in setting up the connection and tearing it down right away, this wasn't a problem at first, because most web servers were not getting hit hard enough for the webmaster to worry about performance issues. HTTP worked well.

HTTP was intended to serve the HyperText Markup Language (HTML), but note that there is nothing in the HTTP specification that says that the server must serve HTML. HTTP can serve any document type. MIME types were later added to the headers created by web servers to help the client know what to do with the document type received. "Well-known" port 80 was quickly assigned to HTTP, freeing users from typing the port number in a URL and securing HTTP a place in the */etc/ services* file of Unix servers around the world.

Be sure to distinguish between browser page views and HTTP hits. From a user's perspective, he or she simply loads a page, gets text and graphics and maybe an applet or audio clip. The download seems unified. From the server's perspective, there is no page view, only a series of requests for files: first an HTML file, then some images, then an applet and a video. The server does not know or care that the initial HTML file contained references to later files that it serves. In fact, when responding to requests from multiple clients, it is common to see in the server log files that the replies to those clients are actually interleaved in time. The operation of sending a file to a client is referred to as a hit on the server, or as an HTTP operation.

Stateless and connectionless

HTTP is stateless, meaning that the protocol does not have any provision for memory about what the server or client has done in the past; multiple states for the server or client do not exist. HTTP is also called connectionless, because there is no persistent connection between server and client. (At least, there wasn't until HTTP 1.1.) Every page the user requests appears to the server as if this were the first time it has dealt with this user. The server simply sets up another connection and returns the requested page. This allows the HTTP protocol to be very simple, which in turn allows it to be rapidly implemented on every kind of machine that speaks TCP/IP.

Connectionless protocols contrast with typical client/server transactions, where the client opens a connection to the database (in two-tier) or application server (in three-tier) and the server keeps the connection open until the client explicitly logs off. The client/server user can be in different states: logged in, authenticated, editing a document, and so forth. Statefulness is essential for many complex functions, such as authentication and transaction processing. Although not provided by HTTP, statefulness and/or persistent connections can be provided by extra software written using CGIs, Java, or CORBA. The actual state mechanism can be cookies passed back and forth between browser and server, information logged on the server and indexed by the requester's IP address or cookie, or direct socket connections, among other mechanisms.

Connectionlessness does have the good side effect that HTTP scales much better than client/server. When a client is disconnected, which from the server's point of view is nearly all the time, the server does not need to maintain any network resources for that client. This means that a single HTTP server can support far more clients than if the connections were continuous.

Ironically, even though HTTP is connectionless, the individual HTTP connections are carried over TCP, which does maintain the state of a connection in order to assure that all packets in a transmission are received and assembled in the correct order. There is considerable overhead in setting up or tearing down a TCP connection, known as a *three-way handshake*. See the "TCP" section earlier in this chapter for a more detailed explanation of TCP and performance. The real TCP performance hit comes from the fact that this handshake must be performed by server and client for every file sent, both for the HTML and for each embedded image, applet, etc. It might have been a better choice to use UDP, which does not require any initialization, and to leave the checking for packet completeness and ordering up to the browser, but that's not the way things happened.

Asymmetric

Note that HTTP data transfer is very asymmetric; requests are quite small, in the tens or perhaps hundreds of bytes, while replies are much bigger. So the output from the server is much more likely to be a bottleneck than the input to the server. Even though the throughput from the server is much larger, the number of packets flowing in each direction is similar because the client needs to send TCP ACKs back to the server to acknowledge data packets.

Text-based

HTTP is a text-based protocol, so it is possible to interact with a web server simply by telnetting to the server port (usually 80) and feeding it HTTP commands via the keyboard:

```
% telnet www.umich.edu 80
Trying 141.211.144.53...
Connected to www.umich.edu.
Escape character is '^]'
GET / HTTP/1.0
HTTP/1.1 200 OK
Date: Sun, 08 Feb 1998 18:35:25 GMT
Server: Apache/1.2.5
Connection: close
Content-Type: text/html
<html>
 ...
```

Seeing what a browser is up to is a little trickier, since the browser must make the first move. You can't just connect to someone's browser and start giving it commands. You can, however, write a little "server" that will accept a browser request and print out the request verbatim. In this way you can see exactly what the browser sends to the server. Here is the code for such a server written in Java:

```java
// give listen port as argument, eg: java EchoServer 8080
import java.io.*;
import java.net.*;

class EchoServer {
    public static void main(String[] args) {

        try {
            byte    buf[] = new byte[1024];
            int     len;
            Socket s;
            String replyHeader = "HTTP/1.0 200 OK\r\n" +
                                "Content-type: text/plain\r\n\r\n";

            ServerSocket ss = new ServerSocket(new Integer(args[0]).intValue());

            while (true) {
                s = ss.accept();

                BufferedInputStream bis = new
                    BufferedInputStream(s.getInputStream());
                BufferedOutputStream bos = new
                    BufferedOutputStream(s.getOutputStream());

                len = bis.read(buf); // get the request

                bos.write(replyHeader.getBytes(), 0, replyHeader.length());
                bos.write(buf, 0, len);
                bos.close();
                bis.close();
            }
        } catch (Exception e) { System.out.println(e); }
    }
}
```

Compile and run it:

```
% javac EchoServer.java
% java  EcoServer 8888
```

Now make a request from Netscape to retrieve the document at *http://localhost:8888/* and you see your own request echoed back to the browser:

```
GET / HTTP/1.0
Connection: Keep-Alive
User-Agent: Mozilla/4.51 [en] (X11; I; Linux 2.2.5-15 i686)
Host: localhost:8888
Accept: image/gif, image/x-xbitmap, image/jpeg, image/pjpeg, image/png, */*
Accept-Encoding: gzip
```

```
Accept-Language: en
Accept-Charset: iso-8859-1,*,utf-8
```

The same request from Internet Explorer shows this:

```
GET / HTTP/1.1

Accept: application/vnd.ms-excel, application/msword, application/vnd.ms-powerpoint,
image/gif, image/x-xbitmap, image/jpeg, image/pjpeg, */*
Accept-Language: en-us
Accept-Encoding: gzip, deflate
User-Agent: Mozilla/4.0 (compatible; MSIE 4.01; Windows NT)
Host: localhost:8888
Connection: Keep-Alive
```

In this request, you see several name:value pairs being sent by the browser. Note the use of the Connection: Keep-Alive header, which keeps the TCP connection open for receiving all of the embedded items in the page, such as images. Keeping the connection open is the default behavior of HTTP 1.1, but this requires the Connection:Keep-Alive header under HTTP 1.0. For a detailed explanation of browser-host communication, see *Web Client Programming with Perl*, by Clinton Wong (O'Reilly & Associates). Also note that Netscape 4.51 accepts *gzip* encoding, but Netscape 4.04 does not.

Compression

One of the header name-value pairs of interest from a performance perspective is the kind of compression used. There is currently no standard for compression of web documents, but most web servers are capable of producing the name:value pair Content-encoding:gzip to indicate the use of *gzip* compression of web documents and most browsers are capable of decoding *gzip*ped documents. Remember that not all files can be compressed (or else you could compress every file down to a single bit) so sometimes it's not worth the time involved in applying compression and decompression to a web page.

Cache control

Another header name-value pair that can help performance is the If-Modified-Since header, which tells the server to return the document only if it has been modified since the last time the server looked at it. You can achieve a similar effect with the HTTP HEAD command, but this may involve two connections to the server: one to get the header of the document, and another to get the document if the cached copy is obsolete.

The If-Modified-Since header can fulfill the request in the same connection that checks the currency of the document. It is automatically added by the browser for documents in the browser's cache. The server can send back an Expires header that forces pages to expire from the cache after a certain amount of time. This has a legitimate use, say, for pages of stock prices, but it has been abused to get a more accurate hit count for advertisements (at the public network's expense), since advertisers are otherwise not able to tell when an ad has been viewed out of the browser's cache.

The trailing slash

A URL pointing to a directory is technically supposed to end in a slash to indicate to the server that the URL points to a directory. Nonetheless, most people leave off the slash, forcing the server to figure out that the user is requesting not a file, but a directory. Servers figure it out, but they have to go through the step of looking for a non-existent file first, which slows things down. They could then give you the index file for the directory you gave them, but in practice, servers respond with a redirect to the client, adding to network traffic and delaying the eventual response. It is better for your server if users provide the correct syntax with the trailing slash, so if you publish a URL or embed links in HTML, use the correct syntax, e.g., *http://patrick. net/dir/*.

For example, Apache 1.2.4 responds with an HTTP redirect, sending a `Location:` URL back to the client, which is the same URL with a slash appended. If we request a directory named *dir* without the trailing slash from a server at *patrick.net*, this is what we would see on the network:

```
% telnet patrick.net 80
Trying 127.0.0.1...
Connected to patrick.net.
Escape character is '^]'.
GET /dir HTTP/1.0
HTTP/1.1 301 Moved Permanently
Date: Thu, 14 May 1998 03:41:58 GMT
Server: Apache/1.2.4
Location: http://patrick.net/dir/
Connection: close
Content-Type: text/html
<HTML><HEAD>

<TITLE>301 Moved Permanently</TITLE>
</HEAD><BODY>
 <H1>Moved Permanently</H1>
The document has moved <A HREF="http://patrick.net/dir/">here</A>.<P>
</BODY></HTML>
Connection closed by foreign host.
```

HTTP 1.1 improvements

The World Wide Web Consortium (W3C) has considered the shortcomings of HTTP 1.0 and made a large number of performance improvements, which are part of the HTTP 1.1 specification. This specification is available at *http://www.ics.uci.edu/ pub/ietf/http/rfc2068.txt*.

The most significant improvement is the use of one TCP connection to retrieve multiple documents, known as persistent connections. This provides an economy of scale, since the overhead of setting up and tearing down the TCP connection is spread over several documents.

By examining the header lines in the request issued by Netscape browser Version 1.0, you can better understand persistent connections even though they do not show "HTTP 1.1" in the server logs. The persistent connection timeout becomes an important web tuning parameter, especially when most clients are on slow connections, because each open connection consumes memory and other resources. When you have a great many HTTP 1.1 clients on slow connections, you accumulate so much simultaneous overhead that you should probably turn down the time of inactivity allowed before the connection is closed. You can see how many connections are open at the moment by running *netstat*, grepping for ESTABLISHED, and then piping that to *wc -l*, like this: **netstat | grep ESTABLISHED | wc -l**. Note that persistent connections work only for static content, not for CGI or server API output.

In addition, HTTP 1.1 allows multiple requests to be pending simultaneously, so you can issue another request before the current one has finished. This is known as pipelining. HTTP 1.0 forced each transfer within a single TCP connection to finish before the next one was allowed to begin. Browsers deal with this HTTP 1.0 restriction by opening several simultaneous TCP connections to the server, but it is no longer necessary for them to do so.

Downloads of a range of bytes in a document are also now allowed; previously, documents had to be downloaded in their entirety. Byte-range downloads allow users to download part of a document to see whether they want to load the rest, then continue on to the rest without starting over. This also helps in cases in which the transfer has been interrupted by a network failure.

Finally, HTTP 1.1 specifies MD5 digest authentication, meaning that a user password can be validated on the client, which not only is far faster than sending it to the server for validation, but also increases security because the password is never sent over the network in the clear. In summary, you should definitely use HTTP 1.1 if you can. It is already part of the Apache server and Netscape Enterprise Server 3.0. Internet Explorer 4.0 reports that it uses HTTP 1.1. Netscape Navigator 4.0 reports that it uses HTTP 1.0 but has some 1.1 features, such as persistent connections.

HTTP proxy request format

HTTP proxies accept HTTP requests in a slightly different format. Because your browser has connected to the proxy and not directly to the desired web server, the browser must tell the proxy which server to connect to. So rather than saying GET / HTTP/1.0, the browser says GET / http://server/index.html and leaves the protocol up to the proxy.

Byterange downloads

HTTP and HTML were created at CERN by Tim Berners-Lee to serve scientific papers on advances in physics. No one thought about serving just a few bytes from the middle of a paper, so the original specifications had no mechanism for requesting and serving only a fraction of a web page, and browsers had no method of incorporating a few bytes into a cached page. Either you got the whole page or you didn't. This worked well enough, but it eventually became evident that a great deal of bandwidth could be saved by having a mechanism to download only part of a document. This was especially true for dynamic content. Usually only part of a dynamic page will be different each time you get it—that is, only some data will be different, not the formatting. Consider a stock quote page. The user is looking for the number, not all the surrounding formatting and images. If you could make just the number reload, you could improve the user experience and save bandwidth.

There are a few ways to reload just a part of a page, but they are all fairly kludgy and have serious drawbacks. For example, you could use a tiny frame to encapsulate a quote, and then use an HTML META "refresh" tag to reload just that tiny frame at regular intervals, but hitting the browser's reload button would still reload the entire page. Another option is to make a tiny applet that reloads the data, but then you have to start up a Java VM, which is time-consuming, and the entire page would still reload when that reload button gets used.

The good folks at the W3C (*http://www.w3c.org/*) knew about this problem and so they included support for fractional page downloads in HTTP 1.1. Fractional downloads are also known as "byterange requests" or "partial content." Apache includes support for byterange requests, as do Netscape web servers. Servers that accept byterange requests output the Accept-ranges: bytes HTTP header, so you can manually check whether your server accepts such requests with *telnet* and a little knowledge of HTTP. For example, here I manually telnet to an Apache server running on my local machine and just ask for the headers for the root page:

```
vahe% telnet localhost 80
Trying 127.0.0.1...
Connected to localhost.
Escape character is '^]'.
HEAD / HTTP/1.1
Host: vahe

HTTP/1.1 200 OK
Date: Wed, 01 Aug 2001 17:17:23 GMT
Server: Apache/1.3.9 (Unix)  (Red Hat/Linux)
Last-Modified: Mon, 30 Jul 2001 05:41:56 GMT
ETag: "54802-86d-3b64f3a4"
Accept-Ranges: bytes
Content-Length: 2157
Content-Type: text/html

Connection closed by foreign host.
```

Now that we know we can, let's try to actually request just a few bytes in the middle of a page. We do it by issuing the "Range" header in the request:

```
vahe% telnet localhost 80
Trying 127.0.0.1...
```

```
Connected to localhost.
Escape character is '^]'.
GET / HTTP/1.1
Host: vahe
Range: bytes=1000-1008

HTTP/1.1 206 Partial Content
Date: Tue, 31 Jul 2001 17:36:37 GMT
Server: Apache/1.3.9 (Unix)  (Red Hat/Linux)
Last-Modified: Mon, 30 Jul 2001 05:41:56 GMT
ETag: "54802-86d-3b64f3a4"
Accept-Ranges: bytes
Content-Length: 9
Content-Range: bytes 1000-1008/2157
Content-Type: text/html

TTOM></a>Connection closed by foreign host.
```

We see that we have bytes 1000–1008 (which is 9 bytes, since we count from 0):
"TTOM></a>". So it all works fine.

Hey, that's great. Our server can respond correctly to a byterange request. Now let's
make a byterange request from the browser. Hmmm. Browsers do not include that
ability. You could write a Java applet to make the correct HTTP request, but the
result would not be integrated into the current HTML page. Actually, there is some
vestigial ability left in a few browsers, but it's inconsistent. It seems to have been
added years ago, and is not well known or used. After much searching and experimentation, this URL worked in Netscape 4.61 on Linux (note that the space before
the semicolon is required):

```
http://localhost/index.html ;bytes=1000-1008
```

Unfortunately, it actually displayed only those bytes in the browser. What I really
want is for those bytes to be integrated with a cached version of the same page.
Through elaborate trickery, I did manage to get Apache to send a "206 Partial Content" response to Netscape, just as if the browser issued the correct HTTP byterange
request, but still the browser displayed only those bytes. IE, on the other hand, simply ignores the "206 Partial Content" response if it has the whole content already,
and does not work with that kludgy "bytes=" kind of URL.

So we see that even though we have some ability to make the request, we have not
had the ability to integrate the response into a cached page. Maybe someday there
will be an easy standard way to tell the browser just to refresh a few bytes and it will
issue the appropriate HTTP request. But that day is not here, though it seems that
PDF readers do already have that ability.

Even though byterange requests are not supported directly in browsers, there is a
new development in browsers that does allow integration of part of a page into an
existing page. The Document Object Model (DOM) is a standard way to represent
and access the internal tree structure of a HTML document. At the top of the tree we

have the initial HTML page, then its images and subsidiary frames as branches and so on. The exciting thing about the DOM is that there is a JavaScript API for accessing and changing the tree structure of a document in the browser. The catch is that the DOM API is available only in IE 5.0 and NS 6.0, and is different in each browser.

HTTP and filesystems

If you think about it, the Web is really just a huge filesystem. The fact that most of the files are HTML or images is irrelevant. It is entirely possible to write a filesystem driver that would mount the entire web in a directory so that all of your usual programs would work. If you execute files, they would download from the remote web server and execute; if you open a spreadsheet file, it would also download and would open in your spreadsheet program. If you are a Unix type, you could *grep* directly from web pages. For example, if the HTTP filesystem driver mounted the web as */web*, you could *grep* like this:

```
% grep "sales rank" /web/www.amazon.com/exec/obidos/ASIN/1565923790
```

All other Unix commands would also work, but directory listings would not work unless the remote web server were set up to allow that. Also, most data would be read-only. The Web would be similar to putting a CD in your local computer and mounting it in the filesystem.

Another project begging to be done is mounting database tables as files so that they can be manipulated just like ordinary files, but with a save request being mapped to an SQL insert statement.

FTP

The file transfer protocol (FTP) is an older cousin of HTTP. FTP uses many of the same design patterns as HTTP (for instance, status numbers to indicate connection results) and the setting up and tearing down of a TCP connection for every data transfer. FTP is different from HTTP in that it sets up a TCP control channel connection and leaves that connection up as long as the client desires to remain connected.

The principal thing you need to know about FTP with respect to the Web is most browsers understand FTP and accept URLs beginning with *ftp://*. Downloads using FTP have better performance than HTTP downloads, probably because HTTP has more overhead and breaks long downloads into chunks. The browser knows enough to send the anonymous user ID to anonymous FTP sites. FTP fits the model that the TCP protocol was created for: relatively large transfers and infrequent connections.

NNTP

Network News Transport Protocol (NNTP) is usually used only for replicating articles posted to Usenet news groups, but can also be used to replicate web content, in effect distributing a site around the world for quick access. It also makes censorship of a web site much more difficult.

CORBA

The Common Object Request Broker Architecture (CORBA) is a specification for software object interaction across multiple platforms. CORBA has been under revision for many years, and it recently had some acceptance because it works with Java, but now it looks like it may be replaced by Enterprise JavaBeans (EJBs). It allows access to legacy applications from anywhere on the Web by wrapping the applications in an object-oriented interface definition language (IDL). A component called an Object Request Broker (ORB) directs requests for services to the appropriate object. Java ORBs can be downloaded from the Web, making CORBA servers available to any web client that understands Java. Netscape now includes Visigenic's ORB. Other Java ORBs are available from Iona, Orbix, and Expersoft. There are also publicly available Java ORBs, such as JacORB.

There is not much performance information available on CORBA. It seems that the principal performance issue with CORBA is the number of times data must be copied between buffers in order to fulfill a request. In particular, the serialization of parameters to remote calls is very costly. Each parameter must be converted to a form that can be passed across the network, and all of its dependencies must also be passed if not present on the remote side. Still, CORBA clearly has an advantage over CGI in that you can invoke methods and services across the network without starting a process just to handle that call.

CORBA scales well in theory, but in practice I have not seen any successful implementations of high-volume CORBA, while I've seen several failures. Objects can run on as many servers as you need, with the ORB dispatching method calls to appropriate objects, or even creating new objects if need be. Disadvantages of CORBA are that it is unnecessarily complex and that it does not gracefully handle remote object instantiation failure. The lookup of named objects itself is intrinsically slow, though flexible.

It is interesting to compare CORBA to simply using a web server to run a CGI or servlet. The DNS lookup of the name of the server running the CGI is analogous to the CORBA lookup of a named object. A big difference is that web forms are intended for human consumption, while CORBA calls are only for machines.

Remember that it's about a million times slower to instantiate an object over the network than it is to do so locally, and there is often no good mechanism to deal with instantiation failures or partial failures, which are much more likely over the network. Distributed objects work well for cases in which most of the work is local computation, with occasional communication, but not very well in cases in which lots of objects have to move back and forth across the wire.

The Voyager product from Objectspace (*http://www.objectspace.com/*) had better performance than CORBA in simple *ping* tests I ran and is more elegant and easier to use. It is a freely available distributed object system for Java, but it does not yet specify integration with legacy systems, as CORBA does. It will eventually include CORBA compatibility.

X

Redirected X displays can easily use up all the bandwidth you throw at them. Every blink of a cursor, the flying stars of the Netscape logo—every change to the display will generate network traffic. A busy screen saver redirected over the network is especially bad. You don't want your web server on a network that is being used for such traffic.

Key Recommendations

- Set a larger timeout for initial TCP retransmits for the Internet, because the Internet is slower than a LAN.
- Increase the TCP listen queue if you know it is overflowing.
- Don't let unused connections hang around for more than half an hour (not eight hours, as TCP originally specified). Use an HTTP 1.1–compliant web server and browser if possible.

## CHAPTER 16

Server Hardware

In this chapter, we revisit computer hardware, this time from the server perspective.

Even though each client receives exactly as many bytes as the server sends, the server hardware needs to be more powerful than client hardware because the servers must be capable of handling many clients simultaneously, and usually capable of generating dynamic content as well.

On the other hand, it is common for small web sites to overestimate just how much server power they really need. If your server is handling only one client every several seconds, then you can probably make do with the same hardware that would make a good web client. For the majority of sites, the network connection is more likely than server hardware to be the limiting factor.

Server tuning is the subject of many entire books, and the subject is much larger than I can present in a single chapter. For in-depth detail, some good books on the subject are *System Performance Tuning*, by Mike Loukides (O'Reilly & Associates); *Sun Performance and Tuning, 2nd Edition*, by Adrian Cockcroft (Prentice Hall); *Configuration and Capacity Planning for Solaris Servers*, by Brian Wong (Prentice Hall); and *Optimizing Windows NT*, by Russ Blake (Microsoft Press).

Box on a Wire

A web server is essentially remote storage that copies data from its RAM or disk to the network connection upon request. It may not be a simple copy, since dynamic content or database access may be involved, but from the user's point of view, your web server is just one more mass storage device.

Now, does a disk drive have a windowing system? No. Similarly, your web server does not need a windowing system, a video card, a monitor, or even a keyboard! In fact, a windowing system occupies a great deal of RAM and CPU, so it is a drain on server performance. You don't have any choice about windowing overhead if you're using a Windows or Mac web server, but on Unix systems you can simply turn off X Windows.

NT and Unix have an additional reason not to use a windowing system: the currently active window has a higher execution priority than other processes. On Solaris for example, processes belonging to the currently selected window are bumped up in priority by 10 points (out of 100 or so). If you're not very careful with the windowing system, you can hurt web server performance simply by moving the mouse. It is better to do web server administration remotely over one or more *telnet* sessions from a different computer.

Web servers without monitors are known as headless servers.

Good I/O

The fundamental distinguishing feature of server hardware is high-performance I/O. Commodity PC hardware is limited by its legacy I/O subsystem, while server hardware is designed around I/O and can easily have 10 times the I/O performance of the best PCs.

Multiple Busses

Servers usually have separate busses for L2 cache, I/O, RAM, and peripherals. This reduces contention and allows the use of appropriate hardware for each bus. Server busses may be packet switched, in the sense that a request is made over the bus and the bus is released until the response is ready, allowing requests to be interleaved with responses and improving throughput. Bus throughput is critical for servers, because a great deal of what a server does is simply copy data between network devices and storage devices.

Fast Disks

Servers should have separate high-speed SCSI disks for content and logging. Traditionally, IDE disks have not been acceptable, however the IDE standard has evolved, and now some IDE drives rival SCSI in performance. Striping data over disk arrays is highly recommended in order to allow seeks to proceed in parallel.

Lots of Memory

Servers should have large amounts of RAM to reduce disk accesses. A good rule is to allow enough RAM to hold the complete OS and the most frequently accessed parts of your data set. Servers also tend to have large L1 and L2 caches, and may have the cache split between data and instruction caches, because data and instructions have different access patterns. The only memory faster than L1 cache is the set of registers on the CPU. Many megabytes of L2 cache is becoming common, but the physical distance of the cache from the CPU, even just an inch, significantly reduces the effectiveness of the cache. Unfortunately, the effectiveness of caching for server CPUs is reduced by the context switching that happens with every network interrupt. HTTPD code and network-handling code displace each other from the caches.

Device drivers occupy kernel memory and kernel memory is not pagable. Therefore, unneeded device drivers reduce your effective amount of RAM. Unneeded device drivers should not be loaded.

Scalability

A server should be scalable to smoothly handle an increasing workload. Unix workstations have far more capacity for scaling by adding CPUs and RAM than PCs. Unix workstations scale up to 64 or 128 CPUs, depending on whom you ask, while PC hardware cannot generally handle the contention between more than 4 CPUs, as of this writing. Workstations also have better I/O bandwidth and more RAM expandability.

Network Interface Card

The Network Interface Card (NIC) provides the connection between the network cable and the server's bus. NICs fill a conceptually simple niche, but their variety reflects the many permutations possible between network cable, cable signalling protocol, and host computer bus. NICs take an incoming serial stream of bits and output a parallel stream onto the bus, and vice versa. Until recently, it could be assumed that the network connection would be far slower than the CPU and bus, but LAN network speeds have been increasing faster than CPU and bus speeds, so it is no longer a safe bet that your network card can be handled by your machine. Still, at the interface to the Internet, you can be fairly sure that your server will be more constrained by Internet access than by any other component, save perhaps disk.

NICs have on-board buffers, and a bigger buffer always gives you more flexibility. The buffer has historically been important for holding outgoing data until the network can deal with it all, but as mentioned, that situation is reversing, so in the future the buffers will tend to hold incoming data, waiting for the computer. In either case, a larger buffer makes a buffer overflow and consequent data loss less likely. Lost TCP/IP data is simply retransmitted, adding to overhead. Typically, 8-bit Ethernet cards have 8K buffers, while 16-bit cards have 16K buffers.

When a NIC has a complete unit of data from the network and is ready to forward it on to the computer's bus, it generates a hardware interrupt, which forces the CPU to save its current state and run the network card interrupt handler, which retrieves the data from the NIC's buffer and fills a data structure in memory. Therefore, a critical performance factor is how many interrupts per second the CPU, memory, and bus can handle from the NIC.

Another important measure of a server is how quickly it can get data from RAM or disk out to the network interface. This involves copying data from one place in memory to another, which is typical of server activity. Data is copied from the server's memory to the network interface card memory. Given a 1,500-byte outgoing Ethernet packet, the OS must copy it—probably 4 bytes at a time—from RAM or cache out to the NIC buffer, so this copy would require 375 bus cycles to complete. The bcopy or memcpy library calls are often used here, so the efficiency of your server's implementation of these library calls is significant.

This is also where the implementation of TCP/IP in your kernel becomes significant. If you have a poor implementation, it probably means the wait between the NIC's interrupt and the retrieval of a packet from the NIC's buffer is large, so additional packets arriving on the NIC may not find sufficient buffer space and may be dropped or overrun data in the buffer. This results in a costly retransmission of the lost packet.

You will get the best performance from the most recent network cards. Many network cards can now be upgraded by loading new code into their flash memory. The latest non-beta release of this code should give you the best performance.

It is possible to sidestep the use of the CPU for retrieving NIC buffer data by using a "busmastering" NIC, which is capable of moving data directly between the NIC buffer and the machine's memory without interrupting the processor. Busmastering cards have a performance advantage over non-busmastering cards, but are more expensive, because they need more on-card intelligence. Intel has specified a method for interfacing NICs directly to PC hard disk, called the I20 specification, which will need operating system support. I20 should be available by the time you read this.

Bus

A bus is a set of parallel wires (usually 32, 64, 128, or 256 wires, plus error and protocol-handling wires) embedded in a board forming the backbone of the computer. Other components, including CPU, disk, memory, and network cards, are connected to each other by their shared bus.

There may be more than one bus in a computer. PCs may have only one bus connecting everything. Server hardware, however, typically has at least two separate busses: a high-speed bus for connecting memory to the CPU, and a slower bus for connecting I/O to the CPU. System busses lag CPU speed by a large margin, meaning that CPUs spend a great many cycles simply sitting and waiting for the bus to catch up. On the other hand, busses are usually faster than network connections. As already mentioned, this has been changing recently. Fast Ethernet, for example, runs at 100 Mbps, which is more than ISA or EISA busses can handle. Gigabit Ethernet runs at 1,000 Mbps, which is even more of a challenge. At gigabit rates, the server bus and CPU generally become the bottleneck, especially if the CPU is trying to do database access or run CGI applications at the same time.

While a throughput of 4,224 Mbps from a 64-bit 66 MHz PCI bus is technically possible, your true throughput will be far lower because of contention, network packet overhead, OS implementation, and many other issues. 10 Mbps is good TCP/IP throughput for a PC. A Sun Ultra 1 should get much better than 40 Mbps of TCP/IP throughput. (The advertised rates you see will be the far higher theoretical rates.) The 66 MHz PCI bus exceeds memory access speeds, moving the bottleneck to RAM.

Multiple PCI busses, provided on some Compaq PCs, may give you parallel access to peripheral devices. Sun uses the IEEE 1496 standard for its peripheral SBus, but recently started building machines with PCI peripheral busses, so you can use off-the-shelf PCI cards if you install Sun-specific device drivers. Sun implements 64-bit PCI at 66 MHz for the throughput needed for 622 Mbps ATM, gigabit Ethernet, and Fibrechannel.

Memory

It is difficult to exaggerate the time difference between accessing memory and accessing disk. Although in human terms there is little perceptible difference between a 100-nanosecond write to RAM and a 100-millisecond write to hard disk, there is literally a factor of one million between them, comparable to the difference between 1 second and 10 days. The perceptible difference comes in repeated access, when the value of having enough memory quickly becomes clear.

RAM Characteristics

Most physical chip memory these days is Dynamic Random Access Memory (DRAM). *Random access* refers to the fact that you can access any location on the memory chip with equal speed. *Dynamic* refers to the fact that the memory is repeatedly being refreshed because the charge on each individual cell is constantly leaking away.

DRAM was invented during the 1980s when it was realized that memories could be made much denser by storing a bit on a single transistor rather than on a set of transistors, with the caveat that the entire chip would have to be constantly refreshed because of the charge leakage problem. The older kind of memory is now referred to as Static Random Access Memory (SRAM). SRAM uses flip flops, sets of 4 or 5 transistors that keep state by refreshing each other. SRAM is more expensive and not as dense as DRAM, but has far faster access time, on the order of 20 nanoseconds rather than 80 nanoseconds for DRAM. SRAM is used for L2 caches.

DRAM has dropped a lot in price recently. You should be able to find commodity DRAM for $3–5/MB as of this writing.

Even though RAM is very fast relative to disk, it is not infinitely fast. Most RAM these days has better than 100-nanosecond access time. Let's compare that to a 1000

MHz CPU, which has a 1-nanosecond clock cycle (1/10 9 = 1ns). Most instructions on an Intel CPU take from 1 to 5 clock cycles to complete and may require additional memory accesses to retrieve operands. Even at 5 clocks per instruction, the CPU would still have to wait an additional 45 idle clocks for the next instruction. This is an overly simplified example that ignores the bus, pipelining of instructions, and superscalar CPUs (which execute more than one instruction at a time), but you can see that, in general, CPUs are much faster than the RAM serving them.

RAM itself is often rated in wait states for a particular CPU. Each cycle that the CPU has to wait for the RAM is a wait state, so the best RAM for your CPU has zero wait states. Wait states are the reason CPUs have caches, which are a special kind of RAM kept on board the CPU (L1 cache) or very close to the CPU (L2 cache). Cache memory can be accessed at full processor speed. Caches overcome some of the mismatch between bus/RAM speeds and CPU speeds by keeping frequently used data and instructions close to the CPU. Note that some kinds of memory chips have on-chip caches too—that's how EDO, BEDO, and SDRAM differ. The rated speeds for RAM are only theoretical maxima because, in reality, there are latencies internal to RAM between row and column assertion.

Multiple memory controllers allow multiple RAM access setups to proceed in parallel, for greater overall throughput.

CPU

Look at any PC advertisement. The first specification given is usually the CPU speed, because PC buyers like to be able to compare numbers, and this is an easy number to use for comparisons. Ironically, most PC systems are not balanced: a high-power CPU is wasted on an inferior bus and disk. (On the other hand, the CPU isn't really wasted from the PC maker's point of view if that's what gets you to buy the system.) A low-end Intel Pentium CPU running at 500 MHz will end up spending most of its time waiting for its EISA bus and IDE disk. What you really want is a fast bus, a low-latency disk, and a lot of RAM. Systems sold as servers are generally better balanced, because they are rated on actual throughput.

Still, sometimes you are really utilizing 100 percent of your CPU and could benefit from more power. Extensive database searches or calculations, generating graphics on the fly, or running server-side Java may all tax your CPU to its maximum. Use readily available Unix tools to monitor your CPU usage. Run *vmstat 1* for a while and look at the last three columns, which are usually user, system, and idletime. If the idle time is usually very low, say under five percent, then you may need more CPU power. You can measure the same things with *top* or *perfmeter*.

How much CPU power you need also depends on the speed of your client connections, the size of the content being served, and the number of clients. Say you're serving a large (100K) file to hundreds of clients at the same time. If the clients are all on high bandwidth connections, maybe you can serve the entire file in the time you have to run before the OS runs another process.

Solaris timeslices are 10 milliseconds by default, but that can be changed. Whether you can efficiently serve the file in the number of timeslices you get will depend on your I/O subsystem. If the clients are all on slow bandwidth connections, then you'll spend most of your time switching between processes, and a good CPU will become more important than the I/O subsystem.

A critical point to remember is that when the Internet becomes congested, say at peak times of the day, even fast clients look like slow clients to the server. The kind of server you need changes from one with the best I/O possible, to one with the best CPU possible and a great deal of RAM to hold all the concurrent connections. (Thanks to Jim Barrick of Keynote for that tip.)

CPU Construction

Let's take a look at CPU construction with an eye on performance. At the most basic level, after a reset, the CPU reads the instruction from a hardwired start address in memory (usually not address zero), executes it, increments its internal program counter to one, reads the next instruction, executes it, and so on. This is a bit of a simplification, but not much of one. The instructions are probably of variable length, so the next one may not be at the next address, and the CPU may need to load operands in order to execute an instruction. It is very likely to jump to an instruction at a nonsequential address, depending on the result of the previous instruction, but the basic pattern holds: read instruction, execute, increment program counter. In fact, if all of memory were filled with "no op" commands, the CPU would just zip right through all memory in sequence. (And it wouldn't take very long: this is pretty much what happens in the memory check when you boot.) When you reached the end, the CPU would just wait for an interrupt in its idle state.

Many optimizations have been done to help the basic "fetch, decode, execute" process along. For example, CPUs now pipeline instructions, meaning that they don't read just one instruction at a time from memory, but read several, queuing them up and executing portions of them at the same time. This reduces memory-access overhead and speeds execution, but sometimes the next instruction is not at the next memory location, so the pipeline breaks and additional memory accesses must be done. Some CPUs actually look at the upcoming code and use branch prediction algorithms to preemptively read from the most likely part of memory for the next instructions.

CPUs also run at different core and bus frequencies. The Pentium, for example, has one bus to the outside world, the "frontside bus," which is 64-bits wide and runs at the PCI clock rate (66 MHz), but fetches instructions from its internal cache and runs internally at a higher rate. The frontside bus of Sun Ultra CPUs is 128-bits wide and runs at 83 MHz or 100 MHz.

When a CPU is referred to as 32-bit or 64-bit, this doesn't mean that it's worth four dollars or eight dollars, but rather that memory addresses are 32- or 64-bits long. On the other hand, a 2-bit CPU actually would be worth about a quarter. The number of bits refers to the size of a pointer, and therefore also determines the address space available. 32-bit machines have a 4 GB address space, and 64-bit machines have such a humongous address space that I don't know how to describe it. The Pentium chips are all 32-bit; the UltraSPARC and Alpha are 64-bit. There currently isn't much 64-bit software available, but if you are writing custom software and need a very large address space and extreme performance, a 64-bit CPU may be useful to you. The AltaVista search engine uses custom 64-bit software and needs it, because each of the search engine machines has more than 4 GB of RAM.

32-bit software will run on a 64-bit version of the same chip, but you will not necessarily see any performance advantage. It is generally true that software may run on a CPU without being optimized for that CPU. This is true of the SPARC line, for example. Any SPARC executable should be able to run on any SPARC CPU, but it may not have particularly good performance unless it was specifically compiled for that CPU. A good compiler like *gcc* will give you multiple options for each CPU family so that you can take advantage of the latest chip features. Type *man gcc* for more information. Sun's C compiler has a similar *-xchip* option to tell the compiler which SPARC chip to optimize for.

How much bandwidth can a particular CPU handle? According to Brian Wong's book, *Configuration and Capacity Planning for Solaris Servers*, a Sparc 5 can fill a 50 Mbit/second line, which is about the same as a T3, but you won't have any CPU cycles left to do anything else. An Ultra or Pentium Pro is capable of saturating a 155 Mbit/second ATM connection.

CISC instructions are of different sizes, and there are more of them. RISC instructions are generally all the same size, so it is easier to build a RISC CPU for efficiency. There are also fewer RISC instructions (hence the name), so you need to use several of them to get the same effect as with one CISC instruction, and the size of compiled code is larger. You're trading processor speed against storage. Intel CPUs are all CISC and backward compatible to the 8088, but now have a RISC core. Most CPUs now come with a built-in floating-point unit (FPU), which is an enormous advantage over software floating-point calculations, but few web sites use floating point for anything.

Remember that any digital algorithm implemented in software can also be implemented in hardware, and vice versa. The difference is performance: hardware implementations can be a thousand times faster or more. The Java Virtual Machine (JVM) is in effect a CPU (and some other runtime components) implemented in software. The logical performance enhancement is, therefore, to implement it in hardware. The first Java chips are already coming to market, but don't expect an immediate thousandfold gain in performance. The bytecodes of the JVM are easily translated into hardware; yet more than half of the time, running Java programs are not simply executing bytecodes but are performing more complex actions, such as object creation, that are already in native code in the JVM. Eventually, these actions will be accelerated by hardware also, making Java programs as fast or faster than native code on other platforms.

An HTTP server could also be implemented directly in hardware for speed. Dedicated HTTP chips would also make it easier to embed the HTTP protocol in consumer devices, so that your radio or VCR could be queried and controlled from any web browser. Of course, chips are much more difficult to upgrade than software, but when was the last time you upgraded anything on your VCR?

Symmetric Multiprocessing (SMP)

Enterprise-level applications often need more CPU power than any single-CPU machine can provide, but getting an application to effectively use multiple CPUs can be tricky. If you are lucky, your application may be able to run on separate single-CPU machines. Web servers scale this way. But many applications, such as databases, need to run on a single machine.

If your application must be run on a single machine, you have to add CPUs to scale it. One strategy for using multiple CPUs in that machine is to run multiple processes and have them communicate via the various forms of interprocess communication, such as semaphores and shared memory. The operating system will automatically allocate different CPUs to different processes. But interprocess communication techniques are not especially portable.

Native thread libraries provide a way to use multiple CPUs in a single process, and can be relatively portable, but native thread programming is difficult. Java thread programming, by comparison, is simple. Not only is Java thread programming simple, but programs using Java threads are extremely portable, and Java threads have been advertised as scaling well on multi-CPU machines. As we'll see next, this has not been entirely true in recent versions of Java, but there are some simple things you can do to maximize Java multithreading performance on multi-CPU machines.

Getting multiple equivalent CPUs to cooperate in a single machine is known as Symmetric MultiProcessing (SMP). Running in a single-CPU machine is known as uniprocessing. SMP machines usually have CPU modules that plug into a bus. In theory, you add capacity by buying more CPUs and plugging them in. Unfortunately, because of the problems of coordinating CPU activity and the fact that most applications spend a great deal of time waiting for I/O rather than using CPU, you don't necessarily see twice the throughput with two processors that you see with one. You may even see that performance is worse with multiple CPUs. For software that hasn't been designed to run on an SMP system, moving from one CPU to two may get you no more than a 30 percent increase in performance. For CPU-intensive programs designed for SMP, you may see an 80 percent or 90 percent increase in performance by adding a second CPU. A lot depends on exactly what the application is doing. CPU-intensive programs, which can run as parallel processes or threads, naturally benefit more than programs which use mostly network and disk.

Java threads can run in parallel on multiple CPUs, but do not do so unless you use a native threads library, which schedules threads in the operating system, as opposed to the "green" threads package, which does thread scheduling within the Java VM, a single process. An environment variable or command line switch is normally used to turn on native threads. Even using native threads, Java does not necessarily use all available CPUs; it depends on how the particular VM was written.

Note that Unix is far ahead of NT in the SMP arena. The most NT can currently handle is 4 CPUs. Even if an NT machine has slots for more than 4 CPUs, performance is likely to decrease if you go beyond, because the operating system is not efficient at partitioning work among more than 4 CPUs. Be careful of demonstrations where the vendor sets up several machines side by side and claims good scalability without mentioning that it is extremely difficult to partition most enterprise applications among several independent machines. Solaris currently scales up to 64 CPUs while gaining benefit from each additional CPU. This means you can start out with a low-end Solaris machine and add more CPUs as you need more power, without reworking your applications or architecture. Assuming, of course, that your application is designed to use SMP.

Testing Sun SMP Scalability

I ran some tests to try to prove for myself that adding CPUs to a large Sun machine would increase performance. A research note about SMP scalability on Linux from Cameron MacKinnon is available at *http://www.phy.duke.edu/brahma/benchmarks. smp*. In this note, Cameron tells how he tests Linux SMP scalability by running multiple processes that do nothing but count to one billion. This should test nothing but the CPU. It's not accessing disk or memory, and perhaps not even the CPU cache. Here is an example C program, which should give your CPU a workout:

```
main( ) { unsigned long i; for (i=0; i<1000000000; i++); }
```

I compiled this program with maximum optimization, e.g., *gcc -O3 -o loop loop.c*, and ran it on a 500 MHz Dell Optiplex GX1 PCI-bus PC with 512 KB cache running Linux 2.2. It takes about four seconds to run.

```
% time loop
```

```
4.02user 0.00system 0:04.02elapsed 99%CPU
```

(I removed some output for clarity.)

Our 500 MHz CPU ticks off one billion clock cycles in 2 seconds. Since we're taking 4 seconds, it looks like we're using about 2 clock cycles per increment of the variable

i. Now what if we run two copies of this program at the "same" time on a single-CPU Linux PC? Of course the processes won't run at exactly the same time because only one can be using the CPU at any given moment. The processes will be scheduled by the kernel and will appear to the user to run at the same time, but the total time taken should be twice as long. And it is. In fact, the time taken is directly proportional to the number of processes we're running. I ran up to 24 processes with the following Perl script, while the machine was otherwise idle:

```perl
#!/usr/local/bin/perl
$| = 1;
$\ = "\n";

for ($procs = 1; $procs <= 24; $procs++) {

    for ($i = 1; $i <= $procs; $i++) {
        if ($pid = fork) {}
        elsif (defined $pid) {
            exec 'loop';
        }
        else {
            die "cannot fork: $!\n";
        }
    }

    $start = time();
    for ($i = 1; $i <= $procs; $i++) { wait; }
    $end = time();

    $latency = $end - $start;

    print "$procs $latency";
}
```

I got the following results:

```
 1  4
 2  9
 3 12
 4 16
 5 20
 6 24
 7 28
 8 32
 9 37
10 38
11 44
12 48
13 53
14 56
15 61
16 64
17 69
18 71
```

```
19 76
20 80
21 83
22 89
23 89
24 93
```

I plotted with *gnuplot* to get the following image in Figure 16-1.

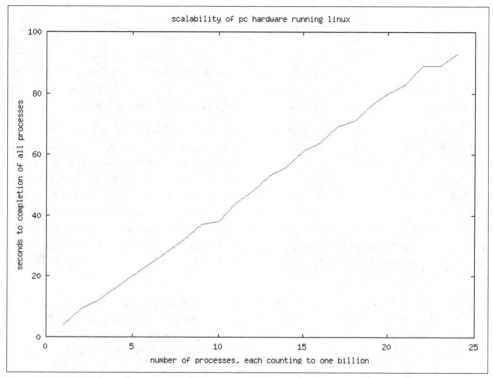

Figure 16-1. CPU-bound processes take proportionally longer to complete

As you run more simultaneous processes, it takes proportionately longer for them to complete. This is exactly what you expect for CPU-bound processes on a single-CPU machine. I have done similar a experiment on Sun hardware, turning off all CPUs but one, and have seen the same linear scaling, but from a different starting point. That starting point for a single copy of the *loop.c* program is about 6.7 seconds on a Sun E450 with one 250 MHz CPU.

A common reaction at this point is to say, "Now wait a minute, the Sun hardware is more expensive than the PC hardware, but runs this test more slowly?" Yes, in this specific case, the test runs more slowly on the Sun hardware, but you can't draw too many conclusions from that. The Sun machine is designed to scale up to many processors, while the PC hardware is not. This adds some overhead. The Sparc CPU was running at half the clock rate of the Intel CPU and uses a completely different instruction set; the Sparc CPU is RISC, while the Intel CPU is CISC. To see how random some simple test results can be, you can simply reverse the order of counting in loop.c, going down from one billion to zero rather than up from zero to one billion, and find that the Sun machine takes exactly half the time it did before, 3.35 seconds, while the PC counts down in exactly the same time as counting up, 4.02 seconds. So now the Sun machine looks faster. What's going on here?

The *gcc* compiler generates fewer instructions on the Sun machine when counting down than when counting up, while it generates the same number of instructions either way on the Intel platform. Remember that the Sparc and Intel chips use totally different instruction sets. The *gcc* compiler just happened to be able to find a slightly more efficient way to count down on the Sparc CPU. You can dump and examine the assembly language generated by *gcc* by using its -*S* option.

Compiler optimizations can be especially confusing. Another difference is caused by changing the lower limit of the counting. For example, if you count down from one billion to 4,095 on the Sun machine, it is about as fast as counting down to zero. But if you count down from one billion to 4,096 or more, suddenly the running time doubles. Note that $2^{12} = 4,096$. When the lower limit is 4,095, the compiler generates a single opcode, but generates multiple opcodes for that same function when the lower limit is 4,096 or higher. If you think about it, a really clever compiler would just set our loop counter to its end value and skip the loop entirely, because the loop has no contents and the compiler can see that. Then the loop would seem to run instantly and the whole test would be meaningless.

We mentioned that Sun hardware is designed to scale up to many CPUs. Does it really use all those CPUs effectively? This is an important question, since CPUs are expensive. Let's start with processes. If we run 1, 2, 3, on up to 24 loop processes on a 12 CPU Sun machine, we see that each additional process adds nothing to the total running time until we exceed 12 processes. For each process more than 12, the total running time increases because we no longer have enough CPUs to run all the processes in parallel. The increase per additional process is about 1/12 of the time to run one process. This increase shows that CPU is shared equally among all the processes. If the work required to run the 13th process were not equally shared among the CPUs, the total running time would increase by more than 1/12, because at least one of the CPUs would be doing more than its fair share of work.

It is possible to bind a particular process to a particular CPU on Solaris, removing the time it takes the OS to choose a CPU from the picture, but I didn't use that feature here. Figure 16-2 illustrates the results. (The total running times are much higher than before because I forgot to compile with the -*O3* optimization switch to *gcc*.)

What if we turn off some of the CPUs and rerun the test? We would expect the rise in the graph to begin sooner. And this is exactly what we see. One by one, I turned

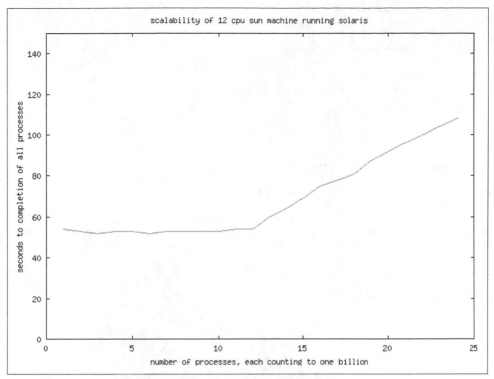

Figure 16-2. Total running time increases after 12 processes

off 11 of the 12 CPUs and reran the whole test from 1 to 24 processes. The result is a
12 by 24 grid of points. Here is the Perl wrapper that ran the test:

```perl
#!/usr/local/bin/perl$| = 1;$\ = "\n";

if ($<) {     # Then we're not running as root.
    die "Need to run as root to execute psradm. Terminating";
}

# CPU numbers are not necessarily sequential.@cpu_array = (0, 1, 3, 5, 8, 9, 12, 14,
16, 19, 20);

for ($cpu = 0; $cpu < 11; $cpu++) {
    for ($procs = 1; $procs <= 24; $procs++) {
        for ($i = 1; $i <= $procs; $i++) {
            if ($pid = fork) {}
            elsif (defined $pid) {
                exec 'loop';
            }
            else {
                die "cannot fork: $!\n";
            }
        }
```

```
    $start = time( );
    for ($i = 1; $i <= $procs; $i++) { wait; }
    $end = time( );
    $latency = $end - $start;

    $cpus_running = 12 - $cpu;
    print "$cpus_running $procs $latency";
}    print;


`psradm -f $cpu_array[$cpu]`;
}
```

Figure 16-3 is a graph of the results.

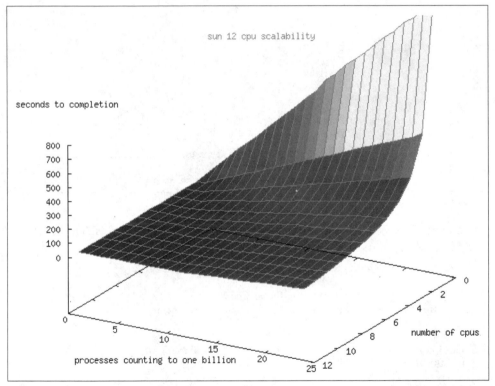

Figure 16-3. Total running time increases sooner with fewer processes

You can see that on the left, where we have fewer processes than CPUs, the surface is flat. The execution time remains constant. But where we have more processes than CPUs, the execution time goes up. This is a great curve. It shows that for totally CPU-intensive processes, not using memory or disk or the network, Sun hardware gives 100 percent bang for every buck you spend on CPUs, at least up to the 12 CPUs tested here.

Now what about CPU-intensive Java threads? Do they utilize Sun CPUs as effectively as processes do? Let's rewrite the *loop.c* program in Java:

```
class Loop implements Runnable {
    public static void main(String[] args) {
        for (int t = 0; t < Integer.parseInt(args[0]); t++)
            new Thread(new Loop()).start( );
    }

    public void run( ) {
        for (int i = 0; i < 1000000000; i++);
    }
}
```

If we compile this and run one thread under Sun's Java 1.1.7 on a 4-CPU Sun machine the execution time is 13 seconds:

```
% javac Loop.java
% time java Loop 1
```

If we compile this and run one thread under the Blackdown Java 1.1.6v5 on the PC running Linux, the execution time is 76 seconds. It's much slower because the Blackdown JDK 1.1 on Linux doesn't come with a JIT, but the Sun JDK does. A simple repetitive loop like this is prime JIT material. There are some open source JIT's for the Blackdown JDK, but I didn't try them. Back on Sun, let's run different numbers of Java native threads and see what the response curve looks like. I ran 1 to 24 threads on the 12-CPU machine. I expected to see a graph just like that in Figure 16-3, flat until 12 CPUs and then rising linearly. What I got what very different (see Figure 16-4).

What's going on here? First of all, it looks like at least two CPUs are being used, because the curve is flat for one and two threads. And it doesn't look like we ever use more than two CPUs, because the running time keeps increasing, though in a stair-step way. The running time doubles at three threads, and stays about there for four threads. This is very odd. We can see exactly which CPUs are busy by using the Solaris *mpstat* tool:

```
% jre Loop 3 & mpstat 1
[1] 17745
CPU minf mjf xcal  intr ithr  csw icsw migr smtx  srw syscl  usr sys  wt idl
  0   22   0  683     1    0  322  233    3   14    0   428    2   1   1  97
  1   23   0  597   301  100  307  223    4   17    0   464    2   1   1  96
  4   24   0  962     1    0  231  149    3   15    0   351    1   1   1  97
  5   23   0  622     1    0  356  257    4   17    0   480    2   1   1  96
  8   23   0 1212     1    0  350  284    3   14    0   461    2   1   1  96
  9   21   0  855     1    0  221  122    4   18    0   350    1   1   1  97
 12   21   0 1816     2    1  196  123    3   15    0   309    1   1   1  97
 13   20   0  896     1    0  323  234    4   16    0   432    2   1   1  97
 16   19   0 1448     3    2  343  258    3   14    0   428    1   1   1  96
 17   17   0 1182    13   11  212  108    3   17    0   322    1   1   1  97
 20   20   0 1212    15   12  340  190    6   27    0   491    2   1   1  96
 24   23   0  846    26   24  461  324    6   25    0   608    3   1   1  96
```

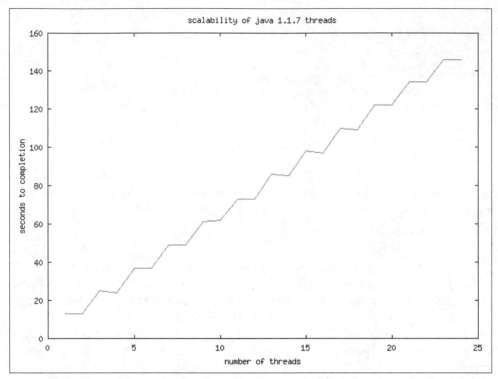

Figure 16-4. Nonlinear increase in running time under Java threads

CPU	minf	mjf	xcal	intr	ithr	csw	icsw	migr	smtx	srw	syscl	usr	sys	wt	idl
0	0	0	0	2	1	142	1	5	7	0	478	0	0	0	100
1	0	0	88	301	101	142	0	4	6	0	67	0	0	0	100
4	0	0	0	0	0	15	0	4	5	0	56	0	0	0	100
5	0	0	0	0	0	27	0	2	8	0	39	0	0	0	100
8	390	0	405	4	0	65	4	3	16	0	1136	60	15	0	25
9	561	0	431	2	0	61	2	17	6	0	809	18	8	0	74
12	0	0	0	3	1	26	2	4	6	0	46	33	0	0	67
13	0	0	0	3	2	91	1	4	17	0	234	0	0	0	100
16	0	0	0	4	2	4	2	2	1	0	0	16	0	0	84
17	0	0	0	2	2	90	0	8	8	0	778	0	3	0	97
20	0	0	0	5	3	191	2	6	22	0	310	0	0	0	100
24	3	0	0	5	4	246	1	5	47	0	376	0	0	0	100
CPU	minf	mjf	xcal	intr	ithr	csw	icsw	migr	smtx	srw	syscl	usr	sys	wt	idl
0	0	0	0	4	0	196	4	4	7	0	667	0	0	0	100
1	0	0	88	300	100	14	0	1	4	0	4	0	0	0	100
4	0	0	0	0	0	18	0	1	6	0	82	0	0	0	100
5	0	0	0	1	1	29	0	2	7	0	46	0	0	0	100
8	0	0	0	0	0	26	0	6	5	0	101	0	0	0	100
9	0	0	0	6	0	7	6	1	2	0	0	100	0	0	0
12	0	0	37103	1	0	45	1	3	16	0	120	0	20	0	80
13	0	0	0	4	2	50	1	1	15	0	52	0	0	0	100
16	0	0	0	8	2	7	6	1	2	0	0	100	0	0	0
17	0	0	44	8	8	41	0	5	11	0	62	0	0	0	100

```
 20    0   0    0     3    2  417    0    9   85    0   650    0   0   0 100
 24    0   0    0    19   18  212    0    5   14    0   122    0   0   0 100
CPU minf mjf xcal  intr ithr  csw icsw migr smtx  srw syscl  usr sys  wt idl
  0    0   0    0     0    0    9    0    1    2    0    11    0   0   0 100
  1    0   0   88   300  100    7    0    1    4    0     0    0   0   0 100
  4    0   0    0     0    0   17    0    0    8    0    66    0   0   0 100
  5    0   0    0     2    2   27    0    1    6    0    28    0   0   0 100
  8    0   0    0     1    0  280    0    3   28    0   427    0   0   0 100
  9    0   0    0     7    0    8    7    1    2    0     0  100   0   0   0
 12    0   0    0     1    0  212    1    4   63    0   738    0   0   0 100
 13    0   0    0     2    2   27    0    6    4    0    52    0   0   0 100
 16    0   0    0     8    2    7    6    1    2    0     0  100   0   0   0
 17    0   0    0     2    2   25    0    4    7    0    56    0   0   0 100
 20    0   0    0     3    2  156    1   13   10    0   292    0   0   0 100
 24    0   0    0     4    3  217    0    4   11    0   110    0   0   0 100
CPU minf mjf xcal  intr ithr  csw icsw migr smtx  srw syscl  usr sys  wt idl
  0    0   0    0     0    0   19    0    3    2    0    44    0   0   0 100
  1    0   0   88   300  100    9    0    5    6    0    14    0   0   0 100
  4    0   0    0     0    0   15    0    1    4    0    56    0   0   0 100
  5    0   0    0     0    0   25    0    1    8    0    30    0   0   0 100
  8    0   0    0     1    0  406    1    4   50    0   624    0   0   0 100
  9    0   0    0     8    0    9    8    1    2    0     0  100   0   0   0
 12    0   0    0     0    0  208    0    1   51    0   739    0   0   0 100
 13    0   0    0     0    0    8    0    2    4    0     0    0   0   0 100
 16    0   0    0     9    2    8    7    1    2    0     0  100   0   0   0
 17    0   0    0     2    2    8    0    1    3    0    19    0   0   0 100
 20    0   0    0     4    4   37    0   13    4    0   112    0   0   0 100
 24    0   0    0     6    6  222    0    8    8    0   108    0   0   0 100
CPU minf mjf xcal  intr ithr  csw icsw migr smtx  srw syscl  usr sys  wt idl
  0    0   0    0     0    0    3    0    1    4    0     0    0   0   0 100
  1    0   0   88   300  100   23    0    6    2    0    76    0   0   0 100
  4    0   0    0     0    0   18    0    1    9    0    40    0   0   0 100
  5    0   0    0     2    2   36    0    3    6    0    40    0   0   0 100
  8    0   0    0     1    0  403    0    4   56    0   627    0   0   0 100
  9    0   0    0     7    0    9    7    1    4    0     0  100   0   0   0
 12    0   0    0     0    0  209    0    0   42    0   732    0   0   0 100
 13    0   0    0     0    0    7    0    1    4    0     3    0   0   0 100
 16    0   0    0     8    1    8    7    1    2    0     0  100   0   0   0
 17    0   0    0     2    2    9    0    2    4    0    30    0   0   0 100
 20    0   0    0     3    3   22    0    3    5    0    63    0   0   0 100
 24    0   0    0    16   14  222    1    6    8    0   107    0   0   0 100
[output truncated]
```

For three threads, *mpstat* shows that during any given second, either two CPUs are busy, or one CPU is busy. So it looks like the 1.1.7 jre is not distributing its work across two CPUs effectively. The third thread is assigned only to one of the two CPUs in use and it doesn't ever using more than two CPUs, which is the bigger problem. As we did previously, let's turn off CPUs one at a time and run from 1 to 24 threads for each number of CPUs. Figure 16-5 is a graph of the results.

You can see that having two CPUs is much better than having one, but aside from that, additional CPUs aren't doing anything for us. (You can also see a point where

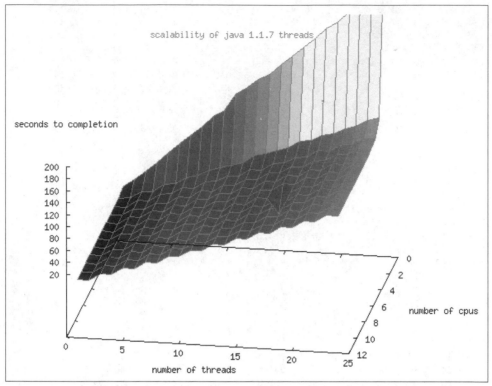

Figure 16-5. Additional CPUs ineffective with Java threads

someone else logged into this machine and ran a test, causing the dip in the graph.) So it seems that Sun's 1.1.7 jre is not scaling well on Sun's own SMP hardware. An email conversation with a Sun employee confirmed that the Java 1.1 mapping of native threads to LWPs (Light Weight Processes, also known as kernel threads) was probably not creating more than two LWPs. LWPs are the entity that actually runs on a CPU, so no more than two CPUs could be used. All of our user-level threads were mapped to an equal number of native threads, which were then mapped to only these two LWP's. There are three ways to fix this scalability problem:

1. You could stay on Java 1.1.7 and write a native method to call the Sun thr_ setconcurrency API (*man thr_setconcurrency* for more info), which can tell the Solaris thread library to create more LWPs. But this destroys your program's portability.

2. You could upgrade to Solaris 8 and use its single-level thread library, which maps user-level threads directly to LWPs. You use this library by setting LD_ LIBRARY_PATH appropriately.

3. You could upgrade to Java 1.2.2, which automatically uses thr_setconcurrency to set the number of LWPs to the number of processors in the machine. Running Java 1.2.2 requires patching Solaris 2.6.

I chose the third way. I reran the previous test on Java 1.2.2 on a patched Solaris 2.6 and got the results shown in Figure 16-6.

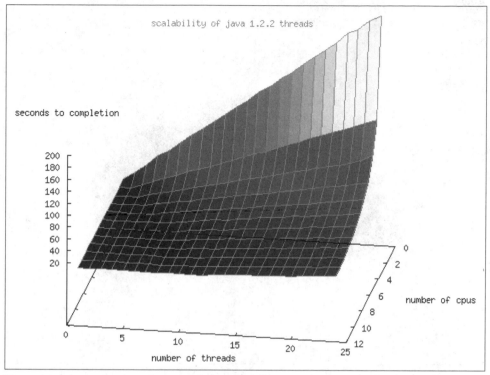

Figure 16-6. Java 1.2.2 fixes the scalability problem

Now that's more like it! We see our familiar flat surface on the left, and no jiggles. It looks like all our CPUs are getting used to run Java threads, and each additional CPU is fully utilized. So Java 1.2.2 would fix the scalability problem I saw with Java 1.1.7. Unfortunately, where I work, it is hard to make major changes like patching the operating system and changing jres in a busy production environment, so we couldn't do that right away. What we could do right away was run more Java 1.1.7 processes and load balance across them. That should make better use of the CPUs, even if each process used only two CPUs.

I found a servlet to use as a more realistic test of web site performance than simple counting threads. The servlet did extensive String manipulation and generated a lot of HTML. I modified it to loop a hundred times through the String manipulation and then throw away all that HTML, returning only a few bytes to say that the servlet ran successfully. The idea was to test CPU performance, not network capacity. I also specifically avoided disk and database access so that we were not testing that by mistake either. I ran the servlet on Weblogic 4.5.1 on Java 1.1.7 on Solaris 2.6. I set the number of Weblogic execute threads to 15. Because this servlet would be accessing main memory and not just CPU cache, I did not expect to see perfect CPU scalability. And that's not what I got, but I was still pretty pleased with the results (see Figure 16-7).

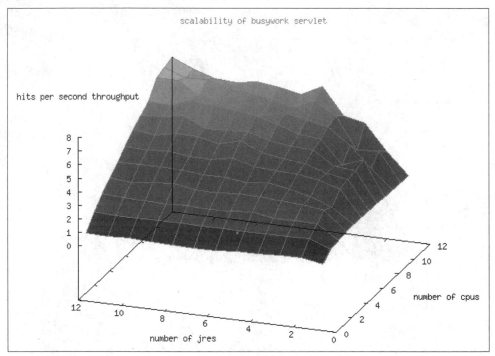

Figure 16-7. Load balancing among several Java 1.1.7 threads

Notice that this is a throughput graph, not a time-to-completion graph, so higher numbers are better. The peak is 12 CPUs and 12 jres. With just one jre, we see that applying more than two CPUs gains us nothing; throughput does not increase. This is what we expect if each 1.1.7 jre can use only two CPUs, but increasing the number of jres increases the benefit you get by adding CPUs. On the other hand, time spent waiting on an IO-like disk or network will increase the number of jres you can use, because blocked jres will not use CPU time, leaving it free for other jres.

To be even more realistic, I ran a similar load test against a page generated by extensive database queries. Since we introduced a new bottleneck, the database, we see that the gains from adding jres and CPUs just aren't as significant. After adding the second jre or fourth CPU, performance levels off at a limit imposed by the database (see Figure 16-8).

To summarize, the Sun 1.1.7 jre does not use more two 2 CPUs on Solaris 2.6 on Sun hardware. This can be fixed by adding a native method, upgrading the operating system, or upgrading the jre. A workaround is to simply run more jres. Sun's hardware does scale well, but it may take a little work and testing get the most out of it.

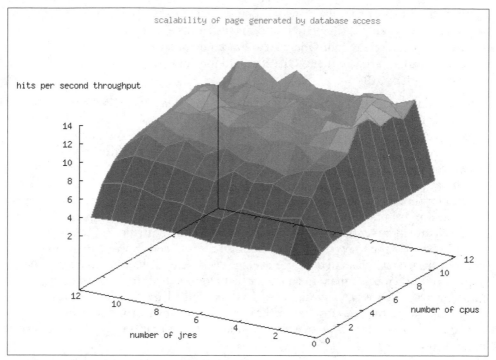

Figure 16-8. Database imposes its own limits on scalability

Disk

Next to your Internet connection, the parameter most likely to affect the perceived performance of your server is the speed of its hard disks. If everything seems reasonable but your performance is still lagging, the problem may be your disks. Remember how much of a penalty it is to go to disk rather than RAM. The relationship between a 100-nanosecond RAM access and a 10-millisecond disk access is the same proportion as 1 second to 28 hours, a factor of 100,000. And that's assuming a fast disk. So we want to avoid disk access wherever possible. If we have to hit the disk, at least we want to hit fast ones.

Disk Architecture and Parameters

Hard disks are literally that: hard platters coated with a magnetic recording material. There are usually multiple platters in a single hard disk unit. The unit is called a *spindle*. Each platter surface has an associated arm that swings in a wide enough angle to be able to position the data-reading and writing tip of the arm over any point on the radius of the platter. The disks generally start rotating when you boot up your computer and continue until you turn off the power. Laptops and other power-conscious machines may spin down (stop) the disk after a certain period of inactivity, but you should disable this feature on any such machine to be used as a web server, because there is usually a several second wait for the disk to spin up again.

Current hard disks typically rotate at 7,200 or 10,000 rpm. Since the disk has moving parts—for example, the platters and the disk arms—it is the part of your system hardware most likely to fail. One way to gracefully accept the failure of a disk is to have a redundant array of them. One standard for doing this, which we'll talk about in a bit, is called RAID.

The most important disk parameter is *maximum seek time*, which is the upper bound on the time it takes for the disk arm to move to any track. Disk arms are subject to forces of inertia when starting and stopping movement, and it is this inertia, as well as the physical distance the arm must travel, that limits overall disk performance. When the disk arm stops over a track, it tends to jiggle a bit, and the disk must wait for the arm to settle down before reading data. Latency for disks is defined as the maximum time needed for any sector on a track to come under the read/write head once the arm is in position. Latency is inversely proportional to disk speed. Seek time is usually much larger than latency, and therefore is the bottleneck. Seek time is also more important than raw throughput because disks spend most of their time seeking, not transferring data. To reduce average seek time, disks often try to queue up requests and then order them in a manner that reduces the total amount of motion of the disk arm. The exact algorithm used is determined by the disk controller, but disks usually use the "elevator" algorithm, in which the disk arm moves in one direction for as long as there are queued reads and writes in that direction before reversing direction.

The best average performance is halfway between the spindle and outermost cylinder, because the arm has the least average distance to travel. You may see some benefit in putting the most frequently hit filesystem in the middle cylinder.

Disks have memory caches of their own, used primarily to speed up writes to the disk system. The utility of a large disk cache depends on whether you're doing a lot of writes. Web servers read a lot of content and write only small records to log files, so the utility of large disk caches is debatable.

You will get better performance from a disk that is physically on the same machine as your web server software (a local disk) than from one mounted across a network, but a very high-speed connection, such as Fibre Channel, tends to blur this distinction.

Your web server should probably have at least two disks: one for content and one for web server logging. If you can afford it, consider yet another disk for the operating system itself, which has its own disk needs. Use the faster disk for serving content, because serving is a more intense operation than logging and is directly relevant to perceived performance. Users don't care if you log their access; only you do. You can also increase performance further by using another disk for your swap space. As much as possible, balance the load across all your disks to get the most from each of them.

A separate disk controller card for each disk will reduce contention. If you use a single controller for several disks, make sure that controller has a maximum transfer rate that is equal to or better than the sum of the maximum transfer rates of all the disks connected to it.

Solid state disks are now on the market. These disks use nonvolatile memory, either flash RAM or battery-backed RAM, and use a SCSI or other disk interface, so they appear to the system to be ordinary disks. There are no moving parts, so they are unlikely ever to break, unlike ordinary disks. Access time is thousands of times faster than that of a rotating physical disk. The main disadvantage to solid state disks is cost, which is comparable per megabyte to that for system memory. Another disadvantage is that system RAM is faster than solid state disks, so if you have money to spend, you'll get more performance from spending it on system memory. Still, if you have filled your webserver to its maximum with memory, a solid state disk could be more cost effective than upgrading the web server machine itself.

IDE

The standard sort of disk you get with a PC is known as an Integrated Drive Electronics (IDE) disk. This is a commodity disk, not very expensive, but without high performance, reliability, or scalability. IDE disks should be fine for your web logging needs, but they are not suitable for a high-performance web content disk or database.

EIDE

EIDE is an extended version of IDE. Because it was not designed from scratch but carries some of the legacy problems of IDE, it is also not particularly scalable, but has better performance than IDE.

SCSI

Higher-performance disks use the Small Computer Software Interface (SCSI) standard. SCSI is the interface the disk uses to talk to the computer, not a type of disk per se, but disks that connect via SCSI are referred to as "SCSI disks." These disks are designed to scale from single small systems up to large arrays.

SCSI disk controller cards may contain cache memory or have the ability to interleave requests to different disks for higher throughput. If you are interleaving requests, you will get the best performance by balancing the load across equivalent disks.

You can also coordinate the use of multiple controllers with SCSI. You should use *iostat* or *sar* under Solaris to monitor the performance of each disk to be sure the load is balanced. Up to 7 SCSI 1 disks or 15 SCSI 2 disks can be daisy-chained, with each disk up to 6 GB in size.

Plain SCSI transfers data at 5 MB/sec to 10 MB/sec. Wide UltraSCSI provides 40 MB/sec (320 Mbit/sec) interfaces, and this is currently the most common variety of SCSI. Wide UltraSCSI disks typically run at 10,000 rpm and have very low seek and latency times. Narrow UltraSCSI provides 20 MB/sec (160 Mbit/sec) interfaces.

Both wide and narrow UltraSCSI allow cable lengths up to 3 meters, which sounds like a lot, but can be constraining for large configurations. Differential SCSI increases the allowed distance to 25 meters but is otherwise the same. SCSI is evolving, with UltraSCSI 2 now available (80 MB/sec) at 12 meters.

SCSI is more expensive than EIDE, but it is well worth the extra cost. You should serve all of your content from SCSI disks.

Fibre Channel

You may be able to replace SCSI connections with Fibre Channel connections for better performance. Fibre Channel is a serial connection standard commonly used on Unix servers but still rare on cheaper hardware. Its key advantage is it is suitable both for connecting peripherals to a server and for connecting servers to each other, up to a distance of 10 kilometers, in theory. It competes with SCSI, which is limited to 10 meters, one-thousandth the distance.

You can currently get 100 MB/s (200 MB/s full-duplex) with Fibre Channel. Fibre Channel was intended for use with optical fiber, but you can use coaxial cable or twisted pair if you want to give up most of the distance advantage for cheaper wire. Fibre Channel lets several servers share the same disk, unlike SCSI, and can be switched or shared, like Ethernet. Because you can talk directly to disk with Fibre Channel, you can remove some of the latency you'd otherwise have with converting from Ethernet protocol to SCSI and back.

Fibre Channel is intended for servers and would be wasted on an ordinary PC, which would not be able to fill the wire. Fibre Channel's future is not clear, because Ethernet and SCSI are already in place with clear upgrade paths, and Fibre Channel does not integrate well with them.

RAID

Redundant Arrays of Inexpensive Disks (RAID) are an example of how you can achieve high performance from a collection of relatively low-performance components. The idea behind RAID is to set up a collection of disks in which every bit of information is on at least two disks, so that any one disk can fail with no interruption in service. Because of the number of disks, you can use cheaper disks that have a lower reliability. As a bonus, the performance of RAID systems is very good because the system can run multiple requests in parallel, and because smaller disks may have lower seek times as a result of their physically smaller platters. For example, four 2G drives will usually have better performance than one 9G drive.

RAID is usually sold as a package that appears to the host machine as a single large disk. Striping is a similar concept, where access to contiguous blocks of data is spread out over multiple disks, increasing the potential for parallelism and reducing seek times because of smaller platters. See Brian Wong's book, *Configuration and Capacity Planning for Solaris Servers* (Prentice Hall), for more details on RAID.

Typical Disk Performance

Hard disks now typically run at 7,200 rpm and have the ability to do about 100 random I/O operations per second, or up to 500 sequential I/O operations. There are also many 5,400-rpm disks (with the ability to handle about 75 random I/O operations per second) and 10,000-rpm disks (with the ability to handle about 140). One hundred random operations per second implies a seek time of about 10 milliseconds, since a majority of access time is seek time.

Disks on PC systems are capable of a sustained 8–16 Mbit/sec throughput, while the same disks on Unix systems can achieve 32–40 Mbit/sec because of Unix optimizations for disk access. One problem with Unix filesystems is the inodes and superblock must be updated when you write to a file, forcing a lot of seeks. BeOS, which uses a proprietary journalling filesystem, doesn't seem to have this issue.

To estimate the number of disks you'd need to support your hit rate from disk (and not from memory), take your average rate of hits per second, multiply by three to get your assumed peak rate, and multiply that by two to get the peak I/O rate you'll need from your disk. Remember that you need to do a read of the directory to get the permissions for a file (the open( ) system call) before you can read the file itself (the read( ) system call). So if you're getting 30 hits/second on average, your peak rate is probably around 90, and you'll need 180 random I/O operations per second from your disk to prevent your users from experiencing noticeable delays. So you would need two RAIDed or striped 7,200 rpm disks to handle that. Going backwards, we can derive a rule of thumb that a 100 I/O operations per second disk should be able to handle a system getting 17 hits/second on average. Actually, you might be able to do better than that, because the OS will cache directory names and inodes, saving some lookups.

8 to 10 disks per stripe is probably optimal because of the overhead of device management. Striping helps performance only if you have multiple disk controllers. Otherwise, the single controller itself becomes the bottleneck.

Fragmentation

As a disk fills up, it becomes progressively harder to find enough contiguous space to write new files, so new files are written in fragments at multiple places on disk. Reads and writes of fragmented files require multiple movements of the disk arm, slowing access. Fragmentation becomes a more significant problem as the disk gets very full, so it is a good idea to leave at least 10 percent of any given disk free.

Disks on heavily used Windows and Macintosh machines need regular defragmentation, and these systems include defragmentation utilities. Unix disks tend to fragment more slowly because of better disk write algorithms, but eventually they too will need defragmentation.

The most effective way to defragment a disk under Unix is to back it up to tape, reinitialize the filesystem with *mkfs*, and then restore the filesystem from tape. This task is a little easier if you combine it with one of your regular backups.

It is often possible to track down the process that is abusing a particular disk. For example, on Solaris you can use *iostat -x* to see if any disks have particularly high service times (svc_t). If you find such a disk, say sd15, you can then look at the links */dev/sd15** to see which disk controller, target, disk, and slice sd15 maps to. Say sd15 maps to c0t0d0s0 (controller 0, target 0, disk 0, s0). Then you should be able to use the *mount* command to see which filesystem is mounted on */dev/dsk/c0t0d0s0*. From there, you can use the *fuser* command to see which processes are currently using that filesystem. For each of those PIDs, you can *truss* to see who is writing. It's tedious, but it may help you figure out who's bogging down the disk. Unfortunately, this all becomes harder to do if you are using a more modern large system with SparcStorage Arrays and the Veritas filesystem.

Disk Activity and PID

Disk activity is a major inhibitor of performance, but as far as I know, there is no way to find out which process is responsible for any given moment of disk activity. Perhaps it's not possible, given that write and reads may be aggregated, or that some filesystem flushing is done by the kernel and not any particular process.

Key Recommendations

- Don't worry about CPU for static content; just concentrate on having a good network connection, fast disk, and enough memory.
- Buy enough RAM to keep the entire HTML document tree in memory.
- Use SCSI rather than IDE disks.
- Use separate disks for log writing and content reading.
- *http://www.sun.com/sunworldonline/* is a good resource for Sun-specific tuning questions.

## CHAPTER 17

Server Operating System

The operating system sits between the hardware and the web server software, translating the web server's request for services into hardware actions and delivering data from the hardware back up to the web server. The server hardware has a maximum performance that is fixed by its physical specifications. You can approach this maximum performance by appropriate configuration of the operating system. The question for web servers is how to configure the operating system to take requests from the network, find the correct file to return or run the correct program, and push the result back out to the network, all as fast as possible.

Except for a brief comparison of Unix versus Windows NT towards the end, this chapter focuses squarely on Unix. A survey at *http://leb.net/hzo/ioscount/* from April of 1999, admittedly a bit old but the most recent I could find, found that about 75 percent of all web sites run on Unix of one kind or another, with Microsoft OS's accounting for another 24 percent. Among Unixes, the most common were Linux at 27 percent, Solaris/SunOS at 20 percent, and BSD at 16 percent.

Unix and the Origin of the Web

Networking has been central to the development of Unix. Unix was originally developed around 1970 as a research project by AT&T Bell Laboratories, building on multiuser and multitasking ideas from the Multics government research project of the 1960s. Since AT&T was barred from selling software because it was the U.S. telephone monopoly, it allowed universities to use the source code for education and research. The University of California at Berkeley, in particular, continued development on the TCP/IP implementation in the Unix kernel. The Berkeley group introduced enough changes that Unix was split into two main camps for about 10 years: Berkeley Unix and AT&T Unix. Around 1988, these were merged into System V Release 4 (SVR4) Unix, but derivatives of the two original camps continue to exist, such as BSDI and SCO.

The HTTP protocol and the first web server were both developed on Unix platforms and are natural outgrowths of previously existing Unix work. HTTP inherited many characteristics of FTP, but extended FTP with automated requests. The first popular web server software, the University of Illinois' *httpd*, was a classical Unix daemon. At that point, all Unix machines had TCP/IP networking ability and FTP by default, so the technological jump from the existing file transfer protocol to the web protocol was much smaller than would be expected from its subsequent impact on the world. As almost all Unix machines were networked, it was a trivial matter to retrieve *httpd* from the University of Illinois and start it running on your local machine. There was no charge for the software, since it came from a tax-sponsored research project. Web usage exploded because the Internet was primed and ready for a new and simpler front-end.

Web servers and clients were quickly ported to other platforms, such as Windows, the Macintosh, and even mainframes and the AS/400, but the majority of web servers remained on Unix platforms. Unix proved superior in stability and performance because of its longer development history and open nature. Simply put, more people have been able to contribute to and debug Unix for longer than any other operating system. Development of proprietary platforms has been limited by the number of paid employees of any one company, while Unix benefited from the work of the entire academic and Internet community. (An interesting hybrid approach between proprietary and public code is Netscape's desire to capture the creativity of the Internet community by releasing the source code to its browser for inspection and improvement. The Netscape browser source code is available at *http://www.mozilla.org/*.)

Unix Flavors

It might be said that the Unix market enjoys competition, but it could also be said that the Unix market suffers from competition. The problem has been that individual vendors have created their own versions of Unix that are incompatible with all other versions. This means that a binary executable for one version is usually incapable of running on any other Unix, even if the hardware is identical.

The problem is gradually being solved by several forces. First, the SVR4 standard has become dominant. An old joke goes that Sun succeeded in uniting the Unix industry, but unfortunately it united the industry in a coalition against Sun. Nonetheless, SVR4 is now the de facto standard. Programs written to the SVR4 standard have source-level portability to other SVR4 systems, meaning that you should be able to recompile the code for each system without changes. Second, the increasing popularity of Sun Microsystems' Solaris implementation of SVR4 means that Solaris is becoming the de facto standard for binary-level portability, while the future of most other versions of Unix is in doubt, with the exception of Linux (which is not Unix in a legal sense). Finally, as more applications are written in Java, small differences between operating systems will become irrelevant. Systems will be forced to compete on performance and cost, not compatibility.

In the following sections we'll go over the major versions of Unix used for web serving.

Solaris

Solaris is Sun Microsystems' (*http://www.sun.com/*) version of Unix. When the Berkeley-derived SunOS was made compatible with SVR4, its name was changed to Solaris. There are versions of Solaris for Sun's SPARC hardware as well as for the Intel x86 architecture. Solaris on the SPARC hardware has the largest Unix market share, so you can be reasonably sure that any commercial multiplatform Unix software will be ported to Solaris first, debugged, and probably optimized for Solaris. This is important because software vendors do not have the resources to port and optimize for every version of Unix.

Solaris has the largest market share for web servers partly due to its performance and reliability, but also because Solaris has the largest share of the computer science education market. Students who learn to program and administer on Solaris systems tend to keep using it once they go out into the business world.

One of Solaris's strengths is its efficiency in memory allocation, which happens so frequently that it has a large impact on overall system performance. Memory allocation is accelerated by hardware called with special opcodes available only to the OS, not to applications.

Solaris 8, the latest version as of this writing, comes with default parameters more appropriate to web services than previous versions, so a web server run out of the box on Solaris 8 will not need much tuning. Solaris 8 also includes many fundamental improvements that increase web server performance, such as a more efficient TCP/IP stack with more networking code in the kernel rather than user space, and better use of multiple CPUs.

AIX

The AIX operating system from IBM has a reputation to be easy to work with and to have many good tools. Some major corporate web sites run on AIX, which clearly is stable and scalable enough for the most important sites.

Digital Unix

Digital Unix is known for extremely good I/O performance because of efficient disk driver and TCP/IP implementations, which make it very suitable for web serving. Digital Unix is already 64-bit, so it is ahead of most other Unixes there. It is scalable up to very large SMP systems, like the showpiece AltaVista search engine.

Linux

Linux is a free Unix-like kernel originally written for the Intel architecture, but it since has been ported to the Alpha, PowerPC, and even Sun's SPARC. The project was started by Linus Torvalds of Finland. Remember that Linux is just a kernel and not the utilities that allow user interaction with the kernel. Linux comes in distributions from various organizations, usually including GNU tools such as the *gcc* compiler and *bash* shell, as well as a version of the X Window System called *XFree86*.

The scalability of Linux is not as mature as that of Solaris. Until recently, you were limited to 256 simultaneous processes and there was no multiprocessor support. Still, Linux is as robust and high-performance as many commercial versions of Unix, and switching between processes is considerably faster than on Solaris.

There is an information page on Linux at *http://www.li.org/* (and a competing page at *http://www.linux.org/*). Excellent free support is available via the many Linux Usenet newsgroups, and paid support is supplied by companies like Cygnus. Now that Oracle has been ported to Linux, Linux is being accepted by the business community as a serious platform. There are several high-volume web sites that run the free Apache server on Linux.

Irix

Irix is the version of Unix developed by Silicon Graphics for the company's high-performance graphics workstations. It runs only on Silicon Graphics hardware. Silicon Graphics hardware has been optimized for graphics manipulation, but many of the graphics features, such as very quick memory and disk access, are also useful for high-performance web serving. Unfortunately, Irix is not as well supported as Solaris by software vendors like Netscape, so there is often a delay before the Irix version is available. See *http://www.sgi.com/* for extensive information on tuning Irix for running web servers.

BSD

The Berkeley Standard Distribution of Unix (BSD) is similar to Linux in that it tends to be favored at smaller web sites and runs on Intel x86 hardware. Unlike Linux, BSD development includes not just the kernel but all of the utilities and documentation as well. BSDI (*http://www.bsdi.com/*) and FreeBSD (*http://www.freebsd.com/*) are derivatives of BSD, and have continued the development of Berkeley Unix.

Mach OS

The list of Unix versions used for web services would not be complete without Mach OS. Mach was developed at Carnegie-Mellon University and provided the foundation for the NextStep operating system, on which the original implementation of

HTTP was built by Tim Berners-Lee at CERN in Switzerland. Mach OS is the kernel in Macintosh OS X. It is a microkernel, proving almost nothing but access to the hardware. Things like filesystems and process control are add-ons.

Let's take a look at how Unix works, keeping in mind the performance perspective.

System Calls Versus Library Calls

An operating system is fundamentally a way to abstract the hardware into a set of calls you can make from your program. These calls run in the kernel and are the only way to interface with the hardware. They are very different from calls you may make to libraries, though from a programming point of view they look similar.

The original Unix system calls were read, write, open, creat (sic), close, fork, exec, wait, and exit. Dennis Ritchie gives a good explanation of what was done and why in "The Evolution of the Unix Time-sharing System" at *http://cm.bell-labs.com/cm/cs/ who/dmr/hist.html*.

Processes and the Kernel

Unix work is divided up into processes, which you can think of as tasks to be done. Each process has a unique process ID, which is simply an integer and an owner, along with priority and many other attributes that you can see with the *ps* command.

Unix is multiuser and multitasking, so many processes belonging to many users can be running concurrently. (NT, on the other hand, is multitasking, but not multiuser.) Of course, Unix processes are not all running at exactly the same time; it looks that way because the operating system is letting each process run for a bit of time, then interrupting it and letting the next one run, more or less in round-robin fashion. The process that does the scheduling runs in the kernel and is known as the *scheduler*. Processes are scheduled in terms of "clock ticks," which are hundredths of a second, so every process is allocated at least one one-hundredth of a second when it starts its turn. The scheduler itself typically takes much less than that, around one millisecond. This is known as scheduling latency. Scheduling latency increases as the number of tasks to be run increases.

The kernel is some address space and tasks that do scheduling and other fundamental functions, such as directly interfacing to the hardware to display something on-screen or to write something to disk. Only the kernel has direct access to the hardware, and the kernel is accessible to user programs only through the system calls that define its interface. This has a couple of benefits: the kernel can prevent user processes from doing naughty things with hardware, such as reading someone else's files from disk. Also, the system calls can be the same regardless of the underlying hardware, making the program's source code portable. SVR4 is mostly a specification of system calls, so software written to use just those calls should compile and run on any SVR4 system.

Scheduling

To be more precise, the scheduler does not use round robin exactly, but assigns each process a priority and uses a system-dependent algorithm to decide which process to run next based on that priority, how long a process has waited, hardware interrupts, and other factors. The more processes you have running, the poorer performance you'll get from each one. Changing from one user-level process to another is called a *context switch*. A context switch is rather expensive because it may require clearing out certain caches, such as the address translation cache in the memory management unit (MMU), and saving and restoring registers. Switching into kernel mode (a system call) is much faster than switching between user processes, but this also takes some time.

Look at your load average with the *perfmeter* if you have it. If you have a single-CPU machine and see a load average above two (meaning more than two processes are waiting to run on average), and if the CPU utilization is also high, you probably have too many processes running and should think about removing some nonessential processes. Move some load to another machine, or upgrade your hardware. On the other hand, if you see a high load average but low CPU utilization, your system may be misconfigured, the running application may be misbehaving, or you may have a bursty load.

Scheduling processes must take some time, but I could not measure the scheduling time on my Linux PC, probably because the maximum number of processes (250 or so) was not sufficient to tax the CPU. I estimate that scheduling time must be measured in microseconds.

A server dedicated to a single process would have almost no scheduling or context switch time. Taken to an extreme, it is also possible to eliminate the operating system entirely and run only the application. The "Exokernel" project mentioned at the end of this chapter takes this direction.

"Real-time" operating systems such as QNX provide a known upper bound on how long it will take to accomplish any given task. This is very different from the situation on Unix and most other operating systems, where is simply is not known how long any particular amount of processing will take. In practice, there is not much advantage to using a real-time operating system for web serving because the Internet itself is indeterminate and Unix is usually fast enough.

Kernel Context

Limiting hardware access to the kernel has some associated performance penalties. First of all, you must switch to kernel mode to get access to the hardware. Then there is a delay because data has to be copied first from a buffer on the device to the kernel, and then from a kernel buffer to the user process (or in the other direction).

All of this means that there is an indeterminate amount of time involved in Unix hardware access. However small that time interval happens to be, you cannot be sure it will be the same every time you access the hardware, so you cannot yet use Unix for real-time applications, such as flying a fighter plane. For that, you need a real-time operating system, or RTOS. There are real-time priorities of 90 or greater under Solaris, which have precedence over even system-level tasks, but real-time programming under Unix still involves some uncertainties.

There's a trade-off here in Unix in that kernel routines are much faster in accessing hardware, such as the network and disk (most of what a web server does), but good development and maintenance dictate partitioning into user and kernel level rather than having one massive kernel. As of the migration from SunOS to Solaris, the kernel is multithreaded and each process is assigned a kernel-level thread for increased context-switch performance.

Unix and httpd

For web serving, what you want to know about your operating system and hardware is how fast you can get an interrupt from the network interface card, go into kernel mode to get the data, and go back to user mode. You want to copy the request and the output only once within the OS: from/to the device driver's buffer in the kernel to/from the user process. Good implementations of TCP/IP do only one copy, and some experimental systems do no copies at all but simply reallocate the ownership of a buffer between the user and the kernel.

When a web server machine receives an HTTP request, it must schedule some CPU time for the *httpd* daemon to handle the request (see Figure 17-1). Note that *httpd* runs as a user process, so it has lower priority than kernel processes. It must wait for them and share what time is left over with other user processes, so the fewer other processes running, the better.

If you can afford it, you should dedicate your web server and not run interactive terminal sessions, database applications, NFS or DNS services, etc. This advice conflicts with the use of Java applets for client-server–type applications, because the default security model for Java applets is to allow access only back to the web server from which the applet originated. This means that the web server machine must not only serve the applet, but also deal with requests from that applet for services such as

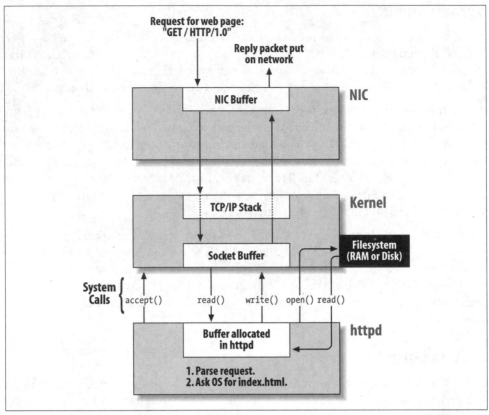

Figure 17-1. The OS and web server handling a request

database access. There are many solutions to this dilemma, such as signing the applet so that it can access other machines, using *appletviewer*, or turning off the browser's network security (only in an intranet), writing a small redirector daemon that copies data from a receiving socket on the web server to another socket on another machine, or mapping the IP address of the web server to a set of machines with one of the load balancing products mentioned in Chapter 3.

That socket buffers will be of size SO_SNDBUF and SO_RCVBUF, which are set by the web server with a call to setsockopt( ). If the web server attempts to write more than SO_SNDBUF bytes to the socket, it will be forced to sleep until the socket can be drained. The TCP/IP stack will take chunks of size MSS or smaller from the socket buffer, but data will not be removed from the socket buffer until it is acknowledged by the client, so slow clients can cause socket buffer overflow. This will cause the web server to be put to sleep. The TCP/IP stack will generate IP packets of size MTU from the MSS segments. If the segment + 40 bytes is more than the MTU, the segment will be distributed across several IP packet fragments. The IP packets will then be passed to the network interface card buffer. If the NIC buffer is full, the packet is discarded and an error is sent to the IP layer, and then on up to the TCP layer, which will try to retransmit again in a few moments.

Solaris Network Cache and Accelerator

Solaris can maintain a cache of web pages in kernel space, which significantly increases the number of HTTP operations per second that a Sun machine can handle. This works natively with Netscape Enterprise Server, and requires a few more pieces with Apache.

For most users, the actual speed of the web server itself is not a bottleneck, so this acceleration is not necessarily worthwhile. Client connection speed to the Internet, dynamic content generation, and database speed are all more likely to improve the client experience. Still, for very busy sites, SNCA seems useful in reducing hardware requirements by simply loading a kernel module and a few other pieces.

Linux khttpd

A similar feature in Linux is the kernel-level web server called *khttpd*. *khttpd* runs within the kernel as a device driver and speeds up serving of static pages. It passes requests for dynamic pages on to a user-level web server, such as Apache. It is still a work in progress, and is not fully HTTP 1.1 compliant yet, but is good enough to be useful. For more information, see *http://www.fenrus.demon.nl/*.

Reducing the Load on the OS

If your web server is going to access a large database, consider using FastCGI or opening a socket to a separate machine running the database and leaving it open. Some "middleware" products will manage a single open connection to a database for you. Interactive sessions, though seemingly innocuous, generate lots of interrupts (for example, one with each keystroke and many with each mouse movement).

You might also increase the priority of your web server process, which you can do as *root* by making the appropriate system call. This could be dangerous on a heavily loaded web server because other essential functions may get starved for attention, possibly crashing your server.

Another trick that may improve performance is to configure the scheduler to use longer timeslices, also known as *quanta*, for each process. This will sometimes help a CPU-bound system by reducing the time spent in the scheduler. See *Essential System Administration*, by Aeleen Frisch (O'Reilly & Associates), for details on how to configure the scheduler under AIX and Solaris.

When I wrote the first edition of this book, I wondered at this point if it would be practical to put a web server directly into the kernel to avoid the overhead of changing into and out of user mode. Since then, Linux 2.3 and 2.4 have included a static-page web server called *khttpd* directly in the kernel as a loadable module. Requests for dynamic content are passed to a user-level web server. The *khttpd* web server is configured via the */proc* filesystem. I haven't tested *khttpd*, but I expect that its performance for static pages is extremely good, probably the best you can get for Linux.

One problem with loading additional modules is that loading drivers increases the kernel size, and the kernel is not pageable. This effectively reduces the memory available to other applications.

Process Creation

The creation of new processes under Unix is done through the fork system call, which copies a process and assigns the copy a new process ID. This is usually followed by an execsystem call, which reads a new executable from disk (if not already loaded) and starts it in the current address space. The disk access takes about 50 milliseconds, and the process creation itself maybe 10 milliseconds. The newly created process consumes something like 50K in the kernel for record keeping as well as its own memory in user space as reported by the *ps* command.

The fork and exec method is not a particularly efficient way to do things, but it is simple for the programmer. It was expected that new process creation would not occur very frequently, so there was no incentive to make it very efficient. It is exactly this inefficiency that limits the scalability of CGI, which creates and destroys a new process for each hit. The reason fork and exec are two separate system calls is that fork was intended for use in a client-server environment, in which the ability to generate a new copy of a server process for each client is desirable.

To get around the expense of new process creation, the concept of threading was introduced. Threads are separate strands of execution within the same process. It takes far less time and fewer resources to create a new thread than to create a new process—as much as 100 times less. In addition, switching between threads is very quick. Your entire process still has to wait for the scheduler to run it before any of the threads in that process can run, but the advantages of quick thread creation and switching are still very great. If you have a Symmetric Multiprocessing (SMP) machine, i.e., one with multiple equivalent CPUs, you can often run one thread on each CPU and take advantage of parallel execution. This is possible with Java threading, but by no means guaranteed. Another advantage of threads is that an entire process can avoid being blocked on I/O by assigning the I/O operation to a single thread and letting only that thread block. Finally, threads share file descriptors, which is a mixed blessing. The utility of shared file descriptors depends on your application.

It is quite simple for a Unix user to create a process that forks out of control. Just create a shell script, and include in it the command to run that same shell script. For example, make a file called *x*, and within that, just put the character x. Make that file executable and run it. You will quickly create so many *x* processes that you will run out of some resource. How quickly and what resource are interesting questions. Here's one way to find out how many processes a particular user can create: modify *x* to run *ps* as well:

```
ps -ef | wc -l
./x
```

Now when you run this, look at the highest number attained. I got to about 317 before paging slowed the system down to a crawl. I changed the *x* script, removing the `ps-ef | wc -1` line, and just watched *top* instead. I got up to 371 processes this time, but then *x* crashed, though the Linux kernel itself remained up. Still, the system was inaccessible while it was forking madly, and this could be considered a simple user-level denial of service (DOS) attack that most Unixes seem vulnerable to. I believe mainframes have stricter controls on individual user activities and this is one reason they are a bit more reliable than Unix. Adrian Cockcroft reports that Solaris can overcome this particular problem by setting `maxuproc` in */etc/system* and rebooting. For example:

```
set maxuprc=100
```

Address Space

When a Unix process requires more RAM than is physically available, it is still possible for the process to run, using part of the disk as its memory space. The memory on disk is known as virtual memory because it is not real RAM and the part of disk used for it is called the swap space. Memory is segmented into pages, so the term for storing some of a process's address space on disk is referred to as *paging*. If an entire process is suspended and moved out to disk, we say the process is *swapped out*. A basic rule of thumb is that paging is acceptable, but not desirable, while swapping is an indication of a serious memory problem that will hurt your performance.

You will necessarily see paging in when you start a program, because it must be read from disk, and you will see paging out when programs have been idle for a long time. Neither is an indication of any problem. In the long term, you should monitor your paging and swapping activity with *sar* or *vmstat*, but *perfmeter* gives a good visual indication of how things are going at the moment. If you see continuous paging or any swapping activity, it would improve performance to figure out why it's happening and fix it, probably by buying more RAM or reducing the load on the machine. Tuning memory parameters is a large subject. For more information on Solaris memory parameters, see *Sun Performance and Tuning*, by Adrian Cockcroft and Richard Pettit (Prentice Hall).

Every process in Unix gets its own independent address space and is unaware that its memory space is actually mapped to the far smaller physical RAM installed on the machine. Most machines are currently 32-bit and therefore have a 4 GB address space. You may know that many Unix machines have room for more than 4 GB of physical memory, yet run 32-bit operating systems. This leads to the question of how a 32-bit kernel can refer to memory outside the 4 GB range. The answer is that the virtual address system uses more than 32 bits to refer to physical memory. For example, Solaris uses a 36-bit physical address space. This means that even though each 32-bit process is limited to 4 GB, you can have many, and the kernel can manage them.

There is a unified dynamic memory pool, meaning that processes and the filesystem share RAM, with the filesystem's buffer cache occupying whatever memory is not needed by other processes. This buffer reduces disk reads and writes, improving performance, but it may give you the false impression that you're running out of memory when, in fact, processes still have plenty of room to grow by displacing the buffer cache. On Solaris, the scan rate of the pager (sr in *vmstat*) and the number of pages moved in or out per second are much better indications of whether you're short of memory than the amount of memory reported as free by *vmstat* or other tools. Also be aware that various tools like *sar*, *vmstat*, and *top* may all have different definitions of what it means for memory to be free. Some deduct memory that a process would like to reserve from the amount calculated to be free even though that memory is not actually in use.

Copying in Memory

Copying data from one part of memory to another is at the core of web servers. Web servers read in a file from disk to one area of memory, then copy it to another part of memory (a buffer) to output it to the network. It would be more efficient simply to have the kernel change its designation of what the memory is than to copy it byte by byte to another part of memory. Some kernels are actually smart enough to do this by changing page table pointers, but only if the item is an exact multiple of the page size. This is why trailer encapsulation in the IP protocol was invented. It would be interesting to experiment with the size of web pages to see if they were faster if they were multiples of the system page size.

Reclaiming Memory

When a process asks the operating system for more memory, the operating system will probably just make a note of the request and reserve the memory, but not actually count it as in the process until the process actually tries to use it. When the memory is freed, it is immediately given back to the operating system and the process size is reduced. This is often a point of much confusion. Here is an example you can try for yourself. You can download it from *http://patrick.net/software/freetest.c*.

```
#include <sys/types.h>
#include <sys/stat.h>
#include <stdio.h>
#include <errno.h>
#include <unistd.h>
#include <string.h>

main(int argc, char * argv[]) {

    void *buf;

    buf = (void *) malloc(20000000);
    printf("reserved\n");
```

```
        sleep (10);

        bzero(buf, 20000000); /* memory won't look used unless you clear it */
        printf("in use\n");

        sleep (10);

        free(buf);
        printf("freed\n");

        sleep (10);
    }
```

If you compile it like this:

```
% gcc -o freetest freetest.c
```

and then run it while looking at the output from *top* (sort by memory size if that's an option in your version of *top*), you'll see that the memory usage of the program is tiny until you actually run the bzero line, which tells the operating system to clear that memory. Using the memory caused it to be included in the size of the process. Then freeing it causes it to be given back to the operating system.

This is different from Java, where most VM's readily take memory, but do not usually give the memory back to the operating system until the process exits. Instead, they return the memory to the Java "heap," which is its own private store of memory. Here is the equivalent program in Java, available from *http://patrick.net/software/ freetest.java*, so you can see this for yourself:

```
class freetest {
    public static void main(String[] args) {

        System.out.println("not allocated");

        try { Thread.sleep(10000); }
        catch (java.lang.InterruptedException ie) {}

        byte[] array = new byte[20000000];
        System.out.println("allocated");

        try { Thread.sleep(10000); }
        catch (java.lang.InterruptedException ie) {}

        array = null;
        System.out.println("freed");

        try { Thread.sleep(10000); }
        catch (java.lang.InterruptedException ie) {}
    }

}
```

More memory is usually better, but even if you can add all the memory you want, your system will just run slower past a certain number of threads or processes because of context switching no matter how much memory you have. Also, having more memory may itself slow you down slightly because it takes some operating system overhead just to manage the memory.

There are many tools that measure memory usage, and it seems none of them give the same results as any other. *top* sometimes seems to report very wrong numbers. Other ways of looking at memory are with commercial tools such as Measureware, the */proc* filesystem, *vmstat*, the *prtmem* command from Richard McDougall's RMC-mem package, *ps*, *memtool*, and raw kernel statistics. One reason for all the differences is that they may count text, heap, stack, and bss, or any combination of those; they may or may not include shared libraries; they may count virtual memory or only physically resident memory; and they may include filesystem buffers and other buffers, or perhaps not.

The Filesystem

While everything in Unix is considered to be a file (including data, executables, directories, and devices), the most common type of file is the regular file, which is simply a stream of data bytes, as opposed to a directory or device file. Within regular files, there is no distinction in Unix between text files and binary files. Our principal concern in serving web content is how to access regular files as quickly as possible. In order to understand the issues involved in access speed, we have to know a bit about the Unix filesystem.

There are many kinds of filesystems in use in Unix systems, but the most common kind is the Unified File System (UFS), derived from the Berkeley Fast Filesystem. UFS filesystems consist basically of inodes, directories, and data blocks. Inodes are typically 128-byte records on disk that describe files. Each inode contains a list of pointers to the data blocks on the disk that make up a file. Given the number of pointers in an inode and the size of the data blocks, we can see that each inode can point to only a fixed amount of data storage. The size of the data blocks is often 512 bytes or maybe 2 kilobytes by default, which is fine if you have a lot of small files, but it is suboptimal if you are going to be serving only a few large files. A 2 KB block size means you could fit one million 2 KB files on a 2 GB disk. For larger files, at least one of your inode pointers must point to a sort of second-level inode called an indirect block that contains pointers to other data blocks. And this can continue on to doubly indirect blocks, but there is a performance penalty in accessing parts of large files through an extra level or two of indirection. Smaller disks with fewer inodes are faster because there is simply less to search.

If you are going to have mostly very large files, you will get better performance by increasing the size of the data block rather than using the default indirection, at the expense of more wasted disk space for small files. With UFS, you have a choice of block sizes ranging up to 64 kilobytes. Changing the block size is platform-specific and is done when you create the filesystem. The point is that you can tune your filesystem to serve a certain size file at the best speed. Remember that web content often has a bimodal distribution, with many smallish (10 KB to 20 KB) files for text and images and a few large (greater than 1 MB) files for downloaded software, audio, high-resolution images, etc. One solution is to have HTTP links point to a server with a filesystem tuned for serving large files for the big downloads, but the gain in filesystem performance would be swamped by long download times over slow network connections. In the case of streaming video, it would help to have a dedicated server with a specially tuned filesystem.

Another kind of filesystem on Solaris is the temporary filesystem, tempfs. If you look in */etc/vfstab* on a Solaris system, you will see that */tmp* is usually mounted as a tempfs filesystem. The unique thing about tempfs is it attempts to keep everything in RAM rather than on disk. This means that writing to or reading from */tmp* under Solaris is far faster than reading or writing anywhere else. The drawback to using tempfs is it goes away on reboot and everything in that filesystem is lost. Also note that tempfs doesn't guarantee that your files will be in RAM; it just makes an attempt to keep them there.

That said, you can use tempfs in various ways to help server performance. If your web server is constantly retrieving data to serve out to clients, say stock quotes, you'll probably want to write the data to */tmp*. This kind of data is volatile anyway, and fast access is very important. On Solaris, you can *man tempfs* for more information.

Filename Length

You might guess that shorter directory and filenames are faster to access, but how much faster? Here is a tiny C program to explore this question.

```
#include <sys/types.h>
#include <sys/stat.h>
#include <stdio.h>
#include <errno.h>

main(int argc, char * argv[]) {

    int i;

    struct stat *buf;

    buf = (struct stat *) malloc(sizeof(struct stat));

    for (i=0; i<100000; i++) {
        if (stat(argv[1], buf)) {
```

```
            perror(argv[1]);
            exit(1);
        }
    }
}
```

If you compile this program like this:

```
% gcc -o stat stat.c
```

you can run it on a directory called "t" and one called "thisname" and see that it takes about 1.37 seconds for "t" and 1.45 seconds for "thisname". For example:

```
% time stat t

real    0m1.370s
user    0m0.270s
sys     0m1.100s
```

Since we *stat* the file 100,000 times, each access takes about 1.37 / 100000 = 0.0000137 seconds, or 1.4 microseconds. *stat*ting "thisname" is about 6 percent slower. A 1-character directory name is not that much faster to open than an 8-character directory name. Still there are at least two valid reasons to use very short filenames: smaller log files and fewer bytes transmitted in requests and replies.

Full Filesystems

The most common and most painful problem with filesystems is that they fill up. As a filesystem approaches 100 percent full, any program writing to that filesystem will slow down dramatically. The performance of web servers, application servers, and databases will all go down as the filesystem nears 100 percent capacity. When the filesystem is full, the application is likely to crash, though well-written programs may exit gracefully. Operating systems typically crash when the root filesystem is full. So both for performance and reliability, it is critical to monitor how full important filesystems are and to keep application and system log files in particular on a nonroot filesystem. From any directory, you can run *df -k* and see exactly how full that filesystem is. For example:

```
% cd /opt/apache/logs
% df -k .
Filesystem        1024-blocks  Used Available Capacity Mounted on
/dev/hda2          3857447 1224872  2432993    33%    /opt
```

This tells us that the filesystem holding our Apache log files is only 33 percent full—that is, running at 33 percent of capacity.

Directories

A directory is a special kind of file that contains a list of filenames mapped to inode numbers, as well as information for each file, such as permissions and the time the file was last accessed. The directory structure of Unix is a linked list. When you refer to a file via a pathname, such as */dir1/foo*, the kernel searches linearly through the names in the root directory until it finds the name *dir1* and gets the associated inode number. It then uses that inode to find the datablock called *dir1* and looks linearly through that data for the filename *foo*. When it finds the name *foo*, it has the associated inode and finally knows exactly where on the disk to find the data in the file *foo*. This is a rather involved process, as you can see, so you will in general see better access performance from a path with fewer components and even a slight advantage from short filenames and directory names.

If you must have long names, try to differentiate them at the beginning of the name instead of at the end so that whatever string compare function the OS uses to look up the name will have an easier time. So, for example, instead of naming web content files as *regional.daily.report.12.3.1998*, *regional.daily.report.12.4.1998*, etc., name them *3.12.1998.regional.daily.report*, *4.12.1998.regional.daily.report*, etc. (Netscape Navigator's disk cache tends to violate this principle, but there's not much you can do about it unless you're ambitious enough to modify the browser source code.)

This doesn't mean, however, that you should put all of your files in the root directory or create any other huge directories. Directories are searched linearly for a name matching the one requested, so huge directories will give you very poor performance. The recommendations for keeping file paths short and for keeping directory sizes small conflict if you have a great deal of content. Which one wins? Consider that each element of a path is an indirection that requires disk movement if the elements are not already in memory, while searching through a linked list of directory names in memory is repeated string comparisons. To balance the time spent in each, several hundred elements per directory is probably optimum. On the other hand, once filesystem structures are looked up, they are cached, so subsequent accesses favor having longer paths rather than larger directories. You would have to run some benchmarks with your content organized in different ways to find the optimal numbers, but 100 files per directory is reasonable. Some systems have Directory Name Lookup Caches (DNLCs), which reduce the disk access for directory lookups.

The Veritas VxFS filesystem uses hashed directories for very fast lookups but is an extra-cost commercial product. See *http://www.veritas.com/*.

The kernel contains an inode table that serves as a cache for recently opened files. Its size is determined by a constant compiled into the kernel, often MAXUSERS, or INODE or NINODE for SVR4. Linked lists, such as directories, do not cache particularly well because they don't consist of contiguous memory, but increasing the size of the inode table should help access time somewhat.

Filename length could possibly influence how long it takes to retrieve a file, since the requested filename has to be compared to each file in the directory until a match is found. I did a test on Linux, creating 2K files named *a*, *aa*, *aaa*, and so on, up to 25 *a*'s in length. One hundred serial retrievals from Apache always took a total of 1.8 seconds regardless of name length, so each one was about 18 milliseconds and any time difference was smaller than one millisecond. It seems that filename length does not make much of a difference, but perhaps under heavy load the results would be different, especially because logging might take significantly longer.

Filesystem Caching

When you read a file on Unix, the filesystem stores it in a cache, known as the filesystem buffer cache, so that you can avoid a disk access if you use the file again soon. In SVR4, the cache is whatever memory is free at the moment, so the cache size grows and shrinks dynamically. On other Unix systems, the cache is usually a dedicated part of the process's address space. When SVR4 reclaims memory from the cache, it chooses memory that has not been recently used; this method is known as the Least Recently Used (LRU) basis.

When you write to the buffer cache, the changes are not written to disk immediately, but queued up for later, more efficient writing. This is different from the Mac and Windows 95 and 98, which synchronously commit writes to disk at the time the application considers the data written. Windows NT has now adopted the Unix approach. This makes Unix and NT systems more vulnerable to data loss in the event of power outage, but higher-performance otherwise. It's one more trade-off.

You can easily see the buffer cache in action by editing a file you have not recently used, closing it, and opening it again. The second time will be much faster, because both your editor and the file are in the buffer cache the second time around and so do not have to be retrieved from disk. This sort of caching helps HTTP servers quite a lot because the same files tend to get requested over and over.

Directory Name Lookup Cache

Given how much disk work can be involved in looking up pathnames, Solaris has a cache for directory lookups, called the DNLC. You can see the cache hit rate with the *vmstat -s* command. Look for "cache hits." The percentage should be 90 percent or better. Otherwise you should probably increase the cache size. You can see the current size of the DNLC as root like this:

```
# adb -k /dev/ksyms /dev/mem
?U
ncsize
^D
```

To increase the cache size, change */etc/system* to include a line like this:

```
set ncsize=xxxx
```

Fragmentation

The layout of a filesystem on disk tends toward disorder after many reads and writes, with the result that a new file will typically be stored in fragments fit into the available holes in the disk. This hurts performance, because writing and accessing fragmented files forces many motions of the disk arm. If your filesystem has been well used for writing many files, you may want to try a disk defragmentation utility or simply dump the filesystem to tape, reformat the disk, and write the files back onto disk. Do not make an image of the disk on the tape with *dd*, *dcopy*, or other disk copy utilities, because that image will itself be fragmented. Write out the files as files.

You should definitely defragment on Windows, but it is not as critical on Unix systems because better algorithms mean Unix files are more likely to be contiguous on disk. Unix writes out whole blocks to disk, while Windows tries to optimize write speed because writes are generally flushed to disk immediately in Windows due to its susceptibility to crashing. Unix flushes files to disk intermittently via a process called *fsflush*, meaning data is greater risk if the system crashes, but it is less likely to crash so it's not much of a problem in practice. Other things that cause synchronous writes to disk are simply having too much data pending, closing a file, or exiting a program (which causes files to be closed).

When you put the files back to disk, you can play another trick: write related content together. For example, write an HTML file, then write the images referred to by the file. When you go to access the HTML file and need the images that go with it, the disk arm stands a good chance of being in exactly the right place to get the image files, thus improving performance. Your frequently accessed files are likely to be in the buffer cache already, so this technique will help them only on the first read; it is more suited to large collections of infrequently accessed files.

If your disk is too full, it will rapidly fragment because it will be difficult to find contiguous space to write files, and performance will suffer. Try to keep your disk under 90 percent full, especially if you're writing to it and not simply serving static content. If your disk is nearly 100 percent full and performance is intolerable, you may want to try to take advantage of any available space on the disk, such as space the disk itself reserves for temporary storage. How this is done varies with the disk and operating system, but it may be as simple and dangerous as using a tool like *fdisk* or *tunefs* or the Linux *fips* utility to increase the size of a disk partition. I don't know the details, and you didn't learn about this from me if something bad happens to your disk. You did back everything up, right?

Remember what happens when a file is accessed? Among other things, the permissions of the file as stored in the directory are checked against the user ID. This takes time and is not necessary for a dedicated web server isolated from your internal network. If you're a kernel hacker, you can change the kernel to skip the ID check. This means that all users would have access to all files on the machine, but it's not as dangerous as it sounds if there is nothing on your web server except content that you'd like to be public anyway, and if login over the network is disabled. The hazard to your web server is greater on the Internet than on your intranet, because hackers are known to commandeer web sites for distribution of "warez," illegal copies of software, and you'd be making it a bit easier to do so. Note that running the web server as *root* is not the same thing as disabling permissions, even though *root* has access to all files. The permission check is done even for *root*.

Another thing that happens when a file is accessed, but which is pointless for web servers, is the updating of the file-access time in the directory. It is pointless because the file will be accessed repeatedly, and the access times will be recorded in the web server log in any case. This is particularly important if your HTML files are being read from NFS, where the access time write requires additional network traffic. See Chapter 15 for information on NFS. You'd need to make serious modifications to your filesystem to stop update times from being written, or you can mount a filesystem as read-only.

Avoid symbolic links in your content tree because they are not only a level of indirection but also require additional two-disk accesses: one to read the link's permissions (remember that a link, like everything else in Unix, is a file) and another to read the contents of the link, which tell you where the target file is located. A symbolic link is a text file containing the path to the target file, marked so that the operating system uses it as a link and not a text file. Hard links, however, can be used with no additional time penalty because they map the link name directly to the inode of the target file, just like the proper filename. But hard links cannot be used to cross filesystems, while symbolic links can.

Keep your PATH and LD_LIBRARY_PATH short and pointing first to the libraries your web server will actually use. If you don't, you'll waste a lot of system calls when executing CGIs or other new processes. Here we should have */lib* first in our LD_LIBRARY_PATH, but it is last instead, causing a lot of wasted open calls:

```
% echo $LD_LIBRARY_PATH
/usr/openwin/lib:/usr/ucblib:/usr/dt/lib:/usr/lib:/usr/local/lib:/lib
```

Here's what happens when we run a CGI (you can see by tracing system calls with *truss* on Solaris or *strace* on Linux). The entire library path is searched before the library is found and opened at the end of the path. We should have had */lib* first in the LD_LIBRARY_PATH:

```
open("/usr/openwin/lib/libc.so.5", O_RDONLY) = -1 ENOENT (No such file or directory)
open("/usr/ucblib/libc.so.5", O_RDONLY) = -1 ENOENT (No such file or directory)
open("/usr/dt/lib/libc.so.5", O_RDONLY) = -1 ENOENT (No such file or directory)
open("/usr/lib/libc.so.5", O_RDONLY) = -1 ENOENT (No such file or directory)
open("/usr/local/lib/libc.so.5", O_RDONLY) = -1 ENOENT (No such file or directory)
open("/lib/libc.so.5.2.18", O_RDONLY) = 3
```

There is some hazard in changing your LD_LIBRARY_PATH because you may suddenly find that certain programs depended on certain versions of the libraries and are now using a different version.

It is entirely possible to serve content off a CD-ROM. However, since CD-ROMs run at far slower rates than disk drives, this is not recommended for performance reasons.

Another trick to save memory and speed up file access is to use Unix memory mapping of files, via the mmap( ) system call. This allows you to deliberately put a data file in RAM so that multiple CGI or other processes using that file will all be referring to part of memory rather than disk. Reading a file will bring it into the buffer cache anyway, but it is more efficient to bring it in via mmap( ), because mmap( ) will map the file directly into the user's address space, while read( ) and write( ) will copy the data into the kernel first, and from there into user space. Once the file is in memory, you can use pointers to access data in the file, which is far quicker than the standard I/O routines. Memory-mapping files requires programming in C rather than, say, Perl or Java. Use *man mmap* for more information. BSD and Solaris can map files to memory, but Linux 2.0 cannot.

Finally, note that most Unix shells and web servers understand constructs like ~user to be a shorthand for the user's home directory. So when you see URLs of the form *http://server/~user/file.html*, the web server has to resolve that tilde to a user's home directory. This can be done in several ways, such as by an NIS lookup or reading the */etc/passwd* file, but it takes significant time in any case. The classic way is to open the */etc/passwd* file and scan down for the user, then move over to get his or her home directory, which is time-consuming even if */etc/passwd* is cached in RAM and lookups are hashed. It is still expensive to look up ~user many times per second, especially if you don't have *cachefs*. In general, it is a bad idea to use ~ in pathnames on heavily loaded web servers.

The Windowing System

There is no need for a windowing system on a web server, middleware server, or database. Users will not benefit from it, because they can't see the server's screen. Far from benefitting, users will suffer from a windowing system because it uses CPU and a great deal of RAM. Eliminating use of the windowing system also avoids problems caused by process priority shifting depending on where the mouse is at any given time. On most windowing systems, it is standard practice to automatically increase the priority of processes running in or started from the currently selected window. A web server is likely to suffer when an interactive user is sitting at the keyboard, running jobs with higher priority.

You can see this for yourself with a simple experiment. Say you start a single *httpd* process from an *xterm* under Solaris. Here's a little *sh* script that will show you the priority of that *httpd* once per second on Solaris. In the output, the priority is the number in the seventh column from the left.

```
while true
do
ps -cle | grep httpd
sleep 1
done
```

As you move your mouse out of the *xterm* and click into some other window, you'll see the priority of *httpd* drop by 10. When you move your mouse back into the *xterm* where you started *httpd*, you'll see its priority increase by 10. This is probably not what you want for a dedicated web server.

It is quite straightforward to avoid starting X on Unix systems, and to do maintenance in terminal mode or through *telnet* sessions. Windows and the Mac do not give you that freedom; you are forced to expend resources on their windowing systems even if your machine is a dedicated web server.

Even on Unix, certain server class applications, unfortunately, seem to need a windowing system. An example a friend gave me is a servlet that generates a GIF dynamically using *java.awt*. The *java.awt* package needs to open an X display to render GIF images, even if the image is generated off-screen. The solution was to start up a "virtual" X-server, using the *Xvfb* command. *Xvfb* creates a virtual framebuffer X-server, thus avoiding the need for a graphic device on that machine.

Versions and Patches

You should use the latest nonbeta version of your operating system with all patches, because performance improvements are always being found and security holes blocked. You can see what version of the OS you are using when you boot up, or by using the *uname -a* command on most versions of Unix. You should be aware that patches often introduce their own bugs, so check performance immediately after installing a patch. The Solaris Internet Server Supplement (SISS) patch for Solaris 2.5.1 gives about a 20 percent performance boost to Internet services under Solaris 2.5.1, both on Sparc and Intel CPUs. The SISS also gives you WebNFS (a filesystem for the Web) and the Java virtual machine for multi-CPU machines. SISS 1.0 is incorporated into Solaris 2.6. Under Solaris, *showrev -p* shows you the patches installed.

Configurable OS Parameters

Here we will go over optimum parameters for running a web server. Note that Unix systems are shipped with a generic kernel, optimized not for any particular use, but for acceptable performance for general use. See Chapter 15 for information on configuring TCP. You can see the current settings in a Solaris system by viewing */etc/system* or *grep*ping for ndd from *inetinit*. In general, Solaris 2.6 is already tuned for web serving, so you shouldn't have to modify anything to get the best performance. Here are a few of the most basic parameters you may want to tune on Linux or another OS. Remember to back up your kernel and configuration files before changing anything.

Number of File Descriptors

File descriptors are positive integers by which the kernel keeps track of open files and network connections per process. If your web server software has a large number of open files and connections in a single process, it is possible to run out of file descriptors, meaning that you will not be able to accept new connections or open new files until old connections terminate or files are closed. For network connections, the accept( ) system call will fail. What happens after that depends on your version of Unix; it may log an error to the system log or print a message on the console, among other things.

Old versions of Unix had a file descriptor limit of 20 (as OPEN_MAX in *limits.h* for SVR4), but every system has increased it far beyond that. It is not unreasonable to want several thousand file descriptors.

The *limit* or *ulimit* shell commands and C functions can be used in Unix to change the maximum number of file descriptors on a "soft" basis up to a "hard" limit compiled into the kernel or set at boot time.

You can see the hard limit under Solaris by running *sysdef* and looking for the string "file descriptors." You can set the hard limit under Solaris via set rlim_fd_max=1024 in */etc/system* and rebooting. Solaris systems function with up to 4096 file descriptors per process, but do not guarantee the stability of the operating system beyond that.

You can see the current soft limit for any running process under Solaris with the */usr/proc/bin/pfiles* command. You can run *lsof* on Solaris to see how many file desciptors are allocated for every processes. I have a copy of *lsof* for Solaris 2.6 on my web site at *http://patrick.net/software/*. You can also look in the */proc* filesystem for actual links to the currently open files for any process. You can set the default soft limit under Solaris via set rlim_fd_cur=64 in */etc/system* and rebooting.

Setting rlim_fd_max over 1024 will break the select( ) C library call, yet the Netscape Enterprise Server 3.0 does not seem to crash until you set it to more than 3000. Programs written to use poll( ) rather than select( ) can use more than 1024 file descriptors without breaking because poll( ) refers to an int file descriptor, while select( ) refers to an fd_set, which is defined to be of size FD_SETSIZE, which is 1024 on Solaris and Linux. You would need to have the source code to know which way your particular web server was written, and from there exactly how many file descriptors you can safely use. You can sometimes fix a program written with select( ) to use more than 1024 by altering the source to define FD_SETSIZE to be larger than 1024 before including <sys/types.h>. Or sometimes, makefile options allow you to choose between select( ) and poll( ).

The FILE definition in the *stdio* library will handle only 256 file descriptors, so a program that uses the FILE definition can open only 256 files.

Here are the ways to change the hard limit on file descriptors per process for several operating systems:

Solaris
    Set rlim_fd_max in */etc/system* and reboot.

Irix
    Run *systune -i* and set rlimit_no_file_max and rlimit_nofile_cur and reboot.

AIX
> Run *smit* and check the kernel-tuning parameters.

HP-UX
> Run *sam* and check the kernel-tuning parameters.

Linux
> The hard limit is 256 in Linux 2.0, and 1024 in Linux 2.1. To change it, you have to change the source code and recompile the kernel.

Number of Processes

The maximum number of processes allowed to any one user can also be set with *ulimit* up to the hard limit defined in the kernel. Linux has a hard limit of 4,000 simultaneous processes. Solaris allows a very large number of processes, so you'll run out of other resources first.

Network Buffers

Note that the web server's response is written to a network buffer, also called a socket buffer, and not directly to the client. This allows the OS to take care of forwarding data back to slow clients, freeing up a thread in the web server. If the network buffer is too small, the web server has to write the response in buffer-sized chunks, waiting for each chunk to drain before it can write the next one. The OS should have the right number and size of network buffers to handle your connections without either wasting memory or forcing the server to block while waiting for an available buffer. Network buffers belonging to clients who have ungracefully disconnected for whatever reason are a major source of wasted memory on web servers; this is one reason to turn down the TCP keepalive interval.

The size of socket buffers can be set with the options SO_SNDBUF and SO_RCVBUF to the C-level call setsockopt( ), at least up to a limit compiled into the kernel. High-volume servers with lots of RAM will benefit from larger buffers. A small receive buffer size is a way of limiting the backlog of incoming data. Enter *man setsockopt* for more details.

Apache has a SendBufferSize directive to allow a webmaster to control the size of socket buffers without recompiling the source code. A larger socket buffer will result in a larger TCP window being advertised. Here is a comment from Apache's *httpd_main.c* source file:

```
/*
 * To send data over high bandwidth-delay connections at full
 * speed we must force the TCP window to open wide enough to keep the
 * pipe full. The default window size on many systems
 * is only 4kB. Cross-country WAN connections of 100ms
 * at 1Mb/s are not impossible for well connected sites.
 * If we assume 100ms cross-country latency,
```

```
 * a 4kB buffer limits throughput to 40kB/s.
 *
 * To avoid this problem I've added the SendBufferSize directive
 * to allow the web master to configure send buffer size.
 *
 * The trade-off of larger buffers is that more kernel memory
 * is consumed. YMMV, know your customers and your network!
 *
 * -John Heidemann <johnh@isi.edu> 25-Oct-96
 *
 * If no size is specified, use the kernel default.
 */
```

Memory Limits

You may also specify the maximum amount of memory that a process may use via the ulimit system call or *ulimit* user-level program. This can put a cap on the amount of damage done by a runaway CGI. Unfortunately, some systems do not implement this correctly, allowing processes arbitrary amounts of memory.

Note that device drivers increase the size of the kernel, and the kernel is not pageable, so you should eliminate all unnecessary device drivers to save that memory.

Flushing Frequency

Writes are not necessarily synchronous in Unix. When you write to a file, the change happens immediately in memory but it is not committed to disk until the operating system gets around to it. In this way, you get better write performance, since writes appear instantaneous to the user but can be queued up in the most efficient order by the disk controller. The downside is that when the write to disk does happen, it runs to completion, meaning that other tasks must be put off during the write, so the user may notice a delay.

One way around this is to use a Direct Memory Access (DMA) disk controller card, which controls the transfer of data between memory and disk without use of the CPU. Once the transfer is initiated, the CPU can return its attention to the user so that disk writes do not affect responsiveness.

If you don't have a DMA disk controller, you can trade-off memory usage against the frequency of writes by writing to disk at longer intervals. Note that the writes may take longer, since more data has accumulated and that loss of power before a write puts more data at risk. Sixty seconds is a good amount of time to wait, rather than the default of 30 in Linux. In Linux, change */etc/rc.d/rc.S* to have this line: /sbin/ update 60 &. Under Solaris, the synchronization load is spread across five-second intervals by the *fsflush* process.

Priority

You can tell some operating systems to increase or decrease the priority of certain processes with the *nice* command, if you have sufficient privileges. *top* has an interface to *nice*, and Solaris has the *priocntl* command, which provides the finest level of priority control. Here is an example of using *priocntl* to increase the priority of four processes to the highest priority in the time-sharing category:

```
# priocntl -s -c TS -m 20 -p 20 -i pid 7645 7646 7647 7648
```

Timer Interrupt

Most Unix-like operating systems keep track of time in units of 1/100 of a second via an interrupt called the timer. The timer interrupt happens every 0.01 second, then the scheduler runs and decides who gets the next 0.01 second. This is fine for most uses, but it does impose some limitations—for example, that a program cannot sleep less than 0.01 seconds.

The timer is configurable on most systems. On Linux for Intel CPUs, you can edit the line:

```
#define HZ 100
```

in */usr/include/asm/param.h*. However, beware that changing the timer requires you to recompile all your modules.

Unix OS Monitoring Tools

Most versions of Unix collect performance metrics once per second from the kernel, so most Unix performance monitoring facilities do not allow a sample rate of greater than once per second. You wouldn't want to do much more monitoring of general statistics anyway, because the measurement itself would significantly add to the load. Read the manpage on each of these for more detailed information. The following sections describe the major monitoring tools and provide some example output on a heavily loaded web server.

ps

The most basic tool to let you know what's going on is *ps*, which displays all your processes along with information on CPU and memory usage. The options to *ps* vary a great deal with OS, so you need to read the *ps* manpage on your system for more details.

The "Berkeley" version of *ps* is has some features to recommend it, like the ability to display the percent of CPU used per process. It lives at */usr/ucb/ps* on Solaris and the manpage is available via *man -s 1b ps*.

An important point to remember is Berkeley-style process priority numbers are oppo-site from SVR4 priorities, but Berkeley-style priorities are the default for most versions of *ps*. In SVR4, higher numbers mean higher priority. You can display SVR4 priority with the -*c* option. Here's a listing sorted by priority and edited a bit for clarity:

```
% ps -cle | sort -k 7 | tail -25

F S UID PID PPID CLS PRI ADDR SZ WCHAN TTY TIME CMD

8 S 10002 24097 24060 TS 58 61518010 346 6101627e ? 0:01 xterm
8 S 10002 27452 24102 TS 58 61216cd8 1297 6101663e pts/15 0:14 xemacs
8 S 10003 10417     1 TS 58 60602668 370 60aebd36 ? 0:00 xterm
8 S 65533 21162 21161 TS 58 613d6670 346 610162a6 ? 0:00 xterm
8 S 65533 21305 21174 TS 58 612ff9a0 257 6194b156 pts/30 0:00 tcsh
8 S 65533 29569 27210 TS 58 612f0cd8 231 61017f16 ? 0:00 httpd
8 S     0   135     1 TS 59 605f0cc8 203 604d3c96 ? 0:00 in.named
8 S     0   312     1 TS 59 607ce020 214 607ce1f0 ? 0:02 nntp
8 S     0 19112 19104 TS 59 60efb998 109 60efbb68 ? 0:00 tail
8 S 10001 12530     1 TS 59 60c0a008 725 60c0a1d8 ? 0:02 java
8 S 10001 20646     1 TS 59 60b26660 726 60b26830 ? 0:01 java
8 S 10001 29165     1 TS 59 6183ecc0 723 6183ee90 ? 0:01 java
8 S 65533 11391 11386 TS 59 60029338 1209 60029508 ? 0:40 java
8 S 65533 27224 27210 TS 59 61a1acd8 231 60d13e10 ? 0:00 httpd
8 S 65533 29602 27210 TS 59 618e0000 231 60d13290 ? 0:00 httpd
8 S  6443 11302 11301 TS 60 60028cd8 240 6152e0a6 pts/18 0:00 tcsh
8 S 65533  4437 27210 TS 60 61a2e020 231 60d13350 ? 0:00 httpd
8 S 65533 19921 27210 TS 60 60065338 231 60d13310 ? 0:00 httpd
8 S 65533 29603 27210 TS 60 6120a668 231 60d13190 ? 0:00 httpd
8 S 65533 29604 27210 TS 60 618eece0 231 60d13210 ? 0:00 httpd
8 S 65533 29605 27210 TS 60 61988008 231 60d13250 ? 0:00 httpd
8 S 65533 29606 27210 TS 60 61a0e020 231 60d132d0 ? 0:00 httpd
19 S     0     3     0 SYS 60 60122678 0 1043e194 ? 64:08 fsflush
19 T     0     0     0 SYS 96 10416c88 0 ? 0:00 sched
19 S     0     2     0 SYS 98 60122cd8 0 10439f10 ? 0:00 pageout
```

perfbar

perfbar is a free, real-time, X-based tool for viewing performance of Solaris machines. It shows bars of CPU going up and down. Pretty cool if you can find it. I haven't seen it recently.

perfmeter

perfmeter is a very simple graphical tool for viewing the performance of the disk, net-work, CPU, and so forth. It gets its data from the *rpc.rstatd* daemon that ships with many flavors of Unix. *perfmeter* comes bundled with Solaris, but there is a freeware open source version from *http://rstatd.sourceforge.net* or *http://www.koeniglich.de*. Set it up to view everything to get the best feel for which components affect others. You'll have an easy way to see if your CPU is overloaded, for example, or when there is network traffic when you didn't expect it. *xload* is a similar tool for Linux.

Figure 17-2 shows what *perfmeter* looks like on a Sun Ultra 1 with 64 MB RAM, running Solaris 2.5.1. I hit this machine with a load generation tool that asked for a 55K binary file 250 times in 35 seconds. So the server was being hit about 7 times per second, and the throughput was about 3 Mbit per second.

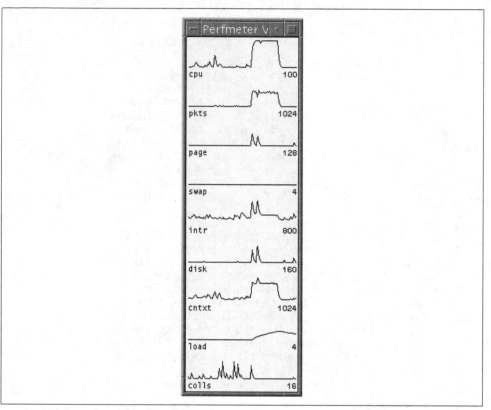

Figure 17-2. Image of perfmeter

perfmon

perfmon is a tool that allows user-level code to access the performance counters in the Sun Ultra series and Intel PentiumPro series CPUs. Its use is not trivial because it requires the installation of a device driver on every machine that is to run it and the writing of code to use this driver. See *http://www.cse.msu.edu/~enbody/perfmon/design.html* for more information.

rstat

rstat is an RPC client program I wrote to get and print statistics from any machine running the *rstatd* daemon. See Chapter 4 for much more on *rstat*.

rup

rup is useful for seeing which machines running *rstatd* are on your local LAN and what their load averages are, as a first glance at the network.

hstat

hstat is a Sun proprietary tool for profiling Sparc CPUs. It is available only through Sun and not supported.

top

top is a wonderful tool for continuously seeing which processes are at the top of resource consumption at the moment. It is rather like a self-refreshing *ps* that lets you sort the output in several ways. The following is some sample *top* output:

```
last pid: 1867; load averages: 1.29, 1.38, 1.40 13:57:59

196 processes: 173 sleeping, 1 running, 21 zombie, 1 on cpu
CPU states: 61.2% idle, 11.7% user, 24.5% kernel, 2.7% iowait, 0.0% swap
Memory: 371M real, 106M free, 260M swap, 181M free swap

PID   USERNAME PRI NICE SIZE  RES   STATE TIME   WCPU  CPU   COMMAND
29390 giacomo  8   0    10M   10M   sleep 0:02   1.51% 2.94% buildindex
27210 fred     -25 0    1848K 1384K run   348:16 2.31% 2.36% httpd
2807  root     33  0    133M  117M  sleep 22.8H  2.67% 1.46% dataserver
1074  patrick  33  0    1880K 1648K cpu   0:00   0.35% 0.27% top
27643 jeffrey  33  0    12M   4824K sleep 67:00  0.15% 0.08% java
2302  jeffrey  33  0    5648K 5224K sleep 0:05   0.02% 0.05% java
8450  root     33  0    2136K 1592K sleep 0:38   0.01% 0.03% sshd
99    root     -3  0    904K  680K  sleep 9:30   0.02% 0.01% defrouter
117   root     33  0    2120K 1176K sleep 3:02   0.00% 0.00% rpcbind
315   root     33  0    2000K 1000K sleep 1:37   0.00% 0.00% lpd
12828 root     33  0    1672K 816K  sleep 1:09   0.00% 0.00% sshd
445   root     33  0    8248K 904K  slccp 0:43   0.00% 0.00% backupserver
11391 aloysiu  34  0    9672K 5368K sleep 0:39   0.00% 0.00% java
1     root     33  0    440K  192K  sleep 0:36   0.00% 0.00% init
330   root     33  0    2904K 1888K sleep 0:30   0.00% 0.00% defcon
140   root     23  0    1760K 1184K sleep 0:21   0.00% 0.00% inetd
217   root     33  0    1504K 1144K sleep 0:20   0.00% 0.00% syslogd
346   root     33  0    1480K 736K  sleep 0:20   0.00% 0.00% at
213   root     33  0    2752K 1568K sleep 0:10   0.00% 0.00% automountd
```

One problem I had with *top* is it showed 2 GB of memory on a machine that I know had 4 GB. Perhaps it has some internal limitation.

top has a convenient feature: it runs once and exits unless it has a terminal. This is what you want if you're running *top* from a *cron* job or as a CGI on a web server. You can also force it to run once and then exit by using the *-b* option. This is useful if you want a list of all the processes, rather than just the top few. In this case, just give it the *-b* option and the number of processes to display, for example: *top -b 2000*.

Finally, *top* has the advantage that it will tell you which processes are swapped out to disk by marking them with <swap>. This information is not available with *ps*.

xload

xload is bundled with Solaris and shows a self-updating graph of system load.

System Call Tracers

Do you ever wish you could see what's going on inside your computer while it's mulling over some seemingly simple question and driving you crazy? Well, you can, sort of. You can see exactly which system calls are being executed and what the parameters to those calls are with one of the system call tracing utilities, such as *truss* on Solaris or *strace* on Linux. Other versions include *ktrace* and *par*. Shared library calls can be seen using *sotruss* under Solaris 2.6. See Chapter 9 for a *trace* of what happens when a request is made of a web server.

Tracing is especially useful for finding out that an application is doing single byte reads or writes, which is terribly inefficient. In Java, the problem is easily fixed by using buffered reader/writers rather than single-byte IO. If you run *truss -t read,write -s\all -p (process id)*, you should see the following:

```
read(49, "     B\r\n T R 0 8 0 6 5 9".., 8192)    = 8192
read(49, "                       J".., 8192)      = 8192
read(49, " 2 4 9      B          D ".., 8192)     = 8192
read(49, " 0 0 3 2 9 . 8 9 0 0 0 0".., 8192)      = 8192
read(49, " . 0 0 R                 ".., 8192)     = 8192
read(49, "             B\r\n T R 0 8".., 8192)    = 8192
read(49, "                        ".., 8192)      = 8192
read(49, " 4 4 1 3 2 4 9      B    ".., 8192)     = 8192
read(49, " 0 0 0 2 4 5 6 1 5 . 0 3".., 8192)      = 8192
```

You should not see this:

```
read(49, " C", 1)                                 = 1
read(49, " C", 1)                                 = 1
read(49, "  ", 1)                                 = 1
read(49, " 0", 1)                                 = 1
read(49, " 2", 1)                                 = 1
read(49, " 3", 1)                                 = 1
read(49, " 0", 1)                                 = 1
read(49, " 0", 1)                                 = 1
read(49, " 7", 1)                                 = 1
read(49, " 5", 1)                                 = 1
read(49, " 6", 1)                                 = 1
read(49, "  ", 1)                                 = 1
read(49, " 0", 1)                                 = 1
read(49, "\r", 1)                                 = 1
read(49, "\n", 1)                                 = 1
read(49, " T", 1)                                 = 1
read(49, " R", 1)                                 = 1
```

```
read(49, "  2", 1)                          = 1
read(49, "  3", 1)                          = 1
read(49, "  4", 1)                          = 1
read(49, "  5", 1)                          = 1
read(49, "  6", 1)                          = 1
read(49, "  7", 1)                          = 1
read(49, "  8", 1)                          = 1
read(49, "  9", 1)                          = 1
read(49, "   ", 1)                          = 1
read(49, "  B", 1)                          = 1
read(49, "  U", 1)                          = 1
read(49, "  Y", 1)                          = 1
read(49, "   ", 1)                          = 1
read(49, "   ", 1)                          = 1
read(49, "  D", 1)                          = 1
read(49, "  L", 1)                          = 1
read(49, "  R", 1)                          = 1
read(49, "  S", 1)                          = 1
read(49, "   ", 1)                          = 1
read(49, "   ", 1)                          = 1
read(49, "   ", 1)                          = 1
read(49, "   ", 1)                          = 1
read(49, "   ", 1)                          = 1
read(49, "   ", 1)                          = 1
read(49, "   ", 1)                          = 1
read(49, "  7", 1)                          = 1
read(49, "  7", 1)                          = 1
read(49, "  7", 1)                          = 1
read(49, "  6", 1)                          = 1
read(49, "  5", 1)                          = 1
read(49, "  .", 1)                          = 1
read(49, "  0", 1)                          = 1
read(49, "  0", 1)                          = 1
read(49, "   ", 1)                          = 1
```

Network Snooping Tools

Do you ever wish you could see what's going across your network connection? The *snoop* utility that comes bundled with Solaris will show you exactly what's being transmitted across your segment of the network. You have to be *root* to run it because it allows you to see absolutely everything, down to the content of the packets. *tcpdump* is a similar utility from the Stevens TCP/IP book with source code available from *ftp://ftp.uu.net/*. *etherfind* is another similar tool.

netstat

netstat shows the status of network connections. This is very valuable for determining which connections are up and whether you are wasting a lot of memory holding connection buffers for unused connections. On Linux, *netstat -c* will start displaying an updated network status every second, which is very instructive if you make a few requests from your browser while running it. Here's some sample output from *netstat*:

```
% netstat -at
Active Internet connections (including servers)
Proto Recv-Q Send-Q Local Address Foreign Address (State)     User
tcp        0      0 *:700          *:*             LISTEN      root
tcp        0      0 *:netbios-ssn  *:*             LISTEN      root
tcp        0      0 *:nntp         *:*             LISTEN      root
tcp        0      0 *:auth         *:*             LISTEN      root
tcp        0      0 *:6000         *:*             LISTEN      patrick
tcp        0      0 *:sunrpc       *:*             LISTEN      root
tcp        0      0 *:pop3         *:*             LISTEN      root
tcp        0      0 *:www          *:*             LISTEN      root
tcp        0      0 *:finger       *:*             LISTEN      root
tcp        1      0 cn2.cab:1584   nik.null.com:www CLOSE_WAIT patrick
tcp        1      0 cn2.cab:1580   nik.null.com:www CLOSE_WAIT patrick
tcp        1      0 cn2.cab:1579   nik.null.com:www CLOSE_WAIT patrick
tcp        1      0 cn2.cab:1578   nik.null.com:www CLOSE_WAIT patrick
tcp        1      0 cn2.cab:1577   nik.null.com:www CLOSE_WAIT patrick
tcp        1      0 cn2.cab:1576   nik.null.com:www CLOSE_WAIT patrick
tcp        1      0 cn2.cab:1575   nik.null.com:www CLOSE_WAIT patrick
tcp        0      0 *:time         *:*             LISTEN      root
tcp        0      0 *:uucp         *:*             LISTEN      root
tcp        0      0 *:ftp          *:*             LISTEN      root
tcp        0      0 *:chargen      *:*             LISTEN      root
tcp        0      0 *:netstat      *:*             LISTEN      root
tcp        0      0 *:daytime      *:*             LISTEN      root
tcp        0      0 *:systat       *:*             LISTEN      root
tcp        0      0 *:discard      *:*             LISTEN      root
tcp        0      0 *:echo         *:*             LISTEN      root
tcp        0      0 *:printer      *:*             LISTEN      root
tcp        0      0 *:shell        *:*             LISTEN      root
tcp        0      0 *:login        *:*             LISTEN      root
tcp        0      0 *:2049         *:*             LISTEN      root
```

netstat is quite slow to run on both Linux and Solaris. On Solaris, there is a much quicker way to display connection status with *ndd*:

```
% ndd /dev/tcp -get tcp_status
```

vmstat

Use *vmstat* to give you a snapshot of your memory situation in an ASCII format that varies between Unix versions. Your scan rate and page-out rate under Solaris are an indication of whether you have enough memory. You want to keep both of them low. Here's some sample output from *vmstat*:

```
% vmstat 1

 procs memory page disk faults cpu
 r b w swap free re mf pi po fr de sr s2 s3 s4 s1 in sy cs us sy id
```

```
0 0 0 352 888 0 534 18 3 7 0 0 0 1 0 1 271 1 418 3 6 91
6 0 0 192960 111528 0 2139 0 0 0 0 0 0 0 0 488 2780 1106 4 23 73
1 0 0 196128 112136 0 4412 0 0 0 0 0 0 0 0 1086 3193 2511 7 33 60
0 0 0 194016 111416 0 3419 0 0 0 0 0 0 0 0 689 1977 1722 2 22 76
0 0 0 193664 111296 0 4319 0 0 0 0 0 0 0 0 890 2597 2231 2 28 69
1 0 0 195608 111992 0 4100 0 0 0 0 0 0 0 0 887 2341 2210 4 23 72
0 0 0 196480 112256 0 1234 0 0 0 0 0 0 0 0 390 924 785 2 7 92
0 0 0 194720 111720 0 1616 0 0 0 0 0 0 0 0 360 1095 738 2 8 91
0 0 0 189440 110016 0 2900 0 0 0 0 0 0 0 0 701 1767 1732 2 20 78
1 0 0 195040 111768 0 5486 0 0 0 0 0 2 0 1 1046 3969 2729 10 32 58
0 0 0 194280 110808 0 4147 0 0 0 0 0 0 0 0 787 2368 1984 2 27 70
2 0 0 191816 110152 0 5556 0 0 0 0 0 31 0 0 1122 3268 2840 4 38 58
0 0 0 194368 111528 0 3784 0 0 0 0 0 0 0 0 750 2157 1914 4 18 78
2 0 0 194776 112064 0 4684 0 0 0 0 0 0 0 0 893 2607 2316 4 28 67
0 0 0 195424 111888 0 2366 0 0 0 0 0 1 0 0 526 1433 1240 4 16 81
0 0 0 195424 111888 0 3650 0 0 0 0 0 0 0 0 758 2381 1896 2 24 73
0 0 0 194368 111592 0 4166 0 0 0 0 0 0 0 0 830 2405 2108 3 24 73
0 0 0 194368 111528 0 3430 0 0 0 0 0 0 0 0 676 2116 1724 2 22 76
0 0 0 194360 112000 0 3988 0 0 0 0 0 0 0 0 772 2266 1896 2 26 71
```

sar

sar provides much the same information as *vmstat*, but can save data in a compact binary format suitable for long-term statistics gathering. *sar* itself provides display options for the data collected. It is much more complete and flexible than *vmstat*. Here's sample output from *sar*:

```
% sar -c 5 5
SunOS pokey.patrick.net 5.5.1 Generic_103640-12 sun4u 02/17/98

15:03:46 scall/s sread/s swrit/s fork/s exec/s rchar/s wchar/s
15:03:51 2418 5 84 79.64 0.60 1126 537
15:03:56 1703 3 58 57.80 0.00 478 505
15:04:01 1676 10 57 51.70 0.00 640 523
15:04:06 2553 14 93 84.83 0.00 739 559
15:04:11 1807 4 60 56.80 0.60 965 556
```

How Many Connections Can My Server Handle?

It is enlightening to set up as many connections as possible to your web server, just to see what limit you hit first. Use the various system-monitoring tools described earlier while running the following script. Note that this script may crash your server or your test client machine, so use it only on machines you can afford to crash. You may need to run multiple copies from several different test machines to max out your server, in which case you'll need to add the highest number output from each copy. I can get about 3,500 connections on my Sony Vaio laptop running Linux 2.2. It seems you can set up far more connections from a single process than the *ulimit* number of file descriptors configured. You can download this program from *http:// patrick.net/software/maxconn*.

```
#!/usr/bin/perl

use Socket;

die "Usage: maxconn <host> <port>\n" unless $ARGV[0];

$iaddr = gethostbyname($ARGV[0]);

$proto            = getprotobyname('tcp');

while (1) {
    print "$n\n";
    $n++;
    socket(SOCK, PF_INET, SOCK_STREAM, $proto) or fail("socket: $!");
    $paddr            = sockaddr_in($ARGV[1], $iaddr);
    connect(SOCK, $paddr)                or fail("connect: $!");
}
```

How Many Processes Can My Server Handle?

It is also interesting to see how many processes a server can handle and what resource runs out first. The following is a small C program that simply forks and waits for the child to exit, rapidly building up to the maximum number of processes your machine can handle. Again, it may well crash your machine, so use it only on a machine you can afford to crash. It is downloadable from *http://patrick.net/software/fork.c*. Compile it like this: *gcc -o fork fork.c*.

```
#include <unistd.h>
#include <stdio.h>
#include <errno.h>
#include <sys/types.h>
#include <sys/wait.h>

main( ) {
    int pid;

    pid = fork( );

    if (pid == -1) perror("failed: ");
     if (pid ==  0) {
        printf("child\n");
        execl("./fork", "");
    }
    else
        printf("parent\n");
    wait(NULL);
}
```

Since each child process is new, we can't simply have a counter as we did with the previous Perl script. I used *top* to see how many processes my Linux laptop could get up to. It was about 500 processes, then *top* gave up with a "help!" message and my

---

laptop was furiously swapping. I killed the parent with ^C and things returned to normal; all the children exited.

If you leave out the wait statement, then you have a truly evil little program that you cannot kill so easily. The parent exits and the child forks a new child and then exits and so on. This means no process is around long enough for you to even hunt it down with *ps*. They constantly fork and exit, not overflowing your process table, but using up plenty of your CPU. The secret to killing this mutant it to run the above program with the wait statement to use up enough resources that it can no longer fork! Once one of the children cannot fork, the chain is broken.

How Quickly Can My Server Fork New Processes?

That evil little program can be modified to do something useful: it can tell us how quickly we can fork new processes. We have to add a little timing code, and a limit on the number of children to fork, and then we just use the unfashionable goto statement to have each child go back up to the fork statement. Because each child process is created by a fork system call rather than an execl call, it is identical to its parent and the counter is preserved. You can download it from *http://patrick.net/ software/forktime.c*.

```c
#include <unistd.h>
#include <stdio.h>
#include <errno.h>
#include <sys/types.h>
#include <sys/wait.h>
#include <time.h>

main() {
    int pid;
    int count = 0;
    time_t      t;
    struct tm * tp;
    char        timestr[20];

    t = time(NULL);
    tp = localtime(&t);
    strftime(timestr, 20, "%Y %m %d %H %M %S", tp);
    printf(timestr);
    printf("\n");

    there: pid = fork();

    if (pid == -1) perror("failed: ");

    if (pid ==  0) {                    /* child */
        if (++count > 10000) {
            t  = time(NULL);
```

```
            tp = localtime(&t);
            strftime(timestr, 20, "%Y %m %d %H %M %S", tp);
            printf(timestr);
            printf("\n");

            _exit(0);
        }
        else {
            goto there;
        }
    }
    /* only parent can get here */
    _exit(0);
}
```

Running this copy, I see from the difference in time output by the first parent and the 10,000th child (7 seconds) that it takes about 0.7 milliseconds to create a new process on my Linux laptop. It seems that I need not have forked the processes in a chain, from parent to child, because the parent does not continue until the child is running and returns a process ID. I also modified the *fork* program to fork a fixed number of times, and replaced the execl statement with an _exit(0) to make each new child exit. I got various errors when I tried to fork 1,000 processes in this way, but I could fork 500 processes. If I printed "child exiting" on each iteration, then it took 50 milliseconds to fork. If I printed only the process number, it took 27 milliseconds to fork. If I printed nothing at all from the child process, again it took about 0.7 milliseconds to fork. This shows that even minimal IO takes much more time than forking.

Unix Versus NT as the Web Server OS

All of this is not to say there is no competition for Unix as a web server platform. It is simple to set up a web server on any Windows or Macintosh machine and get reasonable performance, as long as the load is light. But for heavy loads, the only competitor to Unix for a web server platform is Windows NT. The creators of NT applied many of Unix's features, such as the concepts of a kernel, user processes, and preemptive multitasking, to the design of NT. Let's take a look at what each OS has to offer.

NT Pros and Cons

NT has the traditional Microsoft advantages of close integration with other Microsoft products, a consistent look and feel, and GUI rather than command-line administration for those who don't like to type commands and don't want or need a fine level of control. NT has the ability to run some legacy Windows applications. NT can run on cheap commodity PC hardware, but so can many versions of Unix.

NT does not have especially good performance or scalability for web serving. See the article "The Best OS for Web Serving: Unix or NT?" by Barry Nance (Byte Magazine, March 1998) for one experiment confirming this. More important, NT is very unstable compared to Unix, frequently crashing or requiring reboots, which is a serious drawback to using it for important sites. NT comes with no remote administration and no multiuser mode.

Running a high-performance web site on PC hardware is also difficult. Scalability is limited by the PC's legacy I/O architecture, which was never intended for large loads. By some estimates, you cannot handle more than about 250 concurrent transaction processing users on even the best PC hardware. PC hardware is also generally less reliable than true workstation hardware, because it is built for the mass market, where cost rather than reliability is the driving factor.

Microsoft also has some credibility problems. Their "Wolfpack" scalability demonstration used the easily fudged debit-credit benchmark, rather than the more reliable TPC-C and TPC-D transaction processing benchmarks. And Microsoft has been accused of misrepresenting the capability of NT workstation relative to its NT server edition. The cheaper NT workstation was limited to 10 open connections, allegedly because it couldn't handle more than that; users were supposed to pay much more for a supposedly higher-performance version. A binary *diff* showed that the executables were identical, except for a few bytes that were presumably a switch allowing more connections.

Unix Pros and Cons

Unix operating systems are very robust, usually capable of running for many months and sometimes several years without rebooting. Equally important is that Unix has much better scalability than NT, allowing a small site to grow by adding hardware such as CPUs and I/O controllers to existing machines rather than requiring multiple new machines to handle increasing load. Finally, Unix has better performance, partly because it is usually run on better hardware than commodity PCs.

A large majority of high-performance web sites run on some version of Unix, so the issues are well worked out. A professional Unix system will typically have a higher entry-level cost than NT, even if the price/performance ratio at that level is better. If cost is a big consideration, there are many versions of Unix that will run on the same commodity PC hardware as NT and provide the same or better performance, such as Solaris x86, Linux, and BSDI. Pricing for Solaris is similar to that for NT.

Unix also requires more highly trained system administrators, although GUI tools for the Unix-averse are available, such as Sun's Netra product line, and the free Webmin tool from *http://www.webmin.com*.

The Exokernel

A group at MIT has developed a tiny kernel-like thing that does nothing except provide access to hardware to multiple applications. The applications can include various operating systems as well, but they do not need to. So it becomes possible to write a web server that maximizes the use of hardware resources, completely bypassing all operating system overhead. The Exokernel group did this with their "Cheetah" web server and provides graphs of some impressive results at *http://www.pdos. lcs.mit.edu/exo.html*. While this is exciting, web server speed is not usually a problem. Database speed and dynamic content generation speed are much more important, so these perhaps would see more benefit from the Exokernel approach.

Key Recommendations

- Don't write back the file-access time. Either mount a filesystem as read-only or change the filesystem source and recompile.
- Use short paths.
- Don't use symbolic links.
- Don't run a window system on the server; use terminal mode.

## CHAPTER 18

Server Software

Web servers accept requests and return replies. The reply can be a static page, custom dynamic content, or an error. While there is a lot of variation in performance depending on load, an individual request for a static page typically takes only one-tenth of a second from the time the request arrives at the server until the response is pushed back out. Modem latency, Internet latency, and even browser-parsing time are all likely to be larger than that, so a lightly loaded web server will not be a bottleneck.

A heavily loaded web server is another story. Web servers tend to go nonlinear when loaded beyond a certain point, degrading rapidly in performance. This chapter is about why that happens and what your options are for getting the most out of your web server software.

The Evolution of Web Servers

While their basic function has remained the same, web servers have evolved quite a bit from over the years.

Servers Spawned from inetd

The first generation of web servers were just another Unix service launched on demand from *inetd*, which reads */etc/services* on startup and listens to the ports specified. When a request comes in on one of *inetd*'s ports, it launches the program specified in */etc/services* to deal with requests on that port. This requires calling the fork( ) and exec( ) system calls: fork( ), to clone *inetd* to get a process, and exec( ), to write over that process with another process that can service the request. This mechanism is intended to conserve system resources by starting up daemons only when they're needed, providing better performance for everything else.

As an example, consider *ftpd*. Watch the list of processes running on your system, say with *top*. When a request comes in on port 21, *inetd* launches *ftpd*, and you will see *ftpd* appear in the list of processes. When the FTP session is over, the *ftpd* process goes away.

Originally, *httpd* was launched the same way, but from port 80. Trouble started when servers were loaded above one or two hits per second and couldn't keep up. Remember that a single HTML page can have many embedded images, so one page can generate enough HTTP operations to reach the maximum load of an *inetd*-spawned server. The *inetd* mechanism trades off more startup time for reduced overall system load, but this trade-off works only under very light web serving loads. For anything more, system load is actually increased by the many startups of *httpd*, and performance for both the local machine user and the web client is reduced. Avoid launching *httpd* from *inetd*; run a standalone server instead.

Configure Apache's *httpd.conf* like this:

```
# ServerType is either inetd, or standalone.

ServerType standalone
```

Forking Servers

A step up from using *inetd* to fork( ) and exec( ) is to use an instance of *httpd* to simply fork( ) another copy of itself to handle the request, with no need for an exec( ). This was the original intent behind the fork( ) system call, and it works reasonably well for the client-server world, but because HTTP requests arrive so frequently and are of such short duration the time spent in creating a new process is larger than the time spent actually servicing the request. The early CERN and NCSA servers were forking servers.

Another improvement came with the Apache server. Apache servers are preforking. For example, when Apache 1.2.4 *httpd* starts up, it immediately starts five additional servers by default to handle multiple simultaneous requests from one browser or from several concurrent clients. Apache will increase the number of server processes in response to a heavier load; this works well even for very large sites, but it is memory- and CPU-intensive.

Threaded Servers

To match the lightweight and transient nature of an HTTP connection, server programmers have been turning to threads. Threads are independent streams of execution within a single process. Thread creation and context switching is on the order of ten times faster than for processes. Still, once you have a process created and ready to handle a connection, the bottleneck is in servicing the request rather than the overhead of managing server processes or threads, so you don't see a full tenfold increase in performance with the threaded server.

Netscape Enterprise 2.0 and up are threaded servers and can currently serve several thousand connections per second. Apache 2.0 supports preforking as well as threading, via their Multi-Processing Module (MPM).

Keepalive Servers

An additional improvement in performance is available by keeping TCP connections open for serving multiple files in one request. This technique is known as persistent connections, or "keepalive," and is part of the HTTP 1.1 standard. Most browsers and servers now understand keepalive connections even if they don't fully implement HTTP 1.1. Browsers will indicate that they understand keepalive connections by sending a Connection:keepalive header with their request. Both preforking and threaded servers use keepalives.

A performance hazard to keepalives is that clients may disconnect without notifying the server, which then has an open connection consuming resources indefinitely. To prevent too many such connections from accumulating, most implementations of keepalive come with a timeout parameter so that unused connections will be closed.

System Calls Made by a Web Server

Here's a system call trace (to trace all requests made of the operating system) on Linux 2.0 of what Apache 1.2.4 does in response to a request from a browser. To make this trace, I simply started Apache with one child process and traced that one process while making a request from a browser. You usually can't tell why an application decided to make a particular system call, but this is still a very valuable technique for figuring out where a server is spending its time. I used a similar trace by Dean Gaudet to decipher what is happening here.

(The lines are numbered to simplify the discussion afterwards.)

```
 1  # strace -p1147
 2  accept(16, {sin_family=AF_INET, sin_port=htons(1034), sin_addr=inet_addr("127.0.0.
    1")}, [16]) = 3
 3  fcntl(18, F_SETLKW, {type=F_UNLCK, whence=SEEK_SET, start=0, len=0}) = 0
 4  rt_sigaction(SIGUSR1, {SIG_IGN}, {0x80596c0, [], SA_INTERRUPT|0x4000000}, 8) = 0
 5  getsockname(3, {sin_family=AF_INET, sin_port=htons(80), sin_addr=inet_addr("127.0.
    0.1")}, [16]) = 0
 6  setsockopt(3, IPPROTO_TCP1, [1], 4)      = 0
 7  brk(0x80b3000)                           = 0x80b3000
 8  read(3, "GET / HTTP/1.0\r\nIf-Modified-Sinc"..., 4096) = 336
 9  rt_sigaction(SIGUSR1, {SIG_IGN}, {SIG_IGN}, 8) = 0
10  time(NULL)                               = 988240305
11  stat("/home/httpd/html", {st_mode=S_IFDIR|0777, st_size=2048, ...}) = 0
12  lstat("/home", {st_mode=S_IFDIR|0755, st_size=1024, ...}) = 0
13  lstat("/home/httpd", {st_mode=S_IFDIR|0755, st_size=1024, ...}) = 0
14  lstat("/home/httpd/html", {st_mode=S_IFDIR|0777, st_size=2048, ...}) = 0
15  brk(0x80b6000)                           = 0x80b6000
16  stat("/home/httpd/html/index.html", {st_mode=S_IFREG|0644, st_size=2488, ...}) =
    0
17  lstat("/home", {st_mode=S_IFDIR|0755, st_size=1024, ...}) = 0
18  lstat("/home/httpd", {st_mode=S_IFDIR|0755, st_size=1024, ...}) = 0
19  lstat("/home/httpd/html", {st_mode=S_IFDIR|0777, st_size=2048, ...}) = 0
```

```
20  stat("/home/httpd/html/index.html", {st_mode=S_IFREG|0644, st_size=2488, ...}) =
0
21  lstat("/home", {st_mode=S_IFDIR|0755, st_size=1024, ...}) = 0
22  lstat("/home/httpd", {st_mode=S_IFDIR|0755, st_size=1024, ...}) = 0
23  lstat("/home/httpd/html", {st_mode=S_IFDIR|0777, st_size=2048, ...}) = 0
24  open("/home/httpd/html/index.html", O_RDONLY) = 4
25  open("/etc/localtime", O_RDONLY)     = 5
26  read(5, "TZif\0\0\0\0\0\0\0\0\0\0\0\0\0\0\0\0\0\0\0\3\0\0\0\3\0"..., 44) = 44
27  read(5, "\236\246H\240\237\273\25\220\240\206*\240\241\232\367\220"..., 920) =
920fstat(5,
28  {st_mode=S_IFREG|0644, st_size=1000, ...}) = 0
29  mmap(0, 4096, PROT_READ|PROT_WRITE, MAP_PRIVATE|MAP_ANONYMOUS, -1, 0) =
0x40014000
30  read(5, "\377\377\235\220\1\0\377\377\217\200\0\4\377\377\235\220"..., 4096) = 36
31  close(5)                            = 0
32  munmap(0x40014000, 4096)            = 0
33  select(4, [3], NULL, NULL, {0, 0})  = 0 (Timeout)
34  write(3, "HTTP/1.1 304 Not Modified\r\nDate:"..., 197) = 197
35  time(NULL)                          = 988240305
36  write(17, "127.0.0.1 - - [25/Apr/2001:16:11"..., 66) = 66
37  close(4)                            = 0
38  rt_sigaction(SIGUSR1, {0x80596c0, [], SA_INTERRUPT|0x4000000}, {SIG_IGN}, 8) = 0
39  read(3,
40  0x809eb24, 4096)                    = ? ERESTARTSYS (To be restarted)
41  --- SIGALRM (Alarm clock) ---
42  close(3)                            = 0
43  rt_sigprocmask(SIG_SETMASK, [], NULL, 8) = 0
44  rt_sigaction(SIGURG, {0x8058700, [], SA_INTERRUPT|0x4000000}, {0x8058700, [], SA
45  _INTERRUPT|0x4000000}, 8) = 0
46  rt_sigaction(SIGALRM, {0x8058910, [], SA_INTERRUPT|0x4000000}, {0x8058910, [], S
47  A_INTERRUPT|0x4000000}, 8) = 0
48  rt_sigaction(SIGUSR1, {0x80596c0, [], SA_INTERRUPT|0x4000000}, {0x80596c0, [], S
49  A_INTERRUPT|0x4000000}, 8) = 0
50  fcntl(18, F_SETLKW, {type=F_WRLCK, whence=SEEK_SET, start=0, len=0}
```

At line 2 you see the accept( ) system call, because the server recognizes a request for services from IP address 127.0.0.1, which is the local machine. Then you see an fcntl( ) call to unlock access to that accept call. This is because access to accept is serialized to avoid the problems described in *http://www.apache.org/docs/misc/perf-tuning.html*.

At line 4 we see some signal manipulation with rt_ sigaction( ). This is to cause children to die off when their parent sends them a SIGUSR1 signal, but only if they are not in the middle of serving a result.

At line 5 we get information about the socket to enable the use of virtual hosts.

At line 6 we turn off the Nagle algorithm, also known as "slow start," because it is not compatible with the short-lived nature of most HTTP connections.

At line 8 our request is read from the network.

In line 16 we see one of the many stat calls. stat( ) is used to find out file information necessary for headers like Content-Length and Last-Modified, as well as to decide whether a page has been modified since the last time it was retrieved.

At line 29 we see that the file is mmapped prior to being served, as are all static files under Apache.

At line 34 we finally begin to write a response back to the network.

At line 36 we log the transaction to our log file.

At line 50 we finally lock access to the accept routine again, to serialize access to it.

How Servers Fail

A preforking server with a fixed maximum number of processes (for example, the MaxClientsparameter in Apache's *httpd.conf*) handles that many clients at one time, and no more. Additional requests are not picked off the operating system's TCP listen queue by the server, and the user is met with an annoying hang in the browser. Once the listen queue is full, clients may still hang waiting for the OS-level connections to be completed. The ignored connections have no impact on the server's ability to handle the requests that it does accept. Similarly, threaded servers hit the maximum number of threads (for example, the MaxThreadsparameter in Netscape Enterprise's *magnus.conf*) and refuse to service any more. I wish the server would send an immediate reset to the browser, but I haven't been able to get that to happen.

But let's say that we configure an infinite number of processes or threads, set the TCP listen queue to "infinite," and then overload the servers by increasing the number of client requests. What happens?

Not only are there too many client connections competing for CPU time, but the overhead of scheduling those processes or threads consumes an ever larger percentage of CPU time. Eventually, the CPU spends almost all of its time scheduling and no real work is done. If you were to graph throughput against number of simultaneous connections, throughput would peak at a certain number of connections, and then fall off as you moved beyond that number.

Performance degrades faster for nonthreaded servers because of the larger overhead of scheduling and switching between processes rather than threads. CPU load rises as the number of processes to schedule increases. Memory is also depleted faster in the forking server, because processes incur greater overhead than threads. Still, degradation is fairly linear, because the impact is distributed across many fairly small processes.

Threaded servers hold up better at first because of lower overhead in context switching between threads, slowly dropping in performance as more threads are scheduled and switched, until memory is low enough that the machine begins to swap. The downside to threaded servers is that swapping out the huge process with all the threads is a sudden large hit to performance. This is why Netscape advises you to run 4 processes with 32 threads each rather than one process with 128 threads. Another problem that happens with threaded server is thread deadlocks that occur only at very high loads, which makes them hard to debug.

Slow clients have more impact on memory than fast clients because each slow client ties up buffers concurrently with other slow processes. This means that a server fails sooner when most of the clients are on slow connections. Keep in mind that when the Internet is heavily loaded, say in the afternoon, it looks to the web server like everyone is on a slow connection. Fast clients benefit more than slow clients from server I/O improvements.

Memory Leaks

Some web servers slowly leak memory—that is, they allocate memory and lose all references to it, meaning that memory cannot be used or reclaimed. This eventually makes the server process so large that it has to be restarted. If restarting the web server significantly helps performance, you may have a leak. If you can't get a bug fix, the next best thing is to schedule regular restarts of the web server software or, in the worst case, to schedule regular reboots. You can monitor the size of your *httpd* processes with *ps* or *top*. Server vendors can and do run leak-finding tools such as Purify (*http://www.rational.com/*) on their products, but the aggressive release schedules mean that they don't have time for extensive usage tests with Purify.

Configuring Apache and Netscape Web Servers

Server vendors try to tune their servers as best they can for general use before they send them out to you. They certainly want you to get high performance. The reason you might change things is that you know more about your particular needs than they do.

First, here are some general tips that can apply to whatever server you use:

Short pathnames
> The less you log, the faster it will go. Shorter pathnames for content are written faster, use less disk space, and provide faster lookup. If you want to see an excellent example, check out Yahoo!'s pathnames. Directories and files are often only a single letter long.

No time conversions
> Another trick is to not do any time conversions during the logging step. The Java Web Server, may it rest in peace, used to convert from Greenwich Mean Time (GMT) to local time on every hit by default, unless you specifically told it not to.

Buffered log files
> Most log files for web servers and middleware and other kinds of servers are now buffered, meaning that they are held in memory until a sufficient number accumulate to warrant writing them all out to disk, or until a timer expires. Turn on log file buffering. This provides a substantial performance benefit at the expense of a little memory.

Configuring Apache

Apache, by far the most successful web server, is used on more than half of all web sites. It can be freely downloaded from *http://httpd.apache.org/*. Apache was derived from the old NSCA server via many software patches, therefore the name: "a patchy" web server. One of the best features of Apache is its price: it is freely available along with source code.

Apache has been a preforking server, but a threaded version is now available for Unix and NT. Apache is said to run CGI programs efficiently. Support, via Usenet newsgroups, is probably better than support for any commercial server, and free.

Apache supports Java servlets via the Tomcat project and has real-time performance monitoring tools and an optional log format that tells you how long each transfer took. (See *mod_log_config.html* in the server documentation.) Try to ensure that the server has been compiled with the latest C compiler and libraries for your server platform, or compile the server yourself.

See Dean Gaudet's notes about Apache servers from *http://www.apache.org/docs/ misc/perf-tuning.html* for internal details.

AllowOverride

In the kind of full-path authentication used on Apache and some other servers, the current directory and each parent directory (up to the system root, not just up to the document root) are searched by default for a *.htaccess* authentication file, which must be read and parsed, if found. You can speed up Apache by turning off authentication for directories that don't need it, like the system root, by putting the following in the *access.conf* file:

```
<Directory />
AllowOverride None

</Directory>

<Directory /usr/local/mydocroot>
AllowOverride All (or any of the other AllowOverride options)
</Directory>
```

Even better, if you don't use *.htaccess* files, don't look for them at all:

```
<Directory /usr/local/mydocroot>
AllowOverride None
</Directory>
```

The general web performance tip of keeping paths short takes on added importance for web servers that use directory-specific access control like Apache. Each directory traversal takes time not only because it follows the filesystem's linked list and checks Unix permissions, but also because of the web server's access control, such as *.htaccess* files, which are even less efficient. See the system call trace earlier in this chapter.

BUFFERED_LOGS

For better performance, compile Apache with *-DBUFFERED_LOGS* so that log file writes are deferred until a certain number of bytes are accumulated. That number is the POSIX constant PIPE_BUF.

MaxClients

You'll get much better performance by running only the number of server processes your RAM can hold. If you run too many, you'll start swapping and performance for each will drop. How many can you run? It's tricky because some parts of each *httpd* process are shared with others, but a good rule of thumb is Apache is 1 MB per process.

If you have only 128 MB RAM, then don't try to run any more than 128 processes, even if you often have more than 128 concurrent users. Anyhow, you'll probably be limited by other factors at 128 processes.

You can configure the number of *httpd* processes in Apache with the MaxClients directive. You don't want to run too few *httpd* processes either, because you need enough processes so that fast clients never have to wait for a slow client to finish and free up a process.

Persistent connections

Turn on persistent connections, also called keepalives (KeepAlive On in *httpd.conf*), and set the number of allowed requests per connection high (MaxKeepAliveRequests 100) to save the overhead of setting up new connections. Set the timeout fairly low, say 15 seconds (KeepAliveTimeout 15) to reduce the impact of dead or very slow clients.

Turning off reverse DNS

Turn off runtime DNS reverse lookup. The server is given only the IP address of the calling browser. This reverse lookup is what lets the server use the fully qualified name in CGIs and in the server's log file. You don't really need reverse DNS because log file analysis programs such as the *logresolve* program that comes with Apache can look up names offline, and CGIs can do a reverse lookup themselves if they really need to.

The hazard to DNS is it uses blocking system calls, which hang the entire server process until the call completes. DNS calls can take a noticeable amount of time for a single user, so a server servicing many users sees a large drag on performance from DNS lookups. As of Apache 1.3, reverse DNS is off by default.

In Apache's *httpd.conf*, do the following to turn off DNS lookups:

```
HostnameLookups off
```

Do not restrict by domain

From Dean Gaudet's Apache Performance Notes, we see that using any "allow from <domain>" or "deny from <domain>" directives will hurt performance twice because a reverse DNS lookup is first done to check the domain of the client browser, then a normal DNS lookup is done to be sure that reverse lookup is not a fake. Restricting by IP address alone does not have this performance problem.

Set FollowSymLinks

Another tip from Dean is to set Options FollowSymLinks because this will avoid the lstat system call that would otherwise have to be performed on every element of a path, including a symbolic link every single time you use that link. Here is an example of how to configure it:

```
DocumentRoot /www/htdocs
<Directory />
     Options FollowSymLinks
</Directory>
```

Note that this effectively turns off security for symbolic links, so users could then make a link point to any readable file on your server and actually serve that file.

FancyIndexing

One problem I had with Apache is the fancy indexing. If FancyIndexing in *srm.conf* is set to "on," then whenever you access a directory lacking an *index.html*, an HTML listing of the directory contents is generated on the fly and returned to the user. The problem with the fancy version of this directory listing is it assumes that you have installed the icons that ship with the server in the */icons* directory. If you fail to install these icons, users will see broken links for those icon images. Even worse, every time you go back to that page a bunch of useless network traffic is generated by looking for those icons, holding up the rendering of the page. This occurs every time you view the directory page, even if you set your browser to always use cached content and never check the network, because the missing images are not in the cache. I suppose you could install the icons, but I just set FancyIndexing to "off."

Use specific index files

Instead of using a wildcard such as:

```
DirectoryIndex index
```

use a complete list of options:

```
DirectoryIndex index.cgi index.pl index.html
```

in which you list the most common choice first.

MaxRequestsPerChild

This is the number of requests a child process will be allowed to serve before it is killed. The idea is to pre-empt memory leaks in the Apache code and in the system libraries. The default under Apache 1.3.9 seems to be 100, but this is much too low. Set it to 10,000 to avoid much of the overhead of spawning new child processes. Keep an eye on the size of your *httpd* processes and if they don't seem to grow, you can probably safely increase it to 100,000 or more.

Some notes on sizing Apache

For Apache, which handles load by dishing out requests to many child processes, you want to initially start as many processes (StartServers) as the number of simultaneous connections you expect. Ten or so is plenty for small sites, though that would be inadequate for very busy sites. Those processes will all be prespawned and waiting for incoming connections.

If you configure too many, then the select( ) call will have too much work to do. If you configure too few, you will find yourself forking at a time you can least afford to, though as of Apache 1.3, forking rates double every second—that is, one child is forked the first second, then two the second second, then four the third second, and so on as long as connections are pending. This should be fast enough for most sites to cope with variations in load.

The minimum (MinSpareServers) should be the average number of processes, plus a few for variation in load. The max should be the maximum the machine can handle, usually determined by memory size.

Using mod_status

If you include mod_status and set Rule STATUS=yes when building Apache, then on every request Apache will perform extra timing calls so that the status report generated will include timings. This slows down performance, but gives performance data. Take your pick.

For more information

See *http://www.apache.org/* and *Apache: The Definitive Guide*, by Ben Laurie and Peter Laurie (O'Reilly & Associates), for more information on all of these directives.

Configuring Netscape

Netscape is a multithreaded commercial server, which can be purchased from (*http://home.netscape.com/*). It is the second most popular server on Unix platforms after Apache. Netscape's servers are now managed by a cooperative venture between Sun

Microsystems and AOL that is called iPlanet, so Netscape servers are sometimes also called iPlanet servers. I believe the preforking Commerce Server and entry-level Fast Track Server have been phased out in favor of the multithreaded Netscape Enterprise server.

The major difference between Apache and Netscape is that Apache remains a preforking server (except on NT), while Netscape servers are multithreaded. The primary configuration files for Netscape Enterprise servers are *magnus.conf* and *obj.conf*, both of which are found in the *suitespot/https-<server name>/config* directory. The *magnus.conf* file is the main configuration file read at startup time. The *obj.conf* file controls content-related issues, such as access to directories.

Netscape servers work through the following seven Server Application Functions (SAFs) for each request, as configured by the *obj.conf* file. Steps may be skipped as appropriate. You can write your own SAFs by programming to the Netscape API and referring to the resulting *.so* file in *obj.conf*. These are also known as server "plug-ins." Each SAF returns a response code to the server, telling whether it succeeded, whether to continue, and for the service step, what headers should be returned to the client. Do not use gethostbyname or gethostbyaddr blocking system calls in your plug-ins, because you may block the whole server process:

1. Authorization Translation, where user-supplied information is translated into a user ID and group ID
2. Name Translation, for doing something out of the ordinary, like redirecting requests
3. Path check, for existence and permissions
4. Object Typing, where objects are mapped to MIME types so the appropriate HTTP header can be supplied
5. Service Selection, for returning the static file, running the CGI, and so on
6. Update log
7. Error handling and informing the client of the error

Number of processes

Folklore has it that the number of *httpd* processes should be one less than the number of CPUs on SMP machines. This reserves one CPU for the operating system. For example, on an 8-CPU machine, set the following in *magnus.conf*:

```
MaxProcs 7
```

Number of server threads

Configure the server only for the maximum number of threads the RAM will support. Especially if you generate a lot of dynamic content, be aware that a slowdown in your middleware or database or mainframe will cause threads to remain in use longer than usual, with the result that you may see a surge in the number of threads in use. If you run out of web server threads because they are all tied up, users will not be able to do anything at all on the web server, not even get an error page!

You can run each process as single-threaded processes if your plug-ins are not thread-safe, but you'll lose some performance. You may want to run only one process with 128 maximum threads for easiest programming, but under heavy loads you'll get better performance from 4 processes with 32 threads each, for the reason just mentioned. In *magnus.conf*, set:

```
MinThreads 4
MaxThreads 32
```

I have heard that you must also set:

```
PostThreadsEarly on
```

Otherwise you will never use more than the minimum number of threads.

Turning off reverse DNS

An explanation of why you want to turn off reverse DNS is given above for Apache, and in detail in Chapter 9. As of Netscape Enterprise 3.5, DNS lookups are off by default. In Netscape's *magnus.conf* file, do this:

```
DNS off
```

And in the AddLog directive in *obj.conf*, do the following:

```
iponly=1
```

Persistent connections

Limit persistent connections to 15 seconds so dead clients do not use up resources. Set this in *magnus.conf*:

```
KeepAliveTimeout 15
```

But you also want to have a lot of those connections so that they are there if clients are really using them. Set:

```
MaxKeepAliveConnections 500
```

The default is 200, which may be enough. Be careful that you don't set it so high that you run out of file descriptors for that process. Most web servers run with 1,024 file descriptors (settable with the *ulimit* command) but that includes not only connections, but every file the web server has open. If you run out, your server may crash.

File cache

Netscape servers have an internal cache of files. cache-size is the total number of URLs cached and can be set high for better performance, at the expense of using more memory. The effective limit is the number of file descriptors available per process, which can be discovered or set with *ulimit*. See Chapter 17 for more on file

---

descriptors. On the other hand, if all your content is generated dynamically, it may be better to set the cache size low to conserve memory.

I've never been certain of the utility of this cache, given that the Unix operating system itself will cache files in memory. Another problem with the Netscape cache is that the server will constantly poll to see if the file on disk has changed, which adds to overhead. If you know you are not going to change your static files frequently, set the cache-init PollInterval to 30,000 (which is 8 hours) to keep the check from happening too frequently.

The caching seems to be done by mapping the files to memory. The mmap-maxparameter specifies the maximum amount of memory set aside for memory mapped files; units are in kilobytes. This should be about the same as the total amount of static data you are serving. If you have about 10 MB of static data, you should set this to 10,240. Never set this above the amount of RAM you can actually spare for caching, or you will have to go to the disk for the content and lose the benefit of caching.

max-file is the largest file to keep in cache. You would rather not have the occasional use of very large files push everything else out of the cache, so set this limit at, say, 1 MB.

In *obj.conf*, do the following:

```
Init fn=cache-init cache-size=512 mmap-max=10240 max-file=1048576
```

There is also a directive_is_cacheable option in the Request structure. Your API Server Application Functions (SAFs) can use this option to tell the server that identical URL requests can use a cached response, so the API does not need to be run again. Use this option when the response does not depend on the user's IP or browser, but only on the URL.

pwfile

The following will load */etc/passwd* into memory for faster access to files referred to by paths that contain ~:

```
Unix init-uhome pwfile=/etc/passwd
```

CGI timeout

This will limit CGIs to 60 seconds in case they hang:

```
init-cgi timeout=60
```

RqThrottle

Unlike Apache, the critical sizing parameter for Netscape is threads. When Netscape runs out of threads, it hangs, not even servicing existing connections. And when one process hangs, your load balancer will increase the load on the others, perhaps also pushing them over the edge. New connections will still be accepted by the machine with the hung web server, up to the TCP queue length, but will never be serviced by Netscape. So a key to configuring Netscape is to set RqThrottle below the number of threads, so that the server will never hang.

Be sure not to set RqThrottle too low, either, or users will be able to connect, but will have to wait a long time for a thread to free up. If *perfdump* (see the section "Using perfdump") shows you that WaitingThreads is low, meaning that the number of threads waiting for new requests is low, then you're nearly out of threads, either because RqThrottle is too low, or because MaxThreads is too low.

RqThrottle acts across multiple virtual servers, but does not attempt to load balance.

After threads, you need to watch out for the per-process memory limit. When you hit the per-process limit, the log file will fill with "Fatal, cannot allocate memory" and the process will hang.

Note that threads do not correspond exactly to sockets. You could have only 15 threads and 100 TCP connections going okay, because the sockets are accepted at the OS level and hang around for a while waiting for the application to accept them. They then wait for a little while again after being serviced while the client drains data from the socket buffer.

Disable extraneous features

Several features of Netscape Enterprise Server have a negative impact on performance and should be off unless you really need them:

- Turn off Content Management, Search, and Agents using the administration server.
- Set DaemonStats off in *magnus.conf* to disable some of the statistics gathering.
- Disable ACLFile directives in *magnus.conf* to disable access control lists.

Using perfdump

perfdump is a performance tool built in to the Netscape Enterprise Server. Using *perfdump*, you can monitor socket status, thread count, keepalive data, page cache data, and DNS cache data. To install *perfdump*, add this to *mime.types*:

```
type=perf exts=perf
```

and add the following to your *obj.conf* as the first service function in the file:

```
Service fn=service-dump type=perf
```

Then you need to restart the server. Then you should be able to access *http://hostname/.perf* and see the statistics. You can add a refresh interval in seconds like this: *http://hostname/.perf?refresh=5*. This will cause the information to update every five seconds.

For a detailed description of the information provided by *perfdump*, see *http://help. netscape.com/kb/server/971211-7.html*.

For more information

There is a good iPlanet web server–tuning guide at *http://docs.iplanet.com/docs/ manuals/enterprise/41/scaling/html/estune.htm*.

Some Netscape servers include the Adminserver tool for real-time performance monitoring.

Other Servers

The following sections describe the major web servers and provide some details for the configuration of the Netscape servers. There is a chart comparing features of 125 web servers at *http://webcompare.internet.com/chart.html*, and there are some benchmark comparisons of web servers at *http://www.spec.org/*. Site rankings are from *http://www. netcraft.com/survey/* or *http://www.webcrawler.com/WebCrawler/Facts/Servers.html*. Remember that you can always figure out what server someone is using by telnetting to port 80 of the web server machine and typing in a GET / HTTP/1.0 request.

Boa

Boa (*http://www.boa.org/*) is a very small and basic web server: single-threaded and single-process, but very fast. It has very little configurability, and is intended for small simple sites. It is available for free.

IIS

Microsoft's Internet Information Server, (IIS, at *http://www.microsoft.com/products/ prodref/427_ov.htm*) is very popular because it is bundled with MS Windows. It runs only on Windows and, as of NT Version 4.0, is part of NT Server rather than a distinct product. IIS has an integrated search engine and built-in streaming audio and video, but they work only with Windows clients. IIS can automatically authenticate Windows clients. It comes with a utility that asks your expected load range and does some tuning based on the answers. It is a commercial product. There is an interesting clause in the End User License Agreement for NT:

> No Performance or Benchmark Testing. You may not disclose the results of any benchmark test of either the Server Software or Client Software for Internet Information Server to any third party without Microsoft's prior written approval.

Why Microsoft prohibits independent benchmarking of IIS is left as an exercise for the reader.

Performance aside, the reliability of IIS is quite poor compared to Apache or Netscape. A company called Sysformance in Switzerland routinely measures minutes of outage for major commercial web sites in Europe and finds that the hours of outage per month is consistently two to four times higher for Microsoft-based web sites than for sites run on Apache or Netscape servers. Three consecutive months are profiled by server type at *http://www.syscontrol.ch/d/SWePIX/SWePIX.html*.

Java Web Server

Java Web Server (*http://www.javasoft.com/products/java-serverwebserver/*) was a Java product from Sun's JavaSoft division. It has been discontinued because Sun decided to sell Netscape's server products instead. There may still be a web page on tuning your Java Web Server:

```
http://jserv.javasoft.com/products/java-server/documentation/webserver1.0.2/
administration/performance.html
```

Jigsaw

Jigsaw (*http://www.w3.org/Jigsaw/*) is a 100 percent Java server. It outperforms the CERN server and is comparable to the NCSA server but not as fast as Apache. Jigsaw supports servlets and HTTP 1.1, and it has web-based administration through CGI forms. It is available for free.

NCSA

The National Center for Supercomputing Applications (*http://hoohoo.ncsa.uiuc.edu/*) *httpd* runs at 68,000 sites. NCSA was one of the first web servers after CERN's. It is the ancestor of Apache and Netscape, and through Spyglass, of IIS. Many features found on other servers, like access control and CGI, originated here. It is still only HTTP 1.0 compliant and may never be upgraded. The serious development effort that originated with NCSA has moved to the Apache project, but NCSA is still available for free.

Zeus

Zeus (*http://www.zeus.co.uk/*) claims to be the fastest web server available, and some benchmarks at *http://www.spec.org/* give the claim credibility, such as 1,837 HTTP operations per second recorded on the SPECWeb96 benchmark. The Zeus web server runs as a single process and uses only nonblocking network I/O. Zeus runs best if started as *zeus-q*, which disables some infrequently used access-control features and is run with a very large cache. Zeus is a commercial product.

Missing Features

There are at least two features missing from all web servers:

- As far as I know, there is no web server that logs both the beginning of a request and the end of a response. This would be an excellent performance feature, especially if done with millisecond resolution.

- Another excellent option would be to allow complete log files including all headers and POST data so that log files could simply be replayed to generate load tests, except for dynamically generated cookies. As it is, log files are not complete enough to recreate any particular request.

Proxy Servers

Proxy servers are usually set up at the interface between a large organization and the rest of the Internet, both for security and performance reasons. The main idea behind using a proxy for security is that there will be no direct connections between the Internet and the internal network; when an HTTP request goes out, the proxy intercepts it and makes the request on behalf of the internal user. Or if the proxy already has the page in its cache, the cache will simply return the page to the internal user without ever touching the Internet.

If the page requested is not in the proxy's cache, then the request will be significantly slower because of the extra step of intercepting the request and copying it back from the proxy to the client. On the other hand, for all subsequent accesses, access will be far faster because the page is close at hand.

Proxy caches don't work for dynamic content, or at least they're not supposed to. If your proxy is caching dynamic content, the whole purpose of creating custom content on the fly is defeated. There are a few other twists with dynamic content. The images and other embedded static content on a dynamic page will be cached for an increase in performance, but HTTP 1.1 keepalives may actually hinder this use of cached images and lower performance. It depends on the sophistication of your proxy server. If the proxy checks only the first URL of the connection, it will not realize that it has usable images in the cache. Or, if the proxy gets every embedded image before forwarding anything to the client, the client will see long delays.

Proxies are especially useful in cases in which the entire organization is likely to view a few pages at a certain time, say, when a news release comes out, or every morning when users look at *www.news.com* or *www.cnn.com*. There is also a very large benefit to caching pages from slow sites.

Another great thing about proxy servers is that you can use them to track and filter out obviously non–work-related web requests, such as those to *www.playboy.com*. This spares your Internet intranet bandwidth and helps in general, once users know these sites won't work. There will then be more bandwidth and better performance for truly work-related hits. But don't get carried away with the Big Brother attitude. You want workers to be very web-literate, so you want them to browse a lot. Just cut out the obvious abuses. If browsing performance is very important to your organization, it is doubly important for your proxy server because the proxy has to do both client and server duty.

Intel (*http://www.intel.com/*) has a product called Quick Web that seems to do proxy caching of popular pages and lossy image compression, which means dropping information from GIFs and JPEGs, apparently using their native compression. This makes the images take up fewer bits, but it does not make them any smaller on the screen, so the images are fuzzier.

Apache and Netscape also provide proxy caching software. Remember that your users' browsers must be set up to point to the proxy server. Netscape allows you to specify a URL for automatic proxy configuration, as well as domains for which the proxy should not be used.

Hierarchical Caches

Recent research on distributed caching schemes has led to two implementations of hierarchical caching: Harvest (commercial) and Squid (freeware). They both use the same Inter-Cache Protocol (ICP). Hierarchical caching provides increased perception of performance for the entire Internet, but it requires a large infrastructure to be successful. Squid is being used in an elaborate national caching scheme described at *http://ircache.nlanr.net/*. See also *http://squid.nlanr.net/Squid/*.

Key Recommendations

- Turn off runtime DNS reverse lookup.
- Use a server that understands HTTP 1.1 or at least keepalives.
- Reboot at regular intervals if there is memory leakage.
- The server should not close log files between writes.
- Use recent server software since implementations have been getting better.
- Take advantage of the web server's caching features.
- Optimize for type of content and speed of client connection.

CHAPTER 19

Content

In the end, the Web is about content. The browser, server, and network are all working towards one goal: to push bits from one end to the other. This chapter is about what you can do on the content end to make this happen as quickly as possible.

Size Matters

The network doesn't know or care what type of content you are serving. Bits are bits. Size is all that really matters for network transfer time. Therefore, the most basic performance principle is to send fewer bits and make fewer requests. Try to think of size in terms of download time rather than absolute bits, because how long a human being has to wait is the ultimate measure of success. If most of your users are on 28.8 modems, make a rule that no image can be "larger" than ten seconds. Ten seconds is about 35K if a 56K modem is running well.

Compare Yahoo! (*http://www.yahoo.com/*), which has a very light home page, to CNN (*http://www.cnn.com/*), which tends to bloat. The difference in download time is significant. It's easy to get carried away, so lay down some ground rules and try to get your content developers to care about bandwidth issues. Another example of excellent (i.e., minimal) design is Craig's List, at *http://www.craigslist.org/*.

I personally like all of the web designers I've met, and yet I can't help cringing when I run into them because I spend a lot of my time complaining about their work. Designers like to design, and that usually means writing flashy pages without any consideration of performance. Bells and whistles also introduce browser incompatibilities, make testing harder, and then you have to pay them to harm your site's performance in this way. Applets in particular are a bad idea for content unless they are really contributing something that can't be done with HTML. Servlets are great because you can control their environment, but applets are usually large, have many incompatibilities between browsers, and are much harder to test than HTML.

As Good As It Gets

Let's imagine the fastest possible web page. The page would be at most the size of the largest single packet that could make it from server to client without fragmentation, perhaps 1,500 bytes. We could compress the page with *gzip* if necessary, maybe getting a 2,500-byte page to fit into that 1,500-byte packet. Then let's imagine that we use T/TCP on both ends so that there is only one request packet and one reply packet rather than the usual "three-way handshake." Assuming a 15-millisecond cross-country travel time (near the speed of light), the beginning of that page could be delivered to the client in about 30 milliseconds, with the end of the page following in a time proportional to the connection bit-rate (also confusingly called speed). That's about one-third of one-tenth of a second. That's as good as it's ever going to get. All redirections, frames, images, applets, etc., bring performance down from there.

Caching and Differences

HTTP 1.1 web servers are capable of responding with byte ranges of documents so that browsers can download only the fraction of a document that has changed. This would greatly improve performance, but unfortunately, browsers don't take advantage of this server capability. There is a commercial product called the "Condenser" from FineGround networks that can improve speed by doing something similar. See the Appendix for more on the Condenser. Also, see *http://webreference.com/internet/ software/servers/http/deltaencoding/intro/* for another attempt at specifying how a browser should request a fraction of a document.

HTML and Compression

A slight amount of waste is intrinsic to HTML, because HTML is written in ASCII text. ASCII is defined as using only 7 bits of each byte, so 1 bit in 8, or 12.5 percent is wasted.

A larger amount of waste is due to the fact that text is highly compressible, but no compression is used for most HTTP transfers. It is normal for a text compression program to reduce the size of a text file by half, meaning that file can then be downloaded in half the time. Right now, transmission bandwidth is the bottleneck and CPU power for decompression is cheap, so compressing web pages would seem to make sense, even if it would make debugging problems harder.

Stylesheets may help or hurt performance, depending on how they are used. Linked stylesheets need be downloaded only once and can replace a lot of the formatting HTML you would otherwise need. This reduces network traffic. See *www.w3.org/ Protocols/HTTP/Performance/Pipeline/*. On the other hand, the browser may refuse to display an HTML page unless it can find the associated stylesheet. That is, you have introduced another dependency. On the other other hand, if you embed the stylesheet in the page itself, you do not have the dependency and its additional potential for failure, but you add to the size of every single page, which is going to hurt performance.

gzip

If your browser understands *gzip* encoding, it will include this in its request headers:

```
Accept-Encoding: gzip
```

Large text pages can be sent significantly more quickly in compressed format to a browser that understands *gzip* compression. It is necessary only to gzip the HTML and leave the *.gz* suffix on it for the Apache server to know that you're serving a *gzip*-compressed file and to add the correct HTTP header in addition to the usual Content-type header.

```
Content-encoding: x-gzip
```

Note that you can effectively compress a file only once. Obviously a file can't continue to get smaller with each compression or you'd be able to compress any file down to a single bit. It's kind of fun to *gzip* a file over and over just to see that it gets smaller only the first time you compress it. After that, it actually grows a bit each time. Here's a little shell script that does exactly that, along with some output. Look at the number of bytes in the file (the numbers before "Apr 23"):

```
% while true
more> do
more> ls -l index.html
more> gzip index.html
more> mv index.html.gz index.html
more> done
-rw-r--r--  1 patrick  patrick    2345 Apr 23 14:49 index.html
-rw-r--r--  1 patrick  patrick    1060 Apr 23 14:49 index.html
-rw-r--r--  1 patrick  patrick    1094 Apr 23 14:49 index.html
-rw-r--r--  1 patrick  patrick    1128 Apr 23 14:49 index.html
-rw-r--r--  1 patrick  patrick    1162 Apr 23 14:49 index.html
-rw-r--r--  1 patrick  patrick    1187 Apr 23 14:49 index.html
-rw-r--r--  1 patrick  patrick    1221 Apr 23 14:49 index.html
-rw-r--r--  1 patrick  patrick    1255 Apr 23 14:49 index.html
-rw-r--r--  1 patrick  patrick    1289 Apr 23 14:49 index.html
-rw-r--r--  1 patrick  patrick    1312 Apr 23 14:49 index.html
-rw-r--r--  1 patrick  patrick    1346 Apr 23 14:49 index.html
-rw-r--r--  1 patrick  patrick    1380 Apr 23 14:49 index.html
-rw-r--r--  1 patrick  patrick    1414 Apr 23 14:49 index.html
-rw-r--r--  1 patrick  patrick    1434 Apr 23 14:49 index.html
-rw-r--r--  1 patrick  patrick    1468 Apr 23 14:49 index.html
-rw-r--r--  1 patrick  patrick    1502 Apr 23 14:49 index.html
-rw-r--r--  1 patrick  patrick    1536 Apr 23 14:49 index.html
```

Another option is to compress your content some other way and configure your web server to use a certain MIME type for that compressed content, but you then have to ask your users to configure their browser to launch the decompression utility when a file with a certain content type is received. This requires a bit of work on both the client and server side.

It is best for the server to detect the browser and serve the most compressed content it can, but sometimes proxies cache *gzip*ped content and then serve it to *gz*-ingorant browsers. The result is garbage on the screen. You could include a bit of JavaScript in your HTML to include an explicit reference to a *gzip*ped file only if the browser supports it.

Performance Tips for HTML Authors

Here are some ways that HTML authors can help improve the download time for their files.

Make It Easy on the Server

When composing HTML, try to keep pathnames short, both in number of directories in the path and in the length of each directory name.

You can scale static content easily by partitioning the content across multiple servers and using HTML links to the different servers. To start out partitioning, consider using one server for images, another for HTML, another for applets, etc. Also keep in mind that your HTML can easily refer to other web sites for embedded content, which entirely removes the load from your servers but creates a dependency on the other servers and makes for thorny copyright issues. The Gamelan (*www.gamelan. com*) applet directory does not have applets itself, but simply links to the sites that do, with the authors' knowledge. There has recently been some legal action against a site that was embedding news from other web sites in frames and selling its own advertising in a top frame.

Conversely, if you need to have a link on your page to a site known to be very slow, consider asking the site's administrator for permission to copy the site to your web server.

Make your links explicitly refer to *index.html* files, or end directory references with "/". As discussed in Chapter 15, the trailing "/" in a URL saves the server (and network) the additional overhead of a redirection. Also, explicitly referring to *index. html* saves the server from having to think about whether it needs to do directory indexing. However, be aware that *index.html* is just a convention. Some web servers, such as Jigsaw, do not use *index.html* for the directory index.

If your content is a huge number of files with a fairly even distribution of access, say in a large archive, then your OS's buffer cache and the web server's cache will not be effective. You'll have to hit the disk for most accesses, so don't waste too much money on RAM, but get the fastest disks or disk arrays you can afford, concentrating on seek time. Disk striping should help considerably.

Make It Easy on the Network

The most important thing to do with content, from the network's point of view, is to keep the size small.

If you have a large document, users may appreciate getting the whole thing and not having to click and wait to get more; on the other hand, it may be wise to give them a summary and the first part to see if they really want the whole document. HTTP 1.1's byte-range downloads are capable of downloading part of a document at first, and downloading the rest when the user requests it. This requires a browser and server that understand HTTP 1.1.

Typical HTML size is 4K, which is about two pages of text in a browser. You might want to make the text fit into the MTU, if you know it, so that you'll get it all in one packet. If your MTU is 1,500 bytes, which is common on Ethernet LANs, then you'll see better performance from 1,500-byte HTML pages than from 1,501-byte pages.

Make It Easy on the Browser

Parsing is compute-intensive, so we want to make it easy on the browser. You can do this by eliminating redundant or useless tags, using few fancy features such as nested tables or frames, and giving the browser information it would otherwise have to calculate itself. Also, word-processing programs that generate HTML tend to do rather a bad job, often with extra tags that format blank lines. It is simple but time-consuming to clean this up by hand, so it is worthwhile to write a few simple Perl scripts to perform some substitutions or eliminations for you. Here's an example of a one-line Perl script that removes <BR> tags that are alone on a line. These tags are often an artifact of using a graphical page composition tool:

```
% perl -pi -e 's/^<br>$//i' *.html
```

Don't put much in the <HEAD> of the page, because that section must be completely parsed and acted on before the rest of the page can be displayed. In particular, don't put extensive JavaScript scripts in the <HEAD>. Put the majority of the script near where it is used—for example, within a form that is being validated with JavaScript.

Background images are displayed before the text of the page, so keep them simple or eliminate them. A large single background image, as opposed to background images composed of repeating small elements, can make scrolling painfully slow.

Use the SIZE option to the <IMG> tag to tell the browser the size of the image; this saves the browser some processing time and allows it to lay out the HTML before receiving all of the images. The syntax looks like this:

```
<img src=/images/demo.gif" size height=150 width=100>
```

The Unix file command gives the size of images, and can be used in a Perl script to examine images in HTML source and insert their sizes. There are some publicly available utilities to do this, such as wwwis, or you can write your own.

You can scale an image by including a size that is different from the image's true size in pixels, but it is wasteful to use a size smaller than the pixel size. Scaling an image upward works, but it takes a bit of the browser's time and the image gets coarser.

Frames take some time to retrieve and render. This can be significant for multiple nested frames. There used to be an interesting recursive abuse of frames at *http:// www.vanderburg.org/~glv/* but the link is now down. For older browsers, the ziggurat link off this page tried to use up all the browser's memory, and would crashed it or made it so slow as to be useless. Newer browsers detect recursive frames and refuse to display them.

You can use IP addresses rather than domain names in your links to avoid DNS lookups, for slightly better performance at the expense of flexibility. Note that most operating systems do not cache DNS name mappings, but the Netscape browser itself does. For HTML page links, this puts the IP rather than the server's domain name in the browser's Location box, which might be confusing to the user. For links to images, the user will notice only that the image loads slightly faster.

Make It Easy on the User

Why name your web server "www"? It's easy to type, but impossible to say. Please use one syllable rather than nine—name your web server "web." Instead of "www. company.com," use "web.company.com." The radio announcers of the world will thank you.

The first thing the user will see is the text within the <TITLE></TITLE> tags, so try to make it descriptive enough that the user can decide whether to wait for the entire page to load. Many people don't notice the title, so give them a nice clear label for the page in <H1></H1> tags.

Make every site's home page load lightning-fast, because it sets the tone for the entire site. Users will wait longer for detail pages further in the site, but if they can't get in the front door right away, they may assume the site is down or go away because they're annoyed. You might want to dedicate a server to the initial home page.

Be sure to give text links that mirror image links in case the user has images turned off for faster loading. Many sites are useless without images because no planning was done for text-only browsing. An alternative to putting a text link under each graphic is to offer a link from the home page to a parallel tree for light graphics or text-only browsing. You can use cookies to track whether the user wants a light-graphics version of the site, but cookie-recognition puts a burden on the server, while parallel content adds more content. Always use the ALT text of image tags so people know if an image is worth getting if images are off.

Making all of your site available via text is also nice for blind people surfing the Web with text-to-audio convertors. Similarly, use alternative functionality between <APPLET></APPLET> tags so that users can turn off Java if they need to for bandwidth reasons. The default action of HTML is to ignore tags it doesn't understand, and if Java is turned off, then the <APPLET> tag is no longer understood. The net result is that you can put any valid HTML between <APPLET> tags, and it will be parsed and displayed only if Java is off. I used this in one project to provide an alternative CGI form for a shampoo selector web site. The form did the same thing as the alternative applet. The applet was more interactive and fun but took longer to download.

Don't tell the user about an FTP site or an email address without providing an *ftp://* or *mailto:* link. It's just common web courtesy to make addresses clickable.

Change your web server's 404-file not found page to contain a map of your site so that users don't have to hit the Back button to figure out what the alternatives are on your site. This is a performance issue, because it saves users time. If the link as defined by the HTTP_REFERER variable shows that another link on your site referred the user to a 404 page, set up the server to mail the webmaster about the errors. There's no excuse for having invalid links from within your own site. Users can ask for whatever they want, and should be given a polite answer in every case.

Watch Out for Composition Tools with a Bias

Some Microsoft HTML composition tools make HTML that is painfully slow in Netscape, but very fast in IE. Also, some tools insert MS-only characters that show up as question marks in Netscape, but display correctly in IE.

Keep Up with the State of the Art

Pornographic sites in particular are always pushing the limits of what can be done technically, as well as pushing legal limits. Look under the covers, so to speak, and view page source of HTML and JavaScript on porn sites.

Use an HTML Validator

Valid HTML should parse more quickly and display correctly on multiple browsers. There are a number of free HTML validation tools available:

- WDG validator for HTML 4.0 from *http://www.htmlhelp.com/tools/validator/*
- W3C validator for HTML 4.0 from *http://validator.w3.org/*
- weblint for HTML 3.2 from *http://www1.tu-chemnitz.de/urz/www/html-test.html* (this link in German)

Also consider using the Bobby accessibility standard from *http://www.cast.org/bobby*. It provides a free and excellent analysis of web content from the point of view of disabled individuals so that, for example, a blind user can still get useful information out of your page. Not only is it the right thing to do, but most of the recommendations Bobby makes will actually make your pages more standards-compliant and quicker to load.

For more information on HTML, read *comp.infosystems.www.authoring.html* on Usenet.

The Document Object Model

The latest browsers give the HTML writer direct access to the objects the browser uses internally. There is a standard for these internal objects called the Document Object Model. Access to the DOM is through a JavaScript API in both Netscape 6 and IE 5. By using the DOM directly, many things that would require slow trips to the server side can now be done on the client side, such as sorting table columns by headers, or dynamically converting XML to HTML. In addition, effects are possible that were previously available only with Java, such as client-side animation and 3-D effects.

Graphics

The typical web graphic is 10 KB to 20 KB, which is larger than the typical 4 KB of HTML in a page. The challenge with graphics is mostly how to make them smaller.

Weight Watching

Make images small by reducing size in number of pixels and number of colors (8-bit is usually enough) and using a format with compression appropriate to the image. If you are using 32-bit color to encode the U.S. flag, you can reduce to 8-bit color and lose no quality at all. JPEG compresses photographs better than GIF, but GIF compresses line drawings better. The new PNG format has excellent compression in both cases, but is not supported by all browsers.

Java is often criticized for its long startup time and relatively large memory footprint, but large graphics composed of simple shapes may consume less network bandwidth as simple Java *.class* files than as bitmap images. I used Java's `drawPolygon( )` method in an applet to encode a map of all the rail tracks in the eastern U.S. as sets of points connected by lines. This was not only smaller than a bitmap, but had the added flexibility of easy zooming and scrolling, which would not have been possible with a static image. However, Java is not supported in the standard installation of Netscape 6 and not in IE at all.

Consolidation

Avoid the overhead of sending multiple images by consolidating them into one, saving download time as well as display time. If each image is a link, you can make the composite into an imagemap and retain the functionality. Use a client-side imagemap, in which the URL is chosen by the client, rather than a server-side imagemap, in which the URL is deduced from the click coordinates by a process on the server side.

Use a cached imagemap in place of a frame for navigation to save the download of a master frame and navigation subframe.

Reuse

Reuse graphics wherever possible. The browser's cache is smart enough to find them if you reference them in exactly the same way each time. If you use the same graphic on the same page, note that the browser will try to get it again if you haven't finished downloading it the first time. That is, to be cached and reused, it has to be completely downloaded first.

Psychology

A common trick is to put your graphics at the bottom of the page so users don't notice that they're loading, since they're still reading the top of the page. Be sure to include the image size in the <IMG> tag or you will delay display of the entire page until Netscape gets the image and figures out its size.

If you're designing on a high resolution monitor, it's easy to forget that 640 × 480 is still a very common screen size and create something that users will have to scroll horizontally to see. This makes it more work for users to view your site.

Formats

The following graphics formats are popular on the Web:

JPEG
>JPEG has better compression than GIF for photos but is lossy, meaning that an image compressed into JPEG format cannot be fully recovered. The compression is good enough that most users will not know that any information is missing.

GIF
>GIF has better compression than JPEG for line-oriented images because it compresses line by line of pixels. GIF is not lossy.

PNG
>The Portable Network Graphics format (PNG) is in Netscape 4.0 and higher and Internet Explorer 4.0 and higher. PNG has yet better compression than JPEG or GIF.

Animation
>Animations using either "client pull" or "server push" are now obsolete, and have been replaced by animated GIFs, which not only download quickly but run without any network interaction. Animated GIFs are also quicker to download and

start than Java applets, though their functionality is limited to displaying a series of images. The downside to animated GIFs is they use up a great deal of the client's CPU, even if the user switches from the browser to another application.

VRML

Support for the Virtual Reality Modeling Language (VRML) is now provided in many versions of Netscape with SGI's Cosmo Player plug-in. VRML downloads quickly relative to the level of detail you get but requires a very high performance machine on the client side to be useful.

Audio

Most audio formats encode point-by-point air pressure over time using 8-bit samples, giving 256 possible amplitudes. This technique is known Pulse Code Modulation (PCM). Some formats distribute audio linearly, while others take advantage of the fact that humans hear in a nonlinear way. That is, humans have a harder time distinguishing two loud sounds than two soft sounds, so encodings are assigned more densely at small amplitudes.

All of the following formats use PCM in one way or another:

- Sun's *.au*
- Microsoft's *.wav*
- Apple's AIFF
- mu-law (U.S. telephony)
- A-law (European telephony)

You can also code sound in the frequency domain; that is, the code says something like "play this frequency at this amplitude for this amount of time." MIDI works like this.

The number of samples per second determines the frequency range you can encode: if you have n samples per second, you can encode frequencies up to $n / 2$ Hz. (This is the Nyquist theorem.) The sample size and number of samples per second also determine the size of an audio sample, and therefore its download time as well. In the telephone system, voice is encoded as 8-bit samples at 8 KHz, giving an audio bandwidth of 4 KHz and reasonable quality. Eight bits at 8 KHz comes out to 64 kilobits per second, which is the bandwidth used in telephony between switches for a single voice channel. This is a fundamental limit on the rate of information that a modem can send on a single call over the voice network.

Police and fire department radio systems use a lower resolution and sampling rate or compression to conserve radio bandwidth; this is what gives them that police-radio sound quality. Audio compression for radio has been the subject of many years of research, and very low bit-rate speech, down to 1,200 bits per second or lower, is now possible, although the quality of the signal is artificial.

At the high end, CD quality sound is 44 KHz 16-bit samples in stereo, so you'd need $44100 \times 16 \times 2 = 1.4$ million bits per second.

You can see that it is possible to transmit intelligible speech to most clients on the Internet, but that real-time transmission of CD-quality audio is still not possible. Streaming audio products for the Internet have to cope with the intrinsic unpredictability of IP latency, so they use UDP, which is higher-performance than TCP but makes no attempt to retransmit missing packets. This makes sense, because an audio packet that is even one second late is already useless. In these products, the audio transmission begins with a significant amount of empty time to give the packets a head start. The data coding for any point in time is spread across several packets so that if one of them is lost, the signal will not drop out for a moment, but will degrade in quality for a moment. The whole thing works reasonably well, but sounds more or less like a scratchy AM radio most of the time. You can get a measure of the health of the Internet by listening to Internet "radio stations" from around the country. Streaming audio works quite well on an uncongested intranet, but then again, a conference call works better.

Video

Streaming video gets a better compression ratio than streaming audio, typically 20:1 rather than 5:1 before you really notice the reduction in quality relative to uncompressed data, but since video starts out with far more data, it is even harder to do over the Internet than audio. Video compression depends strongly on the content involved. Videos of talking heads giving the news are easily compressed because each frame is so much like the previous one. Action films don't compress well because there is so much action. Streaming video uses UDP for the same reasons that streaming audio does.

Streaming video is not yet ready for wide use on the Internet but may be useful in intranets. Precept Software (*www.precept.com*) has streaming video for intranets, but it's a Windows-only product. Real Networks (*www.real.com*) does streaming video, too, and has cross-platform (PC, Mac, and Unix) clients and PC and Unix servers. Microsoft Windows Media Player does audio and video streaming.

Key Recommendations

- Send only as many bytes as needed, whatever the content type. Use the ALT part of the <IMG> tag for those who have turned off images.
- Don't assume the user has better than 640 × 480 video resolution.
- Use <SIZE HEIGHT= *nnn* WIDTH= *nnn* > for graphics.
- Reuse graphics; the browser's cache is smart enough to find them.

## CHAPTER 20

Custom Applications

If you are generating dynamic content, you will need to do some kind of programming, even if it is simply inserting HTML-like tags that generate predefined dynamic responses. Custom programming is a likely source of bottlenecks and crashes, and in this chapter we go over some common problems.

Programmers

Programmers vary widely in ability and aesthetics, as all humans do, but when you are paying them, it makes a big difference to you how good they are. The most important point to remember is the best programmers write the least code, and what little code they write, others can easily read and understand. The reason they write the least code is they can clearly see a simple way to accomplish what they need to do. It is amusing that many large software companies grade their programmers on the number of lines of code they write per day. This is exactly the opposite of efficiency. Good programmers often spend their day removing unnecessary and complicated lines of code others have written, so on a really good day, they may actually have produced a negative number of lines of code!

CGI Programs

While plain HTML documents stored on your web server can contain whatever text you like, that text is static. Everyone who requests that document through a web browser will get exactly the same document. Quite often, however, you'd like to customize the response for a particular user. For example, a retail chain store might want to query a database for the user and return the address of the branch store nearest the user. One way to do this is to have the web server run a program that will query the database and format the result in HTML. The first widely available method for incorporating dynamic content like this into web pages was the Common Gateway Interface (CGI) standard. CGI was introduced as part of the original web server, developed at the National Center for Supercomputing Applications (NCSA).

CGI provides a standard interface between web servers and programs that can generate HTML or other web content. CGI got its start as a literal gateway between web servers and older Unix programs that send their output to the terminal, but it quickly became clear that the real value of CGI was that it could provide a web interface to almost any software. Programs started by the web server using the CGI interface are referred to as CGI programs, or just *CGIs*, though CGI is technically the interface and not the programs that use the interface.

The definitive description of CGI 1.1, the current version, is on the Web at *http:// hoohoo.ncsa.uiuc.edu/cgi/*. From here on, I will assume that the reader understands how to write at least a simple CGI program. If you'd like an excellent tutorial on CGI, read *CGI Programming with Perl*, Second Edition, by Scott Guelich, Shishir Gundavaram, and Gunther Birznieks (O'Reilly & Associates). If you already know CGI programming and would like to keep up with the latest developments, read the Usenet newsgroup *comp.infosystems.www.authoring.cgi*.

Server APIs, such as the Apache API, NSAPI, and ISAPI, are a huge performance win over CGI at the expense of portability. Once you've written a program for a server's API, there is a cost to porting it to another server, unlike CGIs or Java servlets. On the other hand, the APIs have no parameter parsing and no separate CGI process. Programs written using the API run as part of the web server process, which means that they can crash the server. Note that some databases are also web servers, which eliminates even the overhead of the separate *httpd* process.

CGI Internals and Performance Problems

Though the CGI mechanism for generating dynamic web content is very versatile, the basic structure of CGI limits its performance. The main performance penalty is that a new instance of the program is executed for each user's request. This process exits immediately after sending its output back to the web server. If the CGI program opens a database connection, the database connection must be reopened for the next instance of the CGI. This load on the operating system severely limits the number of CGI requests that can be serviced per second. CGI execution time is likely to be the bottleneck under any but the lightest loads. CGIs typically take far more CPU and other resources than serving HTML pages. Another inefficiency is that CGIs that are hit more than once throughout the day, say for stock quotes or weather, return mostly unchanged HTML and graphics with only a little bit of new content. This is very wasteful of network bandwidth.

Let's take a closer look at the sequence of events in starting a CGI program and where the performance problems are. When a CGI request comes in, the web server must parse the input URL and the request headers, recognize that the user desires to execute a CGI program, and begin the CGI with the fork( ) and exec( ) system calls. Parsing, fork( ) and exec( ) account for much of the cost of CGI. The server sets up the environment variables and the standard I/O for the child process, then it begins to write the URL-encoded data to the CGI's standard in. The CGI reads the data, stopping when it has read the number of bytes specified in the CONTENT-LENGTH environment variable. The CGI may also read URL-encoded command-line arguments, which are given by placing them after the script name in the URL like this:

```
http://patrick.net/script.cgi?cmd_line_arg
```

It is then up to the CGI to decode the request and decide what to return to the browser. This is the meat of the CGI and varies widely in complexity. When the CGI is done, it outputs its results to the web server, which adds HTTP headers and forwards everything to the browser. Alternatively, many web servers allow the CGI itself to provide all the headers and communicate directly with the client's browser. The CGI then exits.

CGI is also problematic because communication between browser and server is limited to parameters that the browser sends and the result the server returns. Ongoing communication within the same connection is difficult to implement.

Given that CGI performance is poor and that all it can do is reply to a request and close the connection, why does anyone use CGI? There are a number of good reasons that CGI is popular and will probably be around for at least a few more years:

- CGI is conceptually simple.
- CGI is an open standard supported by most web servers, regardless of hardware or operating system.
- CGIs are easy to write and can be written in almost any programming language.
- CGI scripts won't crash a web server (though they will slow down the server) because they run as separate processes.
- Many CGI scripts are freely available.

General CGI Tips

No matter how optimized your hardware and operating system are, it is easy to get truly awful performance with a badly written CGI. There may be no constraint on how long a CGI is allowed to run, so if your CGI is ill-mannered or overloaded, the user will suffer.

We should distinguish here between merely inefficient CGIs, infinite loops, and runaways. Coding for efficiency is a huge topic and is highly language-dependent. We cover efficiency in the section "CGI Language-Specific Optimization Tips," later in this chapter.

Infinite Loops

If your CGI somehow gets into an infinite loop, the web server may well wait forever for the CGI to return results. This, in turn, means that the user will probably be left staring at a blank or partially filled browser for quite some time. Or worse, they'll just hit the Back button and then try again, putting another infinitely long CGI in motion on your server, and thus using up CPU time that produces nothing. CGI programs don't know when the user hits the Stop button on the browser. The program often finds out only when it tries to output HTML and receives a SIGPIPE signal because the socket is no longer valid, but this may depend on the configuration of the operating system and web server.

How to find and kill infinitely looping CGIs

To kill an infinitely looping CGI, you must first find its process ID (PID). The classic way to do this is with the Unix *ps* command. The options to *ps* vary with the version of Unix. Under Solaris, for example, you can list all of your processes like this:

```
% ps -ef
```

Look for unusually large values in the TIME column and note the PID for that process. Note that you can't trust the name given by *ps*, because it can be set on some systems by setting argv[0] in the executing program. Once you have the PID of the looping CGI, you can kill it with the *kill* command, in the following manner:

```
% kill 2353
```

However, this is not guaranteed to stop processes that choose to ignore the TERM signal. If the process is still present after a few seconds, try the *-9* option, as in *kill -9 2353*. This should not be your first option because processes killed with the *-9* option do not get a chance to clean up temp files or finish writing buffered output to a file. The *kill* command may leave a zombie process on the system, which cannot be killed but occupies only minimal system resources. Zombie processes are marked with Z or defunct in *ps* output. If a process is not a zombie but cannot be killed, then it is probably waiting on an NFS call or a stuck device. There are a number of more user-friendly tools for hunting down rogue processes, such as *top*, *skill*, and *killall*.

Runaways

A special case of the infinitely looping process is a process that is not only stuck in a loop, but is also spawning new processes on each iteration of the loop. While an ordinary infinite loop can go on forever, a runaway process uses up its owner's process table in a few minutes at most. One clue that you have a runaway CGI is seeing a large number of processes with the same name and a common parent process ID (PPID) or sequential PPIDs. You should try to kill the common PPID, or, in the case of sequential process numbers, the lowest PPID. It sometimes helps to sort the output of the *ps* command by PPID so you can see patterns more clearly. For example, on Solaris you can do this:

```
% ps -el | sort -k 3
```

A user who manages to use up the process table or memory will see an error message like No more processes or Out of virtual memory, and will be unable to start any new process, even the *kill* program, until at least one process exits. The user may also find that the keyboard has locked up. Just for fun, if you have a Unix system to yourself and have saved all your work and quit your applications, you can easily use up all your processes by creating a shell script with a single command: the name of the script itself. For example, create a file called *x*, insert the single command *x* and make the file executable. When you run *x*, you'll quickly use up all your processes or run out of memory by repeatedly forking shells. Run *ps* a few times, if you can, and you'll see the number of processes created. When you hit the process or memory limit, you'll be unable to fork a new shell, and all of the parent shells will exit. Beware that this little exercise may even crash your machine.

Web server processes, however, typically run as *nobody* and have no controlling terminal, so you will not see error messages, except perhaps in the web server log. The first clue that a CGI has run away will be that the server becomes very slow. If the server keyboard is locked up, it is still usually possible to log in to the machine with the runaway process over a LAN and kill the parent process.

Guarding against infinitely looping CGIs

The best way to guard against infinitely looping CGIs is through careful CGI programming. Be especially sure when using recursion that the recursion will be terminated. When using the fork( ) or system( ) functions, make sure that the created process can not immediately fork( ) itself or call system( ) in the same way. Check to see that the condition of all while loops must eventually be false, ending the loop.

Try to crash your CGIs yourself, before your customers do. Enter bizarre input, including quotation marks, newlines, and other unusual characters.

One trick CGI programmers can use is to set an alarm at the beginning of the script and set up a SIGALRM handler, so that if the script does get into an infinite loop for some reason, it will kill itself when the alarm goes off. For example:

```
#!/usr/local/bin/perl

$SIG{'ALRM'} = sub {
    syswrite(STDERR, "Caught SIGALRM in script.pl\n", 28);
    exit(-1);
};

alarm(5);    # Alarm will go off in 5 seconds...

while (1) {} # We would be stuck here forever if not for the alarm.
```

There is a setrlimit Unix system call to set limits on the consumption of system resources by a process and its child processes. These resources include CPU time, file size, stack size, number of processes, and number of open files. You can achieve the same effect at the shell level with the *limit* or *ulimit* command, depending on which shell you use. Unfortunately, these limits are sometimes not implemented by the operating system even when they seem to be available.

At the web server level, Apache has directives that limit the resource consumption of CGI Scripts. O'Reilly's web site also has a Runaway CGI sanity timer that is set at 10 minutes for server-push CGIs. iPlanet 4.0 has a similar setting in *magnus.conf* called CGIExpirationTimeout.

Don't Keep the Customer Waiting

It's a frustrating experience for users to see that their browser has contacted your site but be forced to wait while you create content for them. If you must do some intensive calculation in your CGI, first turn off I/O buffering ($| = 1 in Perl) and get the content type and some text out to the browser before you take time to create the bulk of your content. If you don't at least get the content type to the browser, it will give up on you after a relatively short timeout and close the connection. You'll end up doing all your calculations in vain. After sending out the header, turn I/O buffering back on ($| = 0 in Perl) for the performance benefit of buffered I/O.

One area where CGIs typically get stuck is waiting for I/O with another part of the computer or the Internet. DNS lookups fall into this category. If possible, avoid DNS by using static IP addresses in your CGI scripts.

If your processing has output that makes sense to view as you are creating it, you should give the user feedback on your progress by using a nonparsed header (NPH) CGI script, which tells the web server not to add headers to the content coming out of the CGI, but to output results directly back to the browser. The great advantage of NPH scripts is that they can keep the connection to the browser open and can output results over a relatively long time. An ordinary CGI, in contrast, has to output all of its results to the web server and close the connection before the web server begins to send the data on to the browser. Another smaller advantage is that the NPH CGI returns its first data to the browser slightly faster than an ordinary CGI, since the data does not have to be processed by the server first. An example of where you might use this technique is a CGI that needs to report back a constantly changing status, as of a stock price.

Under Apache and NCSA servers, all you have to do to transform an ordinary CGI into an NPH CGI is to prefix the script name with *nph-* (for example, *nph-script.cgi*). Note, however, that you are responsible for outputting complete and correct HTTP headers with NPH scripts, which would otherwise be the responsibility of the web server. If you get the headers wrong, the browser will not be able to interpret your output. Also, note that the server cannot log the size of data returned via an NPH CGI.

In iPlanet Web Server 4.1, there is a new *magnus.conf* directive called "UseOutputStreamSize" that will buffer output to the browser. The default size is 8,192 bytes. This is fine for static content, but sometimes you want dynamic content to be smoothly sent to the browser as soon as it is created by a CGI or NPH-CGI. The default setting means that the browser will stall until either the iPlanet web server has an 8K block to send, or until the CGI closes its output stream to the web server. So you get a big delay, then an 8K burst of content, then another big delay. If you need to improve latency and are willing to sacrifice overall throughput, set UseOutputStreamSize very small; for example:

```
UseOutputStreamSize 20
```

The reason this directive was added is that HTTP 1.1 mandates the use of a content-length header, but it is hard for many CGI programs to know in advance exactly how much data they are going to send. Without such a header, the only way the browser knows that all of the content has been received is when the server side closes the connection. But relying on the end of the connection to mark the end of the data is not acceptable because it defeats persistent connections. Now, with this buffer size, the server can send chunks of data of a known size to the browser and still keep the connection for use after the CGI is done. You can also use the new flushTimer directive to send data after a timeout instead of after the data reaches a specific size.

Push State or Processing into the Browser

One good way to speed up CGIs is to reduce the amount of work they do by pushing some of the work onto the browser, which usually spends most of its time idle, waiting for the server to return data or for the user to read the displayed page. An excellent example of this is the use of JavaScript to validate user input on the client side. Sending extra JavaScript validation code to the browser is a small price to pay for the reduced load on the network and server, not to mention the elimination of wasted CGI calls because of invalid input. The CGI itself can be smaller because it doesn't need to do validation, though removing all validation is dangerous. Here is a crude example that checks an input date for correct format before contacting the web server:

```
<HTML>
<HEAD>
<SCRIPT LANGUAGE="JavaScript">
<!-- Hide the script from browsers that don't know JavaScript.
function validdate(lf) {
if ((lf.date.value.charAt(0) < '0') ||
    (lf.date.value.charAt(0) > '1') ||
    (lf.date.value.charAt(1) < '0') ||
    (lf.date.value.charAt(1) > '9') ||
    (lf.date.value.charAt(2) != '/') ||
    (lf.date.value.charAt(3) < '0') ||
    (lf.date.value.charAt(3) > '3') ||
    (lf.date.value.charAt(4) < '0') ||
    (lf.date.value.charAt(4) > '9') ||
    (lf.date.value.charAt(5) != '/') ||
    (lf.date.value.charAt(6) < '0') ||
    (lf.date.value.charAt(6) > '9') ||
    (lf.date.value.charAt(7) < '0') ||
    (lf.date.value.charAt(7) > '9')) {
alert("Invalid date. Please use format MM/DD/YY.");
```

```
        return false
}
else return true
}

// End of hiding JavaScript -->

</SCRIPT>
</HEAD>
<TITLE>stuff</TITLE>
...

<FORM name="dateform" action="/myscript/" method="post">
mm/dd/yy <INPUT name="date" size=8 maxlength=8 value="">
<INPUT name="submit_button" TYPE="submit" VALUE="log on"
onclick="return validdate(dateform)")>
</FORM>
```

JavaScript is also excellent for constructing simple calculators on the client. Not only is the load taken off the server, but the response time is shorter because all of the calculation is done in the browser. Another function is to see what browser and page is in use when an error occurs. Here is a snippet of code that shows this:

```
<a href="javascript:alert ('Agent    = '+navigator.userAgent+
                  '\nBrowser = '+navigator.appName+
                  '\nVersion = '+navigator.appVersion)">version</A>

<a href="javascript:alert ('referrer='+document.referrer)">referring page</A>
```

The downside to using JavaScript for form input validation is that you have to download a little more data, and Netscape and Internet Explorer have incompatibilities in JavaScript support. Another major downside has been that JavaScript just stops functioning when you run out of memory, so a naïve server may think its input has been validated when it hasn't. This means JavaScript cannot entirely remove the burden of validation from the server. However, it can reduce that burden by limiting server-side validation to detecting some key that shows that JavaScript is still running in the client (refusing input if JavaScript is not running). The browser can also refuse to send unvalidated data to the server; one way to do this is simply submit to the form via JavaScript. If JavaScript isn't running, then the form won't be submitted, though the user may not be able to figure out what's wrong. Here is an example. (The link to "#" is just a dummy link to allow us to trigger a JavaScript action.)

```
<html>
<head>
<title>will submit only if javascript working</title>
</head>

<body>
<form name="theForm" action="/cgi-bin/simpleform.cgi" method="POST">
name:<br>
<input type="text" name="theName" value="" size=25>
</form>
```

```
<p>
<a href="#" onClick="theForm.submit( )">click here to submit</a>

</body>
</html>
```

Another way to accept only validated input is to use `document.writeln( )` statements to dynamically create the form. That way, if JavaScript isn't working for whatever reason, the form won't even be printed out.

Cookies

Another browser feature that is useful in reducing server load is cookies. Cookies can eliminate the revalidation of users or their state, or store information about users, so that the CGI does not have to look it up each time the page is accessed. Cookies are limited to 4K of data. HTTP 1.0 browsers will not cache pages that contain cookies. Cookies have an associated domain that requires a DNS lookup. Your browser may have cached the domain name and its associated IP address from your page request, but this is not guaranteed. A link to a copy of the cookie specification is at *http://patrick.net/specs/index.html*.

Java

You can use Java in Java-enabled browsers to eliminate CGIs altogether, but the trend lately has been against including Java support in browsers. Java is a general-purpose language and can make connections back to the machine that served it for access to databases and other facilities on the server machine. While it does take a few moments to start up the Java virtual machine, the benefits can be enormous. For example, I wrote a shipment-tracking applet for a freight company that included a set of data points defining the highways, railtracks, and U.S. borders. Because all map data was downloaded with the applet, it was possible to zoom and scroll far more quickly than is possible with maps drawn with CGI programs, in which substantial network traffic is required for each new view.

You can also use the Java capabilities of browsers to sidestep CGI by making direct method calls to objects on the server. Two standardized ways of doing this are through Java's Remote Method Invocation (RMI) and through CORBA. RMI is easier to program, but it runs more slowly and requires Java on the server as well as the client. CORBA takes a little more time to program, but it runs more quickly and is much more flexible. A third alternative is the Voyager product from Object Space (*www.objectspace.com*), which is simple to program and is high-performance, but is not widely used. See Chapter 21 for much more about Java.

Preprocess Queries and Cache the Results

Do you ever wonder how network news programs can have a detailed obituary story ready within hours of the death of a celebrity? What looks like superhuman performance is actually preprocessing. Television networks keep prepared obituaries of major celebrities on file, especially those who are seriously ill. Obviously, the networks don't know when a given celebrity will die, but since there are a limited number of people whose death would be newsworthy, the networks prepare stories on all of them. The principle here is that the more you limit the input parameters, the fewer possible results there are. A smaller result set means you can do more effective caching of responses.

The point of a CGI is to output different HTML depending on user input and state information; however, if the number of possible input and state combinations is small, it makes sense to run the CGI for all possible input offline and cache each result in a plain HTML file. For example, if a CGI can inform you of tomorrow's weather forecast in 100 cities around the U.S., you will certainly get better performance and scalability by regenerating 100 static HTML pages every night than by running a CGI in response to every query.

Even with a huge number of possible inputs, if there are a few frequently requested pages, it makes sense to dynamically cache those pages. Keep a server-side cache of frequently requested CGI output and have a stub CGI merely return an HTTP Location: response pointing to a static HTML page if the page is in the cache. A good way to prune a full cache is to delete the least recently used pages. This is known as an LRU cache.

AltaVista users can input a query containing any string at all, currently up to 800 characters. Because the data set (all web pages in the AltaVista database) and the uncertainty of what the user will ask for are huge, the effort required to deal with this uncertainty is also huge. But that doesn't mean that AltaVista has to do a linear search though its entire data set for each query. Like most large databases, the AltaVista database is indexed, so the server can simply use the input keywords as an index to the data set and return any results.

An index search is not always faster than a linear search. A linear search has the advantage that the disk heads move only from one track to the next, while an indexed retrieval may require the heads to jump around a great deal. The size of your index and data set determines which method is better. The AltaVista web server also caches the results of the most frequent queries.

As an example of effective indexing, consider a CGI that needs to search through the server's filesystem for a particular file, named *desiree*. While it is easy to have the CGI run the Unix *find* command, it is far more efficient to search a prebuilt index of the filesystem. To build an index of your entire filesystem, you can simply do this:

```
% find / -print > index
```

Now the two approaches to finding the file are the following:

```
% find / -name desiree -print
```

and:

```
% grep desiree index
```

You can time how long these commands take by prefixing them with the Unix *time* command. For example:

```
% time find / -name desiree -print
```

Look at the real (elapsed) time in the output of the *time* command. See the manpage for *time* for more information about your system's output format. You should see that the *grep* of the index is 10 to 100 times faster. This is the benefit of indexing.

You should also notice that if you run either *find* command again soon, it will run more quickly than it did at first. Why is this? It's because your program has been loaded into RAM and probably has not been swapped out, and because the part of the filesystem that you were accessing is also now cached in RAM. This is how Unix operates, and it will automatically work to your advantage.

Another feature of Unix related to caching is the text segment that is the executable code part of programs is shared between concurrent instances. Code shared between concurrent instances of a program is referred to as re-entrant code. For a quick example of the kind of speedup you get by using re-entrant code, start a copy of Netscape and note how long it takes. Then go to Netscape's Menu bar and choose File → New Web Browser. It will start in a flash.

The key is that the code or text segment is already loaded and ready to run. When you get many hits on the same CGI over a short period, the second and subsequent hits use the same text segment as the first hit, meaning that the RAM needed to run the second and subsequent copies is smaller than the RAM needed for the first copy. This also reduces the risk of paging or swapping. For these reasons, the second and subsequent copies usually run faster than the first, subject to the limits of your system. Eventually, the 10th or 100th or 1,000th instance will not have enough resources to run and must be queued or simply dropped.

Almost all browsers have RAM and disk caches so that you can retrieve a previously requested page from cache instead of wasting time loading the same page again. There are some cases, however, where you want to override the browser cache. You generally do not want the browser to cache the output of CGI scripts, so CGI scripts typically specify the Cache-Control header in HTTP 1.1 or Pragma:No-cache header in HTTP 1.0. The hazard to performance is that the CGI writer will use these headers too often, putting an unnecessary load on the web server.

In fact, I worked on one e-commerce project in which the programmers output the Pragma: No-cache header for absolutely every page. The reasoning was that a user might log out and someone else might then sneak up to his machine, click the Back button, and be able to see important financial information. Using HTTPS doesn't help in this situation, because you can click back into an HTTPS session. A better solution might have been to have the logout page pop up a new instance of the browser and then have the logout page close itself. Then the Back button wouldn't work for anyone sneaking up to the machine, but would work for the proper user during his session.

Small Is Beautiful

Smaller programs are easier to understand and to maintain, and they load and run more quickly than larger programs, while reducing the risk of paging or swapping. Though there is always a temptation, known as "creeping featurism," to add features to a program, this should be resisted as much as possible. It runs counter to the well-known KISS principle in engineering. KISS stands for "Keep It Simple, Stupid." Keeping your programs small and quick is also Unix tenet number one of *The Unix Philosophy*, an excellent book by Mike Gancarz (Digital Press).

One way to make CGIs smaller is to move some error checking code to the client via Java or JavaScript, as mentioned earlier. It is much more dangerous to use JavaScript because forms still work when JavaScript is turned off. With a Java form, the input field won't even exist if Java isn't running, so it is harder to submit bad input.

A very simple form of error checking is to use HTML to limit the length of text fields so that users know when they have tried to enter too many characters. For example:

```
<input name="date" size=8 maxlength=8 value="">
```

Scaling Issues

CGI does not scale well. Performance degrades quickly with increased load because of the large load imposed by each CGI process and its child processes. If you have multiple different CGIs using independent data, then the simplest and best way to scale is to run different CGIs on different web servers. The servers don't even have to be in the same country.

If the CGIs do have to share data, another excellent way to scale is to put just the CGIs on additional machines, leaving the web server to decide which machine should run the CGI and the web server as the conduit for returning results back to the client. This is the essence of the FastCGI standard discussed in the "Daemonize It" section later in this chapter. The round robin DNS scheme described does not work with CGIs that maintain state (typically using cookies) because the state information on a particular server must be synchronized with that of a particular client.

Break Up Long Forms into Several Small Forms

Breaking up a long CGI form into several pages does hinder the use of multiple servers for scaling, but it gives you better performance per page. Breaking up long forms also gives you the flexibility to turn a single page into a tree of pages, eliminating the need to send inappropriate questions to the user.

Server DNS Lookup

Be sure to turn off DNS lookup in the web server. Some CGIs expect to use REMOTE_HOST (corresponding to REMOTE_ADDR, which is the IP). This reverse lookup takes time. How you turn off DNS in the web server depends on which server you use. See Chapter 18 for more information.

Debug and Optimize

A final general tip is to test your script offline, where you can time and debug it more easily than from a web server. You can easily write a test script that will set up the environment variables and run *timeprog.cgi*. Ignore the difference between the first and second run; look at the difference between the second and third for the reasons mentioned previously in this chapter.

CGI Language-Specific Optimization Tips

While any programming language that includes the concept of standard in and standard out can be used to write a CGI, some languages are intrinsically more suited to the task than others. In this section, I review the most common CGI languages (*sh*, Perl, and C), point out their strengths and weaknesses for CGI use, and give some language-specific optimization tips. But first, here are a few performance tips general to all languages:

- Keep loops small.
- Use table lookups rather than calculation, where practical.
- Use integer rather than floating-point math.
- Avoid dynamic memory allocation.
- Profile your code and optimize the most used parts.

Shell Scripts

Unix Bourne shell scripts have the advantages of portability across Unix systems, easy file manipulation, and filtering. However, shell scripts are very slow to execute because they are interpreted and because they rely on other Unix programs for advanced functionality, with the result that *sh* scripts tend to fork a lot of new processes. This consumes time and resources. For example, if you wanted your *sh* CGI to search in all the files in the current directory for the word "foo" and output a sorted list of the results, eliminating duplicate lines, the programming is remarkably easy. Here is an entire CGI program that does exactly that:

```
#!/bin/sh
echo "Content-type: text/plain"
echo
grep -h foo * | sort | uniq
```

Although the time it took to write this program is negligible, we pay a large price at runtime. This script starts six processes in response to a single CGI request: *sh*, two copies of *echo*, and one each of *grep*, *sort*, and *uniq*. This is very bad for performance.

If you feel you must write a CGI program in a shell script language, use a more modern shell like *csh* or *bash*. With these shells, you can frequently use shell built-in commands to avoid the overhead of a fork and exec. For example, *csh* has a *time* command that is much faster to use than the */bin/time* program because the built-in *time* executes as part of the shell. You do lose some portability if you rely on built-ins that are unique to the shell you're writing in, but the performance gain is worth it.

If you have to run multiple programs from within a shell script, don't run them all in the background because they will compete for resources. It is better to run them sequentially, so that each program has more resources available to it and will finish faster.

Another tip to use when writing in shell languages is to keep your environment as small as possible. Each fork of the shell (which happens when you execute any external command) must initialize itself. If you keep the number of user-defined environment variables and shell functions small, the fork will be slightly quicker.

Perl

Perl is the most popular CGI language due to its portability (though the portability is easily broken by using the system( ) function to call out to platform-specific functionality), excellent text handling and regular expressions, and extensive library of built-in functions. It is more complex than *sh*, but it has an astounding array of features. A coworker of mine likes to insist that Perl "includes every hack known to mankind." While Perl appears to be an interpreted language like *sh*, Perl scripts are actually compiled just before running, so performance is substantially better, though usually not as good as the performance of compiled C code. It is much easier to write text handling routines in Perl than in C.

Perl looks a lot like an interpreted language, but again, it really isn't. In the shell or another interpreter, each line is read in, parsed, and run. In Perl, first the entire script is read in, parsed, and then the whole script is run. You can see this difference if you put a deliberate syntax error at the end of a shell script. The shell script will execute quite nicely until it hits that error. On the other hand, if you put a syntax error at the end of a Perl script, the script will fail to parse and not even begin to run. Perl is faster than shell scripts partly because it is not interpreted line by line.

Since Perl is so widely used, a lot of effort has been put into Perl optimization. A good place to start reading about Perl optimization is the "Efficiency" section in Chapter 24 of *Programming Perl, 3rd Edition* by Larry Wall, Tom Christiansen, and Jon Orwant (O'Reilly & Associates). Another good source is a newsgroup archive, such as *www.dejanews.com*.

Here are a few basic tips:

- Avoid calling Unix programs if there is an equivalent Perl function, such as sort. This saves the overhead of starting a new process.
- Hashed lookups are faster than linear searches.

- Use everything you know about the pattern you are looking for to reduce runtime load. For example, if you are looking for a pattern that you know occurs only at the end of a line, use the $ anchor to tell Perl it does not have to search the whole line for the pattern.

There is a Perl compiler that generates C code out of Perl scripts. While Perl is already optimized enough that this may not make a huge difference in the actual runtime of the program, compiled C programs do not have the overhead of starting up the Perl interpreter, so for frequently accessed CGIs, this could improve performance considerably. The compiler is currently available from *ftp.ox.ac.uk* in */pub/ perl/Compiler-a1.tar.gz*, and it is distributed with the Perl core as of Release 5.005. Also see *http://www.perl.com/*.

Perl performance can be improved with a Perl module for the Apache web server, known as *http://www.apache.com/*. Because the Perl interpreter becomes part of the Apache web server when you use mod_perl, the overhead of starting the Perl interpreter as a new process is entirely avoided. Users have claimed execution speedups of 400 percent to 2,000 percent by using mod_perl. You may well get better performance out of Perl scripts using mod_perl than out of compiled C code run as an ordinary CGI. You do, however, need to make a few changes to your Perl scripts and web server configuration to use mod_perl. A company called Velocigen (*http://www.velocigen.com/*) offers a similar product for speeding up CGI's.

C

The first CGI programs were written in C, and C is still an excellent choice for cases in which speed of execution is important. Remember that CGI programs written in C are still separate processes, so even if a C CGI program were to execute infinitely fast, it would still have to contend with process-creation time. C is very portable at the source-code level, although it must be recompiled for each platform. There are regular expression libraries for C, but text handling requires more attention to detail than Perl does. C optimization is a large enough topic to merit its own book, but here are some tips to get you started:

- Use your compiler's highest optimization level. For the GNU C compiler, *gcc*, this option is *-O3*. Note that optimizers are not infinitely wise and have been known to slow down, rather than speed up, code-execution time. Be sure to time your program at different optimization levels to make sure you've actually improved performance. Higher optimization may expose subtle bugs in your code; use *lint* to find these problems. The latest compiler is likely to optimize best. Read your compiler's manpages to find out which other options may be of use to you.

- Increase speed by using fewer functions to avoid the overhead of pushing and popping some stack frames. Replacing a function call with the actual code of the function is called inlining code. The speed savings add up if you inline a function that would otherwise be called many times in a loop. Similarly, you can unroll loops for a speed increase: instead of incrementing a counter and making a comparison on each iteration, code all the iterations in a row yourself. Manual inlining and unrolling are considered poor programming practice because they make the code more difficult to read and maintain, so use your compiler's options to do these. The *gcc* compiler has options for both inlining and unrolling. Another disadvantage to these techniques is that both increase the size of the code, meaning that it takes longer to load and is more likely to be paged out.

- Use library calls rather than system calls. System calls are notoriously expensive in terms of time and resources. Even though library calls may end up calling the same system call, the library call is often more efficient in its use of system calls.

- Always use buffered I/O. It is far more efficient to read as much as you can at a time than to read single bytes off the network or from a file. Also, you don't want to keep the user waiting while you read, so put reading in a separate thread of execution if you can.

- Statically link in libraries, rather than dynamically loading shared libraries at runtime. The code will be faster because the dynamic libraries do not have to be found and loaded. As with inlining function calls, this will make your executable bigger and slower to load. Do this only if you have plenty of RAM. This is the *-dn* option on SPARC compilers. Link with the *-lfast* library if you use malloc a lot.

- Use powers of two (1, 2, 4, 8, 16, . . .) in preference to other numbers where you have a choice. Most CPU architectures do power-of-two math extremely quickly, while other numbers require more CPU cycles. This is a result of the nature of the binary arithmetic all CPUs use. You can insure optimum division and multiplication by powers of two by shifting rather than multiplying (e.g., use x << 2 rather than x *=2), but if you have a clever compiler, it will note the opportunity to use shifting and do it for you when translating the C source down to binary. I wrote a map applet in Java that zooms in or out by powers of two. It has to do lots of number crunching to display the map, but does it much faster than it could by multiplying everything by a random integer. See Chapter 16 for Java-specific tips.

- Floating-point math is far slower than integer math and should be avoided unless truly useful. It may help to shift factional numbers up into integer range, truncate them, do integer math, and then shift them back down into fractional range when they need to be displayed.

- Use a code profiler and optimize most-executed sections, rewriting in assembly language if necessary. Use *gprof* to tell you how much time you're spending in each routine and *tcov* to tell you how many times you execute particular source lines. A good commercial tool is Quantify from Pure Software. A rule of thumb is that your code will spend 90 percent of its execution time in 10 percent of the code. Assembly coding is a technique of last resort, given the tediousness of assembly coding, loss of portability, and increased potential for errors.

- Use statically compiled arrays rather than a pointer to malloc'd memory.
- Run *mpstat* for a while to check whether multithreaded programs are making use of multiple CPUs.

See Chapter 16 for a discussion of server-side Java as a replacement for CGI.

Daemonize It

The best way to get CGI-like behavior, with far greater performance and scalability, is a common Unix technique I call daemonization, after the Unix daemons lurking in the background of every Unix machine waiting for events to handle. The basic idea is that, instead of having a CGI start in response to a query and then die, startup a persistent CGI-like process (a daemon) along with the web server. The daemon can even be on a different machine than the web server. When the web server gets a request pointing at the daemon, it simply connects to the daemon, hands over the request, and waits for the results (while still able to handle other requests).

Java servlets run as daemons. Start servlets running and connect to them as often as you like, avoiding the overhead of startup. The fact that Java is interpreted is less significant than the performance gain derived from leaving the servlet running. Servlets are multithreaded, isolating clients from each other. See Chapter 15 of *Java Network Programming*, by Elliotte Rusty Harold (O'Reilly & Associates). Java servlets actually use the CGI protocol for packaging parameters and responses under the covers.

Another method of daemonizing CGIs has been defined by Open Market, called FastCGI (see *www.fastcgi.com*). FastCGI programs are persistent, and they are also extremely scalable, because they can be run on machines other than the originating web server. FastCGI uses a single TCP socket to connect the web server and FastCGI application, unlike the standard CGI method of using pipes and environment variables. This connection provides the environment information, standard in, out, and error, all multiplexed together. Because of this, and the need to run in a loop, source code changes are required to transform an ordinary CGI into a FastCGI.

One downside of FastCGI is that it does not work natively with most common web servers requiring an ordinary CGI stub (Apache is the exception), which reduces the performance advantage. There is a collection of FastCGI performance tuning tips at *http://www.fastcgi.com/kit/doc/fastcgi-whitepaper/fastcgi.htm*.

Recent versions of NT's active server pages are similar in that a loaded CGI service does not exit, but remains resident, waiting for the next request. Apache's mod_perl works the same way.

Daemonized CGIs have a memory leakage hazard because you leave them running all of the time. If the daemon leaks any memory at all, you will eventually lose so much to it that you'll have to restart the daemon. You can try to use *ulimit* to limit the amount of RAM the daemon can use, but this isn't always reliable and you still have to come up with something to do when you hit that limit. A better approach is to make sure your code is clean to begin with. Tools like Purify, CodeCenter, Bounds Checker, or PURE can tell you if you have a leakage problem and often exactly where the problem is. Typically, leakage is the result of failing to clean the heap (free memory) of intermediate stack frames when returning from a subroutine.

Daemons also typically leak database connections, taking them from a pool, but failing to return them, or getting interrupted by an exception before the database release code gets executed.

Note that you can easily bypass CGI yourself and still run server-side programs on machines other than your web server. It is straightforward to set up a program that will accept connections on port 80 and process them, outputting HTML back to the browser. CGI has the advantage that browsers know how to use it to package forms data.

Another replacement for CGI is simply to use a named pipe, also known as a FIFO, in place of an HTML file. Note that named pipes do not take arguments like CGIs.

Finally, you could also write a CGI stub to use shared memory or a memory mapped file to communicate with a resident process if you do not like CGI or FastCGI.

CGI Database Access Performance

The principal performance concern with CGI database access is to eliminate the overhead of opening the database connection for each instance of the CGI. Opening a database connection can be very time-consuming and may require the loading of large libraries. It is worthwhile to buy or write a connection manager that opens the connection only once and brokers CGI requests to it, rather like FastCGI, but for database connections. RDBMS makers have realized this need for a fast or persistent connection and are now releasing products to fill the gap.

Another performance trick is to use one complex SQL query rather than multiple smaller queries, the results of which must be integrated by the CGI process before presentation to the user. Not only is the time spent in the SQL engine shorter overall, but the CGI does less work. Make the database do the work. See Chapter 22 for more tips.

Logging

One important point to remember is not to log too much, just what you need for your records. Don't leave debugging log entries in production unless you are actively debugging. Logging from Java programs is especially compute-intensive because of the conversion of every byte from Unicode to ASCII, so such logging should be minimized or avoided.

NSAPI and ISAPI

The Netscape Server API (NSAPI) is a direct C interface to the web server. Modules written to the NSAPI will run much faster than any other kind of dynamic content, but are capable of crashing the server. See the introduction at *http://developer. netscape.com/docs/manuals/enterprise/40/nsapi/contents.htm*.

Microsoft has a similar and competing API called ISAPI for its Internet Information Server. There is an introduction to ISAPI at *http://www.microsoft.com/msj/ 0498/iis/iis.htm*.

DOM

The Document Object Model is a representation of the tree of tags in a web page, starting with the HTML tag at the root. More than that, it is a JavaScript API for manipulating that tree in the browser. This allows all sorts of effects that were previously difficult or impossible outside of a Java applet, such as sorting columns by clicking on the header, downloading a fraction of a page, and other kinds of dynamic HTML (DHTML). Unfortunately, Netscape and Microsoft each have their own slightly incompatible versions of DOM. See *http://www.mozilla.org/docs/dom/* for more information.

JSP, ASP, PHP

JSP, ASP, and PHP are all server-side schemes for interpreting proprietary HTML tags and scripting for inserting content before serving a page. They are similar to the old "server-side includes" supported at the beginning of web-time. They are easy for newcomers to learn, but they all develop maintenance difficulties. PHP is the most open and perhaps the most popular, since it easily works with the Apache web server. See *http://www.php.net/* for more information.

Key Recommendations

- Set sanity timers in CGIs.
- Get some output from the CGI to the user right away.
- Don't write CGIs in a shell-scripting language.
- Daemonize CGIs.
- FastCGI scales much better than CGI.
- Use `mod_perl` if your CGIs are in Perl and your server is Apache.

## CHAPTER 21

Java

Java has become the standard language for writing server-side applications, and for good reason. Let's take a look at Java performance and the Web.

Java Will Never Be Good Enough for GUI Applications

Netscape tried to rewrite its browser in pure Java and failed. Corel tried to rewrite Word Perfect in Java and failed. The HotJava browser was unbearably slow. Most Java Development Environments are not written in Java. In fact, there are no successful commercial Java GUI applications as far as I know. The variability of clients is too great to allow enough optimization, and virtual machines (VMs) are too big to be quickly loaded and started on demand. This does not mean that there were no successes with Java on the client side. For example, there are applets that display continuously updated stock quotes that are quite useful and effective, but this is because they are very small.

Note that the DOM extensions to HTML now make most things you can do in Java possible from a non-Java browser, such as fractional downloads, 3-D graphics, column sorting, etc. In summary, if you can possibly use HTML in a browser for your GUI, is would be unwise to write an applet or application to do the same thing at greater expense and lower performance. In fact, Java is no longer a standard component of the Netscape and IE browsers.

Java Is Good Enough for the Server Side

On the other hand, Java has been a great success with corporations doing server-side development on cheap Linux or Windows PCs and deploying on big Solaris or AIX servers. The performance of server-side Java is generally acceptable, except for RMI, CORBA, and EJBs, all of which carry a large performance penalty. The server side is explicitly known to the developer and can be controlled to a much larger degree than various clients, giving many opportunities to violate "good" but low-performance OO and Java practices. Also, VM's are simply left running on the server, so VM-startup time is avoided. Another reason for Java's success on the server is the relatively larger amounts of memory available on server class machines, which means less paging and GC.

The Java servlet API specifies how the server should load and execute dynamic page generation class files, or servlets. Performance of servlets is better than traditional CGI but worse than C-language server API programs. For more information on servlets, see *http://java.sun.com/products/java-server/servlets/*.

Performance Problems Intrinsic to Java

So why is Java so slow? Let's take a closer look.

Array Bounds Checking

Java checks the bounds of every array on every access at runtime. Many runtime errors are smoothly handled by array bounds checking, but this necessarily adds time to the execution of your program, because doing something takes longer than not doing it. This is especially noticeable in tight loops. Bounds checking is a welcome relief to many programmers used to C/C++, where a single bad array reference can crash your program.

Blocking Network I/O

Until recently, there has been nothing in Java like the Unix select( ) or poll( ) system calls, which can be used to tell when a socket has data ready for reading by the program. In Java, simply try to read. If there is data, fine, read it. If not, sorry—that read is stuck until there is data to read. That is, all reads in Java are blocking reads, which means that they must be in a separate thread if the entire program is not to hang, waiting for input.

Even if you have multiple threads, blocking I/O is not efficient. First, the reading thread will be awakened and put back to sleep repeatedly. It would be more useful to have a function that could generate an event when a socket has data ready. Second, using one thread per client connection severely limits scalability, since the number of concurrent connections that can be handled by the server will be limited by the number of concurrent threads that can be sustained by the system. Typical numbers are in the 1,000–2,000 range.

JDK1.4, currently in beta testing, has a brand new *java.nio* package that provides nonblocking "select" type functionality for massive server-side scalability. Another option is the "NBIO" open source software from Matt Welsh at the University of California at Berkeley. This implements nonblocking I/O facilities for existing versions of the JDK on Unix platforms. See *http://www.cs.berkeley.edu/~mdw/proj/ java-nbio/*. In fact, Matt Welsh was part of the JDK1.4 *java.nio* "expert" group as well. Certain commercial server software vendors also implement the "Network Connection" handling code in C as a separate module.

Bytecode Interpretation

Java bytecode must be translated into native machine code before Java programs can be run. Doing this at runtime is called bytecode interpretation. Bytecode interpretation is slow, but it takes less than half of your execution time. So even an infinitely fast bytecode interpreter could not improve execution speed by more than a factor of two. The majority of time is spent in things that are already native code in the VM, like GC and object instantiation. Certain fundamental operations like arithmetic and string manipulation are also implemented directly in the VM rather than in the Java class libraries that ship with the VM. Since the VM is usually written in C and optimized for a specific platform, these operations are already as fast as possible.

Bytecode interpretation can be avoided entirely on the server side by using static compilers, which generate native code from Java bytecodes. Also, JIT's are more effective on the server side, where the time spent compiling to native code is a good investment, because the compiled code can be used for many hours or days until the next restart. On the client side, a lot of the work a JIT does is wasted when you close your browser.

Bytecode Verification

Downloaded classes must all be run through the bytecode verifier as a security measure, which takes significant time. This is not a problem on the server side, where you know your own classes and can presumably trust them. Also, server-side applications usually load classes only at startup, then stay running for a long time, so even if you verify them, it happens only when you restart your server application.

Dynamic Method Binding

Java methods are not resolved to memory locations at compile time, as in compiled languages. Unless a method is final, it is located on demand at runtime. Methods are encoded in *.class* files as strings, not addresses. This allows greater flexibility and makes overflow attacks harder, since you don't know where in memory any particular method is going to be. But this also means a lot of runtime overhead of string parsing and method location is going on at runtime, unlike C, where execution jumps directly to the address compiled into the code.

Garbage Collection

Garbage collection (GC) is supposed to happen when the application is idle, but some applications, such as servers, may never be idle. In this case, GC will suspend your application. "Synchronous" GC means GC that happens at the time you ask for it. Synchonous GC is misnamed, because you can't control exactly when it will happen, even if you issue the System.gc( ) call, or its equivalent, `Runtime.getRuntime( ).gc( )`. GC is normally going on in a background thread, which is the normal "asynchronous" case, meaning gc happens only when you are low on memory and the application is idle. Developers have more control over GC in Java 1.3 and beyond.

Another problem is that garbage collection is also usually single-threaded. You can use *mpstat* on Solaris to see that only one CPU is in use while GC is happening. If you have a very large heap, you have a very large single-threaded delay while *gc* happens. IBM claims to have multithreaded garbage collection, and "generational" garbage collection, which distinguishes between transient objects and longer-lived objects.

Indirections

To get at an instance variable, you need a handle to the class first, meaning multiple memory accesses: at least one to get the reference to the object and another to get from the object to the instance variable. As processor speeds far outstrip memory speeds, the problem of memory access will become relatively more important. The VM has to follow several levels of indirection simply to find the class, then has to check for synchronization locking, whether the class access allows you to see it, and so on. There are other locks that might also affect the performance of your application, such as locks for garbage collection, class linking, loading, verification, and thread creation or destruction. The VM can implement these locks as it wishes, leading to variations in the performance of different VMs.

Microsoft's VM was considerably faster than Sun's initial implementation because Microsoft removed one layer of indirection. While Sun had a handle to a pointer to both the data and instructions of a class, Microsoft had only a pointer to a single block containing both the data and instructions, at the expense of slower garbage collection.

i18n & l10n

Internationalization (called "i18n" because there are 18 letters between the i and the n) and localization bloat Java libraries with many foreign fonts, date formats, and other options you may never use. The 2-byte Unicode characters also make strings twice as long as pure ASCII strings. This is not such a problem on the server side, where memory is more abundant, but it gets to be a problem for clients without much memory.

OO

Object Orientation (OO) is intended to help programmer productivity, not runtime performance, and this shows at runtime. One problem with OO is that the loading of a class into the VM forces the loading of all of its ancestor classes. Then, as you download classes, each superclass of any loaded class must be located in the client-side libraries or downloaded. Another problem is that the instantiation of a class may cause other classes on which it is dependent to load and instantiate, and it is often difficult to figure out exactly how many. Again, this is not such a problem on the server side, where the work done loading classes is performed only once for as long as your server is running.

Consider the creation of temporary objects in Java. Java consultant Neil Cannon informs me that a simple statement like the following:

```
Integer.parseInt(new SimpleDateFormat("yyyyMMdd").format(new Date())));
```

creates about 100 temporary objects, all of which must be created only to be destroyed a few moments later.

Another cost to using Java rather than C++ is that all objects are on the heap rather than the stack. This is done to eliminate a source of memory leakage and to improve security, but it requires time to manage the memory of objects on the heap. It's especially bad that most VM's seem to force all threads to contend serially for access to the heap manager. So object creation is essentially single-threaded. If you are doing a lot of object creation on such a VM, that object creation can't benefit from multiple CPUs.

Stack-based

The Java VM stores all local variables on a stack and has no notion of CPU registers. This makes it hard to map the VM to a real CPU and take advantage of very fast CPU registers. C compilers can use CPU registers for quick access to frequently used variables. Java stores parameters and local variables on a stack and has no notion of CPU registers, although a clever VM might. The stack is of indeterminate size, so it is easiest to implement a VM by putting the entire stack in RAM. This in turn means that each frequently used local variable will require RAM access, which is much slower than a CPU register access.

Synchronization

Java's support for multithreading includes support for locking a class or method to avoid data corruption that could be caused by concurrency. Just getting a lock slows down your program. Using the lock slows you down again.

Threading

Java makes threading available to even the most inexperienced programmers, which is not entirely a good thing. Without appropriate synchronization, multithreaded programs are prone to deadlocks or data corruption under heavy load, and the problems are very hard to figure out because they are dependent on subtle timing issues.

If excessive synchronization is used to fix this, the program will run very slowly, because most threads will be blocked on a lock most of the time. Threading also makes programs much more difficult to understand. Instead of code running from beginning to end, you have spaghetti at runtime, regardless of how cleanly the code is written.

Java threads have to be scheduled, either within the VM (green threads) or by the OS itself (native threads). There is no option to use a single-threaded Java. Scheduling time adds to overhead.

The optimum number of threads to use in your servlet runner is an interesting question. If you use too few, work will queue up rapidly. Furthermore, you may limit your capacity to use simultaneous database connections. In Weblogic, each use of a database connection requires the attention of at least one thread. So if you want to have the ability for 50 concurrent users to make a query at exactly the same time, you need at least 50 threads. If you use too many threads, the overhead of scheduling all of the threads will waste most of your time.

I did an experiment using Weblogic on Solaris to run a heavy load of servlets at many different settings for the number of Weblogic Execute Threads. Then I looked at the average and maximum time to retrieve the home page under that load (see Figure 21-1). The result was that the default Weblogic setting of about 15 threads seemed best for latency. As the number of threads went over 70, the CPU spent more time context-switching than doing actual work. So you have a trade-off: more threads for more capacity, but lower performance for each, or 15 threads for optimum performance, but limited capacity.

Coding Tips

Okay, now that you know everything that's wrong with Java, let's talk about what we can do with it.

Use Good Algorithms

The architecture and algorithms of your program are much more important than any low-level optimizations you might perform. Bad architecture and algorithms can make any system seem slow. Premature optimization may be the root of all programming evil (says Knuth) but failure to consider performance right from the start can also doom a program to uselessness. Here are some good guidelines:

- Tune at the highest level first.
- Make the common case fast (Amdahl's advice).

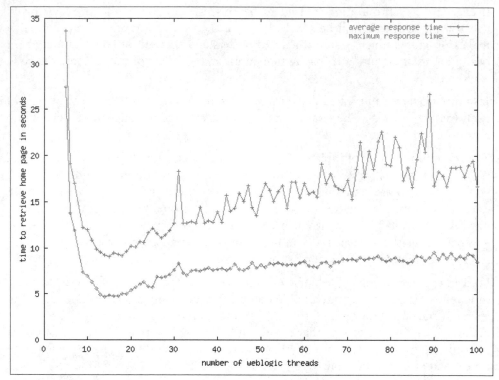

Figure 21-1. Fifteen threads shows lowest latency

- Use what you know about the runtime platform or usage patterns. This violates portability in some sense. In fact, it will hurt later if the platform details or usage pattern changes. For example, optimizations that help before using the Hotspot JIT may hurt with Hotspot.

- Look at a supposedly quiet system to see if it's wasting resources even when there's no input.

Keep Short Inheritance Chains

The cost of creating an object goes up with the size of that object's inheritance chain. Since each superclass must be present before the subclass can be created, there can be a huge amount of network traffic for applets or RMI programs using objects with long inheritance hierarchies. On the other hand, keeping a small chain often conflicts with pure OO design principles. I'd sacrifice OO principles rather than write a very slow program. You will incur OO overhead in Java no matter what. Even with the simplest possible Java class, you have to instantiate an object. For example:

```
class Nothing {}
```

This compiles just fine, and you can see that it will initialize `java.lang.Object`:

```
% javap -c Nothing
Compiled from Nothing.java
class Nothing extends java.lang.Object {
    Nothing();

Method Nothing()
    0 aload_0
    1 invokenonvirtual #3 <Method java.lang.Object.<init>()V>
    4 return

}
```

The *Nothing.class* file produced by the *chapman:10/12/12-23:12* compiler on Linux is 234 bytes, and the *Nothing.class* file produced by the JDK 1.2.2 compiler on Solaris is 259 bytes. The *-O* option makes the file 204 bytes on Linux, but no smaller than 259 bytes on Solaris. Now you can't run this class, because it has no `main()`, but adding `main` would just add a "return" bytecode.

Let's compare this to C. Write a program called *nothing.c* as follows:

```
main() {}
```

When I compile it with *gcc* on Linux, the resulting *a.out* file is 3,695 bytes, which is mostly standard I/O functions. See *Deep C Secrets* by Peter Van Der Linden (Prentice Hall) for more. You can run this, though it doesn't to anything. Adding *-O3* or *-O4* to the *cc* command makes no difference in the executable size.

Use Stack Variables

Class variables require more indirection and take longer to create than stack variables.

Merge Classes

Whether merging classes is worthwhile depends on what you're trying to do. One huge class may contain a lot of code that never gets used, but on the other hand, you have to load and initialize only the one class. Similarly, if you use fewer but larger classes, you'll probably get a slight performance boost because the VM will not have to load as many classes, although this is considered poor OO-programming style. Not only should you reduce the number of classes, you should also reduce the number of objects. That is, reuse a class when you're done with it, if possible, rather than reinstantiating it.

Even for a small class, you'll get better performance by reusing it than by instantiating it twice. The HotSpot designers claim this doesn't help for code run with HotSpot. You can reduce initial applet download time but pay higher runtime penalties by dynamically loading classes as needed with `Class.forname()` or other techniques. This is an obvious advantage over a single large initial load—code that isn't needed won't be downloaded. On the other hand, you'll probably set up a TCP connection for each of these classes at runtime, so fewer classes will help there too.

If you have more than two or three classes, however, you'll certainly want to put all of them into a *.zip* or *.jar* file, which will be downloaded in a single TCP connection. Increasing modularity by putting classes with interdependencies or closely related functionality in the same *.class* file, package, or *.zip* file can take advantage of locality of reference. That is, you often need code that is closely related to the code you're running at any moment, so keeping that code together will reduce time spent searching for it.

Be careful when using packages from the Web. Naive implementations of regular expressions, for instance, can be painfully slow. Use the information you have to reduce the work that the regular expression has to do. I once was looking for a pattern at the end of a long string, and found I got 70 times better performance by anchoring the match to the end of the string (using $) than when I left out that single character.

Use Java Libraries

It's usually faster to use the functions provided than to try to re-implement them. For example, drawPolygon( ) is faster than using drawLine( ) repeatedly.

Do Not Poll

Do not poll for events, as this is wasteful of resources. Use Java's event listeners, especially over RMI.

Finalize Methods

Since nonfinal method names are bound at runtime, if you know you will not override a method in a subclass, you should declare that method as final. Or if you can, declare the whole class as final. This is particularly important in loops. On the other hand, the HotSpot designers claim that there is no additional advantage to declaring methods as final when running with HotSpot. If you can avoid a method call entirely by including the code for one method in another (*inlining*), you will avoid the overhead of setting up the stack and tearing it down again.

Create Fewer Objects

Reuse objects where possible, but one Java performance paper shows that cost of extracting an object from an array in a synchronized way is about the same as creating an object with a shallow inheritance hierarchy and no instance variables. (See *Building High Performance Applications and Servers in Java*, Singhal et al., IBM,

1997) If you are reusing just one object, a "singleton," make it static and create a reinitialize( ) function. Be careful ensure that the use is multithread-safe, since multiple threads may execute the same piece of code.

Java libraries themselves often create unnecessary objects. In some VM's, writing a number to an output stream for display causes creation of a new object for each character, then an object for a String. Singhal also claims that network programs are forced to create a new DataGramPacket object for each UDP packet received, etc.

Beware of Object Leaks

Just because Java does not have traditional pointers does not mean the programmer can't lose track of all references to an object. Repetitive functions are especially prone to create too many objects that never go away. The Visigenic ORB had this problem with orb.init( ). Profiling tools like jProbe or OptimizeIt can help detect these kinds of leaks.

Consider Not Using Accessor Methods

While it is good OO practice to provide accessor methods instead of allowing direct manipulation of instance variables, it also increases overhead by imposing an additional method call. You want accessors to hide the implementation of get and set, and to allow subclasses to change the synchronization of a get or set, but there is a cost.

Use Compound Operators

Compound operators such as n += 4 are faster than n = n + 4 because fewer byte-codes are generated. An optimizing compiler should find these and abbreviate them. Shifting by powers of two is faster than multiplying, but again the compiler should find it. Similarly, multiplication is faster than exponentiation.

Use Int Increments

Int increments are faster than byte or short increments. I don't know why, but it seems to be even more so with JIT's. Maybe it's just that CPU's are optimized to deal with 32-bit int values. Floating-point increments are much slower than any int, byte, or short increment. Probably this is because of the overhead intrinsic to floating-point operations. Double++ is slightly slower than Float++.

Be Conscious of Access Speed for Different Variables

From better to worse here are the fastest to slowest kinds of variables:

- Local stack variables
- Supersuperclass instance variables

- Superclass instance variables
- Class instance variables
- Class static variables

It can help to copy slower-access variables to fast local variables if you are going to operate on them repeatedly, as in a loop. Bitshifts are one-and-a-half to three times more expensive than local var reads.

Local Variables are Faster than Class Variables

Using the following:

```
i = 17;
```

is faster than using:

```
this.i = 17;
```

This is because the class variable requires access to the class before it can access a field within the class. Also, JIT's may put local variables in registers, which are very fast, further increasing performance.

Class Variables are Faster than Array Accesses

Using:

```
this.i = 17;
```

is faster than using:

```
arry[0] = 17;
```

Because each array access requires a bounds check, if you are going to use elements from an array in a loop and the elements do not depend on the index of the array, you'll get better performance assigning the array element to a local variable and using that in the loop. This is known as "loop invariant code motion" because you're moving the invariants outside of the loop rather than recalculating them on every iteration. Array accesses are also generally slower than class variables.

Use Faster Types as Loop Indexes

Because each array access requires a bounds check, if you are going to use elements from an array in a loop and the elements do not depend on the index of the array, you'll get better performance assigning the array elements to a local variable and using that in the loop. For example:

```
local = array[4];

for (int i = 0; i < somenumber; i++) if (i == local) doSomething();
```

Use Native Methods

If necessary for performance, you can write code in a compiled language like C and link it to Java code using the Java native method interface. At first glance, this would seem to destroy Java's portability, but it is not difficult to include pure Java fallback methods that will be used in case your code is run on a platform that does not support your native methods. See *http://www.javaworld.com/javaworld/javatips/jw-javatip13.html* for examples. That is, try to include a native method, but also give a pure Java option that will automatically be used for platforms that do not support that native code. See *http://www.javaworld.com/javaworld/javatips/jw-javatip13.html*.

Use Network Timeouts

Use user-configurable socket timeout options (TCP_NODELAY, SO_TIMEOUT), especially when accessing DNS servers. This will help prevent you from getting stuck.

Buffer Network and File I/O

A common error is to forget to buffer reads and writes, with the result that a single-byte read (or write) gets performance thousands of times, while the read or write could have been done just once with a buffer. It is easy to find these performance disasters on Unix using system call tracers like strace on Linux and truss on Solaris. Just trace your VM as it is running and look for huge numbers of single-byte reads or writes. See "System Call Tracers" in Chapter 17 for an example. java.io. OutputStream is implemented to write a byte at a time, synchronized, slowing down everything.

Use Sockets Rather than URLs

Making an HTTP connection to get a URL is quite easy in Java, but if you need to transfer non-HTML data, you'll get slightly better performance by making a direct buffered-socket connection and moving your data through that. This is especially helpful if you need to get multiple files, since you can use the same TCP connection for all of the files. Also be aware that you can get a further performance boost from using UDP sockets with Java, although UDP is unreliable, meaning you'll have to check the data integrity.

Use UDP

Use UDP rather than TCP if speed is more important than accuracy. This is not a Java-specific recommendation, since it also helps in other languages. UDP use in Java is constrained by the need to create a new object for every UDP packet.

Use Threads

Threads are far easier to use in Java than in C or C++. This is a very good thing, because threading allows multiple streams of execution within a single program, which is critical to writing high-performance applications in Java. One reason threads are so important to Java performance is that before Java 1.4, all Java I/O operations would block the thread they are in (the thread waits until the read or write operation is complete). So you must use multiple threads if you do not want your entire program to hang whenever the network is slow, for example. If you put an I/O read or write into its own thread, the rest of the program can continue in other threads while the I/O thread blocks. The thread with the I/O can then notify another thread (using the well-named notify( ) method) when its operation is complete. Threads also have the advantages of very fast interthread communication via shared variables, parallel execution on multiprocessor machines, a relatively small memory footprint, and very fast context switching.

All applications and applets start out with one parent thread. If you create and run child threads, you may have to force the parent thread to explicitly give up control with the suspend( ) or sleep( ) methods for the child threads to run with acceptable performance.

Note that Java's threading model depends on the underlying operating system and the interactions between the VM and operating system. For example, under Unix, the "green threads" model uses preemptive multitasking, while Windows threads must explicitly give up control. This can lead to differences in behavior across platforms unless the control of threaded operations is carefully thought out. Threading performance also depends on the underlying platform. While the earliest versions of Java did not take advantage of symmetric multiprocessing (SMP) machines, Java 2 (at least the Unix version) will in theory allocate threads across processors on SMP machines, resulting in performance that scales well with the number of processors. In reality, it hasn't always worked out that way. See Chapter 16 for a detailed discussion of Java threads on SMP machines.

Furthermore, green threads are not always slower than native threads. A green threads VM has the advantage of not needing to make a system call to do thread manipulation, but it is harder to implement a green threads VM because all blocking system calls must be wrapped. Green threads may not be able to use more than one CPU on an SMP machine, but you can run multiple VM's and use all of the CPU's that way.

Be aware that you can assign different priorities to different threads, so you can assign a high priority to tasks that are critical for overall performance, while assigning a lower priority to other tasks.

The JVM does not guarantee that your threads will be free of deadlock. Deadlock, when each of two or more threads is waiting for actions that can only be performed by the other, is fatal to performance. It is your responsibility to use the synchronized keyword and Monitor classes to insure this does not happen. Synchronized methods run more slowly than nonsynchronized methods, but synchronization is critical to thread safety.

Use notify

Use notify instead of notifyAll, where possible. notifyAll is much more expensive.

Use Synchronization Sparingly

Synchronization is necessary to let multithreaded programs run correctly, but it does cost something and should be avoided if possible. The more threads you have, the more synchronization will hurt performance, but the more important it may be for correctness. Rather than use synchronization, you could control data access by the design of the application itself, or just write single-threaded code. Synchronization may also cause a method to run more slowly with a JIT than without. The runtime memory allocator itself is synchronized, and so takes a hit there.

Synchronization by default locks on the current object: synchronized means synchronized(this). You can get finer-grained locking by creating a lock object and synchronizing a method on that object. Creating a synchronization object is the way synchronization was originally done, but HotSpot reduced the synchronization overhead to changing just a single bit so that it's very fast, but this is only for synchonized(this), not for synchronization on other objects.

You may be able to get gains by rewriting Java libraries or third-party code to use less synchronization if you don't need things to be thread-safe. For example Vector. elementAt() and Enumeration.nextItem() are synchronized, but you can write your own classes that do the same things without synchronization. Use the Collection library (in Java 1.2 and beyond) classes instead of the old *java.util.* classes. The Collection classes are inherently unsynchronized for higher performance, but provide additional hooks that enable the programmer to impose external synchronization if needed.

You may improve performance of a loop using a synchronized class by putting the whole loop in a block, which is synchronized on that class. This is because each thread will then get a chance to finish the loop before it has to give up the lock.

Keep Synchronized Methods Out of Loops

I/O classes tend to have a lot of synchronization, so you're often better off doing I/O all at once rather than in a loop, because each loop will waste time on locking and unlocking. So you should read an entire stream (for example with the readFully() method) and do any type conversions later on the entire data set rather than looping through a read of a certain type and doing the conversion on the spot.

Watch Out for the Mother Thread

You may have to force the mother thread to explicitly give up control with the suspend( ) or sleep( ) methods to get the child threads to run with acceptable performance.

Counting Down May Be Faster than Counting Up

The VM may be able to do a fast single instruction "branch on 0" rather than several instructions meaning "branch if this not equal to that."

Reduce the Number of Strings

If you profile your program with OptimizeIt, your first reaction will probably be that there are an incredible number of String objects. There are a lot of Strings for many reasons. The Java 1.02 event model is based on Strings. The Java libraries use a lot of Strings. And every object has a toString method, so it must have an associated String object.

JSP is faster than hardcoding Strings in servlets because much of the String manipulation is done at compile time rather than at runtime. Java would have to call the charToByteConvertor foreach print statement to create the output stream otherwise.

Use String Buffers or Arrays

If you are going to do a lot of string manipulation, be sure to use StringBuffers rather than Strings, since extending a String necessarily involves copying the whole thing, while extending a StringBuffer often means filling in space that has already been allocated. Adding on to a StringBuffer is also quite a bit faster than the + operator, which creates a new StringBuffer itself, appends both of the arguments, and converts the result back to a String.

Bare byte arrays are faster than StringBuffers for certain operations, especially if you use System.arraycopy( ). In typical Internet protocol operations, most low-level manipulation is performed on bytes. Use byte arrays rather than Strings to store such data and for related manipulations. Again, the upcoming JDK1.4 release will introduce the *java.nio* package, which has Buffer classes that operate on bytes.

Watch Out for Slow Fonts

Fonts vary in speed of rendering. For some reason it is far faster to display the NY Times font at runtime than some other fonts. This may have to do with fonts built into the VM compared to the indirections in using a loaded font.

Keep the Paint Method Small

Keep your paint( ) method as simple as possible, since it will be called many times. If you have too many calculations in your paint( ) method, the user will suffer greatly while waiting for your applet or application to redraw itself. This is all the more important since calls to paint( ) are queued up by the VM if they cannot be executed immediately. If you have a large paint( ) method and a user needs to scroll or otherwise redraw a lot, the user will probably give up in disgust while the queued up repaint( ) calls are slowly executed, making the screen flash and preventing the user from doing anything else. This problem is especially noticeable when using Windows. If you must do a lot of computation in paint( ), you can use clipping (redrawing just the part of the screen that has changed) to give your machine a fighting chance. Of course, the computation required to redraw a square on your screen goes up with the area of that square.

Double Buffer Where Possible for Smoother Graphics

Double buffer (basically, draw into an off-screen buffer where it happens more quickly, then swap to the screen) where possible for smoother graphics.

Use the Runtime to Do Error Checking for You

If errors are expected to be rare, don't waste time doing an application-level check where the runtime is already doing a check for you—for example, as the ArrayIndexOutOfBoundsException does. Since this check is going to be done whether you like it or not, you could use this to break loops rather than an explicit check of some other loop conditional. For example, instead of this:

```
public class test {
    public static void main(String[] args) {
        int array[] = new int[1000000];

        for (int i=0; i<array.length; i++) {
            array[i] = i;
        }
    }
}
```

you could do this:

```
public class test {
    public static void main(String[] args) {
        int array[] = new int[1000000];

        try {
            for (int i=0; ; i++) {
                array[i] = i;
            }
```

```
        }
        catch(ArrayIndexOutOfBoundsException aioobe) {}
    }
  }
```

The first one takes about 1.5 seconds to run on an old 233 MHz Pentium, the second takes about 1.1 seconds. But it is even faster to just set the array bounds to a local (stack) variable, so this is not a practical example. Another example is avoiding the use of instanceof and just trying to cast and object and call a method on it, catching the ClassCastException if thrown.

Exceptions are expensive to construct and propagate, which is okay if they happen only rarely, but a problem if they are relied on for normal flow of execution. They are, after all, supposed to be exceptional.

Avoid Time Conversions

For some applications that access the date a lot, it can help to set the local time zone to be GMT, so that no conversion has to take place. For example, in the old Java web server, you would set log.time=GMT. Then you won't need a conversion on each hit and the server would run significantly faster.

Be Wary of RMI, EJBs, and CORBA

Distributed object systems sound very cool and work very badly. A major issue is that the serialization that comes with most VMs is poor. If you must serialize, use the "transient" keyword to mark instance fields that are not to be serialized. One alternative to serialization is to use the Externalizable interface and write your own serialization routines, but this is a lot of work. Another alternative is simply to not pass any objects as parameters. Other issues include the excessive copying of data, loading all of the required superclasses and dependencies across the network, and grossly misjudging the latency of the network because everything seems to work fine when first developed and run on one machine. According to Peter Deutsch of Bunyip:

> Essentially everyone, when they first build a distributed application, makes the following eight assumptions. All prove to be false in the long run and all cause big trouble and painful learning experiences: the network is reliable; latency is zero; bandwidth is infinite; the network is secure; topology doesn't change; there is one administrator; transport cost is zero; and the network is homogeneous.

You can see that these are false, but the developer who has client and server on one machine has the strong impression they are all true. So expectations are not correctly managed. One reason the Web works so well is that every remote access is explicitly known to the user, so there is no expectation of a local-speed response when issuing a request for a remote resource.

Compilers

Always use the latest version of any Java compiler, because compilers tend to generate better code in succeeding generations.

Compilers can help performance in the following ways:

Loop invariant code motion
> Things that do not change within a loop should be moved outside of it. This is known as "loop invariant code motion" because you're moving the invariants outside of the loop rather than recalculating them on every iteration.

Common subexpression elimination
> Something like loop invariant code motion. You just do intense calculations once and store the result in a local variable. You may have more total bytecodes, but fewer intense calculations.

Strength reduction
> Strength reduction means using constructs that generate fewer bytecodes or fewer dereferences (for example, using +=). Other examples:
>
> * Making a one-dimensional array variable for extensive calculations on one row of a 2-D or 3-D array. This supposedly saves an iload (load int to local var) and aaload (load reference from array) for each array reference.
> * Using super() to get a reference to the superclass to do manipulations on fields defined in that superclass. Supposedly enables compiler to put in aload (load reference from local variable) rather than getfield (fetch field from object).

Variable allocation
> The first four numeric variables or arguments accessed use shorter bytecodes, so you can speed things up by declaring commonly used variables first.

-0

Compile using the *-O* option to the *javac* compiler, but do so with caution. *-O* will automatically "inline" your final, private, and static methods, meaning that the call to those methods will be replaced with the actual code, removing the runtime overhead of pushing the current state on the stack at the expense of making your code larger.

Note that optimization may bring out hidden bugs in your code. This is usually because the optimizer takes a stricter view of syntax, but it could also be due to bugs in the optimizer, such as inlining things that shouldn't have been. You should thoroughly test your code after optimization. I had a case in which an otherwise one-hour compile took three days with *-O*, then the generated code bombed at runtime.

There is also a commercial tool call "Dash O." It rearranges bytecodes after you compile, optimizing in ways the compiler might not have. See *http://www.preemptive.com/DashO/index.html*.

Profile Your Code

To do code profiling in Java, you can run with the *-prof* option, like this:

```
% java -prof MyClass.java
```

This profile is based on actual execution times, but doesn't count the number of times any set of bytecode is used. The result is a profile file, which is not entirely human-readable. You can interpret the profile file with a number of free tools available on the Web, such as Hyperprof. This will tell you where your code is spending most of its time, and therefore, where you should concentrate your source code optimization efforts.

There is also the *-hprof* option to profile heap and CPU but it leads to 10× inflation in time and code size. The *-hprof* option precludes use of JIT profiler.

The following tools both instrument your code for profiling and display the results:

- Visual Quantify for Java from Rational.
- JavaSpec from the JavaTest part of Sun.
- OptimizeIt, at *http://www.optimizeit.com/*, probably the best known and easiest to use.
- Jprobe from The KL Group, at *http://www.klgroup.com/*. The Enterprise edition can profile remote applications.
- Metamata.
- HAT, the Heap Analysis Tool from Javasoft. Free but unsupported.

If you are profiling and the profiler tells you it can't see into compiled code, then the problem may be that you are running the profiler and a JIT at the same time. Try running the profiler without the JIT. It is also very instructive to start the Java console in Netscape and press 9 in the console window for detailed statistics as the applet runs. Press the question mark (?) to see all the options the console gives you. These options can be very useful.

JVMPI

Java 2 now has a standard Java VM Profiling Interface (JVMPI), but this is for the writers of profiling tools, not for Java application programmers.

Decompilers

Since Java keeps method and class names in the bytecode to facilitate dynamic binding, you can decompile class files and see pretty much everything except local variable names. Here are a few ways to decompile class files:

- *javap -c* will print out bytecode mnemonics, but not Java source. Comes with JDK.
- Mocha will print out Java source. Available from *http://patrick.net/software/*.
- SourceAgain will print out Java source.

There are some "obfuscator" tools that mangle the names in the bytecode, making the decompiled source harder to understand.

OS-Level Profiling Tools

Don't feel inhibited from using more traditional tools on Java processes. A Java process under Unix is just another process, so its network output can be examined with the *snoop* tool that comes bundled with Solaris, and the calls the VM makes of the OS can be seen with *truss* on Solaris and *strace* on Linux. I'm still hoping that someone writes a tool that prints out every Java method call as it occurs.

JITs

Just-in-time compilers (JITs) compile stretches of bytecode (from a single instruction up to an entire method) into efficient native code as the bytecode is being executed. The next time the same stretch of bytecode is to be run, the compiled native code is run instead. For example, loops will run far faster under a JIT compiler because the bytecode does not have to be interpreted on every cycle of the loop. On the first cycle, there is a delay while native code for the loop is generated, and on the second and subsequent cycles, this native code is called and is presumably faster than interpreting the bytecode.

Just-in-time compilers usually help performance substantially, but be aware that they help the most for repetitive code, but are not useful for GUI code. In fact, it's possible that your code will run more slowly with a JIT. One problem is that you really don't want to JIT-compile code that will be used only once, but JITs are not very smart about what they compile (namely, everything). JavaSoft's HotSpot compiler is different. HotSpot collects runtime execution data and uses that data to compile only the portions of the code that are repeatedly executed—that is, the "hot spots." This gives some boost to GUI applications.

JIT's do not help code that is already native, such as the underlying native implementation of some *java.lang* methods. JIT's do not help much with slow object creation time because most of that is already native code. JIT's tend to work poorly on synchronized code.

Here are some JITs, their URLs, the platforms they run on, and whether they're free or not:

Apple (http:// www.applejava.apple.com/)
> The Apple MacOS Runtime for Java MRJ2.0 includes a JIT for Java 1.1.3. It is free for download and bundled with MacOS 8.1.

DEC (http:// www.digital.com/java)
> JDK 1.1.5 on Digital Unix V4.0x only. It is the only 64-bit implementation of Java. Free.

HP (http:// www.hp.com/esy/go/java.html)
> JDK 1.1 for HPUX only. Free.

Kaffe (http:// www.kaffe.org/)
> For Alpha, 68K, PowerPC, MIPS, Sparc, x86. Free.

Microsoft (http:// www.microsoft.com/visualj)
> Internet Explorer for Windows and the Mac. Free.

Netscape (http:// www.netscape.com/)
> Windows 3.1/95/NT, Mac, Solaris. Commercial.

SGI (http:// cosmo.sgi.com/code/index.html)
> Irix. Commercial.

Sun (http:// www.sun.com/workshop/java/jit)
> Windows 3.1/95/NT and Solaris. Free.

Symantec (http:// www.symantec.com/javacentral/index.html)
> Windows 95/NT and Mac. Commercial.

Static Compilers

Java can be compiled into native code and linked to a garbage collection library. This is known as static compilation. Static compilation is against orthodox Sun religion because Sun is afraid that Java code will be compiled and optimized for Windows, but it's simply a no-brainer for Java performance on the server side, where Java code does not need to be especially portable. You can always compile and optimize far better if you have a lot of time to do it than if you're doing it on the fly with a JIT. And you should. There are two ways to compile Java to native: you can first translate Java to C and then compile the C with standard compilers, or you can compile Java directly to native machine code. Here are some static compilation tools:

- Harissa (http://www.irisa.fr/compose/harissa/harissa.html)
- j2c (http://www.webcity.co.jp/info/andoh/java/j2c.html)
- JCC (http://www.geocities.com/CapeCanaveral/Hangar/4040/jcc.html)

- Toba (*http://www.cs.arizona.edu/sumatra/toba/*; applications only)
- TowerJ (*http://www.towerj.com/*)*

If you use one of these, bear in mind that what you produce will not have binary portability, and it will be required to link to a library that performs runtime services, such as garbage collection, usually done by the VM. In addition, you will probably lose the ability to dynamically load regular Java classes (those you have not compiled down to C). If you would prefer to go directly to Wintel *.exe* files, Microsoft's Java compiler is more than happy to help you to do this, as is Symantec's Cafe Pro 2.0.

Virtual Machines

VMs generally improve in performance as time goes on, so you should use the latest version for your platform. Java's 1.1 event handling is much faster than in 1.02. As an example of an improved VM, here are some of the changes from Sun's 1.1 to 1.2 Java runtime environments:

- Each thread keeps its own heap and monitor caches, reducing the overhead of locking and synchronization.
- Loaded classes are able to take advantage of memory compression and to share String objects among classes.
- Object allocation speed is greatly improved, as is garbage collection.
- The 1.2 JDK does not use handles, which are pointers to pointers, but only a single level of indirection to objects. This speeds up object references and allows the elimination of memory fragmentation.

If you know your code will be running on a particular platform, say because it is server-side code, be sure you have the latest VM for that platform. You probably also want a VM written by the operating system vendor because the vendor presumably knows the most about optimizing Java for that OS. So use the MRJ on the Mac, Digital's VM on Digital Unix, and so on. Sunsoft makes the fastest VM for Solaris, including native threads and a JIT, but Sun also makes a "reference-implementation" VM from Javasoft, which is much slower. The faster VM is bundled with Solaris. Sun's Java 2 implementation of the VM now allows the process size to shrink as well as grow. Before, it could only grow or remain constant. Microsoft also makes the fastest VMs for Windows, but be careful when using Microsoft Java products lest you end up writing code that won't run anywhere except on Windows.

Linux has many free VM's: *http://www.kaffe.org/*, The Blackdown VM (*http://www.blackdown.org/*), the Sun VM, the IBM VM, and one from *http://www.hungry.com/*.

---

* Note that TowerJ's support for native threads was missing on many platforms as of this writing. This means that you could not effectively use a multi-CPU machine without running multiple processes.

The most popular VMs for Linux are the Blackdown JVM and the IBM JVM for JDK1.2. The JDK1.2 Sun VM for Linux has poor native thread support, but for Java 1.3, the Sun VM for Linux is quite good.

Some poor implementations of the Java VM may not garbage collect classes at all, meaning you will eventually run out of memory and the VM will stop.

Runtime Options

Java has several runtime options that are worth knowing about. I discuss them in the following sections.

-verbosegc

Setting *-verbosegc* causes Java to give more detail about its garbage collection (GC). Setting this option multiple times actually gives even more information, up to three times: *-verbosegc -verbosegc -verbosegc*. This can be useful in diagnosing GC problems.

-noverify

Bytecode verification is on by default for any class loaded over a network, but not for locally loaded classes, such as those run on the server side. Verification simply confirms that the bytecode conforms to the Java specification. You can use *java -verify* <*class*> after compiling instead. It may soon be possible to turn off the bytecode verifier in browsers (it is off for applications by default). This exposes you to some security risk in return for performance.

-Xmsn and -Xmxn

The *-Xmsn* and *-Xmxn* options (to set the initial heap size and max heap size respectively) are very useful.

Set the initial heap size to the "normal heap requirement" of your program. The default value of 1M is typically very low for server class applications and will cause excessive GC action when the application starts up (due to not enough heap space). Similarly, the default max heap size of 64M is on the low side for server class applications. Increasing that can help to avoid OutOfMemory exceptions as well.

Make Eden Big Enough

Java 2 has "generational" garbage collection, in which objects are first created in a memory space called "Eden" (as in the Garden of Eden). Eden is garbage collected frequently, to take advantage of the fact that most objects are transient. If an object survives several rounds of GC in Eden, it gets promoted to the main heap, which is GC'd much less frequently. If Eden is too small, the Eden GC can start to "thrash," meaning that it fills up and empties constantly, resulting in very high CPU usage and sluggish response time. The solution to this is to set Eden large enough to accommodate your application. Here is an example Java startup parameter that sets Eden to 32M initial and maximum:

```
-Xgenconfig:32m,32m,semispaces:192m192m,markcompact
```

See Java 2 documentation for more about generational garbage collection.

-train

Garbage collection generally stalls the entire Java process, so it is convenient to be able to break up GC into smaller increments. This is especially true for very large heaps, which can cause GC to take more than a minute. The *-train* option in Java 1.3 does this break up, so garbage collection will cause several smaller stalls rather than one long one.

Use Native Threads

Native threads are usually turned on with an environment variable, or via a *-D* option when starting the VM. Native threads usually provide a good performance boost.

Use .jar Files

You should certainly use *.jar* or *.zip* files if you need to download more than one class, because each class requires a separate TCP connection to load (unless you are using HTTP 1.1). Remove things you know you won't use from *.jar* files (if you really know you won't need them).

Java Plug-In

Sun's Java Plug-In is a VM that you can download into browsers such as Netscape or IE. This provides a number of benefits, such as independence from the quirks of Microsoft's VM, and much faster class loading than the Netscape VM. But the biggest advantage is probably applet caching, to avoid repeated downloads of the same large applets.

Applet caching will happen by default using the browser's cache. This is often not acceptable for large applets because the applet may be pushed out of the cache by other content. As of Javasoft's plug VM for the browser version 1.3 beta, it is possible to make applet caching permanent; see *http://java.sun.com/products/plugin/appletcaching.html* for details.

-start_java

Browsers tend not to start the Java VM until you have downloaded some Java, resulting in a delay while the browser initializes its VM before the first time you run Java in a session. With Netscape, you can start Java when the browser is started by using the *-start_java* option.

Java Chips

It used to be thought that Java performance could be brought up to or beyond that of native code on current CPUs by the implementation of the VM in hardware. At that point, the term "virtual" will no longer be accurate. The JVM was designed to be implemented in hardware eventually, and the Java chip should be quite a bit faster for the bytecodes that can be easily implemented in hardware.

Unfortunately, there are bytecodes that require extensive processing to execute (such as declaring a new object) and are not easily implemented in hardware. In some Java software, only 15 percent of the processing is bytecode interpretation by the VM. For these reasons, and because the first Java chips produced were too big and ran too hot, it seems that most plans for Java chips have been cancelled.

Java Benchmarks

The most widely accepted Java VM benchmark seems to be the SPEC JVM98 test. It is available from *http://www.spec.org/osg/jvm98/*. But there are also many others:

Volano
   A scripted chat application. *http://www.volano.com/markvedocs.html*

CaffeineMark
   Supposedly tests can be tailored to get arbitrarily high CaffeineMarks. *http://www.webfayre.com/pendragon/cm2/index.html*

Doug Bell's Benchmark applet
   http://www.javaworld.com/javaworld/jw-04-1997/jw-04-optimize.html

Jonathan Hardwick's Java Microbenchmark
   http://www.cs.cmu.edu/~jch/java/microbench.html

Jack Dongarra and Reed Wade's Linpack
   http://www.netlib.org/benchmark/linpackjava/
   http://www.cs.cmu.edu/~jch/java/linpack.html

Bill and Paul's Excellent UCSD Benchmarks for Java
   http://www-cse.ucsd.edu/users/wgg/JavaProf/javaprof.html

Others
   http://www.cs.cmu.edu/~jch/java/resources.html

Problems with Benchmarks

Java benchmarks often rely on `System.currentTimeMillis()` to get the start and end time for various operations. `System.currentTimeMillis` may take up to .5 ms to execute in itself, and this can't be helped by a JIT because it is implemented as a native system call. You can see that it is a native call by looking at the `java.lang.System.java` source code:

```
public static native long currentTimeMillis();
```

Web Sites with Java Performance Info

If you're still looking for more information on improving Java performance, here's a bevy of URLs for you to peruse:

```
http://www-cse.ucsd.edu/users/wgg/JavaProf/javaprof.html
http://www.cs.arizona.edu/sumatra/toba/
http://www.cs.cmu.edu/~jch/java/compilers.html.
http://www.cs.cmu.edu/~jch/java/optimization.html
http://www.cs.cmu.edu/~jch/java/size.html
http://www.geocities.com/CapeCanaveral/Hangar/4040/jcc.html
http://www.ibm.com/java/education/javahipr/javahipr1.html
http://www.javaworld.com/javaworld/jw-04-1997/jw-04-optimize.html
http://www.netlib.org/benchmark/linpackjava/
http://www.preemptive.com/
http://www.webcity.co.jp/info/andoh/java/j2c.html
```

See also *Java Performance Tuning*, by Jack Shirazi (O'Reilly & Associates).

Key Recommendations

- Use a recent compiler and VM, preferably one optimized for your platform.
- Profile your code and optimize the most-used parts.
- Use threads.
- Use buffered I/O.
- Use HTML rather than Java applets wherever possible.

CHAPTER 22
Databases

The explosion of the Web was partly driven by relatively cheap and easy global Internet access to legacy databases. Most of this information is on mainframes or in relational database management systems (RDBMSs).

There are three standard classes of database access, each with different requirements:

- The individual query of a read-only database, such as AltaVista.

- The very complex query looking for patterns in huge amounts of data, usually for marketing purposes. This is called data mining. In a famous example of data mining, grocery stores correlated sales of all items and found that beer and diapers were often sold together. No one had previously suspected this, but it made sense because both are items that you run out of and may make a special trip to buy. As a result of this discovery, grocery stores now tend to keep beer and diapers close together. Data mining is read-only, and the queries are usually so complex and take so long to run that public web access is not advisable.

- Transaction processing, such as online credit card verification and sales, or bank account access. Transaction processing is rapidly becoming a key area of value for the Web.

These three classes of database access vary in their scalability needs and abilities. The read-only simple access class is easily scaled by replicating the database. Data mining databases generally do not need to be scaled, because so few users will be making queries. Transaction processing databases are the most difficult to scale, because it comes down to writing data to exactly one master copy at any moment, which imposes a significant bottleneck.

Database planning and tuning is a huge field, far larger than all of the work done on tuning web services so far. See *Oracle Performance Tuning*, by Mark Gurry and Peter Corrigan (O'Reilly & Associates).

Do You Really Need a Relational Database?

It is common for web developers to jump to the conclusion that they need an SQL-compliant RDBMS like Oracle, when in fact they have a rather small data set that could be organized as one table. Commercial RDBMSs are expensive as well as non-trivial to install and administer.

When You Need a Professional Database

Here are some indications that you need a professional database:

- You have more than a megabyte of data.
- You have multiple tables and want to do complex queries.
- You need extremely high reliability and performance.
- You need transaction processing abilities.

If this sounds like your situation, then you'll benefit from the performance features of commercial RDBMSs, such as the ability to work from raw disk rather than the OS's filesystem, custom threading models, and query optimizations.

Alternatives

Alternatives to the traditional SQL database include the following. Some of these are low-performance, but make for such easy programming that a low-volume web site should consider them.

The most obvious strategy for a small data set that needs to be searched in simple ways is to download all of the data to the client in an HTML page and let the user use the browser's find function to get to the relevant line. For more complex searching of small data sets, consider writing a Java applet to download along with the data, which presents a search interface to the user and simplifies the query.

For data sets that are too big for your client's access speed, one solution is to search on the server side with an ordinary CGI, on a server API module, or on a Java servlet. The Unix *grep* command is reasonably efficient and very easily used in a CGI. Sometimes *grep*ping a flat ASCII data file has a far better return on investment than any formal database, because the programming is so easy. Perl has easy-to-use hash-tables, and Unix *ndbm* files do a similar sort of hashing, for those inclined to write CGIs in C. C programmers can also read a binary file that is mapped into memory and treated as memory structures directly. This approach has extremely good performance if the overhead of CGI startup can be lessened by daemonizing the CGI or writing a server API module.

Finally, if you feel you need SQL for some complex queries but have a fairly small data set, consider MiniSQL, also called mSQL, from *http://www.Hughes.com.au/*. It is available with source code for a small fee, has good performance, and supports a large subset of ANSI SQL. MySQL is another good choice for small databases, and is free.

Performance Tips

A web site that exists for database access should be planned around the database. First, decide what sort of load the database will have to handle, and then choose web server software and hardware based on that load. The database will probably have to do much more work than the web server, so the database will be the bottleneck.

Prepared Statements and Bind Variables

You can store a preparsed statement in the database with variables in specific positions. These variables are called "bind variables." The performance of prepared statements is much greater than statements that must be parsed and optimized before execution, but there is overhead in setting up the statement to begin with.

Prepared statements are best used when you will be making many nearly identical queries, differing only in the value of specific query values rather than differing in structure or tables. Note that the storage of a prepared statement is rather expensive, so that is the part you want to do only once, not in a loop.

Denormalize Tables

Some performance gains can be had simply by storing the most common data together in the same tables, avoiding expensive join operations. This also makes it easier to write queries, since a single table can then be used where otherwise you would have to do a join. On the other hand, denormalized tables increases the possibility of data inconsistencies, where data that is supposedly identical is different in different tables. Denormalized tables are also harder to administer.

Do Not Create Cursors in Loops

Cursors, memory areas storing the results of a query, are also expensive to create and should not be created inside of loops.

Direct Connections

Direct Oracle connections take more memory, but avoid some of the scheduling overhead of the dispatcher.

Main Memory Databases

If you can afford to cache the whole database in RAM, a technique known as supercaching, do it. Also, if you know something about the kinds of SQL statements that will be executed, you can be ready for them with the correct amount of memory. Complicated joins take a lot of RAM and may even use all of your virtual memory if you're not careful.

Database vendors have a natural advantage in providing the fastest drivers and connectivity for their databases, but the Java DataBase Connectivity standard (JDBC) does give you portability options. The best JDBC drivers talk directly to the database in the database's native protocol. The Open DataBase Connectivity standard (ODBC) slows things down a bit.

Multiple Tiers

The browser/web server/database setup happens to be a three-tier system, but doesn't have all the advantages of three-tier systems unless you plan for them. A two-tier system, in which the web server is also the database, will give you better performance for small numbers of users but may not scale well.

For large numbers of users, three-tier systems can reuse business objects on the web server or application server for both reading and writing without immediately hitting the database again, producing a large increase in performance. A middle tier also lets you join multiple databases to act as one so you can distribute the database. Mid-tier transaction processing monitors can also boost performance by managing access to a database connection, so that the connection does not need to be opened and closed for each query.

Connection Pool Configuration

For a high-volume site, a connection pool is a necessity, not an optimization. The establishment of database connections is very time-consuming, so you don't want to be doing it for every query on your web site. If you are using an application server like Weblogic, it pays to configure the initial size of the connection pool to also be the maximum size. When a connection pool has to grow in size, it take a significant amount of time to set up the new connections. The user is just left waiting during this time. If you set the pool to its maximum size right off the bat, there is no need to wait for the pool to grow and so some responses are much quicker. The downside is that you will be using more of the resources of your database, at the possible expense of other applications.

Queries

A good schema will reduce the amount of work a database must do to satisfy a query. Note that databases now include optimizers, which fall into two categories: rule-based and cost-based. Rule-based optimizes follow a specific set of rules, while cost-based optimizers look at the actual time cost of specific queries. You can give the optimizers hints in comments within your SQL statements:

- Cache the results of the most frequent queries.
- Do the more restrictive part of the query/update first. The second part will have less data to deal with and therefore will run faster.

- It is generally better to have larger granularity of interaction with the database. That is, perform a few large queries rather than many small ones.

- Precompile queries.

- You can push a lot of work onto the database with advanced SQL or stored procedures. Stored procedures also allow the DBA to be responsible for the queries rather than the programmer. The DBA presumably knows more about optimizing SQL than the programmer. Also, stored procedures can be used to enforce certain standards in which queries are made and what else has to happen before or after the queries. It is much easier to change one stored procedure than many SQL statements scattered in C or Java code. SQL is mostly portable, but stored procedure languages will tie you to some particular database.

- Limit locking to the bits of data that you really need to lock. If each query is locking the same table, then they will all necessarily be serialized and performance will suffer. Row-level locking may help.

- A single bad SQL query will create a crushing load on the database. Don't give the general public unrestricted access, not even on your intranet.

Indexes

Build indexes that correlate with what you're likely to be searching for. Otherwise, you've wasted your time building and updating the index, and your disk space in storing it. Creating an index is a simple SQL statement—for example:

```
create index news_index on news_story(user, story_age, already_read);
```

Row-Level Locking

Row-level locking gives a large performance advantage over table-level locking, but not all databases support it.

Combined Web Server/Databases

Some databases themselves are now HTTP servers, eliminating a layer between the client and the database. These can construct HTML on the fly, like CGI, and can maintain state for transactions. They can be configured to use the same database connection for all requests, improving performance tremendously over opening a connection for each request. The downside is that they are proprietary solutions and do not scale well. The applications you write for one of these hybrid servers will not run on the others. The database may allow access across the network to other databases, but then you no longer have the performance advantage of dealing with only one process. The following are a few web server/databases:

- IBM's Merchant Server uses DB2.

- Informix Web Datablade uses Informix.

- NS LiveWire Pro uses Informix, and now Oracle as well.
- Oracle WebServer uses Oracle.
- Sybase's web.SQL uses Sybase.

How Many Connections Can Your Database Handle?

If you generate dynamic content from a database, you may be limited by the number of connections your database can handle. This is a configurable parameter for most databases, but if you configure it very high, you will probably see that you run out of memory or some other resource before you reach the configured connection limit.

Here is a quick Java program that will create an arbitrary number of connections to your database and print them out as it creates them. It is intended to stress and perhaps crash a database, so be careful not to use it on any system that should not crash. It uses the Oracle "thin" driver, but you can modify it to use any driver. Compile with java jdbcCxnTest. The following source code is available from *http://patrick.net/software/jdbcCxnTest.java*:

```java
import java.sql.*;
// Test to see how many simultaneous connections your db can handle.
// Usage: java jdbctest <machine> <port> <instance> <num threads>
// Be sure to up your ulimit if necessary. Eg: ulimit -n 1024
 public class jdbcCxnTest implements Runnable {
    static String where;
    static int     cxn = 0;
    public static void main (String args[]) {
        if ( args.length != 4 ) {
            System.out.println(
                "Usage: java jdbcCxnTest <host> <port> <dbname> <connections>"
            );
            return;
        }
        String host = args[0];
        String port = args[1];
        String sid  = args[2];
        where = "jdbc:oracle:thin:@" + host + ":" + port + ":" + sid ;
        try {
            DriverManager.registerDriver(new oracle.jdbc.driver.OracleDriver());
        }
        catch (SQLException e) {
            System.out.println ("registerDriver failed");
            return;
        }
        for (int t = 0; t < Integer.parseInt(args[3]); t++)
```

```
                new Thread(new jdbcCxnTest()).start();
        }
    public void run() {
        try {
            // use a valid user/password in place of scott/tiger
            Connection conn =
                DriverManager.getConnection(where, "scott", "tiger");
            Statement  stat = conn.createStatement();
            ResultSet resu = stat.executeQuery("select * from dual");
            while(resu.next()) {
                System.out.println(resu.getString(1) + inc());
            }
            while (true) {              // sleep forever
                Thread.sleep(100000);
            }
            // we don't close the connections
        }
        catch ( SQLException e ) {
            e.printStackTrace();
            while (e != null) {
                System.err.println(e.getErrorCode());
                System.err.println(e.getMessage());
                System.err.println(e.getSQLState());
                e = e.getNextException();
            }
        }
        catch (InterruptedException e) {
            System.err.println("sleep interrupted");
        }
    }
    public synchronized int inc() {
        return ++cxn;
    }
}
```

When the Database Is Overloaded

I've tried to overload Oracle by making too many connections too fast, and I haven't
been able to get it to crash during a test. What does happen is that new connections
time out or fail to be made. Some of this may be due to the overflow of TCP listen
queue. See Chapter 15 for information about the listen queue. If an Oracle process is
trying to connect to an Oracle database and logging connections, you'll see errors
like these:

```
TNS-00505: Operation timed out
TNS-12535: TNS:operation timed out
TNS-12560: TNS:protocol adapter error
```

Analysis

There are many well-established ways of diagnosing database problems. Your database administrator should be familiar with some of them. For Oracle, you can try SQL*Net tracing to look at network issues, use tkprof and autoprof to profile queries, or do a database trace. If you know what queries you are issuing, you can manually issue the command set timing on in SQLPLUS to easily see just how long variations on a query take.

Key Recommendations

- Use connection pools.
- If you don't have a large amount of data, consider non-RDBMS options.
- Build indexes.
- For complex queries, do the most restrictive part first.

APPENDIX O

Web Performance Product Lists and Reviews

The following is a list of the major commercial tools using in monitoring, load tests, tuning, or other tasks that someone who reads this book might do. I've tried to isolate most commercial products to this chapter.

Problems with Commercial Tools

Most web performance tools have the same flaws. They do useful things and I'd love to get those benefits, but I have to work around these common problems:

- Most of these tools have GUIs that will not go away. This is especially true for tools that run on Windows. These products literally do not run without the GUI. It is better to deal with a command line and ASCII log files.

  I often need to run tests on the other side of one or more firewalls and get the results. Don't even try to run some Windows GUI–based application remotely through a firewall. You'll waste your time. Even if it used X, it wouldn't work because firewalls by nature will say no to most protocols and ports, including X. Even if the tools include "headless" virtual clients, their controllers are still Windows GUI applications.

- They concentrate on the desktop, which is too far from the server room. You just can't effectively test a server through a low-bandwidth high-latency connection. The network becomes the bottleneck.

- Most commercial tools like to save your work in a compressed format, to put it nicely. To be less generous, I might say that they lock your test and monitoring data into a proprietary format. I want ASCII log files. I can grep them, parse them, run head or tail, or view them in a browser or via *telnet*. There are no hidden bits, no special tools for viewing, and no undocumented weirdness.

- They all want you to learn their proprietary scripting language for writing tests. To put it nicely again, I don't need a new scripting language. Why don't they use Perl? Because they are trying to lock your programming effort into a proprietary format.

- They are very expensive.

Monitoring Tools

A common problem with automated performance monitoring (or automated testing of any kind) is that it does not work well if your content or environment are constantly changing. This is because human intervention is often required to cope with those changes, and human intervention is the opposite of automation. The gains from test automation are generally larger from a static environment.

On the other hand, a coworker of mine effectively used Perl and the DBI interface to validate constantly changing dynamic web pages. He did this by first querying certain database fields for content and then validating that the same content appeared on the web page in the right place. In this way, he got ahead of the "chase" condition in which most test writers find themselves (altering their tests every time a web page changes).

One class of monitoring tools called "transaction trackers" generally claim to provide "end-to-end" visibility of what is going on in your application, often by tagging packets with specific identifiers. This generally does not work well for two reasons. First, requests go through pooling points where packet tagging cannot follow. For example, a web site hit may cause a database query, but if that query is over a connection in a database connection pool, you probably cannot figure out which connection was used. Second, to really gain visibility past the pooling points, in-depth application knowledge and custom programming is required. This means that generic software will not work.

Those points aside, there are many useful monitoring tools on the market. This list only skims the surface:

AIM (http://www.aim.com/)
AIM Technology provides performance measurement software and services for Unix and NT systems.

Baseline (http://www.teamquest.com/)
Baseline is a product from TeamQuest that reports performance of CPU, disk, buffer cache, etc., for networks of Unix and NT machines, locating bottlenecks and providing detailed analysis and alarms. The reports are accessible via a web browser, and there is even a live demo at their web site.

Best/1 (http://www.bgs.com/)
The Best/1 performance products from BGS run on most corporate computers including mainframes, Unix systems, and NT. They not only collect data, but they also feed the data into a capacity-planning tool. You can set performance monitors, alerts, generate reports, and plan additional capacity.

BMC Patrol Knowledge Module for Internet Servers (http://www.bmc.com/)

The suite of Patrol products from BMC monitors all kinds of corporate systems, including web servers. You can set rules to automatically identify problems, then to try to correct the problems or notify you. The Patrol CGI Analyzer lets you monitor CGI performance in particular.

Cisco's NETSYS tools (http://www.cisco.com/)

These tools are designed to monitor networks (routers in particular) rather than web servers, but, of course, the network is critical to your web performance.

CyberGauge (http://www.neon.com/CyberGauge.html)

CyberGauge from Neon is an Internet bandwidth–measurement utility based on SNMP. It supports most routers, but itself runs only on Windows and the Macintosh.

HP Openview tools (http://www.hp.com/openview/rpm/netmetds.htm, http://www.hp. com/openview/rpm/mwds.htm)

The HP MeasureWare agent collects statistics on the performance of distributed systems in general, not just web systems. MeasureWare collects and analyzes application response times and system metrics such as disk, CPU, and network. It is well integrated with the other HP OpenView tools, but stores its data in a proprietary undocumented format, so it's not simple to get it out for other uses with other tools. In other words, it does not intgrate well with the rest of the Unix world. Most users view the data with HP's PerfView management console. Measureware does require the installation of agents on the systems you want to monitor. Measureware can use the Application Response Measurement (ARM) standard to collect application data. HP OpenView can use the Sun agents to get system info.

Netmetrix is an RMON-based network monitoring tool that works with Cisco's IOS. It can extract data from routers for performance monitoring.

INS Enterprise Pro (http://www.ins.com/)

Enterprise Pro is a network monitoring service from International Network Services. They will monitor your web sites and provide web-based reports of latency, throughput, error conditions, and trends.

Keynote Perspective and similar tools (http://www.keynote.com/)

Keynote Perspective is a monitoring service from Keynote Systems, featuring real-time measurement and reporting of web site performance from almost 100 sites around the U.S. The reports can be viewed via the Web and include statistics on latency, so they provide a good overview of how users really perceive your site's performance from various locations. Similar services are available from Service Metrics (*http://www.servicemetrics.com/*), NetCool (*http://www. netcool.com/*), Freshwater Software's SiteScope and SiteSeer services (*http://www. freshtech.com/*), and several other companies. I know of at least one small site that consisted entirely of dynamic content and discontinued using Keynote because its frequent monitoring was increasing the load on their servers beyond an amount they considered acceptable. If you really think about these tools, you find it is in fact remarkably silly to test the Internet for everyone as if load information about this shared medium were unique to them.

Mercury Topaz ActiveWatch (http://topazactivewatch.merc-int.com/)
Mercury Interactive's Topaz ActiveWatch provides a geographically dispersed monitoring service similar to Keynote Perspective.

Multi Router Traffic Grapher (http://www.mrtg.org/)
One very popular free open source tool for network performance monitoring is MRTG-Multi Router Traffic Grapher, by Tobias Oetiker. It is available from *http://www.mrtg.org/* or *http://people.ee.ethz.ch/~oetiker* and is used at many sites worldwide. MRTG uses SNMP and freeware plotting to generate real-time graphs of router traffic viewable over the Web.

ProactiveNet (http://www.proactivenet.com/)
Proprietary API for monitoring, server for gathering on a separate computer, agents which seem to be tiny browsers, displays are HTML, which is nice. Does correlate abnormalities. Can monitor CPU utilization, database-response time, network-interface utilization, etc. Relatively clean interface.

Prognosis (http://www.ir.com/)
Integated Research first became known for its Tandem monitoring tools, but it has since branched out into tools for Solaris and other Unix operating systems. Prognosis, the flagship product, consists of an agent on each machine, which come with an integrated data repository. This means that data is kept locally on the machine it is collected from, not in a central database. Data is compressed to conserve space. Prognosis includes monitors for CPU, IO, network activity, and other system parameters, and includes the ability to trigger alarms at specified activity levels.

RAPS (http://www.foglight.com/)
RAPS, or the Real-time Applications Performance System, is a product from Foglight Software that monitors applications, servers, and networks through lightweight agents that report back to a central server at regular intervals. Collected data can be analyzed to determine current capacity and predict when components will need to be upgraded to handle increasing load. A rules engine can look for certain correlations in real-time data and initiate corrective actions.

Resolve (http://www.crosskeys.com/)
CrossKeys sells a product called Resolve that monitors WAN service-level agreements (SLAs) for frame relay, voice, and ATM. It generates reports that are valuable in determining whether you are actually getting the telecommunication services you are paying for.

Resonate (http://www.resonate.com/)
Although Resonate is really a load balancing tool, it does its load balancing through constant monitoring. It's monitoring information is available in web page format if you use the Enterprise Services Console, and this is very useful for

an up-to-the moment picture of performance. One drawback is that it is rather hard to figure out which machines are being referred to by a Resonate IP address unless you have access to the Resonate console, which few people usually do. Compare this with Round Robin DNS, in which anyone can easily see which IP addresses are included in a DNS name by using the free *nslookup* tool.

SE toolkit (http://www.sun.com/sunworldonline/swol-01-1998/swol-01-perf.html)
The SE toolkit by Adrian Cockcroft and Rich Pettit is actually a Unix system performance monitoring and analysis kit, not a web performance monitoring tool per se. Since the operating system greatly affects web server performance, however, it is a good idea to keep this tool running to collect statistics for analysis. It monitors TCP throughput, TCP connections, TCP retransmits, NIC rates, collisions and overruns, CPU and disk-utility levels, and memory-residence time of applications. The SE package also includes some log file data collection and analysis tools that work with the Common Log File format, but these are written in a custom interpreted dialect of C and run only on Solaris for SPARC or x86.

Symon
Sun Microsystems' Symon reads SNMP, has a Java GUI, and has Solaris-specific agents.

Tivoli (http://www.tivoli.com/)
Tivoli from IBM seems to be a bunch of things. It's a log file warehouse, software distribution system, and many monitoring tools and rules. I haven't used it myself, but have heard that it can easily generate so many alerts that users simply turn it off rather than sift through them all for the significant ones. See *http://www.tivoli.com*, but don't expect a simple explanation from that site.

Veritas FirstWatch (http://www.veritas.com/)
Veritas FirstWatch has a monitoring component that exists only so that Veritas will know when to fail over to a backup machine.

Visual UpTime (http://www.visualnetworks.com/)
Visual UpTime is another WAN service-level management system. It automates the collection, interpretation, and presentation of WAN service-level data for frame relay, ATM, leased lines, X.25, and the Internet.

xperfmon
A free X-based monitoring tool from *ftp.x.org*.

Other tools in this category include *sarcheck* from *http://www.sarcheck.com/*, Oracle Enterprise Manager, NetView from IBM, Sun Microsystems' Domain/SunNet/Site Manager, CA Unicenter, AnySpeed, Transaction Tracker by Measureware, Service Metrics, www.webmeter.net, Network Physics, FireClick, LastMile, and 2wire bandwidth meter at *http://www.2wire.com/*.

Load Generation Tools

There are nearly as many load generation tools as monitoring tools. Again, this list just skims the surface. The problem with load testing tools is tools that record GUI actions like clicks are easy to use to create scripts, but hard to scale because you need as many GUI's as virtual clients. Tools that are not GUI-based, like my own *sprocket* (see Chapter 4), have problems, such as they have a hard time recording SSL and dealing with cases where URL rewriting is used to store state information, but they are much more scalable.

CapCal (http://www.capcal.com/)
> Load testing over the Internet. Stands for Capacity Calibration.

EJB Test (http://www.ejbtest.com/)
> EJB Test is a web-based system that queries your EJB's for their methods and exercises them, drawing graphs of their response time. It is not actually a web performance tool. It is very expensive, with prices starting at $30,000, but does a good job in a difficult situation. EJB's are hard to test because the client piece is usually a proprietary Java GUI using a protocol specific to that application.

eValid (http://www.soft.com/eValid/)
> eValid seems to be a modified version of IE for load testing. It also does functional tests. It records tests via the browser. It is a Windows-only tool, and the demo version is a bit buggy. I didn't understand the performance result charts after doing a simple script.

Mercury Loadrunner
> Loadrunner is a GUI-based scripting tool. Because it is GUI-based, it can record a script even if URL's are keeping state, but those scripts are not scalable. How do you run 1,000 of them? 10,00PCs?

Microsoft Web Application Stress (http://www.microsoft.com/)
> Free, native Microsoft Web capacity analysis tool. Runs on Windows only, specialized for testing ASP and IIS.

PointForward (http://pointforward.compuware.com/scalability/)
> Load testing over the Internet. Owned by Compuware.

Velometer (http://www.binaryevolution.com/velometer/velometer.vet)
> Java-based load generation and response measurement tool for http.

VTS (http://www.sun.com/microelectronics/vts/)
> From Sun Microsystems. VTS is mostly a fault-finding tool, but also used for load testing.

WebSizr (http://www.technovations.com)
> WebSizr is a web loading client that can simulate up to 200 simultaneous HTTP users and record the results. The program runs on Windows only, but it can generate a load to test any HTTP server.

Some other web load tools include ApacheBench from the Apache project, JMeter, *www.webperfcenter.com/*, RadView WebLoad and WebQuantify.

Preloaders

Users on slow dial-up connections might benefit from the class of products that download links in the background while the current page is loading, but the benefit of these tools is slight and it is rude to download many pages you will never even look at.

Preloaders include SpeedSurfer, TurboExplorer, Legion (preloads IP addresses of bookmarks, removing DNS lookup time), *www.SolidSpeed.com*, BoostWeb, *www.fireclick.com*, and Blueflame. Blueflame is a proxy server, which downloads an invisible Java applet that prebrowses for you.

Network Optimizers

The following products can be used to optimize your network connection.

MTU Tuners

This is the class of products that attempts to set your TCP parameters, especially Maximum Transmission Unit, to values most appropriate for your connection. PPP Boost, MTU-speed pro, NetMedic, and Vital Signs (*http://www.ins.com/*).

Optimal Application Expert

Optimal Networks (*http://www.optimal.com/*) is now owned by Compuware Corporation (*http://www.compware.com/*). Optimal Application Expert is a Windows application that captures network traffic and generates various graphs from it. In trying it myself, I found many of the graphs hard to understand, although the use of the tool itself is reasonably intuitive. It is useful because *snoop* and *traceroute* are not standard tools on NT, as they are on Solaris. As is typical for Windows-based tools, the fact that it is GUI-based gets in the way of scripting actions and using resulting data in other applications.

IP Traffic Management Products

One problem with IP is that all packets are treated the same regardless of the latency and throughput requirements of higher-level protocols. This can be solved with one of the recent IP traffic-management products (also known as "traffic shaping" products), quality of service (QOS) boxes, or bandwidth-management products. Some of these products are actually hardware boxes, while others are new software for network hardware.

These products classify and tag IP packets as belonging to different priority levels. When packets are queued up at a router, the traffic shaping product will rearrange the queue depending on priorities. In addition, measurements are taken of network health and of which classes are using what fraction of the bandwidth. Packets from streams that have exceeded a bandwidth allocation may be thrown away. Note that quality of service is relative here: some packets are treated as more important than others, but no guarantee is made about overall latency or throughput. Contrast this with ATM, which does provide hard latency and throughput specifications for different classes of service. ATM can do this, because as a connectionful layer 2 protocol, it has direct control of the physical wire from one end of the connection to the other. IP is a layer 3 protocol and has no direct control over the layer 2 protocol that carries it (ATM, Ethernet, Frame Relay). So you won't find any guarantee that you can make an acceptable voice call over the Internet.

While you can't control the Internet, you can control your own intranet, so you can dictate packet policies and put them into your organization's routers or other network hardware. You may need a single-vendor network to do it, so lock-in is a problem. RSVP, an Internet protocol to accomplish essentially the same thing, has a similar problem because it requires that every router along an RSVP path obey the protocol. A couple of disadvantages to these products are that they add an amount of latency proportional to the number of QOS classes you define, and they don't help at all in cases of extreme congestion, in which packets of all classes may be thrown out anyway.

Here are some of the leading IP traffic-management products:

CheckPoint Software (http://www.checkpoint.com/)
> CheckPoint was first known for firewall software but now has the FloodGate-1 product to allow data prioritization on LANs.

Cisco's Internet QOS (http://www.cisco.com/)
> Cisco is the 800-pound gorilla of IP networking, with by far the largest market share for routers. It is adding QOS features to its router operating system, IOS 11. 1. These features will communicate and synchronize prioritization policy between routers. The product seems designed to keep networks locked in to Cisco.

NetScaler (http://www.netscaler.com/)
> NetScaler 3100 is a rack-mountable hardware product that sits in front of the web server and maintains dedicated HTTP 1.1 persistent connections to the web server, reducing the load on the web server because it has fewer connections to manage by itself. Prices start at $20,000.

Packeteer (http://www.packeteer.com/)
> Packeteer has a hardware product that allocates bandwidth and figures out what sort of web response a client can handle by the rate at which the request came in; it can distinguish a 14.4 client from T1 client and generate a reply that the client can handle.

Sun Bandwidth Allocator (http://www.sun.com/software/band-allocator/)
> Sun's Bandwidth Allocator software is a streams module that performs policy-based bandwidth allocation, for example, to prevent FTP from using more bandwidth than HTTP, or to control which domains get the best service.

Torrent (http://www.torrentnet.com/)
> Torrent supposedly has a guaranteed minimum bandwidth mechanism for IP, not just a reprioritization mechanism.

Xedia (http://www.xedia.com/)
> Xedia's Access Point hardware and software products handle IP traffic-shaping, monitoring, and management. They are mostly appropriate for ISPs.

Content Compressors

There are a few products, such as Gifwizard (*http://www.gifwizard.com/*) and Fineground Networks' Condenser (a proxy), that attempt to compress your web content before or while serving it.

Condenser

Fineground Networks Condenser product (*http://www.fineground.com/*) is a proxy that sits in front of the web server and uses the DOM and JavaScript features of the latest browsers to forward back to the browser only the difference between the page requested and any previous copy of the page the browser may have cached. This of course results in far less network traffic and potentially far better responsiveness. The Condenser uses a cookie to track customers and which pages they have seen. It must terminate HTTPS connections itself, of course, or would not be able to see the content. This may be a problem if you have many HTTPS servers. The size of the condenser's cache may also be a problem. Finally, clever use of JavaScript to allow access to the DOM feature of fractional page downloads can get all of the benefits of the Condenser. Pricing starts at $50,000.

T/X 2100 Series from Redline Networks

Redline's product (*http://www.redlinenetworks.com/*) compresses content and tries to reduce the number of packets through use of proprietary hardware and software. The hardware sits in front of the web server and keeps dedicated connections open to the web server, thus offloading the work of opening and shutting connections. Pricing starts at $59,000.

Hybrid Development Tools/Databases

The following tools integrate proprietary web development tools, clients, and databases.

FileMaker

FileMaker is both the name of a company and its Windows and Macintosh products, which include databases and a web server "connector" that allows publishing of the database to web pages, as well as a proprietary client for viewing data. See *http://www.filemaker.com/*. As a database, FileMaker is more sophisticated than a simple spreadsheet, yet not as complex as a more standard relational database such as Oracle. It is easier to learn than most database products, but the simplification of learning and use comes at the cost of performance and scalability, as well as the hazard that come with learning to do things only in a proprietary way. FileMaker Pro and the "Unlimited" version are single-threaded. FileMaker Server 5, a database server, is advertised as supporting up to 250 concurrent Windows and Mac OS guests. If you know you will not need to scale beyond this level and are running your servers on Windows or Macintosh, File-Maker is a reasonable choice. But for large-scale sites that need very high performance, I would recommend a Unix-based web site.

Microsoft Access

Microsoft Access is another Windows-based database and proprietary client, and is rather like FileMaker. The Access client can also connect to Microsoft SQL Server, a higher-end database, but this will not necessarily overcome the limitations inherent in Access. To quote *http://www.sql-server-performance.com/access.asp*, "If you are really interested in the fastest performance, don't use Access as a front-end to a SQL Server database." It simply wasn't designed for high performance, but instead for ease of learning.

Tango

Tango, not to be confused with a browser by the same name, is a proprietary visual application development environment for the web. You can drag and drop COM objects and JavaBeans onto their application server and connect to ODBC-compliant databases. It is advertised as running on Windows, Macintosh, Solaris, and Linux. Again, runtime performance is sacrificed in favor of rapid development and ease of learning. See *http://www.witango.com/*.

Lasso

Lasso from BlueWorld (*http://www.blueworld.com/*) is a set of web authoring and serving tools. As an application server, Lasso runs on web servers and connects to databases, typically between IIS and SQL Server on Windows. It is multithreaded. Lasso publishes good comparison performance tests of its products against ColdFusion, FileMaker, ASP, and Tango.

Cold Fusion

ColdFusion is yet another visual programming interface and web application server. It is made by Allaire (*http://www.allaire.com/*). It is multithreaded. It uses proprietary extensions to HTML called CFML (Cold Fusion Markup Language). The server runs on Windows, Solaris, HP-UX, and Linux.

Java Profilers and Optimizers

Code profiling is a well-established field for finding where your code is spending its time and how it is using memory. Here are just a few tools that can be used to profile and optimize Java: DashO, OptimizeIt, NuMega, TrueTune, Intel Vtune, Visual Quantify, Rational Performance Studio, and Gnu *gprof*.

Caching Services

There are now dozens of companies willing to mirror your web content at geographically scattered sites. The most popular seem to be Akamai and Inktomi, but there are also ANS (*http://www.ans.net/*), owned by AOL; Exodus Communications; GlobalCenter (*http://www.isi.net/*), which bought ISI; GTE/BBN; InterNex; MCI; and Sandpiper.

Mirroring services and products can save you telecommunications costs because users are closer to content, especially if you are currently running an extranet with dedicated long-distance links. Note that mirroring is also a good way of getting fault tolerance if the system is set up to reroute requests when a server is down. Software to manage the mirroring (that is, to choose the best server for a given request and to ensure that data is replicated quickly and correctly across the servers) is still immature.

Content replication across mirror sites is possible with products from F5 Labs (*http://www.f5labs.com/*), Inktomi (*http://www.inktomi.com/*), Studebaker (*http://www.tigereye.com/*), and Versant (*http://www.versant.com/*).

Professional Services

Most professional service organizations will be happy to work on web performance problems. IBM is by far the largest, but by no means the only such company. Competitors include *www.hudsonwilliams.com*, Sun Professional Services, and myself.

Load Balancers

Load balancing and caching are moving out of dedicated boxes and services and into the network itself, especially into routers.

LocalDirector and DistributedDirector
> Cisco (*http://www.cisco.com/*) sells load balancing products named LocalDirector and DistributedDirector. LocalDirector is a dedicated hardware box that cannot be used for anything else once it is obsolete. It is also a single point of failure and may itself become a bottleneck, though it can be configured in a fail-safe configuration—by having two or more of them as a cluster. Go to *http://www.cisco.com/*, and search for "localdirector" to get more details. LocalDirector rewrites IP headers to redirect a connection to the local server with the most

available capacity. It apparently judges capacity by network usage rather than server machine statistics because it runs no processes on the actual web server. Because of this, it is not a true load balancing tool and may not be appropriate for use with servers of differing capacity. The end user, application, and DNS server have no idea that this sort of balancing is happening; it's transparent to them. This lets many servers share one externally visible IP address, rather like Resonate.

DistributedDirector is intended for geographically dispersed servers. You can either set up a DistributedDirector DNS service that will return the IP of the closest server or you can have it send the HTTP reply status code "302 Temporarily Moved" containing the name of the most appropriate server, which the browser will then use to get the page. DistributedDirector figures out the distance in router-hops and directs the user to the closest server. It does not, however, analyze the performance of the servers and make judgments based on that information, so you may indeed be using the topologically closest server, but that may not give the best performance.

You can use DistributedDirector to maintain one URL that redirects users to your other web servers around the world. One downside of these products is that they are based on proprietary hardware that has a single point of failure, namely the hardware itself. Another problem is that since they map one IP address to many, you have the same problem maintaining state that you do with round robin DNS. DistributedDirector provides a "sticky" option to keep a user hitting the same server for this reason.

Resonate Dispatch

Dispatch from Resonate, Inc. (*http://www.resonate.com/*) is a software-only load balancing tool with no single point of failure. It does not require redundant hardware for failover. Dispatch sets up a single IP address as the address of multiple web servers, rather like Cisco's products. It uses resource-based scheduling to allocate load, so it is a true load balancing tool. Dispatch does maintain state and can be used for transaction processing sites. One problem I've experienced with Resonate that its constant checking of server health can itself be a significant load. The interval between checks can be turned down from every few seconds to once per minute or less, meaning there is more risk that a user will be routed to a down server, but less overhead. Resonate uses up IP addresses and requires some intelligence to maintain but is also happens to be an excellent performance monitoring tool

lbnamed

lbnamed is a load balancing name daemon that allows one DNS name to map to a dynamically changing group of machines. The actual machine chosen depends on the loading of the various machines. A machine may be in multiple groups and so have more than one DNS name under *lbnamed*.

lbnamed was written in Perl by Roland J. Schemers III, and it is freely available from *http://www-leland.stanford.edu/~schemers/docs/lbnamed/lbnamed.html*.

Network Dispatcher

IBM's Network Dispatcher is another load balancing solution which maps a single IP address to a set of servers connected by a LAN. Network Dispatcher chooses a machine according to a set of weights you specify and rewrites IP headers to direct a request to one of the servers, so it is independent of DNS. Network Dispatcher is available from IBM at *http://www.ics.raleigh.ibm.com/ netdispatch/netspec.htm*.

Web Server Director from RND

Web Server Director (WSD) is an intelligent load-balancer for identical-content machines. It is a hardware product supporting two or four Ethernet or two fast Ethernet ports. A single virtual IP address can represent and load balance a "farm" of servers. WSD can handle 512 virtual IP addresses and up to 50,000 servers. The load is balanced according to one of three load balancing algorithms, which allow some servers to operate at higher loads than others. Servers can be configured to backup other servers. Server failure detection is supported physically and/or in the application.

A few other load balancing tools are Arrowpoint, Radware, Sun Bandwidth Manager, and Big/IP.

Modeling Tools

HyPerformix tries to let you model application and network capacity. Optimal Application Expert models network capacity only. I'm skeptical of the utility of modeling compared to actual load testing.

Index

Symbols

(hash mark), 57
~ (tilde)
  as shorthand, 311
  file prefixes, 189
_ (underscore), 74
/ (slash)
  ending with, 350
  in paths, 74
  URLs and, 257

Numbers

100BaseT Ethernet, 47, 222
10BaseT Ethernet, 217
32-bit registers
  CPU considerations and, 196
  improving performance with, 189
  memory addresses and, 270
  memory spaces and, 301
56K lines, 213
64-bit registers, 196, 270
68K emulation, 191
80/20 rule, 164

A

abort intervals, 244
abortive release, 175
absolute performance, 49
Accelerated Graphics Port (AGP) cards, 200
accept() system call, 312
Access Point (Xedia), 419
ACID criteria, 20

ACK, delays sending, 247
Activator Virtual Machine, 184
ActiveX control, 44, 184
Address Resolution Protocol (ARP), 236
address spaces, 301
Adminserver tool, 343
ADSL (Aymmetric Digital Subscriber
        Line), 8, 213
AGP cards, 200
AIFF format (Apple), 356
AIM Technology, 413
AIX operating system
  features, 293
  rpc.rstatd daemon and, 77
  setting file descriptors settings, 314
Akamai, 13, 14, 21, 31
A-law, 356
AllowOverride parameter, 335
aload, 395
<ALT> tags
  HTML authoring tips, 352
  size parameters for images, 12
  text description and, 8
AltaVista, query strings in, 368
Amaya browser, 178
AMI BIOS, 203
amplitude, carrier state and, 206
analysis.cgi, 116–118
analyze command (Netscape), 120
animation, 355
AOL (ISP), 226, 338
Apache servers
  CGIs to run tools, 84
  configuring, 335–338

We'd like to hear your suggestions for improving our indexes. Send email to *index@oreilly.com*.

dynamic content
    as CPU-bound process, 35
    caching, 173
    CGI programs and, 359
    considering need for, 16
    database connections and, 409
    DOM and, 377
    generation trends for, 31
    proxy caches and, 345
    separate boxes for, 29
    server considerations and, 13
    sizing server around, 48
Dynamic Random Access Memory
        (DRAM), 197, 268

E

echo cancellation, 206
echo command, 3, 186
Eden (memory space), 400
EIDE disks, 14, 199, 287
EISA bus, 46, 198
EJB Test tool, 417
EJBs
    cautions using, 28
    considerations using, 17
    Java coding tips, 394
elevator algorithm, 286
eMikolo, 187
emulation
    CPU considerations and, 195
    Macintosh users, 191
    problems with, 102
encoding, carrier signal states and, 206
encryption
    compression and, 146
    HTTPS and, 143
Enterprise Java Beans, 28, 262
Enterprise Pro (INS) monitoring tool, 414
error handling
    causing failures, 139
    error rates, 235
    HTML and, 353, 370
    Java coding tips, 393
    modems and correction, 208
    testing for conditions, 101
/etc/resolv.conf (Linux)
    resolving DNS names, 5
    using different DNS servers, 11

/etc/system
    configuring full-duplex Ethernet, 218
    maxuproc, 301
    viewing current settings, 312
Ethernet
    bandwidth comparison, 46
    bridges and, 216
    features of, 217–223
    latency and, 54
    load balancing and, 27
    misconfigured connections, 16
    network speed and, 38
    performance degradation with, 40
    recommendations, 8
    RMON and, 98
eValid load generation tool, 417
event listeners, 386
Exceed, as X Windows server emulator, 67
exec() system call, 300, 329, 360
Executor emulation, 195
Exokernel, 328
Expect scripting language, 58
Expersoft Java ORBs, 262
Extended Data Output (EDO) RAM, 198
extensions, system resources and, 193
external modems
    cable issues, 209
    checking connection to computer, 3
    send/read lights, 4
Externalizable interface, 394
eXtreme Programming web site, 22

F

failover
    split-brain syndrome and, 140
    system availability and, 43
FancyIndexing, 337
Fast Ethernet
    bandwidth comparison, 46
    busses and, 267
    features of, 221
    recommendations, 8
Fast Page RAM, 198
FastCGI, 49, 299, 370, 375
FDDI
    as alternative to Ethernet, 221
    bandwidth comparison, 46
    default MTU, 217

ifconfig -a command
    Ethernet and, 217
    synchronizing systems and, 101
    viewing interfaces and MTUs, 237
iload, 395
images
    autoloading and performance, 8
    automatic loading of, 181
    composite imagemaps, 165
    consolidation of, 354
    loading with Netscape, 12
    rendering, 195
    scaling, 352
    sizing considerations, 354
<IMG> tags
    including image size in, 355
    performance and, 174
    SIZE option and, 351
indexes
    Apache servers and, 337
    benefit of, 368
    databases and, 408
index.html, 350
inetd process, 77, 329
inetinit, 312
infinite loops, 361–364
Informix Web Database, 408
inheritance chains, 384
Inktomi caching services, 21
inlining
    cautions, 373
    Java coding tips, 386
    -O option and, 395
inodes, 304, 306
INS (International Network Services), 414
INSERT statement (SQL), 261
instance variables, 381
instructions
    clock cycles and, 268
    CPU processing of, 270
Integrated Drive Electronics (IDE) disks
    bandwidth comparison, 46
    disk considerations, 14
    evolution of, 265
    features of, 287
    hard disk standard, 199
    scalability and, 42
Integrated Research Prognosis, 415
Integrated Service Digital Network (ISDN)
    bandwidth and, 8
    broadband ISDN, 46

capabilities of, 211
coaxial cable as alternative to, 212
disadvantages to, 212
web server bandwidth requirements, 47
Intel Quick Web, 346
Intense3D (Intergraph), 200
Inter-Cache Protocol (ICP), 346
interface definition language (IDL), 262
interfaces
    as choke points, 206
    CGI as, 360
    kernel and, 295
    program interconnectibility and, 23
    server speeds to, 267
internationalization (i18n), 381
Internet
    audio quality, 357
    bandwidth limitations of, 51
    bandwidth measurements with bing, 58
    connection time considerations, 49
    cost efficiency of, 60
    getting connected, xii
    hardware considerations, 223–231
    latency on, 205
    performance degradation, 164
    performance statistics, 179
    speed considerations, 161
    URL for socket programming, 172
    web server connections to, 215
Internet Control Message Protocol
        (ICMP), 56, 239
Internet Explorer (Microsoft), 398
    auto completing URLs, 183
    displaying images in, 9
    DOM support, 24
    features of, 176
    gzip decompression support, 178
    HTTP 1.1 and, 258
    memory leaks and, 183
    performance improvements in, 9
    as proprietary platform, 44
    Spyglass and, 171
Internet Information Server (IIS)
    cautions using, 27
    features, 343
    as proprietary platform, 44
Internet Protocol (IP)
    data packets and hops, 13
    features of, 237–240
    traffic management products, 418–419
    trailer encapsulation, 302

Java Plug-Ins, 177, 401
Java programs
  ease of thread programming, 272
  memory leaks and, 135
  monitoring sample, 93–96
  multithreading and, 166
  native threads and, 49
  runtime options, 400–402
Java Virtual Machine (JVM)
  as CPU, 271
  benchmarks for, 402
  browsers and, 367
  bytecode interpretation and, 380
  emulation and, 196
  Linux support, 193
  prestarting, 185
  reclaiming memory, 303
  setting -verbosegc, 16
  startup time considerations, 10
  threads and, 390
  TimeSys, 31
  tuning browsers and, 184
Java VM Profiling Interface (JVMPI), 396
Java Web Server, 344
javac compiler, 395
javap -c, 397
JavaScript
  Condenser product and, 420
  moving error checking to, 370
  Neoplanet and, 177
  proprietary extensions and, 44
  state of the art, 353
  trends in dynamic page generation, 31
  validating use input with, 365–367
Javasoft, 396, 399
JavaSpec (Sun), 396
JCC static compiler, 398
JDBC (see Java DataBase Connectivity
    standard (JDBC))
JDK (see Java Development Kit (JDK))
Jigsaw web server, 344, 350
JITs (see just in time compilers (JITs))
joins, virtual memory and, 406
JPEG format, 354, 355
jProbe (The KL Group), 387, 396
JSP
  HTML tags and, 377
  strings in servlets, 392
jumpers, 201
just in time compilers (JITs)
  Java coding tips, 380, 384, 388
  memory leaks and, 135
  open source JITs, 279

problems with profilers, 396
specifics, 397
synchronization and, 391
System.currentTimeMillis(), 403
JXTA (Sun), 187

K

Kaffe, 398
Keep It Simple, Stupid (KISS), 370
keepalive interval, 245, 314
keepalives (see persistent connections)
KeepAliveTimeout, 245, 336
kernel
  cache for recently opened files, 307
  clock changes and, 101
  device drivers and memory, 266
  Linux as, 294
  memory usage and, 50
  processes and, 295–304
  TCP/IP implementation in, 267
  threads as LWPs, 281
  timing considerations, 105
  upgrading, 194
keyboard shortcuts
  eliminating button usage, 185
  Linux, 183
Keynote Systems
  ISPs and server software, 32
  Keynote Perspective, 414
  measuring Internet performance, 224
  monitoring service, 98
khttpd web server, 299
kill command, 106, 362
killall command, 362
The KL Group, 396
ktrace tracing utility, 320

L

L1 caches
  features of, 196
  purpose of, 269
  servers and, 265
L2 caches
  features of, 198
  purpose of, 269
  servers and, 265
Land Attacks, 114
LANs
  bandwidth/speed considerations, 8
  latency of, 46
laptops, 203

Network Time Protocol (NTP) packets, 240
networks
    buffer features, 14, 314
    cached pages and, 181
    DNS server considerations, 11
    Ethernet and speed, 38
    factors affecting performance, 235
    generating loads, 107
    HTML authoring tips, 351
    modeling tools, 223
    monitoring programs, 249
    optimizer tools, 418
    overloaded hardware, 16
    verifying potential access, 40
    Windows utilities, 190
\n (newline), 186
newline character, 186
newsgroups (Perl), 372
Next Generation Internet (NGI), 231
nextItem() method, 391
NextStep operating system, 294
NFS servers, 15, 41
NIC (see Network Interface Card (NIC))
nice, 316
NNTP server, 15
nobody
    user defined, 138
    web server processes as, 363
non-parsed header (NPH) scripts, 84, 364
notify() method, 390, 391
notifyAll method, 391
-noverify option, 400
NS LiveWire Pro, 409
nscd -d (Solaris), 252
nslookup, 194
Number Nine (video drivers), 201

O

obj.conf, 136, 339
Object Request Broker (ORB), 262
object-oriented (OO) programming, 24, 381
objects
    Java coding tips, 386
    passing as parameters, 394
ObjectSpace Voyager, 262, 367
offered window, 246
offline mode, 5
on-chip cache, 196
Open DataBase Connectivity standard
    (ODBC), 407

Open Market FastCGI, 375
open() system call, 289
Open Transport TCP/IP, 191
OpenBSD, 77
OpenView tools (HP), 98, 414
Opera browser
    capabilities of, 9
    DOM support, 24
    features of, 177
operating systems
    configurable parameters, 312–316
    full filesystems and, 306
    memory for, 50
    power conservation considerations, 11
    purpose of, 291
    QNX, 296
    real-time, 30
    reclaiming memory, 302
    recommendations, 14, 15
    reducing load on, 299
    scalability considerations, 42
    system availability and, 43
    uname -a command, 312
    Unix monitoring tools, 316–320
    Unix versus NT, 326–327
    VM recommendations, 399
    (see also specific operating systems)
operators, 387
OPNET (Mil3), 223
Optical Carrier 3 (OP3), 214
optical fiber, Fibre Channel and, 288
Optimal Application Expert, 223, 418
Optimal Networks, 223, 418
optimization
    based on patterns of requests, 161
    CPU process, 270
    -O option, 395
    performance and, 158
    for usage patterns, 167
OptimizeIt, 387, 392, 396
Options FollowSymLinks, 337
Oracle
    Linux and, 294
    one-box web sites, 29
    outputting Perl DBI data, 80
Oracle WebServer, 409
ORACLE_HOME, 80
orb.init(), 387
Orbix Java ORBs, 262
OSI network model, 222

P

packet sizes
   CPU power and, 230
   error rates and, 235
   for Ethernet, 217
   MTU and, 238
   PPP and, 236
Packeteer, 419
packets
   bastion hosts and, 147
   dropping intermittently, 151–153
   hops and, 13
   maximum IP size, 237
   MTUs and, 217
   NAPs and, 226
   ping statistics and, 224
   routing manually, 227
   snooping example, 218–221
   switched Ethernet and, 221
   TCP/IP and, 267
   unreliability of Frame Relay, 214
   web performance and, 45
   (see also IP packets)
pages (see web pages)
paging
   defined, 301
   memory shortage and, 14
paint() method, 393
par tracing utility, 320
parallel processing, 46, 166
parameters
   configurable for OS, 312–316
   database connections, 409
   in Solaris 2.6, 293
   maximum seek time, 286
   MSL, 245
   passing objects as, 394
   performance monitoring, 53–62
   sizing parameters, 37
   Solaris TCP, 248
   TCP, 241
parent process ID (PPID), 362
parsing
   CPU load and, 195
   CPU usage and, 174
   HTML authoring tips, 351
   Interse, 120
   URLs, 173
partitioning, intranets and, 215–217
patches
   considerations, 139
   recommendations for applying, 312

showrev -p, 312
   using latest, 241
PATH, 310
Path MTU Discovery, 238
pathnames
   directories and, 306
   recommendations for short, 334
Patrol CGI Analyzer (BMC), 413
Patrol Knowledge Module for Internet
         Servers (BMC), 413
PCI bus, 47, 198, 199, 268
PCMCIA slot, 3
Pendragon CaffeineMark benchmark, 114
perfbar monitoring tool, 317
perfdump, 342
perfmeter command
   as rpc.rstatd client, 77
   features, 317
   monitoring CPU usage, 269
   monitoring paging/swapping with, 301
   proxy server loads, 7
   rpc.rstatd daemon and, 76, 84
   system utilization and, 59
   troubleshooting cron interference, 15
   viewing average loads with, 296
perfmon monitoring tool, 318
performance considerations
   analysis.cgi, 116–118
   browsers, 3–11, 173
   causes of server failure, 333
   CGI internals and, 360
   compilers, 395
   component sizes and, 36
   CPU construction, 270–272
   disks, 289
   filename length, 307
   full filesystems, 306
   HTML, 350–354
   increasing system call priority, 299
   ISP usage and, 227
   latest versions and patches, 312
   limiting hardware access to kernel, 297
   network protocols and, 235
   poor NFS usage and, 252
   scalability and, 41
   Solaris and, 293
   swapping and, 301
   TCP limits, 241
   tempfs and, 305
   TP monitors and, 52
   troubleshooting routers, 5
   Unix, 292, 327

memory usage with, 51
process ID and, 362
Telnet example, 86
using CGIs to run tools, 84
viewing PID, 295
pseudo-terminal (pty), 137
pst, 304
PTT (Post, Telephone, Telegraph), 231
public keys, 143, 146
Public Switched Telephone Network
(PSTN), 206
Pulse Code Modulation (PCM), 356
Pure Software (Quantify), 374
PURE tool, 375
Purify tool, 43, 134, 334, 375
pushing spawned processes, 41
PVC (permanent virtual circuit), 214
pwfile, 341

Q

QNX real-time operating system, 296
quality of service (QOS), 214, 418
Quantify (Pure Software), 374
queries
cursors and, 406
databases and, 404, 407
preprocessing, 367–369
SQL, 75
Quick Web (Intel), 346
QuickRoute utility, 190

R

RAID (see Redundant Array of Inexpensive
Disks (RAID))
Rainbow, 144
RAM
bandwidth comparison, 46
databases in, 406
memory shortage and, 8
shared, 302
tempfs and, 305
wait states and, 269
(see also memory)
Ramp Network, 211
random access, 268
RAPS (Real-time Applications Performance
System), 415
Rational Visual Quantify, 396
rdist (Unix) command, 21
read() system call, 289, 311
read-ahead caching, 189

readFully() method, 391
reads
in Java, 379
Java coding tips, 389
Real Networks, 357
real-time operating system (RTOS), 30, 297
Receive WINdow (RWIN), 245
recursions, 363
Red Hat Linux, 77
redirects, 12
Redline Networks, 420
Reduced Instruction Set Chip (RISC), 196,
271
redundancy
hardware failures and, 137
performance improvement and, 167
SMP machines and, 49
Redundant Array of Inexpensive Disks
(RAID), 36, 44, 288
relational database management systems
(RDBMSs), 404, 405
relational databases
performance monitoring and, 75–76
storing results in, 86
storing rstat data in, 78
reliability
Solaris and, 293
typical failures, 133–142
Remote Method Invocation (RMI)
cautions using, 28
considerations using, 17
features of, 367
Java coding tips, 394
REMOTE_HOST (CGI environment
variable), 12, 370
repaint() method, 393
repeaters, 216
replication
solutions available, 21
versus simplicity, 20
requirements, 37–45
resolution, 201
Resolve (CrossKeys) monitoring tool, 415
resolver, 174
Resonate
advantage of, 136
Dispatch, 423
Global Director, 26
load balancing system, 98
Local Director, 26
monitoring tool, 415
recommendations using, 139
system outages and, 142

V

Van Jacobson compression, 240
variables
  bind variables, 406
  instance variables, 381
  Java and, 387, 388, 395
  local variables, 382, 388, 395
  stack variables, 385
vBNS, 58
Velocigen, 373
Velometer load generation tool, 417
vendors
  benchmarks and, 114
  open standards, 44
  reliance on specifications, 36
-verbosegc option
  Java runtime option, 400
  setting Java VM, 16
verification
  bytecodes and, 380
  -noverify option, 400
Veritas
  FirstWatch, 416
  VxFS filesystem, 307
video, 188, 200–202, 357
video RAM (VRAM), 200
VidSpeed 4.0, 201
virtual memory, 301, 406
Virtual Reality Modeling Language
      (VRML), 356
Visigenic ORB, 262, 387
Visual Quantify (Rational), 396
Visual UpTime, 416
Vital Signs Software, 5
vmstat command
  cache hit rate and, 308
  measuring memory usage, 304
  monitoring CPU usage, 269
  monitoring paging/swapping with, 301
  network snooping, 322
  rate of page scanning, 50
  rpc.rstatd daemon compared with, 77
  troubleshooting memory shortage, 14
  using CGIs to run tools, 84
voltage requirements, 197
Voyager (ObjectSpace), 262, 367
VTS (Sun) load generation tool, 417
VxFS filesystem (Veritas), 307

W

W3C validator, 353
wait states
  bus cycles, 198
  performance tuning and, 203
  RAM and, 269
.wav files (Microsoft), 356
wc (Unix program), 23
WDG validator, 353
Web Application Stress tool, 417
web browsers (see browsers)
web pages
  as database alternative, 405
  cached, 10, 11
  delays receiving, 6
  fractional downloads, 259–261
  grabbing, 186
  HTTP HEAD request and, 173
  memory segmented into, 301
  monitoring performance of, 90–96
  Netscape bug reloading, 176
  number of items on, 46
  optimum design for, 348
  SNCA caching, 299
  stripping HTML from, 186
  system dashboard example, 96, 98
  (see also dynamic content)
  (see also static content)
Web Server Director (WSD), 424
web servers
  benchmark tests and, 111
  capacity planning, 41
  causes of failure in, 333
  cautions for programmers, 41
  CGI as interface, 360
  configuring, 334–343
  connection limits, 323
  copying data in memory, 302
  as databases, 408
  development of, 292
  evolution of, 329–331
  features missing from, 345
  forking new processes, 325–326
  functions needed, 297
  HTML authoring tips, 350
  HTTP operations per second, 37–38
  httpd software, 292
  khttpd, 299
  listed, 343–344

web servers *(continued)*
load balancing and, 27
major Unix versions for, 292–295
maximum number of processes, 324
network bandwidth, 47
opening Telnet sessions, 5
overloading, 135
placing on intranets, 215
popular, 32
server silence, 118
Solaris parameters, 293
streaming media sizing and, 40
system availability and, 43
system calls and, 331–333
tuning, 264
typical reasons for slowdowns, 17
Unix versus NT, 326–327
unnecessary processes on, 15
UPSs and, 43
web sites
architecture, 19–33
fundamentals of setting up, xii
HTTP 1.1 specification, 257
outage times for, 344
sizing for purpose, 38
software examples, xvii
static compilers, 398
webget tool (Perl), 60
weblint, 353
Weblogic
CLF and, 124
clustering features, 21
connection pool configuration and, 407
reconnecting databases, 140
threads in, 383
WebNFS, 312
WebRamp M3t, 211
WebSizr load generation tool, 417
WebStone benchmark, 112
WebTV, 177
whatroute utility (Macintosh), 190
wide UltraSCSI, 287
wildcards
cautions with Apache servers, 337
wrong files and, 138
windowing systems
considerations, 311
server hardware and, 264
web servers and, 15

Windows
defragmentation needs of, 289
defragmenting, 309
IE bundling with, 176
Mosaic browser and, 178
Netscape, 175, 398
Network Control Panel, 11
Opera browser and, 177
operating system features, 188–193
round robin DNS and, 251
service packs, 189
terminal mode and, 15
Windows 95
System Monitor tool, 190
Windows NT
clustering and, 44
IE bundling with, 176
scalability considerations, 42
SMP and, 273
taskmanager tool, 189
Unix versus, 326–327
Windows RAM (WRAM), 200
win.ini files, 188
Winsock under Windows, 189
Wintach 1.2, 201
Wisconsin Proxy Benchmark, 114
World Wide Web Consortium (W3C), 178,
257, 259–261
Worldcom, 225
write(), 311
write-behind caching, 189
writeln() statement, 367
writes
defragmenting and, 309
flushing frequency and, 315
Java coding tips, 389
queued up, 308

X

X Window System, 67, 263, 294
Xbench for Xfree86, 201
xDSL, 213
Xedia Access Point, 419
XFree86, 294
xload monitoring tool, 320
XML, 44

-Xmsn option, 400
-Xmxn option, 400
xntpd (Unix), 101
Xon/Xoff flow control, 209
xperfmon monitoring tool, 416
XSL, 31
Xvfb command, 77, 312

About the Author

Patrick Killelea currently works for a major online brokerage, but he won't say which one. He spends his days writing monitoring and load testing tools, and proclaiming the Web to be the one true frontend because of its simplicity, portability, and performance. He thinks Microsoft is not to be trusted with your backend. Patrick knows there are huge web performance improvements yet to be realized using the details of existing open protocols. He is a fan of T/TCP and hopes one day to set up a connection and deliver an entire web page all in a single packet.

Patrick spends his evenings playing with his wife and kids, and is interested in etymologies, obscure religions, and pan-seared salmon with mixed greens and a nice merlot. He likes to get email about web and Java performance issues. Please visit his web site at *http://patrick.net* or email him at *p@patrick.net*.

Colophon

Our look is the result of reader comments, our own experimentation, and feedback from distribution channels. Distinctive covers complement our distinctive approach to technical topics, breathing personality and life into potentially dry subjects.

The animal on the cover of *Web Performance Tuning*, Second Edition is a sword-billed hummingbird. There are over 300 species of hummingbird, all found only in the New World. All of these species are easily identifiable by their long, tubular bills and iridescent feathers. The iridescence is a refraction effect that can be seen only when light is shining on the feathers at certain angles. Hummingbirds range in size from the bee hummingbird, which, measuring 2 inches long and weighing less than an ounce, is the smallest of all birds, to the great hummingbird, which measures about 8.5 inches long.

Hummingbirds are so named because of the humming noise made by their rapidly moving wings. On average, hummingbirds flap their wings 50 times a second; some species can flap as many as 200 times per second. The wings are flexible at the shoulder and, unlike most birds, they are propelled on the upstroke as well as the downstroke. Because of this flexibility, hummingbirds can hover, fly right or left, backward, and upside down. Most hummingbirds have tiny feet that are used only for perching, never for walking. Hummingbirds will fly to travel even a few inches.

Hummingbirds expend a great deal of energy, and they need to feed every 10 minutes or so. They feed on nectar, for sugar, and small insects, for protein. Their long, tapered bills enable them to retrieve nectar from even the deepest flower. Pollen accumulates on the head and neck of hummingbirds while they gather nectar. They then transfer this pollen to other flowers and thus play an important role in plant reproduction.

Hummingbirds appear frequently in Native American legends and mythology, often as representatives of the sun. According to some folk beliefs, they can bring love.

Since Europeans first spotted these beautiful, colorful little birds, they have often appeared in the art and literature of the Old World, as well.

Mary Brady was the production editor and proofreader for *Web Performance Tuning*, Second Edition. Sarah Jane Shangraw was the copyeditor. Darren Kelly and Claire Cloutier provided quality control. David Chu and Julie Flanagan provided production support. Lucie Haskins wrote the index.

Edie Freedman designed the cover of this book, using a 19th-century engraving from the Dover Pictorial Archive. Emma Colby produced the cover layout with Quark-XPress 4.1, using Adobe's ITC Garamond font.

Melanie Wang designed the interior layout, based on a series design by David Futato. Neil Walls converted the files from Microsoft Word to FrameMaker 5.5.6 using tools created by Mike Sierra. The text font is Linotype Birka; the heading font is Adobe Myriad Condensed; and the code font is LucasFont's TheSans Mono Condensed. The illustrations that appear in the book were produced by Robert Romano and Jessamyn Read using Macromedia FreeHand 9 and Adobe Photoshop 6. The tip and warning icons were drawn by Christopher Bing. This colophon was written by Clairemarie Fisher O'Leary.